SELF-PROMOTION

FOR THE

CREATIVE PERSON

D0979954

BOOKS BY LEE SILBER

NONFICTION

Self-Promotion for the Creative Person

Career Management for the Creative Person

Time Management for the Creative Person

Aim First!

Notes, Quotes & Advice

Successful San Diegans

The Guide to Dating in San Diego

FICTION

Summer Stories

Tales from America's Finest City

SELF-PROMOTION
FOR THE
CREATIVE PERSON

GET THE WORD OUT ABOUT WHO YOU ARE AND WHAT YOU DO

LEE SILBER

THREE RIVERS PRESS • NEW YORK

Published by Three Rivers Press, New York, New York.
Member of the Crown Publishing Group.

Random House, Inc. New York, Toronto, London, Sydney, Auckland
www.randomhouse.com

THREE RIVERS PRESS is a registered trademark and the Three Rivers Press
colophon is a trademark of Random House, Inc.

Printed in the United States of America

Design by Rhea Braunstein

Library of Congress Cataloging-in-Publication Data
Silber, Lee T.
Self-promotion for the creative person : get the word out about who you are
and what you do / Lee Silber.—1st ed.
p.   cm.
Includes bibliographical references and index.
1. Vocational guidance.   2. Career development.
3. Creative ability in business.   I. Title.
HF5381 .S596 2001
650.14—dc21   00-067304

ISBN 0-609-80626-2

10   9   8   7   6

FIRST EDITION

This book is for all creative people who wish
they could remove the "self" from self-promotion
but also realize that they need to promote themselves.
You can do it—and better than you think!

ACKNOWLEDGMENTS

If you are reading this, give yourself a pat on the back. Savvy self-promoters always read acknowledgments. One of the reasons is to find out who is helping the author and then figure out how to get them to help you, too. The other reason is purely voyeuristic. It gives you a peek into the personal life of the writer. (Whether he thanks his wife first or last could mean the difference between "Isn't that sweet" or "Holy cow, that marriage is in trouble.")

I won't drag out the suspense. First and foremost, I want to thank my wife, Andrea. Being married to an author isn't easy. Sure, there are perks like book tours to Hawaii and Florida. There is also the "I'm living with a madman" part. Sometimes she'll be watching television and just smile at me as I storm past (cursing to myself) on the way to my studio to play the drums. (That's what I do when I'm stuck and can't think of what to write next.) Other times she'll bring me coffee before going to bed (I like to write late into the night) and then wonder where I am in the morning. (It's not what you think. After drinking all that coffee I can't sleep, so I like to sneak off to the Denny's down the street to write.) After eight books she now understands my writing patterns as I go from panic (How am I ever going to write this book?) to published (big release party, hooray), and takes it all in stride.

Not only is it fun to say my agent's last name, Lopopolo, it's even more fun to be able to spend time with her as our relationship changes from author/agent to author/friend. Toni Lopopolo is the kind of agent every author dreams about—experienced, excited about your work, and extremely competent. In fact, I was reading a book about agents and, lo and behold, there is an interview with Toni, and she was praising (and promoting, I might add) me. Now that's my idea of a super agent.

When I turned in the manuscript to my previous book, *Career Management for the Creative Person,* my editor at the time decided that after reading it she needed a career change. (Nice endorsement for the book, though.) Just as I was growing attached to her replacement, Jessica Schulte, she also left (to work on children's books). Those were just two of many editors I have seen come and go at Three Rivers Press, but there was none I was more saddened to see leave than Peter Guzzardi. Not only is he an excellent editor, but he is also a very cool guy. (He has an outstanding singing voice and sang with my band when he came out to California.) When he told me he was leaving, I was crushed, until he told me about my new editor, Becky Cabaza (Now I say, "Peter who?"). I went from great to greatest. How did I get so lucky? I'm in author heaven.

In this book you will read about the importance of mentors (and networking), and the following people will always be included in my acknowledgments because I owe them all (big-time) for their help and support. First, I'd like to thank my mentors, Mary-Ellen Drummond, Joseph Oppenheimer, and Harriet Schechter. I am also fortunate to be able to count on people like Susan Guzzetta and Troy Larson.

In the past I worked with Beth Hagman, who had a real knack for figuring out my creative spelling of words and making sense out of my stream-of-consciousness style of writing. This is the first book In years that I didn't have Beth to lean on. Instead, I turned to my dictionary-reading, thesaurus-toting mom for guidance. It was just like when I was a kid: "Clean up that hanging participle" and "Mind your p's and q's."

Finally, I want to thank the readers of this book and other books in this series. As a creative person myself, I know how important it is to be able to connect with others who understand what it's like to live a creative life. I write these books for us so that we can learn from each other and share ideas about how to get ahead and finally find the freedom to do what we really love—create. I encourage you to contact me (www.creativelee.com) if you need additional help, want to share information for future books in this series, or just want to talk to someone who understands. Thanks for being there for me. I'm here for you, too.

CONTENTS

Introduction   *xi*

1. **I Create, Therefore I Am?** (Why You Must Make
   Yourself More Marketable)   **1**

2. **You Can't Be Everything to Everybody**
   (Writing a Right-Brain Marketing Plan)   **18**

3. **Show Off** (Get Your Ass Out There)   **50**

4. **Do the Hustle** (Persistence Pays Off)   **80**

5. **Walk Tall and Carry a Big Shtick** (Make Yourself
   More Memorable)   **111**

6. **Image Is Everything** (You Are the Message)   **142**

7. **It Takes a Village to Raise a Business**
   (It *Is* Who You Know)   **174**

8. **Raving Fans** (Making the Most of Word-of-Mouth
   Marketing)   **200**

9. **Show and Sell** (Selling Without Selling Out)   **238**

10. **Full Court Press** (Positive Publicity)   **278**

11. **Surf This!** (Internet Marketing)   **302**

Contact Information   **319**

Bibliography   **321**

Index   **325**

INTRODUCTION

Ask a creative person for a few ideas on how to promote a product, and they will likely be able to quickly rattle off several clever concepts without much effort. Ask them how to promote themselves, and they will scratch their head and then begin pulling their hair out in frustration. Self-promotion is one of the most difficult things a creative person must do. It is also the most crucial.

What separates the successful creative person flush with fame, fortune, and a rewarding career from the struggling artist? It's not talent or luck. It is the ability to promote themselves and their work that gets them the exposure needed to stand out from the crowd and make it big—whether they're an author, actor, artist, or accordion player. Self-promotion is the key to success as a creative person.

When you take a look under the hood to see what makes us tick, it's easy to understand why self-promotion is a common problem for creative people. For instance, right-brainers (creative people) have a notoriously short attention span, and most books about marketing and self-promotion are incredibly technical and boring. This book changes that by being solution-oriented, relevant, and fun to read—anything but boring. It is chock full of entertaining (and educational) examples without all that marketing mumbo jumbo you find in many of the other books on the subject. This book is written specifically for the right-brained, creative person who desperately wants to know how to promote himself and his work, even if that means you work in the corporate world (bummer) and want to know how to get noticed and get ahead.

Creative people want to create. Many feel that promotion is both a waste of time and beneath them. Self-promotion can be a creative endeavor, and this book discusses how to make this necessary evil both honorable and easy. You'll read about fresh, creative, offbeat, and cost-effective ways to promote yourself. If you maximize your creativity and craftiness, self-promotion can be a right-brained affair. This book shows you how to do just that.

Most creative people are divergent thinkers—their minds skip from one new idea to the next, tending to wander. You can take this right-brain trait and use it to make self-promotion feel more natural. Being able to juggle several things at once can be a tremendous asset when it comes to promotion. We'll discuss working in short bursts, and easily switching off from one promotional idea to another while making sure your efforts support and feed one another. The book is even written so that you can pick a topic and start there. It doesn't have to be read in chronological order. Go ahead, skip around—but promise me that you will eventually finish reading the entire thing.

Often, the highly creative (and expressive) person will find it challenging when it comes to communicating and translating what they do. This book not only helps you clarify what you do, but also shows you how to articulate it to others in a sound bite kind of way. This kind of focus helps the multitalented creative person explain what they do clearly and concisely, which is vital to any promotion.

Emotion plays a key role in almost all creation, but it can get in the way of promotion. Rejection in the form of poor reviews, bad press, and a lack of support from a publisher or record label can be devastating. We'll discuss how to detach and distance yourself from what you do to survive and thrive, even when it seems like the world is against you. The tone of this book is upbeat for a reason—somebody is going to get publicized, profiled, and promoted, so why shouldn't it be you? You've worked hard and you deserve that recognition. You have to believe that. Yes, it's difficult to make it in creative fields, but it's impossible with a negative outlook.

It is true that many artists are indeed starving artists. This does not mean they can't continue to promote themselves. (A lack of promotion is probably part of the reason they have not yet achieved sought-after elusive fame and fortune.) The free and almost free promotional ideas in *Self-Promotion for the Creative Person* encourages readers to maximize their creativity and minimize using money to get the word out.

The biggest challenge facing the creative person is competition. It can be daunting when you read statistics about how many writers will actually have their works published or how many actors actually make a living at their craft. That is precisely why this book is so valuable. It shows the reader how to stand out from the crowd, start a buzz about their work, use word-of-mouth advertising to enlist raving fans, align themselves with VIPs (very influential people), and create marketing materials that act as salespeople when they aren't around to do it themselves.

In short, by implementing the tips and techniques in this book, you will blow the competition away with clever and creative self-promotional strategies. You can use these ideas right out of the box or—and this is what I suggest—you can apply some of your creativity and build on it, or morph the promotional idea into something original. The information and ideas you'll read about will work, *if you work them*. There are tons of ideas that you can use to promote yourself whether you are pressed for time or lacking in money (they're all in here). There is even a chapter about how to make the rather daunting task of self-promotion more manageable and create a right-brain plan of attack.

One thing you can do *right now* is grab an index card or two and, as you read, write down the self-promotion suggestions you feel would work for you in your situation. Make a note of the things you are going to do right away on one card, and on the other note the things you'll do later. There are more ideas in this book than even a master self-promoter could use in a lifetime, which is why I want you to pick a few things you will do right now so you'll see immediate results.

SELF-PROMOTION
FOR THE
CREATIVE PERSON

I CREATE, THEREFORE I AM?
(Why You Must Make Yourself More Marketable)

"Business is the act of extracting money from another man's pocket without resorting to violence."
—Max Amsterdam

It's called self-promotion for a reason: If you don't do it yourself, it usually doesn't get done! It's definitely a do-it-yourself proposition. It's an overwhelming proposition to make it big in the arts, and impossible if you don't take a proactive role in your promotion. This book will take the mystery out of marketing. It can't force you to embrace the concept, but it will teach you how to do it. It is the willingness (and ability) to market yourself and your art that increases your odds of making it. A lot of creative people have talent, but few have the know-how or desire to promote themselves. This isn't anything new. Throughout the years, creative people have grappled with the conflict of creating great work and then being expected, and forced, to sell it. "There should be a single Art Exchange in the world, to which the artist would simply send his works and be given in return as much as he needs. As it is, one has to be half merchant on top of everything else, and how badly one goes about it!" Guess who said that. Give up? Ludwig van Beethoven.

I am not saying you have to like it, you just have to do it. (It is easier when you can find methods of promotion that you can at least tolerate.) For better or worse, we live in the age of media. Promotion (*self*-promotion, or having others help) is a necessary evil for the creative person who just wants to gain a little exposure for their art, let alone achieve fame and fortune. Simply put, if nobody knows you exist, it doesn't matter how good your work is (unless this is a hobby for you, in which case I guess it doesn't matter as much).

The business world and the art world are (unfortunately) interlinked. Sometimes it feels more like a business than an art form. You can't ignore one or the other. You need to make money, and you should be getting paid for what you do. I don't know what your dream is, but for most of us it is to be able to earn a comfortable living while working on projects that we enjoy or are passionate about. Is that too much to ask for? I don't think so. Both of those goals (to make money and work on art that motivates us) are the direct result of a successful self-promotion campaign. So suck it up, get over your squeamishness, and do it, because the reward is worth it.

I'm not saying it's easy. You send out your résumé, distribute your brochure, network like mad, write a stellar proposal, force yourself to make cold calls, and schlep your portfolio all over town, sometimes with little luck. It takes a lot of your time, time you'd rather be creating. It's not just in the beginning, either, it's like that all the time. It's a business and you are the product. That means you have to sell the product—constantly. So you have two jobs, innovation and marketing. The more you accept that and learn how to do it, the easier it becomes. As you will learn from this book, it doesn't necessarily have to take a lot of time or money to do it well.

I have also found that when you are the creator, it is hard to step back and come up with ways to market your creations. For some reason, all that wonderful creativity dries up and you end up blocked and frustrated when it comes time to create your own marketing materials. Another phenomenon I have encountered is that after working on creating something for months, the last thing you want to do is promote it. You are ready to move on to the next great idea. Fight the urge to abandon your "baby." Your creations need you to raise them until they are self-sufficient.

One thing I'm sure of is that you can't wait to be discovered, or for that time when others promote you. I know so many creative people who don't understand that creating something is less than half the battle and that the real work has just begun. I know, you are an "artist," but you must also become a salesperson, booking agent, performer, publicist, pitchster, promoter, publisher, presenter—in other words, you will wear many hats. (We have to juggle all that goes with being an artist with all the other responsibilities that go with running a business.) This takes an incredible amount of your energy and enthusiasm away from your real work. You can get help with the promotional side of your business, but in my opinion nobody can promote you as well as you can promote yourself. This book is designed to help you do it yourself. You *can* do it. You know you *should* do it. Let's agree, you *will* do it. Let me help.

If you aren't marketing yourself, you're falling behind someone else who is. You need to embrace the concept of self-promotion and actively engage in it or else you will always be on the fringe. You need visibility and credibility. You can accomplish both by writing articles, speaking in public, putting up a first-rate website, writing a book, or associating with a well-known person in your field. Do good work and it's a little easier, but they won't always find you. You have to market yourself. *Every* successful creative person does it; even the *super*-successful still promote themselves. This book is loaded with helpful ideas (from ads and attitude to word of mouth and websites) to make it easy for customers to find you, talk you up, and get you to the next level (wherever you are—beginner or best-seller).

We will cover all kinds of inexpensive, innovative, and effective ways to get the word out about who you are and what you do; how to reach a larger audience and build a loyal fan base as well as getting the media to recognize you for your efforts. It's about getting influential people to say yes to you more often, whether you're an actor, artist, carpenter, cartoonist, comic, dancer, designer, entrepreneur, film-maker, landscape architect, musician, or involved in any other type of creative endeavor. You will learn how to compete (and win) against bigger competitors by tapping niches and doing the creative things the large players can't do. We will discuss how to improve your marketing materials, create an effective promotional plan, take action, and have fun along the way. This isn't brain surgery, and it doesn't have to be boring, either.

☆ ———————————————————————————

FAST FACTS

If you don't think promotion is important, here are some famous inventions whose inventors (sadly) remain unsung due to a lack of self-promotion. For instance, do you know who invented the answering machine? Edwin Peterson in 1945. How about the crossword puzzle? Arthur Wynne in 1913. Windshield wipers? Mary Anderson in 1903. Power steering? Francis Davis in 1926. The ATM? Luther Simjian in 1960. The Egg McMuffin? Herb Peterson in 1973.

Why Creative People Don't Do It

"If I go into Universal and even mention the word 'art,' security forces will come and take me away."

—*Terry Gilliam*

Don't you think I'd rather spend all of my time making art rather than marketing it? I would love to just write books all day, sitting by the pool sipping a cool drink, and never have to write another press release, design another brochure, or cold-call booksellers trying to line up another book signing. I know, get real. Books don't sell themselves. Today's creative person has to wear many hats, from publicist to promoter. The trick is to learn to love it. (With today's technology, I can still sit by the pool and promote.) Technology aside, you still have to use your imagination to create simple, effective, and creative methods to market, and then you have to act on those ideas. I realize it isn't quite that simple. I mean, if you are blocked as an artist, you can imagine the big boulders your brain puts in your path when it comes time to devise an approach to promotion. I know, I know. Somehow some of us have managed to overcome and manage to market. So will you, if you can accept the idea that you should.

We have been conditioned to think that somehow hype and mainstream success are bad things. But you don't have to struggle to be a "real" artist. Being paid well for your art is not selling out. Enough already with the myth that to create great work you can't have widespread appeal. Do you really believe that? We must stop feeling guilty about our success as artists. What's so bad if a lot of people love what we do? Does that lessen the quality somehow? I don't think so. "If you're in jazz and more than ten people like you, you're labeled commercial," laments jazz great Herbie Mann. It can be so frustrating remaining in obscurity while you watch other less talented people make it. Many artists get cynical, bitter, jaded, and give up. (You can see them playing at a Holiday Inn lounge near you.) I like the attitude Metallica has to promotion. When pressed by an interviewer about whether they have sold out, they replied, "Yes, we sell out. Every seat in the house, every time we play." That rocks!

Instead of promoting yourself, you can hope people will magically discover you, and then you won't have to market at all. It's true, there are some self-promotional things that are easier and more palatable than others. If you don't like interaction with others, you can still do a website, newsletter, or postcard mailing. Maybe you don't like detail work but have no problem talking up what you do. Find what fits into your comfort zone and start there. After that you can begin to face your fears. As an example, I don't mind going in to booksellers to talk to the store managers about my books. I'll sign the books they have on hand and encourage them to order more. No big deal. But I went beyond my comfort zone recently and found it felt fantastic to both break the rules and be a guerrilla marketer. I made up a bookmark-style tab that sticks up and says, "Are you in your 'Right' mind? Take the quiz in chapter one to find out." I inserted them in each copy of my book. One day I had a wild idea: I decided to slip postcards with my book cover and ordering information in every *other* book in that section of the store. Yikes! The risk of possibly getting caught was worth the reward of selling more of my books.

Let's talk about the fear of rejection and failure. It will happen—often. Get used to it. It's extremely hard to put something of yours out there and have people criticize it. It takes a really strong person to not take it personally. You must validate yourself, rather than rely on others. Stop worrying that they will "find you out" and that you are a fraud. (You deserve good things to happen to you.) There is also the fear of selling. Relax, it's not your father's selling. The hard sell went out with eight-track tapes. Now it's all about forming mutually beneficial long-term relationships. It's a soft sell with warm leads. You can do that. There is also the fear of selling out. Look at self-promotion as another outlet for your creativity, and when it works, it's very fulfilling. In many ways it's an art form. There is the fear that you may waste your money on marketing. Good. Be very cautious about how (and how much) you spend your marketing dollars, and look for free and inexpensive ways to do it. Which leads us to a fear of technology. Everything is easier and cheaper on the Internet, but maybe you've been afraid to try it. This is a real fear. You *must* make an effort to at least understand the possibilities available to you online.

Finally—and I left this for last because it is big—there is the fear of public speaking. We will talk about how to make this a part of your marketing and where you can go for help in polishing your presentation skills to the point that you will want to get out there and speak.

What It Takes to Be a Self-Promotion Superstar

"Advertising isn't a science. It's persuasion. And persuasion is an art."

—William Bernbach

1. There must be a market. (Even if it's not a massive market.) It is naive to believe "If you build it they will come." You have to build something they want and will pay for (and then promote the hell out of it). You can't expect that if you create whatever mousetrap you feel like creating, people will beat a path to your door (and gladly pay your price for it). The fact is, you need to know if there is a market (even if it's a small one) for what you do. You have to get your mind around the idea that publishers, studios, labels, galleries, retailers, and even clients want to make money. They want creative people and marketable creations. This doesn't necessarily mean you have to compromise yourself or your art. If you can find an outlet, or people who will pay or appreciate what you do the way you want to do it, that's all being marketable means.

Just find some people (who are willing to buy) to sell to. This said, you have to understand that people's preferences can determine your promotability. If, for example, you write poetry, it will be harder to promote yourself and your work than it would be if you took those same words and wrote a hit song. Sorry, that is a fact of life in marketing. Many creative people have had a nice career living on the fringe. You don't necessarily have to turn into a lip-synching teen idol to make it in music—or any other creative endeavor. There are areas in the arts where, no matter how hard you try, there simply is little or no market, or there may have once been but that market is now extinct. Move on and come up with something newer and better. Reinvent yourself. Focus on reaching people, and reaching the right people. This book is for the creative person who wants to reach a hundred people or hundreds of thousands. As long as these people want what you are marketing, then that is a market.

2. You need a marketing mind-set. When I graduated from art school my parents wanted to know (rightfully so) if their money was well spent. "So, what did you learn?" they asked. To be honest, many of the tangible things I learned (like specific techniques) are obsolete. But I am grateful for (I should call my folks and tell them this) the marketing mind-set I picked up (or was programmed with?). Not only was I taught that it's okay to want to promote yourself and your art, but to always be on the lookout for opportunities to do so. To use your creativity and imagination to come up with unusual and offbeat ideas to get the word out. That self-promotion is an art and a worthy pursuit and a necessary part of being an artist. It also is an understanding that *everything* about marketing is about your audience and not about you. What's important to *them*? What do *they* need? Want?

You know who seems very comfortable with self-promotion? Madonna. How else can you explain a run like hers? She is controversial and overexposed (in more ways than one). She's a nonstop producer, a master of manipulating the media, and she's up on trends and even creates them. It's her "look at me" attitude along with a little talent that makes her so marketable.

If Madonna is the anti-Christ, as some have said, then here's a little angel. Charlotte Church, the teenager with "the voice of an angel," has made classical vocal music more mainstream. The Welsh soprano admits that she wouldn't listen to a classical musical station—too boring. So she's making it more accessible to a whole new market, young people like herself. Even classical musicians can target an audience, take an innovative approach, and turn themselves into a brand name. They may take some heat from traditionalists and critics (people who are frustrated artists who were unable to make it big themselves), but it's worth it.

3. Marketing know-how. It's not enough to want to be promotable—you also have to know how to do it. There are so many amazingly innovative and creative people who design and invent such neat stuff, but when they hand out their marketing materials I'm struck by how boring, complicated, and bad they are. (You can do a lot of damage with poor promotional materials.) It has never been easier to be your own publicist, promotional director, and graphic designer, but just because you can, doesn't mean you should—at least not without a little training. That's why this book will be so valuable. It's a crash course in promotion. Though there are countless types of creative people, in many different fields, there are some universal truths and timeless techniques that will work, regardless of your medium. (Define what you do, articulate it in a way others will understand and respond to, and package it and promote it as creatively and effectively as possible.)

The only thing not covered in this book (and you will need to stay on top of this) is the new and ever-changing opportunities that technology is making available to the savvy marketer. You will want to use every weapon at your disposal. You can mourn the way things were or move forward and make use of these mostly mind-boggling marketing weapons. Even so, one thing that will never change is the ability to turn what you are offering into benefits for those to whom you are marketing. Decisions are usually not logical ones, but if you can elicit an emotional response by playing on people's desires and dreams, you will succeed.

4. Light up your desire to market. When you see other (and far less talented) creative people making it big and enjoying their fame and fortune, you, of course, want to strangle them—slowly. You mistakenly believe they were just lucky. True, some were in the right place at the right time, but most mastered marketing or had people around them who did. You must think and act like an artist *and* a businessperson. When you come around to the realization that you must market and make yourself more marketable, you'll be amazed at how things will "magically" start happening for you, too.

You'll also notice that people who can make you a star—in whatever creative field you're in—will treat you differently (decidedly better) when you understand how to promote yourself and are willing and able to do so. You can't be modest or humble when promoting yourself. Once you get a taste of success yourself, it's like a drug, and you'll want the recognition, respect, and raving reviews to continue.

A long time ago I came to grips with the fact that publishers want media-savvy authors. That's why I tell authors that they need to become more self-sufficient when it comes to marketing themselves and their books. In the past all an author had to worry about was producing a promising book, but now they have to promote like mad, too. Publishing is a business, and publishers want a return on their investment. That means forming a strong alliance with an editor (who can help create a buzz for your book within the publishing house). I even flew across the country to ask (beg) my publisher for additional support from the promotional department. (This is where having sales skills come in handy.) Although the publisher assigns you a publicist, that doesn't mean you just sit back and wait for them to do all the work. These in-house publicists may be working on as many as ten books at a time. You can be the squeaky wheel, which helps, but you should also do promotion on your own. Many of my fellow authors are not willing to do this. They don't feel it's part of their job description. "I'm a writer, not a publicist." That's too bad. They should rethink that job description thing, because if they don't, they won't have any jobs to describe.

5. Focus on marketing effort and action. Marketing is not magic, it's a plan and an attack. Without one or the other, a plan or an attack, you may win a battle or two but you will lose the war to a competitor who is more organized, aggressive, and consistent. As you will learn in this book, a plan can be as simple as a one-page outline of who your audience is and the best way to reach them (plus a few other minor details and deadlines). Your efforts don't have to be all-consuming, either. Maybe you decide to make Monday a marketing day or use your lunch break for promoting yourself. You set a goal of securing at least one promotional opportunity a week and then you DO IT!

It's not as impossible or mundane as it sounds. Marketing is many things, some of them both fun and creative. Going to a bookstore and chatting with the manager to see what's hot and what's not. Taking a reporter to lunch. Donating your time to a charity and rubbing elbows with some of the movers and shakers in your industry. Giving the best show you possibly can. Going to a gallery opening of a friend or as a fan of an artist.

If you do nothing, nothing happens. Your creations sit in a drawer and maybe someday you pull them out and show your grandkids and tell them, "I could have been . . ." Think about how sad that would be. Just a little promotional effort on your part is better than none at all. Focus on what you think you can do now, with what you have. Promise me you will at least try some of the suggestions in this book. Please. Even if it's just burning your old boring brochure. It's a start!

6. Develop a never-say-die attitude. Yes, there is an insane amount of competition today. Yes, it can seem like an impossible proposition to get anyone to pay attention to you. It seems more and more like a have-and-have-not world for the creative person. Those who have been able to land promotion for themselves and their work and those who haven't had any luck. The fact that some are getting promoted should give you hope. Now it's your turn.

"Great, so what do I have to do?" Outthink, outhustle, and outlast your competition. I am not going to lie to you, it's not easy, but it is doable and that means that YOU CAN DO IT! You may not see results right away, but then, marketing isn't a short-term proposition. It takes patience, persistence, and consistency. You may plant many promotional seeds and have to wait for them to bloom and grow into something you can see. The good thing is that once you start to see results from your efforts, they will multiply. Opportunities will start coming to you. It seems like they are gifts from a higher power; maybe they are, but it's more likely they're more earthly and the fruits of earlier labor.

Promotion and publicity beget more promotion and publicity. When James Michener had an idea for a book, all he had to do was call his publisher and tell them what he was going to write. The rest of us have to write a proposal, pitch the idea, and pray that we get a deal. It takes time, but once you build momentum you will have to start *turning down* promotional opportunities for fear of overexposure. Keep your chin up, and whatever you do, keep trying, because your big break is waiting just around the corner. You have to believe that.

7. Be willing to be a do-it-yourself marketer. One of the great things about the Internet is that it has *never* been easier to be self-sufficient when it comes to promotion. With access to some amazing tools, self-promotion is now a do-it-yourself proposition. Stockbrokers and travel agents may not be the only professions in danger of becoming extinct. We probably won't be adding publicists and promoters to the endangered species list anytime soon, but many of the functions they perform we can now do ourselves, for a lot less money. Look at what's worked in the past for these professionals and then do it yourself. If you can, why not do a bang-up job on behalf of yourself? Why would I even mention this? I mean, all these years the goal was to get help with promotion (and hopefully have someone else pay for it). The problem is that more and more creative people are either being dropped by their labels and publishers and are going the independent, self-published route, or they're finding out that the publicist assigned to them is overworked, overwhelmed, and underpaid. They are doing the bare minimum, and you have to ride them just to get them to do that.

With the demise of many smaller, independent retailers who understood and appreciated good work and would take a chance on an up-and-comer, it's a tougher sell with the "big box" superstores. If their chain buyer doesn't like you (or doesn't see any sales potential), you could be in trouble. Fortunately, the market is fragmented and independents are bypassing the corporate structure to make and market art to targeted customers who are both loyal and long-term. Can't land a record deal? Form your own label and release your own CD. That's why I want to teach you how to do your own promotion, even if you don't have to. (Chances are you will need to.)

8. Make time for marketing. Someone once commented to me that marketing equals success and no marketing equals "Would you like fries with that order?" Ooohh. Harsh. Want to hear something even harsher? Whatever time you have available to spend on your *art,* take that number and divide it in half and use it for *self-promotion.* I'm not kidding. I know, you are working on that big project now and you'll get to it later. There is *always* something that will get in the way of making time for marketing. You have to schedule it in. We are *all* too busy to market. But some of us make it a priority and find ways to fit it into our busy schedules. Do it as a warm-up before doing your creative work, or do it during the downtime during your day. (You can't create all day long, can you?) Let me ask you this: How much time do you spend monthly on marketing now? Is it enough? Do you have all the business you need? Are you exactly where you want to be in your career? The way to make it big is to not major in the minors (doing things that in the big scheme of things are a waste of time), but swing for the fences and try to hit home runs (things that help you big-time in the long term). If you will devote at least a little more time to marketing yourself, you will see it is time well spent. It pays off, even if it's just an hour a day. By the way, if you need help with time management, I have just the book for you: *Time Management for the Creative Person,* by ME. (How's that for self-promotion?)

9. Set aside some money for marketing. It can cost tens of thousands of dollars to promote even a minor musician's CD. There is the mailing, phone calls, press kits, advertising, release party, and review copies of the new CD. Just throwing money at marketing is NOT the answer. It does take money to make money. But good promotion takes more than money. It takes creativity. Less money and more brains (and balls) are better than a big budget with no focus, no idea of who the target is, and no clue about how to package the product or service to appeal to the emotions and needs of your market. (Focus doesn't take finances.)

Unless you are willing to invest in yourself and your future, you aren't serious or committed enough about your art. For a budding actor it can cost as much as $5,000 just to get started (union dues, head shots, video, résumé, mailing costs, and acting lessons). Think of it as an investment in yourself. You owe it to yourself (and your art) to promote it. The trick is to try to do it as cheaply as possible. It can be cheap, but it's never free. (Even building a website and using Internet marketing is not entirely free.)

No matter what creative field you are in, to be seen as serious and professional, you'll need tangible materials. Many industries have minimum requirements for proper promotion. What are your industry's standard promotional tools?

Innovation and motivation can overcome a lack of money for marketing, but you will need a little dough, though. If you're reading this and living out of your car and collecting aluminum cans to get by, then I say food first, rent second, and business cards third. If you aren't living on the street but have to scrape change out of your ashtray to pay for gas, I would recommend business cards *and* flyers. For everybody else, maybe cut back elsewhere in your life to find the funds for self-promotion. (Drink domestic beer instead of imported beer.) Keep your day job. (You can use their copier and computer, and the paycheck comes in handy.) Use what you have by bartering your services for other services you may need. I'll be honest with you, you need high-quality promotional materials. I don't care what the label, publisher, or gallery told you, their efforts are not going to be enough. You have to do something. Put your money where your mouth is or use other people's money, as one enterprising filmmaker did. He got corporate sponsors and then convinced them to send him to Park City, Utah. Only he didn't have his film showing at the Sundance Film Festival. Instead he showed it in a nearby bar on the main street.

Too much money for marketing makes you stupid and lazy; too little makes it difficult to do anything. Think of it as an investment in yourself and your career. Hey, we're building a brand here. Then you can go about outsmarting and outhustling the competition on a shoe-string budget.

10. Use offbeat marketing techniques. You can't survive in the crowded, competitive creative fields unless you are willing to not only embrace self-promotion, but also do it in a big, bold way. Thankfully, this doesn't mean spending a lot of money. In fact, just the opposite is true. If you can come up with some screwball gimmick, you should be able to garner exposure in the form of free publicity and word of mouth. This is the one time when breaking the rules and being the off-the-wall, creative thinker you are really pays off. By applying unconventional thinking to publicity and promotion, you can increase sales without spending much money on marketing.

Look at what makes you unique. Any interesting hobbies? Do you enjoy surfing or skydiving, or scuba diving with sharks? Do you have a hidden talent for something outside of your field, like being a musician in addition to a graphic artist? I have used all of these angles in promoting myself, and they worked extremely well. It's a "hook," and the media loves anything out of the ordinary.

Another author includes recipes in her mysteries. She was able to capitalize on her culinary creativity by attracting the attention of food editors, who gave her books more print coverage than book reviewers did. She "gets" that it's up to the author to play a more integral role in the promotion of their books. Otherwise the books will bomb (no matter how well-written they may be). That's why we're referring here to mainstream marketing as well as unorthodox and low-cost approaches to self-promotion.

11. Be willing to meet and greet your market. It is wishful thinking to believe you don't need to do any promotion because people will come looking for you. What-ev-urrr. You need to know your market intimately. Get to know them and *listen* to them when they tell you what they want. It is arrogant and foolish to ignore your core fans and what they're telling you. So many of us have paid our dues on the road, promoting, you might think it's just sour grapes, that we want others to suffer also. That's not it. Much of self-promotion is just showing up and doing your thing, which, when you enjoy what you do, is no big deal. One of the biggest (and in my opinion) best chapters in this book deals with this aspect of promotion. Check it out.

12. Have an ability to market (sell) your stuff. I have heard people say, "Oh Jim, he's a born salesman." Hmmm. Funny, I have never heard of the birth of a salesman. Selling is something anyone can (and should) learn. There comes a point in every creative person's career when he realizes that he is in business for himself (even if he has a "job"), and that he has to sell himself and his creations. It's always a difficult pill to swallow. To make it go down a little bit easier, let me assure you that it isn't the kind of cram-it-down-their-throat style of selling you may be afraid of. It's more like building a relationship with people who can benefit in some way from what you have to offer and who appreciate what you do. It's also a little bit of psychology and common sense, as you get into their heads and their shoes and you figure out what they want and need and how to best give it to them.

You are actually more of a consultant than a salesperson. You are providing goods or services that will entertain, enrich, or enhance your customers in some small (or big) way—maybe even make them money. It's a win-win in every sense of the word. You do something wonderful for them, and they tell all their friends and associates—making for lots of warm leads and no more cold calls. Whew!

It starts by being able to describe what you do in a few words. Focus is probably not a creative person's strong suit, but it is essential when you are selling something. Selling starts with being able to answer the inevitable question, "So, what do you do?" Being able to answer in a concise and catchy way can open a lot of doors. We will show you how to focus and communicate—in other words, sell. Until technology allows our creations to make cold calls, network, and sell themselves, this is something we all need to learn how to do.

13. Market through word of mouth. Coming up with new and innovative ways to make your customers and clients say WOW! is the start of your word-of-mouth campaign. With the current state of customer service in this country, this isn't all that hard to do. It means being reliable, professional, and exceptionally good at what you do, and then going one step further and giving them a little something extra. Something they didn't expect. When you exceed the expectations of others, they will start to spread the word. For example, a few words from Oprah and a book becomes a best-seller. (Every book that has been an Oprah Book Club selection has rocketed to the top.)

Combine your efforts with those of other creative people and pool your resources. Instead of competing, find ways that you can complement each other. An example is an illustrator and a graphic artist doing a co-op mailing to ad agencies. Be consistent; you never know when your monthly mailing will finally click and someone will say, "Oh, I have the perfect . . ." Surprise—word of mouth is a proactive thing. You don't just wait for others to start talking you up, you have to prime the pump first.

14. Find marketing mentors and support people. Successful self-promotion is usually a process that requires the help of several key people along the way. Don't worry if you don't know anyone who can help you yet. We will cover how to enlist the help of others later in the book. Let's first discuss the difficulty many creative people have in asking for, and accepting, help from others. Many of the creative people I know (myself included) are Lone Ranger types. We prefer to work alone and do everything ourselves. But there comes a time when we can't do it all ourselves and we have to start looking for a trusty companion, our Tonto.

We may need help from fans, family, or friends. Maybe we need professional help from a publicist, website designer, or a distributor. It also means having a good working relationship with your agent/manager as well as publicists and promotional people. They can help you if you let them. Even the talented Elvis Presley knew he needed a manager, and Colonel Tom Parker was that man.

Most of all, find a mentor who can give you good advice, and please make sure you nurture your fans. You may have figured out by now that creating positive word of mouth is a *huge* part of marketing. We cover it extensively in this book, along with building a network and fan base of people who believe in you and want to help you when they can.

15. Develop an ability to plan and organize marketing efforts. Without some kind of system to stay on top of your promotional efforts, you will end up all over the place doing double the work and wasting an incredible amount of time and energy. In my opinion, the most important part of promotion is follow-up. It is almost impossible to do this without at least a simple plan and system to keep track of your promotional efforts. Otherwise, things can get out of hand so fast you'll be overwhelmed and give up.

Other aspects of a successful marketing campaign are referrals and word of mouth that come from networking and staying in touch with people. This requires a method to manage your mailing list (preferably with some sort of software program). It is so easy to get wrapped up in our art and forget to show up for an interview or meeting. A planner is another must-have for a promoter.

Marketing requires discipline, structure, and a coordinated plan. (I know, yuck.) But chaos doesn't enhance your promotional efforts. It's hard, because you don't get paid for promotion. You get paid to produce. So why spend any time on it? Don't, and see what happens. It could get real ugly. It's a part of your job description. Treat it as such or you'll lose your job. (It's more important than what you are working on now.) Make it a commitment! Schedule one day a week for follow-up. Give yourself a deadline for that flyer, newsletter, or ad. Then do it!

A Real-Life Example of Self-Promotion Success

"I'm a small vineyard. And I'm not willing to sacrifice the way I make wine to get into Safeway."

—Tori Amos

Best-selling author Rebecca Wells's first novel, *Little Altars Everywhere,* was published by a tiny Seattle press with no money for promotion. The unknown author and sometime actress had a friend who knew someone at National Public Radio's "All Things Considered." The friend gave the producer a copy of the book, and Wells was a guest on the show. That interview was heard by a man in Blytheville, Arkansas, who bought the book for his wife, who loved it. She also happened to run the town's bookstore and began recommending it to everyone who came into the store. (The same thing happened in several other cities, where the book developed a small but loyal following due to word of mouth.) This caught the attention of an editor in New York who published Wells's second book, *Divine Secrets of the Ya-Ya Sisterhood.* When the HarperCollins rep went into the tiny bookstore in Blytheville, the owner ordered a hundred copies—an enormous amount for her. She informed the rep that this was going to be a big book. She also asked that the author come to town to do a signing. Wells made the trip to Arkansas and the place was packed. The author toured the country to increasing crowds, mostly mothers and daughters. It took nearly two years, but *Ya-Ya Sisterhood* became a bestseller with three million copies in print. This story includes several elements of self-promotion, including networking, publicity, building a buzz, mastering your craft, word of mouth, hustle, target marketing, and most of all, it was done without a big budget. This story gives me hope. It can happen for you, me, and anyone willing to do even a little marketing. Let's learn how to create our own success through self-promotion.

Ask a Pro

SARK
Best-selling author of books on creativity
www.campsark.com

What is the ideal environment for creativity?

For me it's night. It's dark. There are no people. I'm alone. And there have been many, many hours of good avoidance in the form of naps, popular magazines, old movies, more naps, and then naps to recover from the naps that didn't work. Oh, and I also need to be very well fed, with perfect snacks close at hand for later.

Okay, now what stops us from being creative?

Procrastination, perfectionism, and the inner critic.

Is there an antidote?

There are fabulous things that are especially geared for each one of those. For procrastination, I have found a way to trick myself into doing something that's not napping, reading popular magazines, or watching old movies. I call them micromovements. These are tiny steps that are five minutes or less in length, because not only do I have a short attention span, I am a perfectionist. Otherwise, most things don't get started and finished. I went from someone who never started anything to someone who is now a prolific author and artist. I also spend a lot of time outside in nature doing absolutely nothing. That is a well I go back to all the time.

You forgot to mention the inner critic.

That's important, too. I meet more people who don't even know what their inner critic is. For example, I was on the East Coast, and out of an audience of three hundred, only twelve hands went up when I asked if they knew what their inner critic was. All these people are listening to their inner critic, not knowing what it is. I did a drawing of my inner critic in my new book, *The Bodacious Book of Succulence,* and my business partner Bridgette is so scared of it she can't stand to look at it without closing the book. It's frightening.

SELF-PROMOTION FOR THE CREATIVE PERSON

16

I noticed you were able to weave a mention of your new book into your previous answer. It shows me you are someone who embraces self-promotion.

I love it. I love it! I love it! I do embrace it. When I was a kid I wanted every day to be show-and-tell day. I was also the "wake-up fairy" in kindergarten. That's what I am doing today. I feel like I still have my magic wand and that I'm showing and telling. I'm a natural, and I really like it. It thrills me to meet people and to go out and speak.

Does it surprise some people when they find out you enjoy speaking and promoting?

People who aren't good at it or are frustrated by a lack of promotion like to picture a crabby author who never goes out-side, walks around in a ratty old bathrobe, and doesn't want to do anything for money. And they will jump on anyone who wants to do it.

What separates the successful artist from the struggling artist?

Completion. The struggle comes when they hardly complete anything or make excuses by saying things like, "I want to do a story, I want to send it out, and I want to get it published," but they don't do anything concrete. It doesn't have to be a big thing, just do micromovements, and then your inner critic can't say you aren't doing anything with your creativity. All my books are made up of micromovements. I was all potential but no completion, and I thought I would live that way all my life.

2

YOU CAN'T BE EVERYTHING TO EVERYBODY
(Writing a Right-Brain Marketing Plan)

"Before you build a better mousetrap, it helps to know if there are any mice out there."
—Mortimer Zuckerman

Thomas Edison's first patent was for an electronic vote recorder. There was no demand for such a thing at the time and Edison earned nothing from his invention. After the frustration from that experience he vowed to never invent anything unless he was sure it would be commercially marketable. In other words, "dig where the gold is" or you'll waste a lot of effort promoting a potential flop. Who wants and needs what we have to offer (and can they afford to pay for it)? Is there a need? Technology and innovation are great, but people won't usually buy what they don't want or need.

Bill Cosby hit it big with "The Cosby Show." The show obviously had national appeal, but it was especially well-received among the core audience it was targeting. Cosby once said, "I don't know the key to success, but the key to failure is trying to please everyone." For example, the first time I ever saw a Mentos (breath fresheners) commercial I thought, "You have to be kidding me, is this some kind of joke?" (This was before the Foo Fighters did a parody of the bizarre commercials in their music video.) It turns out that the European company ran the same ads here in the United States that they ran overseas. Not good. You need the right approach to the right people at the right time. That means using a different approach for different types of people.

When someone is asked, "Who is your audience?" and they reply, "Everyone," you know they're in trouble. It is impossible (and undesirable) to try to turn everyone into a customer or client. The smaller your niche, the less you have to spend on advertising and the more personal attention you can give. This kind of myopic focus allows you to stay in touch with core customers and meet their needs. You get to know what your prospects want and expect from you, and the best way to approach them. Then you can create and sell them almost anything that interests them. The goal is to have a narrow but deep target audience, one that is interested (in you), loyal (to you), and willing to pay (you) for what you do.

When I lived on Maui I was a fan of a local group called Hapa. They played modern Hawaiian music at the old El Crab Catcher in Kaanapali. Slowly but surely they built a strong following, becoming very successful on Maui and then the other islands. They then began picking up fans of slack key guitar all over the country. Much like Keola Beamer, Ray Kane, and Cyril and James Pahinui before them, they made a name for themselves in a very small niche, but one that is extremely loyal. You must focus and be great at something, even if there isn't mass appeal. And once you know who your target is, everything else seems to click into place. When you focus your promotional efforts in one specific area, you'll see the results multiply faster. It's easier to build a name and reputation for yourself within a small targeted group. Since it's a smaller community, word spreads faster and they seem to see your work everywhere. It's easier to open doors when people know who you are and have heard of your work. Then you're able to branch out within that niche and expand. When I ran my surf shop I added wet suit repair, video rentals, and lessons, in addition to the usual merchandise, because we knew what our existing customers wanted. We didn't need new customers, we just turned our existing ones into better buyers.

From running this retail store and others, I learned the hard lesson that you have to give people what they want, and not what you like. I made some bad buys as the "soft goods" buyer before I came up with a system: I would see stuff I would buy for myself, which was my cue that it wouldn't sell. The things I hated almost always sold. Go figure. That system wasn't foolproof, so I would also have some of the "cool" kids come in on days the reps were showing the line and ask for input. These kids were uncanny in picking winners.

Or you can create a niche for yourself. Lane Bryant made pretty and practical maternity clothes to wear outside the home, which was unheard of at the time. In her first ads she included testimonials from doctors and psychologists proclaiming it was healthier to get out and live a normal life when you're pregnant. Sales boomed! She *created* a niche of maternity wear that was comfortable and cool, then went after another segment: hard-to-fit females. Just because you create things the public wants does *not* mean you are a sellout! Two surfers started Dean Miller Hawaiian print bedding by creating limited-edition bed sets in "da kine" designs, with prints that include hula dancers, hibiscus, and hodads. It's something the public wanted (sales are proving that), but it still has soul. It's a labor of love and a passion and a public pleaser. Guitarist George Benson says, "I looked around and I saw other jazz musicians who were limited, guys who wouldn't compromise their talent and wouldn't search for an audience. I don't think I ever compromised my talent, but I did search for a newer audience." The goal is to find the perfect fit for you and what you want to do.

Part of planning your promotion is knowing what your target audience does on a daily basis. What do they read? Where do they hang out? What websites are they browsing? When the founder and CEO of Temps & Co. needed more temps, he found out that the type of temps he needed hung out at Starbucks, liked to shop and go to the movies. (Hmm, this sounds very familiar.) He discovered this by asking for feedback. So he started Job Stores, and made everything about applying for a job as easy as ordering a cup of coffee. The stores were located in malls and looked like a comfy, trendy bistro. The decor and location respond to what the customer wants.

Knowing an audience means figuring out who they are, what they want, and *how much they're willing to spend.* Two women came up with an idea for a customer-friendly art gallery—a gallery for young people just out of college who now have some money to spend, want to decorate their apartment with more than just framed Nagel posters, would like real art, but would never step foot in a regular gallery. So the savvy owners brought in art they knew their audience would want and could afford, and presented it in a pleasing environment. This isn't rocket science, but it is easily forgotten in the rush to build a business. The more you know about your target audience, the better and more focused your promotion becomes. Know where your audience is and how to best reach them. When job recruiters hit the beach during spring break to recruit college kids, they went where the kids were. *That's* what I mean.

It is also handy to know who you DON'T work well with, and to eliminate them as potential clients. It saves time and money and helps you focus on those who are a better fit. It is one way to eliminate some of the endless possibilities for promotion. Otherwise self-promotion is overwhelming, expensive, and too broad. Jeff Scott makes custom handmade guitars in the shape of gargoyles and dragons. He *isn't* looking to compete with Gibson and Fender, but instead this head banger is happily charging $5,000 and up for one of his custom creations. He knows who his target market is and who it isn't. (It is not the classical, jazz, or folk guitarist, so he doesn't bother marketing to them.) You don't have to give in to a trend or target audience if it's wrong for you. You just need to find people who appreciate what you do. There may not be mass appeal for what you do, but you also don't have to compromise, either. Do your art your way and find people who appreciate it.

Define and Refine

You don't want to be running around in circles without a clue about who your target is. Knowing who needs what is a key to success. A niche is a specific area that you specialize in. One man creates golf-related art and sells it through pro shops, country clubs, and ads in golf magazines and newsletters. This niche is good for him because he loves golf and he's found that golfers have the discretionary income to afford his art and it gives him an edge. When I wanted to sell a set of my drums, I took out an ad in a magazine read by musicians rather than the daily paper. I didn't need to pay to reach a million people. I needed to reach far fewer who were more likely to buy drums. It worked. The splintering of the television networks led to what is called "narrow casting." They are programming for specific audiences because they're so splintered. This allows the shows to be more creative. You can take the same approach too.

I think it is also important to define who you are and what you do before you can promote yourself to others. It's called "positioning." How can we explain to others (promotion) what we do if we aren't clear about it ourselves? Having a focus makes it much easier for others to spread the word about you. I know we hate labeling things—it pigeonholes us. But in other people's eyes it helps to define what we do. Besides, it's better to pick a label than let someone else hang one on you. Are you a blues band? Jazz? Rock? Reggae? Country? New Age? Hip-hop? A combination of two of those? Maybe get outside of your label of "I'm a painter." What else do you do well? Any opportunities there? Concentrate on your strengths and market those. Companies get to know you for a specialty, and this *is* the age of the specialist. Just remember, self-promotion starts with the customer, not you. A clear understanding of your audience—the editor, record executive, retailer, or end-user—is invaluable. It influences everything that you do, from presentation to publicity. The more you know about your audience, the more you can create things they would love to have and will gladly pay for.

FAST FACTS

The new customers that corporations are now seeking are under the age of thirty-five. Good-bye BMWs and hello WB.

Tweens	Ages 9–12
Generation Next	Ages 13–17
Generation X	Ages 18–34

Looking for Love in All the Right Places

Aside from all this talk about a niche and a market, we want to remember these are people with emotions and desires. We also want to find ways to make your goals, and the goals of those you want to reach, overlap. It's not about trying to trick people, it's giving them what they want. It's about trying to help them. Consider these points as you ponder that:

It's lonely at the top. There are very few BIG acts. There is a lot more room in the middle and bottom. Yes, try to hit it big, but also take advantage of small markets and a loyal following. Start small and build your following one fan at a time. Start by getting your feet wet and enter at the bottom, then build and expand. When Life's a Beach began selling its Bad Boy beach gear, there was a limited market for that kind of stuff. But after losing control of the company to their partners, Brian and Mark Simo started No Fear, based on extreme sports, which had a broader appeal. They took their knowledge from their earlier success and expanded into a bigger market. Their success with the No Fear brand is undeniable. Where would be an easy entry place for you to begin your marketing? Is there potential to grow and expand?

You can choose a niche, or they will choose you. I was doing a talk at a bookstore, and one of the attendees asked if I would be interested in speaking at their annual regional conference. Sure. At the conference, I was asked if I did any consulting on the side. "Sure," I said. This led to a nice little consulting gig doing makeovers of their marketing materials. Since I was now hooked up with the regional branch, they helped me get work with other offices all over the country.

Every time our band plays, it seems like the entire San Diego contingency of South Africans comes out to hear us. (Half of our band is from South Africa.) It is apparent that our core fans are also from South Africa. So why fight it? It has helped us build a loyal following and guaranteed a good turnout each time we play. (Plus, they're the nicest people.) Look at your existing clients: Do you see any patterns of the type of people who appreciate what you do? Can you build on that?

Be proactive. The Dallas-based restaurant chain Canyon Cafe combs the local papers looking for announcements of people who were recently promoted. Then they mail a personalized letter and gift certificate congratulating them and inviting them to dine with them for free. What ways can you go out and actively recruit new customers? Are you doing all you can to reach new people and win them over?

Find common ground. Can you turn your passion into a profit center? Yes, you can. Find something you are passionate about, and then use your knowledge of the people and their passion for promotional purposes. Using sailing as an example, once you do good work for one person, your name spreads quickly in the small, tight-knit sailing community. (Of which you are a member also. Can you say instant credibility?) Let's say you write fiction and your main character lives on a sailboat. You can target sailing magazines, boat shows, buy boat-owner mailing lists, put flyers up at marinas, post to sailing-related websites, and so forth. Yes, you will also go mainstream, but here's a chance to build a little momentum with a target market that you know intimately and which is interested in what you do. (You can also trade for stuff you can use—like new sails, for instance.) As Chevy Chase said in *Caddy Shack,* "Be the ball." What are your passions, and is there a way to tap into a market that you are already connected to?

Work with your strengths. I am not a technical person. I know what good design is, however. My strength is designing (not creating) websites. I don't want to deal with the details. What are your strengths? Do you offer something that is hard to find? One of a kind? Do you do things better, faster, more creatively? Are you more experienced? More credible? Have superior equipment? Basically, what makes you great?

Compare yourself to your competitor. What do you do better or different than your nearest competitors? A struggling wedding photographer had a special talent for photographing babies. She was unable to find enough work in the highly competitive area of weddings. So she would look up birth announcements in the paper and send parents a beautiful brochure and a discount for new parents. Business is booming. Study the competition and look for holes that aren't being filled, needs that aren't being met. Look for ways you can stand out in a crowded field by being different or the best. Best-selling author Suze Orman writes books about financial management. She doesn't try to compete directly with other self-help gurus like Tony Robbins, Stephen Covey, and John Gray, and thus doesn't dilute her brand. With all the financial management books in the stores, it would seem impossible to find a way to break out. But Orman did by being a little different. She doesn't claim to be holier than thou, and she freely admits to making mistakes herself earlier in her life. She also doesn't make managing your finances seem overly complicated. She talks in terms that most people understand. What do you want to be known for? How will that set you apart?

Find your champion. One artist tied in with a local Realtor who gave her art away as a gift to new home buyers. Once these people got one of her paintings, it seemed they wanted more. This was one of those ideal situations where everyone wins. The artist sold her paintings for full price, the Realtor impressed clients with a really nice gift, and the new homeowner got some great art. After this local success she approached Realtors in other cities and set up similar arrangements in other parts of the country. If she chooses to advertise, she said she would do it in real estate journals. Find someone who is "connected" to a target market you want to reach and team up. Name at least one person who could be your champion and help you reach a target audience.

Be a big fish. Dominate a small niche and end up with fewer customers but more business. These will be better customers. Less is more if they are loyal. Progressive rock was big in the seventies. Trent Gardner is bringing it back. He has turned his passion into an international business and is on the forefront of the revival. The record label he created has resulted in a roster of progressive rock legends that include Steve Howe (Yes), Terry Bozzio (Zappa), Steve Walsh (Kansas), and John Wetton (UK). Is there some area related to what you do where you could be the big fish in a small pond? This is the narrow-niche, deep-pockets theory, and it works because there are so many fish in the sea, but in a small pond you can move right to the top of the food chain.

Use your ethnicity to your advantage. Black consumers spend over $320 billion a year on goods and services. That's a huge target market. Cookbook author Barbara Smith has been called the "Black Martha Stewart." Like Martha, she hosts a nationally syndicated television show from her home (in Sag Harbor, Long Island). The show, called "B. Smith With Style," is the beginning of an empire that will likely also include books and a magazine. The Latin explosion (Hispanic buying power increased 67 percent since 1990) led to the founding of *Latina* magazine. Emilio Estefan (Gloria's husband) built a $200 million empire that includes everything from records to restaurants. The target market is broad-based, but with a focus on Latins. Are you overlooking a specific ethnic target market that you have ties to?

Be gender biased. *Wahine* is a surfing magazine devoted entirely to women who surf. There are also brands of equipment designed solely for women and which are sold through surf shops exclusively for women. I love their names: Salty Sister, Pink Laura, Watergirl, Girl in the Curl, and Surf Like a Girl. In my surf shops we sold women's swimsuits, but I know for a fact that bathing suit buyers did not feel comfortable with us (male clerks) leering at them. So I made sure we had at least one girl working at all times. (I mean, I never knew what answer they were looking for when they would ask, "How does this look on me?") I know fellow women speakers and authors who focus solely on their own gender with great success. It helps them to focus their marketing efforts, while also reaching the segment of the population they know best. (Besides, women make up over 50 percent of the population, and I read somewhere that they control nearly all of the money in the United States in one way or another.) How can you use your gender to form a bond with a target audience? It's nothing new—magazines do it, television shows do it, too. So why don't we do it?

Age before beauty. There is a mad scramble to market to teenage girls online. These sites are trying to offer things that would interest them. What would teenage girls want? Help with homework, boys, and shopping, of course. Oh, and one more thing. What do teenage girls do best? Right. Talk on the phone. So there are chat rooms, e-mail, and instant messaging. Age is one way to narrow your focus and find the right fit for what you offer. Once you know the age of your core customer, you can tailor your approach specifically to them. Advertisers do this all the time. Let's say, for example, you're promoting an offer of some sort for seniors (not high school, think older). It makes sense to make your copy easy to read by using larger type. You would also want to use photos of (active) people the same age. Since seniors are often cautious about being ripped off, make your offer clear and believable. Of course, instead of placing an ad in *Teen* magazine it should be in *Senior Living*. You get the picture. Once you know the age of your audience, you know where to reach them and how to reach them. (It's almost like being able to read their minds.) So, what age group is the best buyer for your product or service?

Be all you can be. Any angle that gives you credibility and makes you "one of them" should be explored. One author, who is ex-military and writes books about the Navy SEALs, does his signings in

Coronado and Oceanside (near two of San Diego's biggest military bases) and is always featured in articles in military papers. Use your rank to reach readers. If you are ex-military, that could be one area to begin to market to.

Local knowledge. One singer wrote a song for his hometown, which was adopted as a theme song. Royalties began rolling in immediately from sales and usage rights. You can be a hometown hero and parlay your regional success into something more. Think national, but start local. You have an edge in your own neck of the woods. You know more people, maybe even have a connection or two with the media. ("Local Person Does Good" is almost always newsworthy, by the way.) Maybe you know someone who knows someone who works for the person you need to contact to sell your creations. Hey, it's a start, and it can lead to bigger and better (national) things. This book is filled with examples of nationally known celebrities who first built a following in their home state. I know I have good luck by promoting first in my hometown and then expanding to a national level. For example, I was hired to give a talk to a national organization's local chapter, which led to a talk at the regional conference, and eventually, ta da, I was asked to speak at the group's national convention. The same thing can apply to a consultant working with a local division of a larger company. Get into one part of a company and you can work your way into other departments. Is there a local angle you could play in promoting yourself? Are you doing all you can do in your own geographic region?

Pray for promotion. "Most Texans think Hanukkah is some sort of duck call," says comedian Richard Lewis. Religion is the perfect example of target marketing. Former Padre and Giant pitcher Dave Dravecky, who lost his arm to cancer, wrote a book called *When You Can't Comeback*. If you look at the number of books sold, it could have been a best-seller, but the bulk of book sales came from Christian bookstores. Who cares? Books sold are books sold. (And royalties are royalties, baby!) After giving public seminars all over the country, I have noticed that a surprising number of my attendees work for a church or temple. A lot. I have deduced that organized religion has some money to spend. Now, I realize I am skating on thin ice here, so let me just say: Don't overlook the church and people who share your beliefs as potential clients and customers. (Lightning hasn't struck me yet, so I'll just keep going.) Churches have functions with lots of people, newsletters, magazines, websites, and other avenues that allow a believer (you) to reach a lot of people. Also, as I mentioned earlier, they need the assistance of creative people to help them run their business, er . . . chuches and temples (and they pay for that help). Amen. Have you used this approach yet?

Go back to the well. Once you know your audience, you can keep creating things they will enjoy and benefit from. Being an expert in an area gives greater name recognition. Bradley Richardson became an "X-pert" since writing *Job Smarts for Twentysomethings.* The book led to a speaking tour of colleges, plenty of publicity, and a nice living. Then the tide turned, and instead of teaching college kids how to survive and thrive in the corporate world, he went over to the dark side and began consulting with companies on how to snare and care for young workers because that's where the market was, but he was able to use knowledge he already had. What other products or services could you offer your existing customers? How could you take what you know, or what you do, and recycle it and sell it again to a new audience?

Look for unconventional markets. Linda Ellerbee once said, "Only dead fish swim with the stream all the time." Find an off-the-beaten path. Find an unconventional approach and angle to reach potential clients. Look for customers on the fringe. Find an alternative to the big stores and the standard distribution channels. Can't crack regular stores? No problem. Urban Juice and Soda couldn't afford to "buy" shelf space in supermarkets for their drinks, so to reach their target market (Gen-X) they sold Jones Soda and Wazu Water in skate shops, tattoo and piercing parlors, and cappuccino bars where there was no direct competition. This resulted in sales into the millions. Have you overlooked any unorthodox and unconventional outlets for your stuff? Whom else could you sell to? Where else could you sell it? What else could you sell? Try to find the most obscure connection to what you sell (use the mind-mapping method to do this) and see if you turn up any new and uncharted territory to promote and sell your stuff. The other day I was in my boat on the bay when I saw a bottle floating in the water. Being the environmentalist that I am, I pulled alongside and plucked it from the water. I noticed that inside the corked bottle was a note. My mind raced with the possibilities. I anxiously pulled the paper out, and scribbled on it was a note from a young girl inviting the recipient to attend her "totally awesome" church (just a few miles away). I applaud the creative approach to promotion, I just don't dig the idea of littering the bay.

Decide whom you *don't* want to deal with. We agree that not everyone is going to be, wants to be, or should be a potential person to promote to. Right? So whom should we promote to? For the answer to that question, let's turn the tables and start eliminating people we don't want to do business with and see what we're left with. First, fire customers who don't pay, don't appreciate you or your work, and are a pain in the neck. See, in order to get better customers, we need to create a void. Don't waste your time and promotional efforts on people who waste your time and efforts by not paying, who don't give a damn about art and artistic integrity, belittle you, cheapen or tarnish your reputation, and are so much trouble that working with them hardly seems worth the effort. Because by continuing to work with and promote to these types, you may be missing out on much better business. So factor in all the abovementioned scenarios and fire or eliminate those you don't want to work with. Always consider the long-term ramifications of your immediate decisions. Yes, you need to pay the bills, but in the larger scheme of things, is it worth working with these people? Do you have anyone you'd like to dump? Describe what your ideal client, customer, or audience would be like.

Stop beating your head against a wall. I know a freelance writer who spent a lot of money promoting work that nobody wanted. She never took the time to ask editors what they were looking for. She was locked in a time warp and kept writing the same things she did when disco was popular (the first time around). Now, instead of writing full-length features, she writes 250 to 500 word "filler" pieces and sells several a month to publications like *Family Circle, Men's Journal,* and *Travel and Leisure.* Find out what is selling. What exactly is the person you are promoting to looking for? What are the exact needs of the market right now?

Turn disadvantage into advantage. High self-esteem is very important when it comes to self-promotion. That said, very few creative people possess it. Maybe it's because what we do is subjective (and subjected to people's opinions), or that we have to deal with uncertainties and insecurities as part of our chosen careers in the creative arts. It's also a fact that we face heavy doses of rejection on an annual basis. (Exposure to rejection has much the same effect as exposure to radiation—it makes you sick.) Yet all the things you can think of as negatives about what you do (and I am sure you can come up with at least a couple) can and must be turned into some kind of tactical advantage. Maybe you put the "small" in small business. That can easily be turned into a positive thing in the eyes of the customer. You can do things faster, and offer more personal attention than your competition. Maybe you lack some expensive piece of equipment and instead you still do it the old way, like a true craftsman, which could make for a very interesting story in a newspaper. Possibly your sales are a little slow. One author went to Amazon.com to find out the ranking of his book (which is based on sales). It was dead last, ranked at over a million (number one is the best). I have to give him credit, he turned the fact that he was ranked last into a promotional point, which the media picked up on, and after a short while he was last no more. List all the negative things you can think of about what you do and come up with at least one positive promotional item for each.

Get creative with distribution. Find small pockets of people and be a leader in that arena. There are plenty of hidden markets and alternatives to the "big box" stores. But there is nothing like selling a ton of stuff with one call. (The same effort it took to sell one thing now results in sales into the gazillions.) What am I talking about? Distributors, wholesalers, and buyers for the chains. Certainly you want the biggest possible market, but you also want to reach them with the least possible effort. Selling your stuff to a middleman may be the way to go. Let them deal with the details and distribution. Target the biggest distributor in your field and make your pitch. It's a lot less effort, and there's a potential for greater sales than if you tried to individually move all your stuff yourself. Once you land a helping hand—help them to help you. Give them marketing materials to help them sell. Stay in touch and update them on media appearances and mailings. Work with them on window displays. Build a relationship and be the squeaky wheel. Who is the leading distributor, wholesaler, representative, retailer in your field? Could you develop a relationship with them? Have them handle your work or represent you? Are you doing all you can do to distribute your work?

Focus on deep pockets. Go where the money is. I have watched so many creative people spend all their time pursuing people with little or no money to spend, and avoiding the big spender. Why is this? Fear. It's easier to go after the smaller, more accessible, and less intimidating target, and maybe even make a small sale or two. But isn't it better to promote to those who have the potential to make your year with one sale? My wife gets a magazine at work that her large company pays for (it has health-related articles). It is easier for the publisher to sell subscriptions to large corporations (who distribute them to their people) than to sell them one at a time on a newsstand. When a friend of mine started her own apparel company, she went right after the biggest department stores and stayed away from the boutiques. Everyone said she was nuts (and had big balls). Guess what? She landed two major chains and hasn't looked back since. Who is the biggest possible client you can imagine? Have you approached them yet?

The grass IS greener. For years jazz musicians have had to go to Europe (now it's Japan) to find a larger audience. Go where the action is, even if it's miles away. Are you having trouble promoting yourself locally? Maybe it's time to look for greener pastures. Think about venturing out a little to reach fresh new faces. Where is all the action in your industry taking place? Do you have a presence there?

Do it deeper. Focus on one target customer but offer a wide variety of goods and services. Ask yourself: What else would this person want that I can provide? What can I add to what I already offer? When a word processor and editor added graphic design, she doubled her business. In the past she farmed out all the design work, but discovering she had the talent and the equipment to do it herself, she did. Then she added website design to her list of services and her business grew again. She was able to ceate and edit copy, design the site for the client, and maintain it. Mind you, these are the same clients she already worked with—she just added additional services they needed. What can you add to your existing line of merchandise or range of services that would be of interest to your existing customers? What other things would your "fans" pay to see you do?

Look for a secondary market. I soon discovered that people were buying my books to give as gifts to their friends and family. So I offered to autograph and mail copies of my books directly to the recipients of the gifts. Just the suggestion of "makes a great gift" seemed to help. This is becoming a big part of my business. Be on the lookout for nontraditional places and people to sell to. What could be a secondary market for what you do?

Match your materials to the audience! Look at your marketing materials. Do they project the kind of message you are trying to convey? Are you high end? Bargain? Somewhere in the middle? Does the layout, color, type, and paper match that message?

A final thought. We all want to find the right clients, people who appreciate us and what we do. They are supportive and trusting, giving us the freedom to be as creative as possible. They benefit from what we do and gladly pay us well for our work. You don't have to change for them. There are people out there who love you the way you are. Find 'em.

☆————————————

FAST FACTS

Book buyers under the age of twenty-five make up the smallest and least likely demographic to buy a book (5 percent). The largest group of book buyers are between the ages of forty-five and sixty-five, accounting for 68 percent of book sales.

Create a Detailed Dossier

Moses led the Jews through the desert for forty years and ended up in the one place in the Middle East that doesn't have oil. Amazing. The lesson as it relates to self-promotion is this: Don't wander and squander your energy, time, and resources. Instead, focus on who and what give you the best promotional possibilities. Look at what worked in the past for promotion and who was your perfect match. List all the reasons why someone would want to work with or buy from you based on why they bought before. Or start from scratch and create a detailed description of your core customer. Start by answering the following questions.

Who:

• Who needs what I have to offer? Create a profile. (Remember, these are people with emotions and desires, not numbers.) What are their needs?

• Can this target market afford me? What's the point of targeting an audience if they can't or won't pay your price? Is there a group of people who will pay for this? How many of them are there? How can I best reach them? Ask yourself: If I were a customer, where would I look for my services and products?

• Make a detailed description of your core customer—the ones you have or the ones you want. Here are some sample questions to get you started: How old are they? Are they primarily men or women? Where do they live and work? How much do they make? What are their likes and dislikes? What's important to them? What are their biggest problems and concerns? What do they need? What do they want? What would be the best way to reach them? What do your current customers frequently ask you for? What are your current bestsellers? Why?

What:

• What are they buying? Why? If not from you, who are they buying from? Why? What would impress them? Sometimes the decision to buy or not buy is illogical. They got a reference from a friend, want to work with an up-and-comer, don't like you, don't like your agent, unknown name, difficult reputation.

How:

• Take the time to get to know current customers. Ask for feedback and listen! Go have a beer together. Do lunch. Send out a questionnaire. When Tom Morey first invented the Boogie Board, he was working for a company called Gordon & Smith. The name he had come up with for this new invention was S.N.A.K.E. He asked the girls in the office what they thought of the name. "Ick, I don't like snakes" was the universal reply. So he changed the name to Boogie Board.

• If things aren't working, ask for feedback on your promotional materials. Why didn't you buy? Even if they did buy, ask: How can we do this better?

• One consultant sent blank paper and crayons and asked customers to write, draw, and color in what they thought of his work.

• Online focus groups. Put up samples of your work and ask for feedback. You get honest responses this way. The answers are a click away. Use your competitor as a model. Look at their website, ads, and anything else you can get your hands on. Sam Walton, the founder of Wal-Mart, would fly around the country (in his own plane) and secretly shop his competitors. He would often get caught. About your competition: Why are you better or different? Look at all areas for answers. Do you do things better, faster, more uniquely? Are you local? Are you a better fit? Do you have better equipment? Are you more hands-on, lower-priced?

• Make a logbook for prospecting. Keep records of why they bought, what they said, how each conversation, performance, or sales call went.

• If you are having trouble answering these questions, make up a questionnaire and ask current clients to provide feedback. Reward them for their efforts and the valuable information they provide.

☆ ─────────────
ACTION ITEM
Come up with a simple message that your target market would understand and relate to, one that highlights your strengths and differentiates you from the competition. What am I selling? (Describe what it is, why it's unique, and why customers would care.)

Quick Quiz
By now you should be able to answer the following questions about your core customers. If you can easily answer ten or more questions correctly, you are in touch with your target market.

1. What makes me better? Different? Special?
2. Who is my target audience? Are they men or women?
3. What general age are they?
4. Where do they live? Hang out?
5. What turns them on? Off?
6. What do they do in their free time?
7. Describe their tastes.
8. Where are they located?
9. How often do they need what I have to offer?
10. What is an extension of existing sales? (Give as a gift?)
11. What type of websites do they go to?
12. How do they like to pay for things?
13. My best clients are?
14. The best way to get their attention is . . . ?
15. Where would they go to look for me?
16. What other products or services would they be interested in?
17. How are they like me?
18. What are they passionate about?
19. Why do they buy from me?
20. Who cares about what I do?

Getting to Know You

"It takes considerable knowledge just to realize the extent of your ignorance."

—*Thomas Sowell*

Ignorance is not bliss. In *The Next Karate Kid* there is a great line: "Ambition without knowledge is like a boat on dry land." That's why it's a good idea to do your homework. Right-brained people like to wing it. But a little research can save a lot of time and money (and embarrassment). For instance, it helps to know the rules of your industry's game. The odds of an unknown author who sends in an unsolicited manuscript to a publishing house ever getting it published are about the same as seeing Ed McMahon showing up at your door to hand you a check. (Not good.) There are certain protocols in the publishing industry. (Getting an agent to submit your manuscript is far better than sending it yourself.) The same is true of the media. Sending the wrong pitch to the wrong publication or person at that publication does not make you look good (and usually fails to garner any good results). Do a little recon. If you are pitching a catalog company, check out their website, get on their mailing list, and call to see who is the decision maker. This knowledge is helpful in many ways, including boosting your confidence level. You find out people's preferences, which gives you an edge. Knowing what their needs are before you send samples is simply smart. The more you understand about the needs and trends of your industry, the more it allows you to target. What studio does what kind of films? Which ones are struggling? What are they looking for? Whom would I pitch to? Read the trades. (In Hollywood it means you read the *Hollywood Reporter* and *Daily Variety*.) Go to an industry trade show or convention and learn as much as you can. Talk to a veteran in your field. This kind of information can prove to be invaluable.

Don't assume. Which of the following countries would you guess has the highest annual theater attendance per thousand people? The United States, Mongolia, Cuba, or Vietnam? The answer is . . . Cuba. (The United States wasn't even in the top ten!) Do your homework! Listen to the needs of clients, get in their heads by asking questions, and take a walk in their shoes. Know what they want. Don't just guess. It's a common assumption that the art will sell itself. Wrong. That people will beat a path to your door without promotion. Wrong again. That customers will drop their current supplier to sign up with you despite the fact you are brand new. Of course distributors will carry your product. NOT! Once you have done some research, you can make educated guesses. As a surf shop owner we were pretty confident that our customers went to the beach, so having a company that flies 300-foot banners with messages on them over the beach made sense. That was a good guess, but it's better to be sure.

Statistics are like a bikini. What they reveal is suggestive, but what they conceal is vital. I'm not sure who said this, but oh how true it is. So look at the numbers, and trust your gut, too. Facts can lie. Sometimes it helps to unlearn what you know and think way outside the box. The "suits" want tried and true, and you present them with "there is nothing else like this, never has been," and it frightens them. Sell your idea with energy and enthusiasm as well as examples of other similar "first time" successes. And for the "suits," find statistics that support your hunches. They don't want pie-in-the-sky ideas, they want to see pie charts.

Talk to people who know. This is why a mentor is so valuable. Do lunch with people who are connected.

Sleep with the enemy. Sleeping with the enemy simply means you get ahold of your competitors' stuff. You should also request information from companies that you are interested in doing business with. Look for areas you can compete with them and things they may have missed.

Test. In direct marketing and even display advertising it is wise to test first. Play new songs and gauge an audience's reaction before recording them. Release a chapter of a new book and ask for feedback. Produce a prototype and let people play with it and give you input on how to improve it.

Listen. Clothing designer Tommy Hilfiger credits his success to listening to the customer. He sees a niche and he fills it fast.

Read. Read your daily paper and your trade magazine and ask yourself when you come across news: How does this affect me? How can I take advantage of this trend or opportunity?

Discuss. Start logging on to online discussion groups, to find out what people in your field are saying and thinking.

Survey. Before a developer of apartments laid one brick he spent months researching the lifestyles of his target market—people who work out of their homes as entrepreneurs or telecommuters. As a result he made sure each house had office space, high-speed access, and a business center in the lobby. Abercrombie & Fitch was once a store for the rich and famous. Today the hundred-year-old company is going after a much younger crowd and caters to college students. They sent people to college campuses to see how students live and what they were willing to pay for a "name."

Get out more. When Amazon.com founder Jeff Bezos began, he needed to learn about the book business—and fast. He went to the American Booksellers Association annual convention for a crash course on the publishing industry and roamed the aisles and talked to key book distributors about his plan to build Amazon.com.

Let your fingers do the walking. The yellow pages are an excellent source of information about your competitors and the market.

Search. Get in the habit of doing a monthly Internet search to see what's new out there related to what you do.

Go to the source. For me, that's bookstores. I spend a lot of time loitering in the magazine section (reading *Publishers Weekly* and the *New York Times* best-seller list) pursuing the recent releases displays to see what's new.

Be a little sneaky. Many times reaching people is easy. Most companies make an e-mail address the person's first initial and last name. Try it. I reach people I want to get to know by looking in the back of their book and going to their website. Aspiring authors should pay attention to the acknowledgments of published books to find out who publishes what and what agent and editor are thanked by the author. Then go to a directory for publishing and look up the address and phone number (and look for the best way to approach them). Look at what they are publishing and find a natural follow-up. See what holes you could fill in a particular publisher's list.

Join an association. Do it for the directory.

Get a rep. Talk to the reps; they are usually very knowledgeable about what's hot and what's not.

Temping. Ad agencies need freelancers, magazines need freelance writers. Learn what they are looking for. You get paid and get good inside information.

The more you know, the better. "A man will turn over half a library to make one book," stated Samuel Johnson. There are all kinds of facts, figures, and studies available on the Internet and the library, and don't overlook your Chamber of Commerce and trade associations.

What's Going On?

"Outside of traffic, there is nothing that has held this country back as much as committees."

—*Will Rogers*

Philip J. Quigley, the former CEO of Pacific Telesis, commented in a speech that if we were to go back in time a hundred years and ask a farmer what he'd like if he could have anything, the farmer would probably tell us he wanted a horse twice as strong that ate half as many oats. He would never have thought to ask for a tractor. Why? Because they didn't exist. Things change so fast it is hard to predict the future, but that doesn't mean we should stop trying. In fact, smart marketers are somehow able to spot trends before they happen and then act on them. It goes without saying that it isn't enough to spot a trend, you have to take advantage of it. Besides, it is always good to show you are "with it" and on the cutting edge of your industry. Sure, you can't predict the future, but you can plan and prepare for the possibilities. You don't want to be left behind or caught by surprises. You want to study trends to spot hidden or developing opportunities that you can take advantage of. How do you spot these trends? Pay attention and be observant, read and research, stay dialed in with colleagues, trust your intuition and hunches. Things are always in a state of flux (now more than ever), so look around and ask yourself: What's selling? Why is it selling? How or where is it selling? Who is buying? As an author I pay attention to the best-seller lists and new release section of the bookstore to see who is publishing what. I talk to my agent, who pays attention to trends.

Someone who has been on top of trends is Aaron Spelling. He consistently reads what people want and then gives it to them. In 1968 he came up with the "Mod Squad," where Peter, Link, and Julie took on the demeanor, fashion, and vocabulary of the times. In 1975 he came up with "Charlie's Angels," a hit bigger than Farrah's hair. (In the seventies he also had "Starsky and Hutch" on the air.) In the greedy eighties he created "Dynasty," and in the youth-oriented nineties he produced "Beverly Hills 90210" and "Melrose Place." That's an amazing track record. It's not as hard to know what's what if you pay attention to trends.

When you spot a trend, ask yourself: How does this trend/change affect me? How can I benefit from it? How can I take advantage of it? What am I going to do about it? When Thermos saw that starter fluid was being banned in some states, they began focusing on and developing high-end electric grills instead of gas and charcoal. They also noticed that more and more people lived in small apartments and condos, so they developed compact and clean barbecues (with three legs) that fit in small spaces and emitted less smoke. Another example: Rutgers University did a study and discovered a 43 percent drop in the marriage rate from 1960 to 1996 due to people getting married later in life and cohabiting instead. (Shhhhh, don't tell Dr. Laura.) So how could someone benefit from this information? How about an online matchmaking service? That's what eCrush thought, too. It's not enough to spot a trend, you also have to act on it.

Keep a notebook or journal and make notes about the things you see and hear that may be trends. Be a sponge. Read everything, especially your industry's trade magazine. Did you know there is an official magazine for arm wrestlers? Yup. It's called *Arm Bender*. There's also a *Horse Illustrated* magazine. (I wonder if they do a swimsuit issue?) Expand your range of knowledge. Take a class (even if you have advanced degrees), browse a bookstore, talk to colleagues, search the Web, and watch TV. Keep up on technology. Don't fall so far behind you are lost; stay one step ahead instead.

In the early 1900s, Charles Dwell, Director of the U.S. Patent Office, made this bold statement: "Everything that can be invented has been invented." Whoops. Add at least one cool new thing to your résumé every quarter. What's new? When microwaves first came out Bev Hans was one of the first to write (and self-publish) a book on microwave cooking. The result of being first was that she sold 750,000 copies. Wow! The more things change, the more they stay the same.

There are patterns that are repeated over and over. Look back at the history of your industry and try to spot patterns. It can almost be considered predictable. My friend Diana Snodgrass, a fashion accessory designer, hoards old fashion magazines and mines them for ideas she can use in her current designs. When Johann Gutenberg invented a new and faster form of printing, an information revolution followed. Guess what? We are seeing the same thing again. In 1990, Tim Berners (not Al Gore) created the World Wide Web, and the revolution is in full swing.

Follow the money. F. Scott Fitzgerald said: "Culture follows money. Money in new media is reshaping culture." Read books by futurists. I recommend Faith Popcorn and Alvin Toffler. After reading *The Third Wave* by Toffler, who saw the future of interactive media, a man named Steve Case decided to act on that information. Now he's the founder of a little company called America Online. Things *are* what they used to be. Look at your past successes for clues about what once worked. Pull out old invoices, press clippings, and portfolio pieces to see what sold in the past. Could it be time to bring back something that was once hot? Turn to an old contact or client again and sell them something different, smaller, bigger, better. It's easier to build on past success than starting from scratch. Look at where you are today. Predict what you think the future holds. Ask yourself: What opportunities are there going to be? What will I need to take advantage of them? (Resources, tools, training, skills, connections.) For example, Broadcast.com found a nice niche in broadcasting live events over the Internet (like the Victoria's Secrets fashion show, oh, yeah). The potential is there to broadcast all kinds of live business events. As a seminar leader, I find this exciting. I was also pleased to read that one trend in the coming years is the need for lifelong learning. People will need to be trained and retrained at a rapid rate in the near future. For me, that's a good thing. Self-learning is a growth industry. (They need books, instructors, and trainers—they need me, man.) By combining online learning with what I do now, I am confident I will have plenty to do in the future.

Timing is everything. Know the best time to produce and promote something (for your industry) and then work backward. For example, golf books sell better in the winter, when people aren't playing. Books on barbecuing sell better during summer, when people are able to use them. Pick your spots and plan ahead. Maybe it's a seasonal thing. Adam Sandler wrote a perennial holiday hit in 1995. "The Hanukkah Song" is a seasonal standard.

That's the Plan, Man

"Songs are all written as part of a symphony."

—Bob Dylan

As I mentioned earlier, creative people like to wing it. We would prefer to go with our gut rather than take the time to study, organize, and plan. We act and react as situations present themselves. The problem with this (as it relates to self-promotion) is that you'll have no target, no focus (there are so many distractions for right-brainers), you'll become overwhelmed, lose interest, and your approach will be hit and miss—mostly miss. You'll end up chasing your tail and running around in circles with your career left to the whims of fate. You'll have a short-range view and make decisions that will harm your chances for long-term success.

Sometimes it isn't the plan that matters most, it's the act of planning. When you break down a goal, it gives you a major reality check. Plans overcome assumptions and give you a reality check. So many self-published authors get sucked into thinking that the more books they print, the lower the per-book price. But how many can you sell? To whom? Do the math first. Then you will start to realize you are going to have a ton of extra copies lining the walls of your garage or basement if you printed how many you thought you needed. (Of course, there is print on demand now.) One nice thing about planning is that it is primarily a left-brain function, and since fear resides in the right brain, while you are planning you are fearless.

Plans get you focused and fired up. It's kind of comforting knowing what needs to be done, and to whom to do it to. It's motivating, too. A written plan is more tangible than some vague idea floating around in your head, and frees up your brain for more important things. A good plan tells you exactly what you need to do in small, easy steps. This can make you get off your ass and do something. Because you know what you need to do, you do it. It's a blueprint of what you want to accomplish with your marketing and how you'll do it, and for whom, using the tools and taking the steps to create the most impact. It helps you define your market (and find new ones you didn't think of before) and how to best reach it with the least effort, and using your creativity instead of money. You'll identify potential pitfalls and plan for them in advance. No more surprises. You'll identify how to get help when and if you need it. It helps you make better decisions, keeps you focused, and it becomes a little easier to make decisions about what promotional opportunities to pursue next. (You'll be less likely to waste money on advertising in a haphazard fashion.) You are more organized (both in your thinking and your actions) and more consistent with your efforts. Finally, and perhaps most important, a good plan creates a vision that you can focus on, and it pushes you to try harder. Deadlines can be very motivating. (Trust me on that.) Many magazines have such a long lead time, you need to start thinking about promotion early. So you have to stay on top of deadlines. You can take advantage of good timing techniques when things are laid out on a time line. Planning also alerts you to duplicate efforts and calls your attention to past mistakes.

It's good to slow down and evaluate where you want to go and to figure out how to best get there. For instance, a plan takes into account what your strengths and weaknesses are. Maybe you like doing mass mailings but hate cold calling. Plan around your weaknesses and take advantage of your strengths. You won't continually reinvent yourself and lose momentum. You'll stay the course, and as a result have more success.

Why wouldn't you do a plan, even a simple one? Most people think they don't have the time (it will save you time in the long run), or they don't know how (keep reading and I'll show you), or they don't think they need one (without one you flail and flounder and eventually drown). They see it as too rigid (read on, it can be and should be flexible). Promotional plans make marketing seem less overwhelming. Make order out of chaos. It gives you some structure, which can lead to peace of mind. Planning takes into account your budget and time. (So you won't waste it.) What you focus on becomes your reality, and a plan gives you something GOOD to focus on. It forces you out of your comfort zone. Smart ideas with a well-thought-out plan, pursued with passion and persistence, will make you prevail. Planning frees you to worry about other things, like your art.

IT ALL STARTS WITH WHAT YOU WANT

"I want to make a bad horror movie so bad I can taste it. I want to be in, like, panties and a T-shirt, brushing my teeth, asking 'Who's there?' "

—Kristen Johnston

The first step is figuring out what you want from your marketing efforts. Then we'll figure out how to get you there through savvy self-promotion and planning. By the way, be careful what you wish for. Do you really want to be touring for eight straight months? Are you able to handle all the pressure and expectations that come with being a media star? Talk to someone who has what you want. Better yet, spend a day with them. Try on this new life for a day.

Plan to Be Spontaneous (Planning the Easy Way)

"The reason that everybody likes planning is that nobody has to do anything."

—Jerry Brown

"When I'm at point A, I can see point E, and I don't get stuck on what will happen at B, C, and D. Ninety percent of the people in the general population are so focused on what might go wrong in the middle that they lose sight of their goals." That was Tom Scott, cofounder of Nantucket Nectars. Martha Stewart once said, "Life is too complicated not to be orderly." That's just like her, isn't it? A *little* chaos isn't such a bad thing. It's okay to be flexible. (But you want to bend, not break away from your promotional plans.) Trust your gut. You can't always predict who your best audience will be. Take advantage of unforeseen opportunities. Keep it simple so your plan is easy to understand and refer to—often. It can be on a napkin or matchbook. One page, even! Still, you must have a written plan. It's a preventive thing. No plan prevents you from promoting yourself well. A simple, flexible plan doesn't cost anything and it can save you a lot of pain. Planning is like the yellow brick road to your dreams. (Look out for the wicked witch.) Here are some points to work through as you put your plan together.

1. What is your main goal as an artist? How much money do you want to make? What do you want to be known for? In a perfect world, you would have what? Describe your perfect day. Perfect clients.

Projects. Work environment. The kind of work you will do. (Quality of that work.) Do you do art full-time and make $60,000 a year and do a book a year? Visualize all of your success. (For example, if you are an author, see your book displayed in the window of your local bookstore. Imagine that large advance and royalty check. Best of all, picture adoring fans wanting your autograph.) It all begins with a clear understanding of what you want to accomplish. Think big, act small. What are your promotional goals? What are you trying to accomplish with your work? How much time and energy would it take to pull it off? What inspires you? What legacy do you want to leave behind? Are you willing to work that hard? Do you need to downsize or expand your goal? Where do you see yourself in a year? Two years? What's stopping you from having it now? Who can help you get what you want? Who has what you want? What steps did they take to get it? What do I offer? Who cares? What's the first thing you think of when you hear your latest project's name? First person you think will buy it? Why? What is your best promotional tool? What promotional tasks do you like doing?

☆ ————————————————————

ACTION ITEM

Make a promotional plan that is a collage of pictures cut out from magazines and catalogs that represent what you hope to gain from your efforts. These are a visual representation of your promotional goals. (Include written captions next to each photo for the whole-brain effect.)

————————————————————————

2. How do others benefit from what you do? What emotions are connected to what you do? How does your service rock? Give one example of where you exceed expectations. What else can you do? What are your strengths? How are you better and different from your competitors? Why should people buy from you? What does your name say about you? Make them think of? What problem do you solve? Why do people buy from you or come to see you perform? What are their goals? How do you help them reach those goals? Most companies brag that they offer the best price, service, and selection. Fine, so what does that mean to a client? Be specific. What's in it for them?

ACTION ITEMS

Make a list of all the things you offer, and next to each one find at least one benefit to others. (Focus on the customers' wants and needs.) Now describe what you do in ten words or less using only benefits.

3. Who is my audience? Who will buy this and why? And for how much? You can't say "everyone." You don't need a lot of people, you need the right people! Describe your core customer. What will they pay? Is it worth it? (If they buy one painting a year at $1,000, that customer is worth $10,000. If they buy one book a year at $15, they are worth $150. If it costs you $15 a year to reach them, is it worth the effort and expense? So, what is the value of each of your customers?) What do they want? What turns them on? What approach works best to reach them? Noticed any trends in them? What do they ask for the most? Do you already provide this? Describe their daily routines or habits. Day in the life. Where would they be most likely to see your creations? Buy it? Best time of the year to reach them? How can you create long-term relationships? Repeat business? How many new clients did you get this year? Why did they switch to you? How many did you lose? Why did they leave and where did they go? Why? Who are your competitors? List all of their products and services. What are they doing? Strengths and weaknesses. Any holes? What is your niche? How are you special? Unique?

ACTION ITEM

Create a day in the life for your core customer. What do they do? Watch? Read? Where do they go? Who else do they hang out with? Create a "to do" list for them.

ACTION ITEM

What are you selling? If the audience gets only one thing from your marketing message, what would you want that to be?

4. How do you best reach them? What's worked the best in the past when it comes to promotion? What hasn't worked? Why? If money were no object, how would you gain the most visibility for yourself and your art? Can any of these things be done for free or cheaply (or can you trade for or co-op with someone)? Do you have the best distribution possible? Do you need an agent or manager or publicist? Are you actively marketing on the Internet? (If not, why not? Go do it!) If you are having trouble coming up with ideas about the best way to reach your target market, go back to question number 3.

ACTION ITEM

If you could not fail, how would you promote yourself? Or, who has all the promotion that you want? How did they do it? Find out and make a plan based on those principles.

5. What resources can I afford to spend on promotion? How much time can/will you spend on marketing? (It's unlikely you'll be able to pursue promotion full-time. Be realistic. You will need to devote some time to it!) Break it down until you get to a weekly number. One hour a day? Two? Where is the best area to focus your time? Which are most likely to be successful? (Publicity, performing, mailings, Internet?) What is your budget for promotion? (You have to spend some money to make money and promote yourself.) How much can you afford to spend on promotion? Break it down. List all the activities you want to do and the cost next to each. Add it up. Where would your promotional money be best spent? What are some free things you can do? Do you need to purchase marketing materials? Airtime? Hire a website designer? This gives you a dose of reality and helps you get rid of the things that don't pay off in terms of money. Forces you to get creative! Time plus money doesn't always equal self-promotion success, but it does increase your odds.

ACTION ITEM

Look for the most cost-effective way. Start with how much you think you will make this year. Then list all the methods you are considering using for promotion. (Ads, flyers, newsletter, postcards, and so on.) Then, next to each tool, break down what it would cost you in dollars each time you use that method. Then multiply that by how often you plan to use that method this year. That will give you the REAL cost of each method. Total that up. Can you realistically afford to do them all? Which ones would be the most effective or most cost-effective?

Final Action Steps

Your plan will never be perfect or complete. Get over it and go forward. Look for the biggest payoff promotional ideas and do them first. Make a things-to-do list (with deadlines) and schedule self-promotion into your weekly routine. Or write down what you will do and when on a time line or wall calendar or make a marketing calendar. Start with small steps. Take it one day at a time. Come up with one thing you will do every day and then force yourself to do it. Momentum is an ally, so stay the course and continue to promote yourself a little bit every single day.

Review your plan and progress from time to time. Is it working? Track the results. Review the numbers. Ask yourself: How will I know if I am successful? What would be some signs of success? (By age forty I will have a website, award-winning book, fan club, top agent, radio talk show, be featured in a national newspaper, and do a book tour in Hawaii, for example.) Test some tasks and throw back the little ones. Focus on what works. When Steve Jobs returned to run Apple, he got rid of the things that the company didn't do particularly well, like printers, and focused on what it did best, desktop and portable Macs for professionals and consumers—particularly design and publishing customers. Be honest: Is the plan not working or are you not working the plan?

Planning for the Right-Brainer

"Greatness is not where we stand, but in what direction we are moving."

—Oliver Wendell Holmes

Don't like rules and structures? Hate the idea of planning? You need at least a little structure or you will be buried by the daunting prospect of promoting yourself. Without deadlines and direction, you will flail about and eventually drown. Not having a promotional plan is a sure way to waste time and money. We need to come up with a creative, flexible plan (and to start a routine to carry out the plan—including an appointment with yourself to do marketing) that gives you simple steps to take. Think big! But get real with a plan that uses your strengths (big-picture thinking and creativity). Use your intuition rather than facts and figures, which will feel more natural. The only catch is that it has to be in written (or drawn) form and on paper (even if it is colored construction paper, even if it's just one page), not something floating around in your head. Otherwise it's not real and you'll become easily distracted and find excuses to stop using the plan.

Visualize the end result and work backward. Use your intuitive powers to decide what to do and in what order.

Create a résumé. Author Guy Kawasaki says you should create a one-page résumé for your company as if it were a person applying for a job. Include experience, education, accomplishments, and references. Create a résumé of how you want things to be, or as if you have already accomplished all of your promotional goals.

Create an artist statement. When people hear my name, I want them to think? I am known for? I want to be known for? I am unique because? My work benefits others how?

Create a journal. Make page one the plan and then keep track of what sold, to whom, for how much, how you reached them, comments from customers. Review regularly and summarize. Highlight key things. Adjust the plan according to your track record.

Create something creative. Turn your plan into a song, story, poem, or painting.

Make it a game. Every time you perform a promotional task or reach a milestone, give yourself points (depending on the difficulty), and when you accumulate enough points, reward yourself with a prize.

Start a file with ideas. Articles about clever promotions others have done. Customer suggestions. Fan mail. Opportunities missed. Things you don't have time for but will do as soon as . . .

Create a collage. Cut out pictures of what you want. Arrange it into a time line or plan.

Create a mock-up. Make a mock-up of the *New York Times* bestseller list with your book at the number one position. Then, under that or in a mind map, what would it take to get there? (Same for the *Billboard* chart.) Conduct an interview with yourself as if you have everything you ever wanted.

Create a marketing calendar. A promotional calendar on the wall is a motivator. You can see it. Start with goals at the top. Make hash marks for gigs or PR. Write in marketing efforts. Gigs. Put how much you made next to the sale or gig. Keep a running total. It tells you where you are and how far to go.

Create a simple one-page plan. This one page is something you can carry around and look at often, and maybe even show people.

Create a strong visual image. Draw a picture of what you want your company to look like. Write a caption to further descibe what you want.

Create a time line. Write your main promotional goal at the top of the page. Make a list of all the things that will help you reach that goal. Then make a long line and add benchmark dates with spaces in between. Next, write in tasks and goals next to the dates they need to be done.

Create a mind map. Put your goal in the middle of the paper and circle it. Then free-associate and circle ideas and categories that support the goal. Keep branching off ideas and action items that will make up your promotional plan. Add an idea or category as needed by adding a new circle or more branches to an existing category.

Follow the leader. Have you ever considered using someone you admire as a benchmark for your promotional plan? It stands to reason that if you follow in their footsteps and do the same things they did, in the order they did them, you will get the same or similar results. Maybe it isn't quite that simple, but at least it's a place to start your promotional plan.

Action Jackson

"Once you've done the mental work, there comes a point you have to throw yourself into the action and put your heart on the line."

—Phil Jackson

Planning is good, action is better. Gandhi once said, "Action is my domain. It's not what I say but what I do that matters most." The hard part (planning) is over. Now it's time to put the plan into motion. The question always is: Where do I start? As I have said many times before, do the easiest thing first. Something that will get the ball rolling and build momentum, something that has an excellent chance of success. Something you may even enjoy doing (I strangely don't mind putting together press kits and mailing them out). Then just start making a series of small steps. Steps so easy you can't *not* do it. Maybe it's something you already know how to do and have done before. "The secret of getting ahead is getting started. The secret of getting started is breaking your complex overwhelming tasks into small manageable tasks, and then starting on the first one," said Mark Twain. You will never be ready. Get over it and go forward. Don't waste time (and squander opportunities) waiting for just the right business card, demo tape, portfolio. Go with what you have. Act and react. If you fall on your face, so what? It's all part of the process. Fix what's "broke" and go on. Make marketing a priority and set aside time to do it, even if it's only a few minutes a day. (I make it a rule, I won't go to sleep unless I do one promotional thing a day.) You can't do it all, so eliminate wasted efforts and work on what works first. As a last resort you can hire someone to do promotion for you, but they will probably charge you a small fortune. Instead, get a calendar and write in what are you going to do each month for promotion. Simple, effective. Give yourself deadlines. Look for tie-ins. Break it down to a daily goal. Force yourself to find a system so you will follow up. (Follow-up is a key!) Don't "what if" and worry about all the details or worst-case scenarios. Don't think too much, act and react. You may be thinking: I don't need no stinkin' plan. I am a rebel. I am different. I'm a by-the-seat-of-my-pants kinda gal. I'm too busy. Okay, try it your way. If it doesn't work, reread this chapter. Deal?

Parting Thought

Stay flexible. John Sebastian, the founder of the Lovin' Spoonful, happened to be in the audience at the original Woodstock. On the second day, the stage filled up with water and the organizers couldn't have anyone playing an electric guitar in those conditions. They asked Sebastian to play an acoustic set. He was a hit.

Ask a Pro

Sue Viders
Art marketing consultant/author
(www.sueviders.com)

What is the first question that needs to be asked when you begin promoting yourself?

What are you promoting? The reason this is important is that when you talk to creative folks, it is not always a product, it could be the person. So the first thing that needs to be decided is *what* is being promoted. However, in all cases, besides stating the obvious, it is important especially for those who offer services to promote the *benefits* the buyer will receive.

What is the most effective form of self-promotion for creative people?

The most effective form of promotion is self! That is, the creative person doing his or her thing. Talking, speaking, having a website, writing about their products, etc. Which translates into "tooting one's own horn, loud and clear." You are the most effective tool, as you believe the most in your product.

What kind of marketing plan works best?

Well, that depends. Are you a plotter or a pantser? A plotter is one who has to get everything down on paper, a line-up-the-dominoes type of person. A pantser (doing it by the seat of your pants) simply does it with no particular rhyme or reason or because it seems like the "thing to do." And yes, the details or the "baby steps" make it all work. Let's assume you are thinking of entering the print market. A pantser will look at all her paintings and say, "I love this one the best, therefore, this is the one I will print," which may or may not work. A plotter will also look at all her paintings and say, "I love this one the best, but," and proceed to enter the image in contests, show it at exhibitions, have a group gathering at her home, etc., to see if the "buying public" really has any interest in it. So which is best? Some paper planning will save hours of frustration and money.

When setting up a marketing plan, what are some of the most important parts?

The most important part of a marketing plan is to get it out of your head and onto paper. Next comes research. This step cannot be overlooked. Unless you know which market segment you are going after, all marketing attempts are money down the promotional drain. So how do you find your niche? Test marketing is the answer. Getting the product out in front of the great buying public to test their reactions. Friends, neighbors, and family do NOT count. Once you know WHO you are marketing to, you can begin to formalize your marketing plan.

What is the biggest mistake creative people make when it comes to self-promotion?

Probably the biggest mistake is NOT doing anything. Many creative people have the misbegotten idea that their creative product is the end-all, be-all product of the century and the world will flock to them. Wrong. The world doesn't give a damn. No matter how great, how inventive, or how wonderful the product is. The only thing that will make you succeed in today's highly competitive marketplace is *marketing*.

3

SHOW OFF
(Get Your Ass Out There)

"It's important who you meet—after all, if you meet forty or fifty people, the one person who will produce your first film might just be there."
—Martin Scorsese

Someone once said, "You have a better chance to be hit in the head with opportunity if you put yourself in the line of fire." That's what this chapter is about. Stumbling into success by putting yourself in a position to trip over it. If you do nothing you . . . (help me here) right, you get nothing. Maybe you have heard that some species of sharks have to keep moving to survive. It is also true of creative people. You can rest on your laurels, or make a commitment to hunt for opportunities that show off your talents. Get out there and show off what you've got, baby, because you are either moving closer to your dream or farther away, and it's up to you to chase it.

It's a fact of life that as writers we are now expected to be promotable. "A person who publishes a book appears willfully in public with his pants down," declared Edna St. Vincent Millay. It's true. The life of a modern-day writer includes doing interviews, book signings, lectures, and workshops. For some of us this is no big deal. Bring it on. But it's also a fact that many writers (and creative people in general) are reclusive. Author Joseph Heller (*Catch-22*) was described as grumpy and antisocial. He even had a doormat on his East Hampton home that read, "Go Away." It's true, we need solitude to write and create, but our creations need us to get out there and promote the hell out of them. They deserve no less. We deserve no less.

You don't have to like it, you just have to do it. Force yourself to step out a little at a time. The next time you have the chance to stand up and stand out, do it! It could be just the break you've been waiting for. Do it now or regret it later. When you force yourself to get out there, good things can happen. Kathy Buckley is known as one of the funniest women in show business and is a five-time nominee for the American Comedy Award for Best Stand-Up Female. It all began when a friend dared her to enter a comedy contest. She came in fourth place and soon was performing in clubs across the country. The fact that she is hearing impaired makes this even more remarkable.

I know this will sound terrible, but I can't tell you how many times I have wished that the drummer performing in concert would somehow be unable to play (and no, I would never try to maim him myself) and the band would ask, "Is there anyone out there who can play drums?" Like the desperate single girl lunging for the tossed bouquet at the wedding reception, I would not hesitate to make my way to the stage. Sound far-fetched? Consider this: In 1973 the Who was performing in San Francisco when drummer Keith Moon (who had downed an animal tranquilizer with booze before going on stage) couldn't finish the set. The Who pulled volunteer drummer Scott Halpin out of the audience and onstage to play with the band. Not only did the teenager play the remaining songs flawlessly, one of the songs he played on was *unreleased*. Be prepared to play anywhere, at any time. As one musician put it, "Get the guitar out of the case as often as you can."

How Having a High Profile Helps

"Happiness is having a large, loving, caring, close-knit family in another city."

—George Burns

You never know who will be in the audience. Treat every performance as if your professional life depends upon it. Blow people away, every time. Vonda Shepard's first big break came at age nineteen when Rickie Lee Jones asked her to play keyboards and sing backup on her tour. But it wasn't until years later that David E. Kelley caught her act in a small club at the time he was developing the hit show "Ally McBeal." He wrote Shepard into the "Ally" plot as an on-camera lounge singer, a role that she reprises on each episode. He also chose the show's theme song from her 1992 album, *The Radical Light,* which had sold less than 6,000 copies. She went from playing for small crowds of well under a hundred people to over 10,000 screaming fans. Her career has taken off.

Getting out and showing off sets off a positive chain reaction. Vivica A. Fox was a struggling actress when she was cast as a doctor on the soap opera "The Young and the Restless." A movie producer's wife watches the show regularly and recommended Vivica when her husband was looking for an actress in his movie *Independence Day*. Her appearance in the blockbuster film gave her career a big boost. Here's still another example of why it pays to perform. My wife and I were walking around Seaport Village (a quaint shopping village on San Diego Bay) when we heard the most amazing Latin band performing. She bought the band's CD and played it at work. When her boss heard it he decided to hire the band to play a private corporate gig. Not only was the band, Nova Menco, paid well to perform, but they also sold a ton of CDs and landed several other gigs as a result.

Go where the action is. Maybe you have to go where the action is. Wes Bentley read the script for *American Beauty* and wanted a part so badly that he flew from New York to Los Angeles to audition in person, claiming that "nobody hires you from a video." He wanted to make it more personal, and felt to do that he had to audition in person. (He got the part as the brooding neighbor, by the way.)

Prove yourself to the skeptics. Another aspect to consider when deciding if you want to hibernate or come out of your cave is this: Not many people want to take a chance on an unknown. If you can build a track record and a following, it is likely the skeptics will take a closer look at you. See, once you get one gig, you're likely to get another. My friends and I call this "breaking the seal." It's sad that many of the decision makers are afraid of risk. Nobody wants to be the first to hire you, so get some experience under your belt, even if you start small. Stop practicing your art and start performing, publicizing, and putting yourself out there.

Good things happen when you get out. An aspiring artist friend was waiting to be discovered. To pay the bills, he worked at a frame shop during the week and decided to try to make something happen (and make money) by selling his art at swap meets on the weekend. As luck would have it, a vacationing art agent from New York was wandering the swap meet in San Diego with a friend when he "discovered" the most amazing art (and artist). Within a matter of months he was able to sell all of my friend's original works, had posters made of his best stuff, and licensed his art for cups, calendars, and cards. Now the lean years are over, and his only problem is being able to produce new works fast enough.

It can lead to bigger and better things. Nothing is too small if there is a chance it could lead to bigger and better things (and most gigs have that potential). I will speak free of charge if I have the opportunity to sell books at the back of the room. If I can sell a couple of hundred books, I can make $3,000. Not bad for a few hours' work.

It's even better when I am paid to speak and sell books. Sometimes I will earn as much as $10,000 for one day's work. Harvey MacKay, the author of the best-selling business book *Sharkproof,* gave a motivational speech to the employees at Ingram, the largest book distributor in the United States. He built a buzz for his book, increased his visibility, and won them over, all of which boosted sales to bookstores.

The media will want you. In many ways the media is pretty predictable. They love things that are controversial, have a human interest angle, and are timely and newsworthy. By getting out to do something in public, you are hitting almost all of the media's favorite things. You and your event are newsworthy, timely, have human interest (you), and, depending on what you do, could be controversial.

Develop a fan following. When you build an audience, sales will follow. There is nothing that builds a loyal following like interacting with fans. Even if your fans are only three feet tall, as J. K. Rowling's are, they will come to see you. Rowling has signed hundreds of her blockbuster Harry Potter books at a stretch for her little fans. You are never too big to get out and meet customers. Makeup maven Trish McEvoy came to my wife's store and gave individual consultations to customers on proper makeup application techniques. McEvoy's trademark is her hands-on, one-on-one teaching system. (She does half the face and then the customer repeats the process on the other half.) McEvoy's client list includes Sharon Stone, Sarah Jessica Parker, and Brooke Shields, and she has a loyal following among other professionals who use her products, especially her precision brushes. She ventures out from her New York salon to visit the department stores where her products are sold, including Nordstrom, and gets more loyal customers as a result.

Get buzzed. Being a musician living in San Diego, I can recall the buzz surrounding Jewel. She built a strong local following by being a persistent and personable performer. We wanted her to make it. Her acoustic sets at intimate coffeehouses started the buzz in the beach areas and led to a cover story in the local paper and a record executive coming to see her play (and signing her to a deal).

Make a name for yourself. It's so much easier to sell yourself when the other person has heard of you. It's now a warm lead instead of a cold call. Try to get out and mix and mingle as much as possible. I know, I know, who has the time? Make it a goal to go to at least one function a month (or more). You may also be the reclusive type. So am I, surprisingly. For all the horn-tooting I do, you would think I am an extrovert. The truth is I am a shy guy. I have to force myself to get out and meet people. Then I consider the alternative to making it as a creative person (a real job) and drag myself out of my comfort zone and get out. It's the lesser of two evils, believe me.

Challenge and stretch yourself. During the Depression, Billie Holiday was earning money as a prostitute until she got arrested and decided to try dancing. It was a gutsy move, considering she was not a great dancer. At her first audition, after failing to impress the crowd with her dancing ability, the pianist asked if she could sing. She gave such a powerful performance of "Travelin' All Alone" that a hush fell over the crowd, some even wept, and when she was done, they threw money at her feet—literally. (And this was during the Depression!) If she hadn't had the courage to go to that audition and try singing, we would never have known her work.

Put some distance between you and your town. When I speak in my hometown (San Diego), I am just another author. But when I do signings and seminars on the road, I am treated like a star. That's why I travel great distances to give talks. Of course, you should begin by building a local following first and then hit the road in search of more fans. I did this by signing with a seminar company that had me on the road one week out of every month in places I never dreamed I would go. For five years I gave all-day seminars, and then did book signings at night all over the country, and the hard work has paid off with massive media, a major mailing list, and, of course, book sales. (Not to mention the fact that my paid day job of giving seminars allowed me free travel to some pretty cool places.)

It never ends. The amazing Lily Tomlin still keeps up a hectic touring schedule in her *Search for Signs of Intelligent Life in the Universe.* Think about how many bands still limp into town for their reunion tour. I happened to be reading the paper the other day and looked at the list of acts coming to the local Indian casino's concert series. Bands I thought were dead have been resurrected. Others are like old friends, like the band Yes, who still have it. Blues legend John Mayall is still going strong at age sixty-six, doing at least 150 shows a year. And then there is the Boss. At age fifty-one, Bruce Springsteen still puts on arguably the best performance of any rocker. His three-hour-plus shows are still a tough ticket to get, and he never fails to bring down the house. The message is to work on your performance skills and get out there and do it.

Places to Expose Yourself (As Well As Your Art)

"We haven't had any underwear thrown at us yet. But if we do— boxers, please. No briefs."

—Martie Seidel, The Dixie Chicks

Out of sight is out of mind. You need to get noticed (in a positive way) anywhere and everywhere and as often as you can. Don't be shy about showing off, because opportunities don't come to invisible people. Rudolf Mendoza, a sculptor in Trinidad, left his homeland to teach art in London. Soon after arriving he lost his teaching job due to budget cuts. He became a street sweeper to pay the bills. Rudolf would make elaborate carvings on the handles of his brooms. A gallery owner noticed the carvings and after hearing Rudolf's story offered to let him show his work in the gallery. Rudolf sold his first work for £500 (or $800) and eventually "cleaned up" by selling enough art to quit his day job for good. Plaster your art or logo on everything. Show off your creations on your car (bumper stickers), yourself (hats and T-shirts), where you hang out, your website, letterhead, fax cover page, office walls, newsletter—everywhere. Look for places that attract the type of people interested in your style of creations but that don't normally display art.

Take it to the streets. Some artists make money selling their work at traveling craft shows and sidewalk art shows, which are regularly held all over the country. You could also stage your own. One woman turned a barn into a co-op gallery and craft show. Many street fairs regularly seek out bands, dance groups, and all sorts of performing artists to liven up an outdoor event. Why not give it a shot?

Do good deeds. One makeup artist who donates her time at burn centers touched the doctors so deeply they asked her to speak at their convention and bankrolled her own line of cosmetics and a book on the subject.

Find unusual places to show off. Don't laugh, but you can display your work in frame shops. Aaron Brothers even sponsors an "Art Faire" that allows artists to show off their work in their chain of stores. Cruise ships have art auctions on board. (They usually sell prints.) Talk about a captive audience. Ask the media relations person at a construction company if you can do murals on the temporary walls surrounding a construction site. Have someone hold a Tupperware-type party in their home to show off your art. (I know a clothing designer who does this with great success.) Living in a Navy town like I do, I noticed that when ships returned from long deployments overseas a local strip club used to send a boatload of beauties to greet them. This worked well until the strippers showed the sailors their not-so-secret weapons.

High tech and high touch. To generate interest (and demonstrate an otherwise difficult-to-explain product), Dell computers took their show on the road. The Dell on Wheels creative promotional campaign consisted of two semitrailers outfitted with Power Edge Servers. On the outside these rigs were giant billboards painted with flames and Dell's logo. On the inside there were comfy leather chairs, large monitors, and enough state-of-the-art equipment to impress the I.T. personnel who receive demonstrations delivered by Dell engineers and product managers. The trucks traveled from city to city, usually setting up in the parking lot of a hotel near a business district. The advantage of this unorthodox approach has been that people can see the solutions for themselves, and not just look at a catalog. They also are able to ask questions and interact with the people who built the system. Many of the spectators who passed through were so impressed by the effort it took to bring the product and presentation to them that numerous valuable one-on-one relationships (and brand loyalty) were developed by these successful tours.

Think outside the box. When times were tough for retailers on Maui, many of the storefronts sat empty. One resourceful artist was able to convince several landlords to allow her to display her art in the vacant storefront windows (some of which were in high-traffic areas). Her improvised rotating gallery directed people to a small out-of-the-way gallery where they could purchase her work. (And they did.) She put brochures and business cards in a rack out front, along with free postcards featuring her art and directions to a permanent gallery selling her stuff.

Galleries aren't the only place to show off. For the fine artist, building a track record means getting into galleries. If you can't get a gallery's attention, try other places to show off, including: church, post office, library, co-op galleries, your home, university galleries, banks, corporate headquarters, art centers, museums, nonprofit centers, real estate offices, coffee shops, doctor's offices, or restaurants.

How to Do It

"I didn't really attend school. I just attended the parking lot,
smoked pot, and listened to Rush eight-tracks in my friend's car."
—Chad Smith, Red Hot Chili Peppers

Now that you are itching to get out and show off, let me give you a few tips to help you make the most of your efforts. It takes some advance planning to make sure there is someone there to see you when you roll into town. First figure out where you want to go and how you're going to get there. Then start working on the media. Put together a press kit and send it well in advance of your arrival. Make a mock-up of a flyer (leave the place and date blank and fill in later for each venue). Look at your mailing list and find friends, family, and fans in the places you are performing who can help you get those flyers out, sell tickets, bring their friends, or contact the media for you.

If you are selling something (other than at the back of the room), make sure your products will be available when you hit town. You really have only one shot to get people to act, and that is right after you awe them with your performance. If your product isn't on the store shelf, the chance of their coming back for it later is slim to none. If you can have your stuff available at the event, so much the better. Always carry extras in your car, case, or carry-on (and if you're selling books, let the publisher and publicist know where you'll be).

Are you thinking to yourself: Oh my God, this a lot of work? That's why you'll need to get help. Work hard to convince your label, publisher, sponsor, or the maker of the product you are pushing to underwrite all or part of your tour (or deal with the details). Be sure to tell them that personal appearances sell products and generate plenty of publicity. If they don't want to offer financial backing, maybe they would be willing to do the legwork and work out the logistics. (Planning a tour is a major undertaking.) Now, when I say "tour," you are probably picturing a band, roadies, and lots of groupies. No, a tour is sometimes just you and your sore back and a few freaky people who want to talk your ear off at each stop. But a tour could also be a carpenter who invented a new tool showing do-it-yourselfers how to use it at Home Depot, a Martha Stewart type demonstrating a line of craft products at a Michael's craft store, or a cookbook author demonstrating how to make a low-fat (but tasty) dish at a bookstore. These freebies are big with the media, and because your expenses are all paid by your sponsor, you get to travel for free and get paid to push your product.

Go where the right people are. Where do your potential fans and customers go? You need foot traffic, yes, but you need the right feet to pass. An illustrator friend married a horse trainer and began painting portraits of horses. His wife's stables were next to the polo grounds, and he had a brilliant idea. On Sundays while the polo games were going on, he painted. Curious people would wander over, wondering what he was painting. After seeing his work, they wanted to know more. He kept a portfolio of his other paintings with him, and sold out of everything he had painted and was commissioned to paint several others. The people at polo games for the most part are loaded, interested in horses, and appreciate good art. As a medical illustrator, he made plenty of money. He painted horses for the love of it and was able to use the proceeds from his "hobby" to purchase a ranch outside of town.

If you can put out the same kind of effort and reach millions of fans or just ten fans, which would be better? I know, it depends. But all things considered, your chance of spreading the word about your talent is better with a bigger crowd. Why would Phil Collins perform at the 2000 Super Bowl halftime show? Let's see, could it be because it's broadcast to millions of viewers? Trisha Yearwood sang "The Flame" to wrap up the 1996 Summer Olympics in Atlanta, and some 3.5 billion people saw the live performance. On Fridays during summer months, NBC's "Today Show" features artists performing outside the studio. Jimmy Buffett, Sting, Ricky Martin, and others took advantage of the chance to perform. Go where you will reach the most people at once.

One stand-up comedienne touring comedy venues across the country decided to hit smaller markets (where she was a big name) as a headliner, places where she had performed the previous year. In her newsletter she asked friends and fans (many of whom she developed while on the road) if they would be willing to help out. Many offered her a free place to stay while she was in town. One of her fans offered to put up flyers and contact the local media if she would send a press kit. Another lined up a paying gig at her church and a book signing at a Borders bookstore. She realized that she was onto something big. She decided to "evangelize" her flock and started sending care packages filled with flyers and press releases to pass out and post, and gave free tickets for their help. She also asked fans and friends for tidbits of local life in a town that she could incorporate into her now customized act. Needless to say, her shows were sold out. The only negative was that the venues were too small to accommodate the crowds, so she added another night.

Create your own Lilith Fair or Lollapalooza. By the time you're reading this I will have already rented a small RV and driven from my home in San Diego to Arizona, New Mexico, Texas, Alabama, and down the Panhandle and west coast of Florida doing book signings in each city until I get to Key West (where I will meet up with my wife to celebrate and recover from this self-financed book tour). I got the idea from Greg Godek, the author and publisher of a series of books on putting romance back into your life. He spent two years (with his wife) traveling the country in an RV to promote his books. The "love machine" was plastered with promotional material, so that while he was driving around he was promoting his books in addition to his bookstore and media appearances.

Make a memorable impression. Dave Hirschkop, proprietor of Burrito Madness, noticed that his college town eatery attracted a lot of after-party patrons. To get rid of the rowdy crowd, he concocted the hottest hot sauce on earth. It was so hot that when mixed with a stomach full of beer the spicy sauce usually pushed people over the edge and outside to "purge" themselves. The hot sauce earned a reputation for its insane spiciness. In fact, that's what Hirschkop called it, "Dave's Insanity Sauce." Dave decided to take the sauce on the road and began bottling it and taking it on tour to food shows. At one show, an attendee had to be taken to the hospital after testing it. This drew a lifetime's worth of attention to the product. People are still talking about it.

Try going against the grain. Look for venues that usually don't have performers or display art. They are usually easier to approach and willing to give it a try. You can promote for the price of a subway token. To get people to come see you perform or present doesn't have to be expensive. A couple of actors in an off-off-off-off-Broadway play got on the subway several stops before the theater where they were appearing and performed a part of the play. They then passed out flyers and invited commuters to get off at the appropriate stop and take in the play. (It helped that they left riders hanging by setting up a cliffhanger before passing out discount coupons.) One band set up and performed in the parking lots of large companies as workers got off and passed out flyers to their show later that evening. Most libraries let authors and others use community rooms for workshops and lectures free of charge. (Hint, choose a library near a bookstore if you are promoting a book.)

Maybe you could tag along with another creative person and split the costs. Touring acts do this all the time. The up-and-comer is the opening act for a major star. Singer and guitarist Jonny Lang ("the Prodigy") has managed to sell over one million albums while touring the world opening for acts like Aerosmith, the Rolling Stones, Buddy Guy, and B. B. King.

It only takes one—one person, that is. A friend of mine had just completed his first student film and was interested in getting work in the documentary film industry. He knew that I knew a person who had a company doing exactly what he wanted to do. I invited him to a party that my documentary filmmaker friend was also attending. Well, Jim somehow got this guy to go to the screening of his student film and was hired on the spot.

Leaving Is Never Easy

"When people don't want to come, nothing will stop them."

—Sol Hurok

The goal is to get your name out there. The best way is to get *yourself* out there. If you can't (or don't want to) do that, at least get your art traveling around for you. One very talented musician did not want to leave the care of his autistic son to relatives while he traveled and performed. Instead, he recorded a demo tape of one of his songs (a heart-wrenching tribute to his son David) and sent it certified mail (along with a cover letter explaining his situation) to a music publisher he found on the Web. To his surprise, they were interested! They cataloged and copyrighted the song and registered it with ASCAP. A few months later he was notified that a big-name recording artist wanted to record it.

Awards: "I'd Like to Thank . . ."

"A ship in the harbor is safe . . . but that's not what ships were made for."

—Unknown

In 1981, at the tender age of twenty-one, Maya Lin won an open competition for the design of the proposed Vietnam Veteran's Memorial. Her idea, now realized in the Washington Mall in D.C., launched her career as an architect and artist. She now runs her own design studio in New York. Countless careers have been launched with an award. Look at some of the winners on "Star Search." There is Britney Spears, Rosie O'Donnell, and Usher Raymond. Usher Raymond? In 1992, he was a "Star Search" winner, and was able to parlay that into an acting career that included roles in two teen films (*She's All That* and *The Faculty*), and his album *My Way* has sold into the millions. Entering a competition (Battle of the Bands, industry-specific awards, or even local talent shows) can lead to media exposure, credibility, and great leads—and that's if you don't win. Add to that prize money, prestige, and plugs galore. You can't lose. It's validation, a third-party endorsement, that your work is good. I'm not saying enter every competition that comes along—some are a waste of time and money—but by being selective you can boost yourself up to the next level.

At the least, it's a chance to display your work and get the attention of reviewers, buyers, and the judges. That's what happened to Katie Hamilton, a star on the San Diego State University women's soccer team, who also wants to make it as a country music star. With no experience outside of singing in the car, she entered a national contest—the True Value/Jimmy Dean Country Music Showdown. She heard about the competition on the radio station that cosponsored the event and thought it "might be fun." She wrote and recorded a song and sent in the tape. Her song "Never Gonna Make It" (ironic title) was one of the eight chosen out of three hundred entries for a regional competition, which she won. She lost in the statewide contest, but the radio station that sponsored the first competition offered to assist her with her musical career. They helped her make a professional demo and put together a press kit and approached record companies in the hopes of landing a record deal. The station's director of marketing was a judge in the contest (and a good judge of talent) with more than thirty years experience in the business. He was the past chairman of the Association of Country Music.

It doesn't have to be the Oscars. Look for awards that are regional or specific to an area you specialize in, like the Golden Rib Award for the best BBQ cookbook. Increase your chances of winning and alerting people to your specialty or something within your geographic area. (I was the runner-up for best book the past two years at the San Diego Book Awards.) There are awards for various ethnicities, and religions as well, like the National Jewish Book Awards. You may have a better chance of winning in a local or trade-specific competition. For example, many paper companies sponsor competitions for graphic artists. Wausau has the Graphics Excellence Program, Hammermill sponsors the Creative Inking Awards, and Gilbert's has the Graphic Greatness Awards. Winners and runners-up are featured in ads and on their websites as well as in graphic design magazines and books. On an even smaller scale, Paper Direct encourages customers to send their designs for the "Show Us Your Stuff" section of their catalog. The reward for those featured is $500 worth of products and exposure in their catalog. Many other graphic design awards also include publishing books and directories that show off the award-winning work. Every industry or locale has an award. See what it takes to enter yours. Keep a record of your award. Tell everyone! (Media, clients, friends.) Include it on the cover of your marketing materials and on your website. Alert the media immediately. Don't depend on the organization giving the award to do it. Take your own photo, if you have to, and send it with your release.

The bottom line is that awards can create more of an awareness and respect and can increase sales, even if you don't win. Being nominated for a Pulitzer or a Hugo can boost book sales. Boyd Willat invented the ultracomfy Sensa pen in 1995. The Plasmium Grip (a cushioned grip) won several awards, as did the pen itself and even the packaging. The awards garnered attention from both vendors and the public, and increased sales.

FAST FACT

According to *Variety,* the entertainment industry hands out roughly 3,200 awards at 332 ceremonies. (There are even awards for the best awards.) Some are weirder than others, from the Silver Sewer Award to the Golden Frog Award. One award that I thought was most appropriate is *High Times* magazine's Stoney Awards Silver Bong. The winner in 2000 was Dennis Hopper. Perfect!

Give Yourself an Award

"Every dogma has his day."

—Israel Zangwill

Depending on the kind of business you're in, give out an award of your own. You could create a best-garden award (if you're a landscaper), or most unusual use for a product (manufacturer), or best patron of the arts (artist), or best gallery (artist), or best club (band), or best fan (anyone). Make it relevant to what you do and what the customer or fan does. Offer as big a prize as possible. Make it so that you can get business out of it. A pet store had a "cutest" and "ugliest" dog photo competition. Many professional photographers entered for the prize money and the publicity. Awards that capture the media and public's attention are most productive. You could also create a Seal of Approval or a "Recommended" designation, which works well with environmental causes. Or choose a hero, give a scholarship, or push a product you believe in.

Much of the attention comes from holding an awards banquet or the presentation of the award. Make it newsworthy or at least a good photo opportunity.

Ask a Pro
Doug Auld
Artist

What awards have you won for your art?

I was given the title of Absolut Artist of the Year by Absolut Vodka in 1993. This led to appearances on MTV, "Entertainment Tonight," and, believe it or not, many articles in the newspaper. I was also part of a yearly event where artists open their studios to the public. I was part of the Hoboken Studio Tour. A guy working with MTV walked into my studio, saw my portraits of celebrities in wildlife, and commissioned me to paint a portrait of Jim Morrison of the Doors. He was putting together something called the Museum of Unnatural History for MTV.

What's your philosophy about getting out there and showing off?

My philosophy is to make good work and put it in public places. For example, my art occupies the walls of an elegant restaurant in Hoboken called Amanda's. I'm able to sell my paintings and pick up some portrait commissions as a result of the exposure. I also always carry photos of my work, and I'm not shy about showing them when in a social situation. My next big thing is a website for my work.

What was the worst experience you have had with displaying your art?

The worst event I ever experienced was showing some of my work in a beauty salon. I did it as a favor to the owner and it was clearly the low point of my career. Still, I think it is all growth. But it's all about a lack of confidence and doubting your skills and your work. Now I know that when you have something really mature and good, you take it to the right place—art galleries and the like.

Make It an Event

"You can't build a reputation on what you intend to do."

—Liz Smith

When one of my best friends moved back from Maui and began to build his custom carpentry business back up on the mainland, he built an amazing workshop from the ground up. When it was done he invited everyone to a party that included a band, sushi, and tons of fun. He also had his creations on display. He got so many referrals and work as a result of this party, he hasn't had to do any advertising at all. (He's so busy, I never see him anymore.) Events like an open house or a release party can be a great way to get the all-important word of mouth and advance buzz started. Beyond the obvious ways to make the event a success (invite the right people and have food), here are some creative clues to an excellent event.

Hold the event in an odd location. For their album *Innuendo,* the band Queen rented the *Queen Mary* (get it?) for their release party. One software company had moved to a larger building but was still leasing their old space, so they turned it into a haunted house for clients and their kids at Halloween. At the same time they held an annual pep rally for clients, with a ghost story theme.

Come up with a strong theme. A sales rep for a line of skate-wear had a fashion show/skateboard demonstration/rave party in an old airport hangar. Everything played off the theme, from the invitations (they looked like airline tickets) to the decorations (vintage flying posters and props).

Make it memorable. I have seen massage therapists, fortune-tellers, magicians, and live animals transform everyday events into happenings that are a little out of the ordinary and thus memorable. Use your creativity to go beyond what people expect. Get them talking.

Have them come to you. One author (and former Navy SEAL) I know invited the media to participate in a hard-core Navy SEAL–type fitness boot camp in the desert. He got great press! On the flip side, a trainer and author set up a retreat in the mountains that included techniques from her book (drumming, singing, meditating, and group therapy), with the media and book buyers invited to attend. This also was received with positive press.

Combine and conquer. For my last book I set up a first-class release party at the Hyatt Islandia Hotel on Mission Bay in San Diego. I rented the entire bar and patio overlooking the marina. The evening started as I hosted my radio talk show live from the event, followed by a miniseminar about the book, and wrapped it up with two sets by my band with me on drums. On the invitation list were past purchasers of books, the media (free food, so of course they came), family and friends, fans of the radio show, and so on. You get the picture—people who have supported me in the past or could be an ally in the future. Not only did the event promote and sell the book, but it also led to bookings for the band, more listeners for the radio show, and media coverage for all three. As a bonus, my editor (at the time) was coaxed into coming up on stage to sing a few songs. All in all, it was worth every dime. (And proceeds were donated to a local environmental organization.)

Team up with the media. By making the media a cosponsor, you can trade for ad space or have an on-air personality MC the event. (Hopefully the host will talk up the event on their show.)

If you aren't a celebrity, get one. I have used celebrities to increase the draw to events, and it works. They don't even have to be the real deal. My friend Arden Bercovitz gives talks as Albert Einstein (he calls his business Einstein Alive), and he's a dead ringer (no pun intended) for Einstein. So I invited him to introduce me at a talk, and he was a huge hit. Maybe you could get actors to dress up like a famous person (I recommend deceased celebrities to avoid any lawsuits) for your event. It makes for great photo opportunities. One guy I know hired *two* Marilyn Monroes (one just wasn't enough). Elvis is always a hit.

Turn a sales pitch into a performance. If you are a performer, one of the cheapest forms of promotion is . . . performing. After spending New Year's Eve at the Jimmy Buffett Millennium Show with 4,999 other Parrot Heads in Los Angeles, I never would have guessed that a few days later he would be playing again to an intimate gathering of a hundred or so restaurateurs. To launch his new Margaritaville tequila, Jimmy invited these lucky folks to a private performance. My friend's mom, who owns a restaurant in Orange County, thought she was going to a regular concert and couldn't believe her luck when it turned out that this was such a small gathering and she was able to meet the man himself. They now carry his tequila in her bar.

Take it to the street corner. Saxophonist Arthur Blythe is an internationally celebrated musician. If I told you that you could find him on a San Diego street corner playing for pedestrians on a weekday afternoon, you would assume he was down on his luck. Actually, Blythe, who tours primarily in Europe, was promoting an upcoming concert in his hometown by blowing his horn in front of the museum he'd be playing at later in the day as part of the "Artists on the Cutting Edge" series. How about music in the park? Organize a display of student art. Do a benefit for struggling artists, a boat parade, something at a retirement community. For your industry, do a "latest trends" presentation or host a panel discussion.

Tie in with a charity. Now that your event involves a charity angle, you can take advantage of free listings (public service announcements) and gain access to their mailing list. One photographer agreed to take pictures of kids for photo ID badges and police registration. He met a lot of parents who hired him for all kinds of work. Or hook up with a corporate sponsor who can underwrite the whole thing. If you are really hard up, you can be the charity. One computer consultant was able to get the clients he worked with to sponsor events all over the country for his own software release presentations. If you need a celebrity, maybe your corporate sponsor can underwrite the cost of getting one or the CEO could speak. (Always try to get a printer as a sponsor in trade.)

Creative invitations. In my opinion, the key component to an event is a creative invitation. It should be clever (and concise), create excitement (I have gotta go to this), and stand out (this is definitely not another boring function!). Play around with the materials, folds, size, color, and content—or do it via the Internet.

Do as I say, not as I do. This is an area where I am both experienced and have established a track record. (That's not to say I haven't had a bomb or two.) On the positive side, we did a midnight-madness sale at one of my surf shops that was really an all-day event with free surfing clinics from pros, a skateboarding clinic conducted by Tony Hawk (with a half pipe out in front of the store), free Rollerblade demos (this was when Rollerblades were brand new), a fashion show (read: girls in bikinis), carnival-style games, a barbecue, and the list goes on, all culminating in an after-hours feeding frenzy for sale-priced merchandise. It was HUGE.

On the flip side, at our other store an event ended with a gang-banger chasing me down the street with *my* gun. (It's a long, long story—and one that does not have a happy ending.) Here are a few more lessons I've learned from these experiences: Add in a charity element to hook the media. Send press releases to different departments at the paper, including the society columnist, business editor, or even the entertainment or currents editor. The more bizarre, the better. (Go for a world record in *Guinness*.) Try to get as much free stuff as you can from vendors, sponsors, friends, anyone willing to help. Make it an annual event. Promoting it online is the cheapest way to go. Give people a token (like a poster, shirt, or hat) with event information on it and the event will live on forever.

Trade Shows

"The most important part of any trade show are the after-parties. That's where the deals really get done."

—Anonymous

Why should you attend (or display, speak, perform, or just party at) your industry's trade show? Let me count the ways. First, it's your opportunity to show off to distributors, buyers, retailers, managers, producers, agents, and so forth. These are basically inaccessible people who are maybe just a little more vulnerable at a show. Then there are the networking opportunities. You may learn something at one of the panel discussions or gain some inside information over a cocktail. Collect business cards and build your mailing list. You can meet people face-to-face. You may meet more important people in three days than you can in three months. It's nice having them all in one place. This allows you to develop relationships, leads, and visibility. Research shows that 86 percent of trade show attendees are the decision makers or influence buying decisions. Choose the right show, of course, or it's a waste of time and money.

As an Attendee

Will work for distribution. Fledgling filmmakers in search of a deal have a good chance to meet someone who can fund their film at the International Film Financing Conference in San Francisco. In addition to the wheeling and dealing, there are excellent networking opportunities as well as workshops by respected industry insiders. Then there is Sundance. This film festival that launched many independent films (most recently *The Blair Witch Project*) is the incubator for many independent filmmakers working with very limited budgets trying to create a buzz for their picture. This festival is vital for many upstarts who hope to make it big in the film industry. It's a chance to mix and mingle with make-or-break people in the biz. In addition to the screenings and publicity opportunities the festival affords, there are panel discussions, technology exhibits, concerts, and, of course, lots of parties.

Bigger isn't always better. (It's how you use it that counts?) You never know what can come out of regional or "niche" conventions. The band Hanson was signed at the South by Southwest Music Festival. Verve Pipe was signed at the eX-travaganza. The smaller the show, the more likely they'll let you play, perform, or give a presentation for industry people who might never have heard you (or of you) if you passed. This is a chance to play for talent buyers from clubs across the country, lawyers, managers, talent agents, booking agents, distribution companies, support staff of all kinds. You never know who is in the room. Maybe you won't get signed, but you are definitely moving in the right direction.

Don't be shy. If there is a person you really want to meet, do your homework. This could be your one shot to impress them. Figure out who the must-meet people are and then come up with some clever way to wow them. Attend the after-parties, where you have can make your move (so to speak).

Hello, my name is ... Throughout the crowded ballroom hundreds of tiny lights blinked on and off. This "bright idea" was Marla Silva's (of Marla's Mania) clever way to help the soft-spoken Helen Anderson, president of Rayvern Lighting, stand out at a conference. The flashing buttons became a collector's item. Another cool idea for an icebreaker was an author who turned her book cover into earrings. One financial planner I know wrote on his name tag, "Financial Planner." Boring. He went and got a new name tag and wrote the word "money" on it. That seemed to pique people's interest.

Play a bigger role. If offered a chance to serve on a panel or conduct a workshop, do it. It is the perfect chance to build your reputation as an industry expert. Try to milk it for all it's worth. Provide the trade show organizers with a bio and photo for the directory. (A fun photo helps you to stand out.) Offer to write an article in their newsletter or magazine. Come up with a clever title or hook for your talk. Do some advance press to announce that you are talking at the event. Promote yourself after the fact by turning your talk into a transcript or article for your newsletter, or post it on your website.

As a Paid Participant

On the show "Party of Five," Charlie Salinger's ex-girlfriend and mother of his child also happens to be a stripper and is now a part-time employee (this *is* a TV drama) in his furniture business. When Charlie is detained and can't make it to the trade show they're in, she decides to get creative and has her fellow strippers pose in bed (the beds they sell) with the buyers. And they wrote a ton of orders. Sex sells, so get the right people working your booth. When I attended the Action Sports Retailer Show as a buyer for women's bathing suits for our shops, I had a hard time concentrating with the models right in my face, and I almost always overbought.

As a paid participant, you want to be the one everybody is talking about. The design of your booth is a good place to start focusing your creative energy. Do more than display. For the "Ultimate Guitar Show—the History of California Guitar Making," Taylor Guitars made and displayed a one-of-a-kind six-string acoustic model made of Hawaiian koa wood. Considering that the attendees of the show included guitar stars like Joe Pass, Eric Clapton, Eddie Van Halen, and Larry Carlton (to name a few), it was good advertising and a show-stopper. You almost have to reach out and grab them by the throat and pull them in. The way to do this includes:

Get motivated. Set a goal of how many people you want to meet. What you want to accomplish. Don't stop until you reach your goal.

Don't be shy. If you're the strong silent type, get someone (a hottie) to help. You have got to meet and greet or do demonstrations (it slices, it dices . . .) or have an icebreaker of some kind. A clever greeting, maybe. Look for things you can compliment passersby on. Have something free you can offer. Come up with a gimmick. I had stickers made up that said, "I was caught being good today" and "I was bad today" and put them on people. A photographer took digital photos of attendees against a tropical backdrop and told them to come back later to pick them up.

People expect freebies. Don't disappoint. Food is a must. Samples are also well-received. Give away something they can wear or show other attendees and that will prompt others to ask them where they got it. At the Columbian EXPO in Chicago in 1892, Henry "the Pickle King" Heinz and his company had an elaborate exhibit but in a bad location (on the seldom-seen second floor). So the Pickle King printed up little white cards offering a free pickle charm souvenir if redeemed at the Heinz booth. So many people came (over one million) to collect their pickle pins, officials had to strengthen the supports of the gallery floor. This led to a lot of publicity, and the pins became a fashion fad.

Make it an interactive experience. Have listening stations, computers with samples of your work, or a video playing to show them while you tell them. Allow people to enter their own name on a mailing list or enter a raffle on laptops. A short demonstration (under fifteen minutes) can't hurt. At a trade show for presenters (who do a ton of traveling), a luggage manufacturer gave a demonstration of packing tips and ended up selling a lot of luggage. At one trade show, one of the manufacturers hired a DJ and literally had people dancing in the aisles.

What is a trade show without promotional materials? Bring plenty of promotional materials. Put your contact information on EVERY piece of literature. Bring press kits and make it a point to go to the media room to hand them out. Follow up quickly on any leads, and you have an edge. Make notes on their cards so you'll remember to follow up and know what materials to send.

Have a theme. One company built their booth using the theme of everything being top secret. They sealed it off and met people only by appointment and called them "secret meetings." Everyone dressed like secret agents, complete with badges.

Make the most of the opportunity. One man had a van with a sign on top and had one of his employees drive back and forth in front of a convention center. Another put flyers about his show specials up in the bathrooms. I know of a vendor who hired a gorilla to give out brochures. No matter what you do, make sure to contact the local media. Maybe you could play in a town the night before a convention.

Do what Dick Clark does. Dick Clark Corporate Productions takes many of the concepts from the entertainment industry to make corporate events less stale and stodgy. As Clark says: "It's all about entertaining people, getting their attention, and communicating the message. To do this, much the same as it is with television, you have to arrest the attention of the person passing by. You've got to captivate them." Put on a show. (I've seen actual game shows at convention booths, photo ops with models, and all kinds of interactive demonstrations. Remember, it's a trade *show*.) At the 1854 American Institute Fair in New York, Alisha Otis gave a dramatic demonstration of the safety device (in case the cable broke) on his elevator. Few people believed that his "safety hoist" would keep the elevator from crashing to the ground, so he staged a demonstration. He had an assistant cut the cable, and his device worked like it was supposed to. Not only did he get a rousing ovation, he got orders.

Throw an after-party. The clothing company Hang Ten had a boat docked off the Chart House next to the convention center for the most wild party after a convention I have ever been to. Another clever vendor offered free limo rides back and forth to your hotel or car.

Ever thought about putting on your own industry trade show?

As a Crasher

One person not displaying at a show hired a couple to dress up like a pimp and prostitute with the company's name embroidered into their custom costumes to hand out samples. (They sold a product called Little Hookers, which were little suction cups with hooks attached for hanging things without making a hole.) People were talking about them later at the dinner, the speaker mentioned it, and the papers picked up the story. Outrageous (or at least out of the ordinary) sells. When one company couldn't get a booth at a computer industry trade show, they had cabbies pass out brochures. The company made it a contest by having secret riders who would pay a cabdriver $100 if they had a brochure handed to them. They ended up giving out $400 in prizes to cabbies and got nearly $15,000 in orders.

To Speak or Not to Speak? Good Question.

"Short, short, I know I'm short."

—Phil Collins, on the brevity of his
Grammy acceptance speech (and his stature)

At a conference on patient relations, the speaker's scheduled time to begin talking came and went. The physicians began to get restless. One doctor had enough, and when he tried to leave he found the door was locked from the outside. One of the doctors started screaming, "This is outrageous! I don't have time to wait for this guy. My time is valuable." Just then the speaker, who was sitting quietly, rose and said, "Ladies and gentlemen, let's now talk about patient relations." Neat story, huh? When you get out there and start giving public speeches, you'll have your own stories to tell. Wait! Before you say, "I would rather swim through shark-infested waters, wrestle with a snake, and eat a bug (sounds like "Survivor") than do any public speaking," let me give you some really good reasons to face your fears and show you how to make it as painless as possible. Once you have something to say, it's not that bad, really.

Giving lectures, seminars, and workshops happens to be my forte, so I could go on and on about why you should add speaking to your promotional plans (and I will), but I realize it's not for everyone. I mean, it's not for people who don't want any fans, publicity, respect, free travel, leads, sales, or extra income. But for the rest of us who are trying to build a career, it can be a key component in our creative lives. Not only because it leads to fantastic opportunities, but also because standing in front of an adoring audience and having them lavish praise on you is reward enough. And there's more.

Speaking is a cheap (and effective) form of advertising and may be the best way to reach affluent, busy people. You earn their trust and it builds up your credibility. It's a fantastic networking tool, too. You don't have to grovel or approach people, they will seek *you* out after your talk. Many times you are being paid to talk and selling product at the back of the room, which can add up to a tidy sum for a few hours of your time. Many times the group or organization you're speaking for will publicize the talk and you with a mailing to their people and put notices in the papers and their own publication. Then there is the free travel. Since most conferences and retreats are in beautiful, tropical, and warm places, you get to go to beautiful, tropical, and warm places, too. (That last item should do the trick and convince you to read on.)

As I said earlier, I have benefited immensely from a willingness to speak in public. Some of my best clients were students first. You can build yourself up in their eyes (and build a relationship), which usually results in referrals. You might think that if you teach the student to fish they will be fed for life. But in my experience, at least with desktop publishing and website design, after hearing how much is involved (and they realize how much they still don't know), many will ask if I can consult on their projects. In their eyes I have become the guru. (How can that be a bad thing?) By educating people through demonstrations, workshops, and classes, they become better customers. You also establish yourself as an expert in the field by conducting workshops or teaching a class.

Good speaking skills also can mean strong selling skills (you know how to get your ideas across), and at the very least you can make yourself look even better with a good acceptance speech. When filmmaker Jessica Yu accepted the Oscar for Best Documentary Short Story Subject, she brought down the house with the one-liner "You know you've entered a new territory when you realize that your dress cost more than your film." The audience went wild, and the fallout from her win and her speech landed her more attention than she could have imagined. You don't have to be a brilliant speaker, but your presentation skills, more than anything I can think of, will help you sell your ideas, master the media, and win fans and influence people.

At his high school graduation, a senior began his speech by reading from prepared text. "I want to talk about my mother and the wonderful influence she has had on my life," he told the audience. "She is a shining example of parenthood, and I love her more than words could ever do justice." At this point he seemed to struggle for words. After a pause, he looked up with a sly grin and said, "It's really hard to read my mom's handwriting."

Join Toastmasters! It's not a cult or new religion—but everywhere you turn people plug it for improving their presentation skills (and boosting their self-esteem). The graduate list reads like a Who's Who. There are over 150,000 members and 8,000 chapters worldwide. (Chances are, wherever you're reading this there is a chapter nearby.) I was a member of the Del Mar, California, chapter for eight great years. Acting lessons help, too.

There is nothing like getting out there and just doing it. Where? How about civic groups like Rotary or Lions clubs or the Chamber of Commerce? You can teach a class at a college, art school, adult school, or create your own class and hold it in a hotel, the library, or your studio. (Consider this: The UCLA Extension catalog is mailed to more than a quarter of a million people.) There are plenty of professional groups, women's groups, church groups—there are just a lot of groups who desperately need speakers. Mark Victor Hanson (*Chicken Soup for the Soul*) spoke for a chuch at their Positive Thinkers Luncheon, which not only paid him but did a massive mailing as well. You could talk at a convention, trade show, craft guild, labor union meeting, banquet, retreat, for corporations, in bookstores, coffee shops, and so on. There are plenty of places to present yourself. Try to get in front of people who might need your products or services or may be able to help you in some way.

I have hit all of the above and some other places that I wouldn't wish on my worst enemy, but the point is, it has paid off. It hasn't all been pretty—I could tell you stories about being hungover, having a rat run across the room, falling off the stage, having the power go out, having people looking at their watch (which I don't mind, but when they start shaking it to see if it is still working, that's not good). I have told the same story twice in one talk, had every kind of equipment failure known to man, and, of course, spoken with my fly open—several times. So what have I learned from all these unfortunate experiences? Here are just a few suggestions to make your speeches less stressful and more successful.

Practice your talk *at least twice!* Focus on your opening and closing comments. Organize your talk so they can easily "get it" and follow along. Don't be boring! You can make any topic more interesting with stories, humor, and enthusiasm. Open with a bang to grab the audience's attention (use a shocking statement, a concern they can relate to, or humor). I like to open with a magic trick, but one guy I shared the stage with outdid me when he unzipped his pants and pulled out a . . . microphone. Smile and make eye contact. You want to win a few friends right away, and this is how to do it. Give them a break—people can't listen for more than ninety minutes (with understanding), and they listen with retention for about twenty minutes. (Break your talk up into twenty minutes or less and involve them every ten minutes.) Show them what you mean with a prop, or an overhead slide, or flip chart example. People remember what they see. Revisit content six times in different ways (games, reviews, interaction), because people need to be told what you're going to tell them, then tell them, and finally tell them what you told them. (Kinda like a newscast does. They preview what's coming up with teasers and then deliver the news.) Metaphors, acronyms, and catchy phrases as well as stories also increase retention. Especially stories. Bail the boring statistics and tell a story or two. If I told you that my friend slid down a cliff, so what, right? So I add more juicy details, like he was climbing out of the ocean in a panic (he thought he saw a shark) and pulled himself up a barnacle-ridden cliff, only to have the water rush out from under him, and when his grip gave out he tore the tips of his fingers off as he slid down, and the bloody stumps (and other cuts) bled like nobody's business into the very water where the alleged shark was. This is a true story, and the message is twofold: One, no matter what, don't panic, it will only make a bad situation worse. Two, stories are better than stats. (Especially true ones.) It helps if you can keep it simple—a main point with several supporting points. Ask yourself: What is the one thing I want the audience to take away from this talk? Build your speech around that point. (Keep that key point in front of you as you outline the talk.) Accept the fact that you won't be able to, nor should you, tell them everything you want to. Determine your objective and then switch hats and decide what they need to hear. Get away from the lectern if you can force yourself to let go. Give them a piece of you—be personal and personable. You should also give them a handout of some kind, but never hand them out during your talk, it's a distraction. For one talk, I gave out black and white handouts and crayons and asked the audience to color them in. It was fun for all. Once people write (or color) in a handout, they start to take ownership of it and keep it. Give out an evaluation form, because you want the feedback (it's so nice to read the rave reviews), and you also want to build your mailing list, so ask for their name and address. Make it more of a performance (we call it "edu-tainment") and less like a lecture. Don't let the technology get in the way of your talk. You are the star, not your handout or overheads. Get there early, test the equipment (and unplug any phones and lock any door that may be a distraction). Use note cards, not a pile of loose papers. Make an outline with key points, and don't read your speech! Ever.

☆ ——————————————
JUST FOR FUN
A teacher asked a student to sum up Socrates' life in four lines. She said: (1) Socrates lived long ago. (2) He was very smart. (3) Socrates gave long speeches. (4) His friends poisoned him. Moral: Shorten your talk.

————————————————

PowerPoint Stinks

Nearly 90 percent of all electronic slides are created in PowerPoint. That's 90 percent too many, in my opinion. Steve Jobs, the cofounder of Apple (and current chief executive officer), also heads

Pixar Animation Studios, the studio that produced top-selling films, including *Toy Story*. He knows a little bit about technology. Jobs stood in front of the standing-room-only crowd of Mac faithfuls at the Mac-World trade show, where the audience was in a rock-concert frenzy as he announced the next generation of Apple's operating system. The only problem was, because of technical glitches he was unable to demonstrate all of the features. As they say, "It happens."

PowerPoint-type presentations are both a blessing and a curse (mostly the latter). They have made presenters lazy. With the advent of technology, we have lost sight that at the heart of every great presentation is the presenter. A person with a powerful message who can, with a few good words, win people over and galvanize them into action. For many years (without fancy props and PowerPoint) people have won the hearts and minds of audiences with exceptional oratory skills. (Sounds like you're a bitter old throwback, Lee.) No, I have found that PowerPoint presentations (of course, I realize that Power-Point doesn't kill, people do) usually suck. I see the same bad things over and over, and it makes me sick. In more darkened rooms than I care to count, I have seen overdesigned, overused (it's like watching someone's slide show of boring vacation photos, yech), and sloppy (typos) presentations that used PowerPoint as a crutch that diverts attention away from the speaker. The funny thing is, these things take a lot of time to prepare, time that would have been better spent preparing the talk itself. Enough said.

Go Where the Action Is

"I moved to Los Angeles because that's where the work is."
—John Cusack

Jackson Pollock moved from Wyoming to New York (with a stop in Los Angeles) because he felt it was the best place to meet people who could further his career. He was right, too. (Not that Wyoming isn't a great place, but for artists, New York was and is the place to be.) I know, it's expensive, competitive, and cold. But as overwhelming as the odds are of making it there, they are probably longer if you live in Little Place, USA. I know that's harsh, but it's true. You may have to move to make yourself more promotable (or have an agent who's located where all the action is taking place). This isn't new. The hot spots change. Seattle was where grunge bands came from. My home-town of San Diego has produced its share of successful bands. But let's face facts. If you are an actor, Los Angeles is the place you have (notice I didn't say "want") to be. (Not many people want to live there, but that's where you have the best chance to make it. Agents, auditions, and almost all the studios are there.) Los Angeles is also an important place for a band to be. For a while it was the center of the universe for rock 'n' roll. Places like the Hollywood a Go-Go and Ninth Street West as well as The Red Velvet, Pandora's Box, The Trip, and The London Fog, to name just a few, launched bands like The Doors, Buffalo Springfield, the Byrds, and many, many more. Sure, hot spots shift. In the 1970s it was San Francisco, and then it was L.A. again, as Black Flag, X, The Knack, the Plimsouls, and Los Lobos launched from there. Of course, if you're a studio musician this is one of the best places to be.

Country singer Trisha Yearwood always wanted to become a professional singer, but growing up, she kept her dream to herself. Her conservative family would have thought it was a crazy idea. She convinced them that the best place for her to attend college (as a business major) would be Nashville. She got her degree and, as we all know, became a big country music star. The key was to go where the action is, and for country music, that place is Nashville. Award-winning jazz violinist Miri Ben-Ari served two years in the Israeli Army and then moved to where the action is—New York City. There she became entrenched in the New York scene, studying by day and playing jam sessions at night. One evening while onstage performing, Betty Carter walked in after her gig next door at the renowned Blue Note. After Miri finished her set, the legendary singer came up and gave her a hug and eventually invited her to be a part of Jazz Ahead, a jazz education program.

Start local and then go where you have the best chance to make it. Actor and comedian David Spade began building his résumé doing stand-up in his hometown of Phoenix, Arizona, yet it wasn't until he moved to Los Angeles and began performing there that things started to happen for him. First, an agent caught his act at the Improv and cast him as a skateboarder in *Police Academy 4: Citizens on Patrol.* Then Dennis Miller, who was the host of "Weekend Update" on "Saturday Night Live," was hosting HBO's Annual Young Comedians Show and told Lorne Michaels, the creator of "SNL," about him. Lorne saw him perform and asked him to join the cast. After six years on "SNL" he landed a role on a popular TV sitcom, "Just Shoot Me," made several movies (*Tommy Boy*), and is a spokesperson for MCI.

Selma Hayek was a soap opera superstar in Mexico, loved by legions of fans, but she wanted more. She decided to start over in the States and moved north (to Los Angeles), even though she didn't have a lot of money (or know how to drive). After landing some small roles on television and in films, she was discovered, storybook-style, by Mexican-American director Robert Rodriguez, who noticed her by chance on a Spanish-language television talk show. He then tracked her down and cast her in *Desperado* opposite Antonio Banderas. Rebecca Gayheart used the $300 she won in a local beauty contest in Kentucky to finance her move to New York, where she landed roles in soap operas. Then, after moving to Los Angeles, she acted in such films as *Scream 2* and *Urban Legend*.

It isn't always New York or Los Angeles where the most talented creative people go to become rich and famous. How about Seattle, for instance? Amazon.com has lured some extremely creative people to the Northwest to work in the editorial side of earth's biggest bookstore (and more). The editorial folks' job is to create opinionated, entertaining guides to Amazon products. There is also the Amazon design team. Where are things happening in your area of the arts?

Cities with the most growth include Boise, Idaho; Gainesville, Florida; Sterling, Virginia; Austin, Texas; San Luis Obispo. The top destinations for people moving are New York, Houston, Los Angeles, Dallas, and Orlando. (According to a survey done by U-Haul International.)

ACTION ITEM
Name one thing you are going to do to show off. When? Now! Put this book down and go do it.

Ask a Pro

Nadya
Clothing designer who lives in Bali
(but does trunk shows in the United States)
nadya@attglobal.net

Why do you prefer doing showings for your custom clothes?

The experience was always personal and social. Bonds were formed, relationships developed. The hours for the showings stretched from morning till night. It was through these bonds and the personal relationships that loyalty and friendship developed. From the beginning it was critical to me that people have a good experience and receive value and pleasure from their purchases. Because it was very personal, they only shared their secret of Nadya Shopping with people they liked. Their enthusiasm was based on knowing they were really cared about. It sounds simple, but for me it is about respect and human values. And I think those should be the tenets of business and marketing. Doing periodic showings twice a year means when people come they shop—or wait another six months. All of my designs are unique, limited-edition pieces. Everyone always remembers the one they missed when they wanted time to think about it. Listening to client feedback is a great benefit of personally doing shows. My ideas are always very exciting for me—my clients, however, always remind me about their needs and what I might be missing.

Are you comfortable speaking in public and interacting with clients?

I was always shy about public speaking, but I sensed the importance of getting over that fear. A friend, writer/astrologer Katherine de Jersey, gave me great advice when I confessed my resistance about speaking in public. She said, "Remember, you'll always be asked to talk about something you know and care about passionately—go for it!" It was great advice.

☆ ⎯⎯⎯⎯⎯⎯⎯⎯⎯⎯⎯⎯

HOW TO BE A STAY-AT-HOME M.O.M. (MULTIPLE OUTLET MARKETER)

"To infinity and beyond."

—*Buzz Lightyear*

Is it possible to be in two places at one time? In marketing it is. The goal is to get your name out there. You don't necessarily have to physically go anywhere, if you don't want to or can't. The important thing is to start the ball rolling so that so many people know you and what you do that leads begin to come to you with little or no effort. To increase your visibility and credibility, you can write a book, build a Web presence, write articles, or become a columnist, garner publicity (radio interviews can be done from home via the phone), and get your art out there on the road. When you record a live performance and package it for sale, for example, your efforts are multiplied each time you sell a CD. You don't have to leave home to get out there anymore. You can teach a class, participate in a panel discussion, and do interviews online, all in the comfort of your home (and you never have to change out of your sweats).

Parting Thoughts

The Dixie Chicks, the Grammy-winning, multiplatinum-selling, hard-touring band of very talented (and savvy) country/pop stars, got their start singing on Texas street corners. People were so enthralled by the free show, they would stop and listen for hours and throw a lot of money in the tip jar (which was a chicken on wheels). The girls made enough money to finance their first of three self-published albums, which sold a very respectable 90,000 copies from the backs of their cars. They also sold hats and T-shirts bearing the band's name. This attracted the attention of bar owners and eventually record labels. Who wouldn't be interested in a band of talented, motivated, promotable (and attractive) performers like the Dixie Chicks?

4

DO THE HUSTLE
(Persistence Pays Off)

*"An artist after many phone calls finally got an appointment
with a local art dealer. The dealer kept him waiting for an
hour, looked through his portfolio, and told him, 'Come back
when you're dead.'"*

—Sam Provenzano

Remember when the knight in the movie *Monty Python and the Holy
Grail* keeps trying to fight even after having his limbs cut off?
Sometimes that kind of dogged determination is the difference
between obscurity and an appearance on "Oprah." In football they say
a player has a "motor" and "finishes every play off." In the creative
arts we call a person who just will not quit despite constant rejection
delusional. Just kidding. It is hard to hear the word "No" over and over
and still keep hacking away. You know there is a "Yes" out there somewhere, so you keep going, working hard to improve, continuing to
promote, despite the emotional scars that rejection leaves on the frag-
ile ego of the emotional, thin-skinned creative person.

Many talented and creative people struggle. The ones that make it
have an intense desire to promote and succeed—an attitude that says,
"You can't stop me." Elzie Alexander is an aspiring stand-up comic in
San Diego. Every Sunday evening he commutes by bus from the
downtown homeless shelter where he lives to The Comedy Store to
make people laugh. During the week he works odd jobs and tests his
material on other residents at the St. Vincent de Paul Village (a very
tough crowd), and he goes to bed every night dreaming of one day
having his own HBO special. I'll bet he makes it.

You do whatever it takes. Drummer Tommy Lee talks about the
early days of Mötley Crüe. "We were like a self-promotion machine.
We went around with flyers and a staple gun and plastered everything." How many people are willing to put out that kind of effort? I'll
tell you, not many. Some, however, do what others aren't willing to do

and end up getting what others (who don't try nearly as hard) want—success. Metallica was willing to work. For two and a half years they built their fan base by becoming road warriors, performing over three hundred shows.

Use your brain (and your back) to get the word out. It's called "sweat equity," and the time and effort is an investment in you. It goes to show it doesn't take money to make it. Elaine Sosa runs a coffee-themed, guided history tour of San Francisco and writes for a travel website. To get going she used a guerrilla marketing effort. She sent letters to guidebook companies, wrote a press release and sent it to 250 magazines and newsletters, created a flyer and circulated it to hotel concierges. Now she gets paid to have coffee with interesting people. Very cool.

Eventually, you wear them down with your effort and persistence. Todd McFarlane was a comic book collector who wanted to create his own comics. He began the pursuit of his dream by sending out drawings to almost all of the comic book publishing companies. For his efforts he received more than seven hundred rejection letters. Most people would have quit at seven rejections. He then began mailing out his portfolio for fourteen straight months before finally receiving an offer from Marvel Comics. He told *People* magazine how his persistence paid off. "Editors knew my package was coming every month. After a while, they said, 'Just give him some work and shut him up.'" McFarlane went on to become the most recognized name in the comic artist field and created *Spawn,* the best-selling independent comic of all time, making McFarlane a millionaire many times over.

Don't get mad, get even. The best way to get even is to succeed and prove people wrong. Author Karen Salmansohn says, "Behind every successful woman is someone who pissed her off." For some, hustling is a habit. Janice Peters is the president and CEO of the nation's third-largest cable TV operator. When she was a salesclerk at Sears (obviously years earlier), she found out that they paid a 10 percent commission on everything you sold in the toy department. So instead of waiting for customers to come to her, she sought them out and offered to help them find what they were looking for. The other clerks would stand around and talk during slow periods, but she made the most productive use of every minute. This was while she was in high school. Her hustle and habits put her where she is today.

What does all this say? Creative people who make it in the arts don't succeed because they are the smartest or most talented—they succeed because they persevere and keep putting one foot in front of the other (and are willing to crawl if they have to), and slowly but surely move closer and closer to success (stepping on the naysayers with each step). I know nobody wants to hear this, but hard work combined with good ideas and talent is the not-so-secret formula for fame and fortune. If it's not a secret, how come everybody doesn't do it? A major reason is that some of the creative person's most endearing traits are offset with some not-so-great ones, like the desire for immediate satisfaction, short-term thinking, and acute fear of failure and rejection. Some face their fears and force themselves to keep on, others wilt and die under the pressure. They give up the dream, get a real job, and sell off their gear. This is not the case for people who are passionate and committed to making it—no matter what. I'm getting goose bumps just writing this stuff. I know I have been tempted to quit at times and get a real job—NOT! I can't tell you how many people told me I wouldn't make it. The line from the movie *Rudy,* "You're five-foot-nothing, a hundred and nothing, with nary a speck of talent," rings true. I can relate to that. (I also love it when he fails on one play and the coach tries to pull him out but he says, "No! Coach, I can do it!") People had been telling me early in my career that it "will never happen" and "Who do you think you are?" and "What makes you think you can beat the odds?" I have proved people wrong again and again, and they have finally stopped betting against me. I believe it's because they know by now I will not give up, give in, or give a damn about what they say. I can't be stopped. I won't be stopped. I dare anyone to try to stop me. Face your fears and move on. "I'm scared by psychological things—like being in meetings at Warner Bros.," says director Tim Burton. But look at his track record of successful films.

What makes creative people keep pushing on and promoting? One word: passion. Singer Diana Krall says, "I'm excited about the music. I play with integrity and I don't compromise my vision. I approach it from an artistic perspective. But I am also aware of the market and the need to sell records so that I can continue to grow. All I am trying to do is make beautiful records that people enjoy. I'm passionate about the songs." You need to approach your art (and marketing of your art) like it's Christmas morning and there is a purple bicycle under the tree. You feel like the luckiest person alive, even if success has eluded you thus far. Force yourself to get outside of your comfort zone. "The producer said, 'Do you have a problem with nudity?' I was like, 'The question is, do you?' Ba-boom. I was bucknaked. Swingin' and hangin'," boasts actor Cuba Gooding, Jr. What's the worst thing that can happen? Big deal, so you get fired. You can bounce back better than before. Stronger, faster . . . Take rejection in stride. "I read the most appalling stuff about myself: 'She has bug eyes,' 'Her hair is like straw.' I was like, 'Okay, I could use a little conditioner,' but—God!" admits Tori Spelling. Don't let *them* get *you* down.

Stay committed. For each of my last two books, I paid for my own book tours. I would fly into a city and rent a car (always with the GPS navigational system), hit as many bookstores as I could during the day, and do in-store seminars at night. It took every ounce of commitment to do this, because I would go into bookstore after bookstore to sign copies of my book, and if I was lucky, they had one or two copies in stock. It was demoralizing to go from a nationally known author with eight books, an agent, and a powerhouse publisher to next to nothing. Standing at the information booth of a bookstore repeating the title for the clerk for the tenth time, I would ask myself (more than once), "Why the hell am I doing this, I could be at the beach?" The beach was beckoning, but something inside pushed me to keep going. "Go the distance," it said. It paid off, too. I made some great connections with key store managers who would take a chance and order a dozen copies of each of my books, only to have them quickly sell out. For example, when I was in the Los Angeles International Airport I stopped by one of the booksellers in the United terminal and convinced them to order more copies of my books. To date they have sold over a hundred copies of each title. One community relations coordinator in Florida built a series of classes around one of my books (much like the *Artist's Way*) and sold a lot of books. Something inside pushed me to keep going (the dream of a big, fat royalty check?) when I was dead tired and didn't want to do any more and only had three people show up at a signing. Then at night, after driving around and doing in-store workshops, I would call more stores from my hotel room that I didn't get to and convince them to order more copies. I didn't get to the beach (much), but I sold lots of books.

Kick Ass, Take No Prisoners

"Go on working freely and furiously, and you will make progress."

—Paul Gauguin

There are plenty of teenage girls who want to be like Britney Spears. (I bet there are many who can sing just as well, too.) But what separates fifteen-year-old Emily Carlstrom from the rest of the wannabe's is her hustle (and chutzpah). Emily went to a San Diego radio station (which also happens to have the number-one-rated morning show in the sixth-largest city in the country) and asked the disc jockeys to play her demo tape. She had her press kit (complete with Glamour Shot photos and a bio). The two hosts, Jeff and Jer, were impressed by Emily and her song, so they played it. (The song is about a cute guy she liked at her high school.) Darn it if people weren't humming along to her song and requesting to hear it again. So the station invited Emily to be an in-studio guest, put up a Web page for her, arranged a concert, and helped her sell her CD and potentially land a record deal. (You can read more about Emily's story in the last chapter of this book.)

Do the legwork. We have discussed that what separates the people who have success and those who struggle is hustle. Talent helps, but if you really want to get ahead and be promotable, you have to be willing to do whatever it takes to make it happen. Something as simple as following up is a good example. Many creative people (and detail work is generally not our strong suit) will send out samples and press releases but fail to follow up. Follow-up is a key component to self-promotion success. But it is a big burden (and you don't want to be a bugger). Yet when you see someone who is a media darling and appearing on all the talk shows, you think to yourself, How come she gets all the breaks? (You also likely think, That bitch doesn't deserve it, either.) What we fail to sometimes see is all the legwork and behind-the-scenes hustle and hard work that go into getting promotional opportunities. As Michelangelo once said, "If people knew how hard I worked to get my mastery, it wouldn't seem so wonderful after all." Actually, I think it is amazing when someone is so disciplined and so dedicated that they will work their ass off to get where they want to go (even if others still think they are an overnight success).

Micromovements. Are you willing to go the extra mile? I know that in my career I started at the bottom and worked my way up by taking baby steps. Obviously, I am not the only one. I know a woman who wanted more than anything to be recognized for her talent as a party planner. Whenever someone in her family (and she had a huge, extended Portuguese family) had a party, she volunteered to turn it into an event. She did a lot of craft-type things and would stay up all night (she had a full-time job as well) making handcrafted tiaras out of beads and coming up with new activities for the kids. Although she wasn't paid, her efforts paid off as family members told friends who told their friends, and a business, Parties on the Run, was born. Musician and author Jana Stanfield knows what hustle is. "In the beginning I told myself I would do whatever it took to make the necessary dollar amount each month—even if I had to work some hours at Taco Bell.

The thought of me in a Taco Bell outfit gave me the push I needed to start creating some gigs, especially when I see there's going to be too much month at the end of the money."

Think big. Even if you think it is impossible, go for it anyway. "No guts, no glory," said Bette Davis. Saying "I can't do it" won't get you anywhere. Instead say, "I'll give it a go and see what happens." It helps if you get lost in the process. Focus on the footwork, or as athletes say, "Take it one game at a time." This helps to keep your fears and worries at bay and out of the way. Quietly do something every day that pushes you outside of your comfort zone when it comes to promotion. Something you think you can't possibly do. No matter what you perceive as a possible deficit. "Your disability is your opportunity," says Kurt Hahn, founder of Outward Bound. Think big, believe big, act big, and the results will be BIG. "No" is only a two-letter word that can't hurt you unless you let it. Don't be afraid to tell everyone what you want to do. Yes, we have all kinds of wild ideas, and some of them never pan out. We're dreamers, and that's part of our charm. Some are awake while working on that dream every day, taking little steps at a time. Prove people wrong if they try to put you and your dreams down. How? Hustle. Hootie and the Blowfish toured for a couple of years in a little van (and they are still together!) before their debut album made them stars.

Commitment. Performance artists Rhodessa Jones and Idris Ackamoor have been able to make a living at their art for over a decade. When the two first met, they both quit their day jobs so they would be committed to making it as working artists. A bold move, but one that has paid off. Stay committed even after you have "made it." You must continue to outhustle the competition. Pianist Jim Brinkman's path to success is the result of perseverance and hustle. The guy already has four gold records and he still will market his music by doing interviews (many times at ungodly hours after a concert) during multicity tours to connect with his fans, known as "Brickheads." When you are hot, you should try to keep it going and use that momentum to your advantage.

Keep the ball rolling. For a while Phil Collins was the hardest-working guy in the music business. He was the drummer and front man for Genesis, formed another band called Brand X that played progressive rock, played drums and toured with Peter Gabriel, released several solo albums, toured, and produced albums for people like Eric Clapton and Philip Bailey. Collins also appeared as an actor on "Miami Vice" and in the movie *Buster,* and won several awards for making movie soundtracks. You can't just kick back after you've made it and live off the residuals or you will be a has-been and a candidate for a "Where Are They Now?" show.

Persistence Doesn't Necessarily Mean You're a Pest

"He doesn't know the meaning of the word quit. He can't spell it, either."

—Robert Thornton

I saw this unattributed quote on a poster and it rang so true to me: "On the road to success, you can be sure of one thing . . . there is never a crowd on the extra mile." It seems that some people give up too soon. I haven't quite figured out where the fine line is between being persistent and being a pest. But people respect (and reward) tenacity. Keep at it, you eventually break through (or in my case, break them). Patience *is* a vital virtue when it comes to self-promotion. I think that the common ingredients in successful self-promoters is having a dream and the determination and discipline to keep at it, and to sell others on that dream through passion and/or persistence. William Faulkner maybe said it best: "Success seems to be largely a matter of hanging on after others have let go." The creators of "South Park," Trey Parker and Matt Stone, were both (by their own admission) geeks in high school. Things didn't get much better in college. (Parker was kicked out of film school for truancy.) The two of them then made funky low-budget films without much positive response. For seven years they kept plugging away. During this time the two experimented (in their apartment) with cutout characters, eventually turning these construction paper cartoons into "South Park" and becoming multimillionaires. They had a tremendous amount of patience.

I hate to wait. Sometimes deals that involve your art take time—lots of time—to develop. The problem is, there is nothing you can do to speed things up. So your mind starts to create these horrendous scenarios. No news is NOT good news. You just have to keep plugging away on other things (juggle several projects at once) and hope things will work out. It doesn't matter how much you worry, that won't help. Worry is a waste of time. Stay calm, think good thoughts, and tell yourself, "I'll deal with whatever happens." By all means keep creating.

☆

ACTION ITEM

Interview yourself, and either make a tape or write a story or article about your success as if it has already happened.

The Time to Begin Is Now

"If you are going through hell, keep going."

—Winston Churchill

Most creative people come up with wonderful ideas—few follow through and consistently promote them and themselves. (We'd rather move on to the next thing.) Those who can stick with it are the ones you hear about. The ones with all the "luck." It is common for creative people to put off promoting themselves. It is not their favorite part of being an artist. Or they have done some promotion, but don't maximize the momentum created by those earlier efforts. You cannot let your guard down—ever. Don't ever forget that the competition is hungry, talented, and proficient, and that the moment you let up, they are passing you by. Taking away opportunities that should have been yours. Leaving you to wonder: What the hell happened?

A freelance artist told me that her most positive promotions came from the final one percent of her efforts. In other words, don't give up too soon. Even if it seems that a promotional plan is a bust, you may be close to realizing a boom from your efforts. She was explaining that after sending out newsletters for several months she was convinced it was a waste of time (and money). Then she landed three commissions in a row with a direct link to her mailings.

The path to promoting yourself is full of challenges. There will be boulders in your way. No doubt about it. What you need to do is look at them with detachment and objectivity and find ways to chip away at them or move them out of the way. When you read about people like Shania Twain, who lost both of her parents in an automobile accident and helped raise her siblings by singing at the Deerhurst Resort in Hunstville, Ontario, before becoming one of the biggest country crossover stars ever, then you look at your minor obstacles and say, "Okay, maybe I am obsessing. If she can do it, I can do it, too."

ACTION ITEM

It would be very easy to say, "If only I . . ." In fact, see if any of these are factors that have kept you from persistent promotion.

If only I had more training or a degree.
If only I had more talent, like so and so.
If only I knew the right people.
If only I lived in a different city.
If only I had more equipment or the right equipment.

But if you finished the sentence "If only I . . ." and your excuse has been overcome by someone else, it's bogus. You can outhustle most people and persist when they would have pooped out. Don't worry about what you don't have; focus on all the things you do have going for you.

Do It with Passion

> "Great dancers are not great because of their technique—they are great because of their passion."
>
> —Martha Graham

Passion and promotion go hand in hand. If you have a dream and are passionate about achieving it, you are more likely to be filled with enthusiasm (which is helpful for the self-promoter) and able to sustain that enthusiasm over the long haul. When you are passionate, it is much more likely you will be able to weather the rough times, the rejection, and even the ridicule for believing in your dream. (You will, of course, have the last laugh.) When you can hang on long enough (or have the good fortune of some early success), there is a transformation that takes place. You can taste it. That keeps you going. Having your first positive review, a feature article, or a successful opening can sustain you through to the next big thing. Of course, when you enjoy the process, you don't have to depend on a media appearance for a lift. Passion is what keeps people plugging away in the film and music business, despite the long odds and constant rejection. Passion takes you from a sleepwalking state to being a person on a mission, willing to do whatever it takes to get the word out, which is what makes for self-promotion success.

I never thought I would be writing about Richard Simmons, but he is the perfect example of someone who is extremely passionate about what he is doing and uses that passion to publicize himself. No wonder the guy is sweatin'. He is everywhere, all the time—"The

Tonight Show," QVC, infomercials, magazines, his own show, book-stores, conducting diet and health seminars for corporations, making personal appearances at exercise studios and at malls across America. I'm not done yet. He also answers e-mails, writes letters, and makes encouraging calls to people on his program. The guy is for real. (I know, I know, ditch the do and the Dolphin shorts, but I respect his accomplishments and commitment to his crusade to help overweight people.)

Passion pushes you to do more than you think you can do. It makes you want to wake up every day and tell everyone about what you are doing. Someone I know from surfing, Tom Lochtefeld, is making waves with his invention. Literally, that's what his invention is: a wave-making machine that can create the perfect tube. This life-long obsession has become a viable career. His invention is in water parks all over the world. Who would have thought that a surfer could succeed to that degree? J. C. Penney said, "Give me a stock clerk with a goal, and I will give you a man who will make history. Give me a man without a goal, and I will give you a stock clerk." (Sounds like a great premise for a film. Oh yeah, it's called *Trading Places*.) Without passion, people are tired all the time. The last thing they want to do is promote themselves or their work. They procrastinate and don't want to work. I have found that if you don't enjoy what you do, you will be far less likely to promote it and will be easily discouraged, feeling deflated and defeated. This makes you and those around you irritable and unhappy.

With passion, a creative person is fired up and ready to take on the world. You want to press on and push yourself, to persevere despite setbacks. You are willing to do the grunt work and have more stamina for the crap that is part of promotion. When you believe 100 percent in what you are doing, you are more enthusiastic and people pick up on that and buy into it. You can see it in their eyes, hear it in their voices, and feel it in their handshakes. Joseph Campbell says, "Follow your bliss, and what looks like walls will turn into doors." Translation: Passion will overcome obstacle and objections. Selling work you love is smart business and brings bliss.

If you have lost that lovin' feeling, one way to get it back is to mix in work that you are passionate about. Doing work that would sell is smart, but it doesn't feed your soul. To your surprise, it might not even make you more marketable. The more you do work that comes from the heart, that excites you, the more likely you will do it well. You are excited about promoting it because you love it, and it is better because you are working with your strengths. Musician Keb' Mo' knows what

I'm talking about. He says, "Before I was doing blues, I was just trying to be a pop songwriter, and the things I wrote didn't have any meaning for me. It just had to be catchy and have a form. In hindsight, I see what was missing from them was heart. And the blues really woke me up to the need for songs to have heart in them." It can be tempting to create work that the market dictates to you it will buy. To some degree you must do this to sell and survive. Doing work that you love, that you do well, *and* that sells is also smart business. You don't have to completely compromise your vision, voice, or vehicle. Maybe you don't sell a million, but you didn't sell out, either. "Since you usually can expect no earthly reward if you write poetry, you have to do it for the love," states Roger Bergman. Please yourself and hope that "the suits" will get it, too. Maybe you have to downsize your dreams just a tad and come to grips with less success but more happiness.

Commercial success does not bring happiness. We hear that and say to ourselves, "Oh, yeah, let me see for myself." Fine, but consider that when singer Gwen Stefani was most depressed was when her band No Doubt was most successful. The good life is *your* version of what the good life is. I have this discussion with my wife from time to time. She will ask, "Why don't you try this or that?" and I will point out that although that may be a more promotable project, I have no passion for it. She'll then point out, "What about the mortgage?" I tell her, "I'd be miserable if I did things for the money or because they may be more marketable." She'll point out again, "What about the mortgage?" I try to explain that there is more to life than a nice home, and she looks at me like I've gone mad. You know what her reply is? Right. "What about the mortgage?" Well, I will not mortgage my soul to make a house payment. Passion is life. Passion is what makes artists create great works. And passion for something is what makes many of us more promotable (and as a result the riches will come, eventually).

☆

ACTION ITEM

Get close to what you are obsessed with. To know what that is, ask yourself what the one thing is you would do for free (but because you do it so well there are people who will pay you to do it). Slow down and take stock of where you are and where you're heading. When impressionist painter Renoir was crippled by arthritis, he strapped a brush to his arm in order to paint. That's passion. What is *your* passion?

In It for the Long Haul

"If you have a burning, restless urge to write or paint, simply eat something sweet and the feeling will pass."

—Fran Lebowitz

Once you form good promotional habits, they become a way of life. Following up becomes second nature. Making the media aware of what you are doing is a monthly mission. Sending a newsletter, updates, and greeting cards to your mailing list every quarter is something you should consistently do. This makes you stand out. Some creative people are lazy and their promotional efforts are haphazard at best. Consistent and persistent not only rhyme, they are also synonymous with good promotional hygiene. Persistence keeps you moving ahead. Little things lead to your big breaks later on.

It's also a mind-set. In the *Rocky* movies, Rocky Balboa almost always gets pummeled in the early rounds. Then, like a champ, he somehow (movie magic?) makes a miraculous comeback. It sometimes feels like you are a bad boxer and people are whaling on you. Your ego is bruised, your feelings are hurt, and you would rather just stay down for the count than take more punishment. In your head I want you to hear the Rocky theme song, da-ta-da-da-ta-da-ta-da . . . and force yourself to keep trying. Self-promotion is a streetfight. You get knocked down, you get up and spit in their face, and say, "My mother hits harder than you. Is that all you got?" I know that when I'm having a tough time promoting myself, every bone in my body says quit. But my heart says, Get up, keep trying. (Or else you'll have to go get a job. That's the smelling salts for me!)

Every freelancer goes through slumps. It's usually a "when it rains it pours" followed by a long drought. It happens. That's when the "fire in your belly" mentality must take over. It's not enough to sorta want it, or to say, "If I don't make it by next week, I'm gonna quit." It's gotta be, "I want this so bad I am not going to quit until I get it. Rejection? So what, it's only temporary. I'm committed!" Remember, if Carlos Santana can come back . . .

It sounds simple. Don't quit. I get it. But in reality, the frustration and even the anger of not getting any publicity, or getting bad reviews, or a lack of business, can be a real motivation killer. You start to doubt yourself, your ability, and even whether you made the right career choice. Stop feeling sorry for yourself. Shake it off and keep at it. I know for many of us there is no backup plan. We blew up the escape route and it is our art or nothing. (It's not a suicidal thing, but it's more of a belief that this is what we were meant to do.) If you can look deep inside yourself and find even a flicker of hope that others will eventually recognize your genius and your talent, then you can use that to keep moving forward—even if it is just a crawl.

I want to let you in on a little secret. I chose to write this chapter when I did because I was in a minor slump. Nothing major, just a lull. I was feeling a little lethargic. I lost the "eye of the tiger." But by keeping my eye on the goal and filling my days with positive action, I am getting back in touch with my kick-ass, you-can't-freaking-keep-me-down mind-set. (See, you *can* channel your anger constructively.) I think I will go put *Rocky III* in the VCR and get fired up and start up the promotion machine again. I hope you find comfort in the fact that everyone goes through these "Why me?" phases. Some of it stems from a sense of "What if they find me out" syndrome. Which, put another way, is fear. Fear limits your success. We all feel it, but the truly successful people work through it. Ask yourself, "If I keep trying and fail again, what's the worst thing that will happen?"

Just for Fun
Match the motivating quote to the person who said it: (a) Mia Hamm (b) Charles Schulz (c) Eddie Murphy (d) Clint Eastwood (e) Paul Lazarus III

1. "You get born only once in this business, but you can die over and over again. Then you can make comebacks."
2. "You may get skinned knees and elbows, but it's worth it if you score a spectacular goal."
3. "Life is like a ten-speed bicycle. Most of us have gears we never use."
4. "Persistence is always a necessary part of the Hollywood success story."
5. "If I get to the point where I look like a basset hound, I'll just play basset hounds."

Answers: 1. (c), 2. (a), 3. (b), 4. (e), 5. (d)

I hate telemarketers. They have no shame, calling at the worst possible time (if you know what I mean). There is also a lesson we can learn from the good ones. They don't take no for an answer. They will call every day, sometimes twice a day, if there is a chance they can make a sale. They wear you down. If you really want something and the person standing in your way isn't cooperating, pick up the pace. Go see them personally. Regroup and try again. Adjust your approach.

Don't whine, don't cry, and certainly don't quit. Use your anger. "Get pissed off, not pissed on," says Karen Salmansohn. It's not a setback but a get-back. Make them understand, prove them wrong. (Success is the best revenge.) Early in my career I went to a big-time literary agent who lives near me. She told me she didn't think my idea would sell. It really made me angry. I listened to why she thought my idea wouldn't work, and fixed it, and then went about showing her up. Proving she was wrong was the fuel that kept my fire burning.

Sometimes it's just that your timing is off. You have the right idea at the wrong time. That's why you can't give up too soon. It's also why you juggle a couple of things at once and diversify. If one deal falls through, no problem, I'll work on something else for a while. Nearly all the networks passed on "The Sopranos." David Chase ended up at HBO and things could not be better. The Emmy Award–winning show would not have been a good fit on network television. After "Baywatch" was canceled by NBC, David Hasselhoff turned the show into a syndication sensation. Bigger (maybe not better) than before. Al Neuharth's first attempt at publishing a paper was a disaster. He may have lost $50,000, but not his confidence. He would later found *USA Today* (which also got off to a rocky start).

I also think that persistence and frequency are linked. You have to keep hitting them over the head before they get it. Harry Beckwith, in the book *Selling the Invisible,* makes this point with the following example: You are driving in your car and you hear a song on the radio and you think to yourself, hmmm, catchy. You hear it the next day and maybe you note the name of the band or the song's title. Two mornings later you start to sing along with the song. (This is the problem with radio programming, no?) The following week you go out and buy the CD. You play the CD at home and now you know most of the words. What if the singer had changed the song every time? (Jazz fans, play along with this analogy, even though I know it's painful.) Would you recall the song if it were different each time? Nope. You don't necessarily have to change your pitch, you just have to keep pitching. Danielle Steel says her success is due to her unflagging optimism and ambition. "After five of my early books flopped, what if I had said, 'Oh, the hell with it—I can't do it'? I'd never have all this. You *have* to keep at it. Although I've been lucky and blessed in my life, my success has not been handed to me—I've worked very, very hard."

Rejection: Fuhgeddaboudit

"The way for a young man to rise is to improve himself every way he can, never suspecting that anybody wished to hinder him."
—Abraham Lincoln

When you think that over a thousand restaurateurs turned down Colonel Sanders and his fried chicken recipe before he sold it, it makes you wonder how many no's it takes to get to a yes. After thirty publishers turned down one of my earlier books, I began to wonder if I should give up shopping it around. It was the thirty-first publisher that said yes. My goal wasn't to see how many rejection slips I could collect. But I did somehow feel that I was getting closer to a yes than another no.

Critics called Robin Williams's early performances lightweight. Adam Sandler's stand-up career began with horrendous reviews. (Later his movies got panned, too, but he is a multimillionaire and seems positively happy about his career.)

I am okay with the fact that the life I have chosen (writer) has its share of ups and downs and critical people. I know that I will constantly be in a state of permanent insecurity, but I have faith in myself and my ability. Every morning I can choose to cave in or keep going. Don't pay attention to critics. It's a little disconcerting that you have to take a test to get a driver's license, but critics don't have to have any credentials before critiquing your creations. So why even pay attention to them? Take the following example of critics who were way off the mark.

"A flash in the pan."
Billboard magazine's review of superstar Madonna, 1983
"Boring and predictable."
Time magazine's review of the popular show
"All in the Family," 1971
"We don't like their sound. Groups with guitars are on their way out."
Decca Recording Co. after turning down the Beatles, 1962
"With your voice, nobody is going to let you broadcast."
CBS producer Don Hewitt to Barbara Walters, 1958
"The singer will have to go."
Rolling Stones manager Eric Easton on Mick Jagger, 1963
"You ain't going nowhere . . . Son, you ought to go back to driving a truck."
Grand Ole Opry manager Jim Denny
after firing Elvis Presley, 1954

"Can't act. Can't sing. Balding. Can dance a little."
MGM executive about Fred Astaire's screen test, 1929

"Asking a working writer what he thinks about critics is like asking a lamppost how it feels about dogs," observes Christopher Hampton. You have to get used to the fact that art is subjective and not everyone will like it. It doesn't mean they don't like you. It's almost impossible not to take criticism personally. It's hard to get used to the fact that not everyone likes and understands your work. It's also difficult feeling that there are people out there who don't like you. There is an on-air personality in my hometown who is very controversial. When I interviewed him a few years ago I pointed out that people had passionate opinions of him—they either loved him or hated him. He said, "That's fine, half the population loves me, the other half, over one million people, don't. That's tough to deal with."

JUST FOR FUN
Which of the following books were first rejected by publishers?

A Time to Kill by John Grisham
The Diary of Anne Frank by Anne Frank
Chicken Soup for the Soul by Mark Victor Hansen and Jack Canfield
A River Runs Through It by Norman MacLean
Valley of the Dolls by Jacqueline Susann
Catch-22 by Joseph Heller
The Postman Always Rings Twice by James M. Cain
Gentlemen Prefer Blondes by Anita Loos
Sanctuary by William Faulkner
Answer: All of the above

Promotion and a Positive Self-Image
"'I'm going to be a big star!' In California, we call that sort of statement 'creative visualization.' In the other forty-nine states it's called self-delusion."

—*Maureen Brownsey*

Dion Sanders is a master marketer. Considering "Prime Time" doesn't play a "glamorous" position like running back (he's a defensive back), he has managed to make quite a name for himself—and not on talent alone. He knows he is good, and he makes sure that everybody else knows it, too. Most of the other players resent him because he showboats, but they respect him because he truly is a great player. During one game he told Rams wide receiver Isaac Bruce (whom he was covering) how to run better routes. That's confidence, or arrogance. It is this distinction, between being self-assured and being an ass, that causes people to play down their talent. As creative people in a very competitive world, we can't afford to be humble. So what if they call us brash or a bitch, that's just their jealousy talking. Keyshawn Johnson, another of football's "flashy" players, confidently titled his autobiography *Just Give Me the Damn Ball*.

Your attitude (positive is a plus) does determine your altitude (how high and far you will go). You have to believe you will make it and deserve to make it and that your work is worthwhile. Most of us find that we lack a little when it comes to confidence. But if you have it, you have a powerful edge when it comes to promotion. You will have the guts to go for it while others watch from the sidelines. People pick up on your insecurities. It's impossible not to notice when a creative person bad-mouths everyone around them or uses self-defeating phrases like "It'll never happen for me," or if they undervalue their time and talents. It undermines everything we're trying to do with self-promotion.

A positive outlook makes it easier to get out of bed and do what you have to do to promote yourself. It isn't easy to promote yourself with a good frame of mind; it's next to impossible when you have a negative outlook on life. Negative self-talk can kill good ideas. (You get a constipated brain. It won't work right if it's filled with garbage.) The mind shuts down or is busy having an inner dialogue about why the market sucks, you suck, the whole goddamn world sucks. Whoa. I got a little carried away. But if you're listening to this "Why even try, there's no way you will sell this, nobody is selling anything now, what's the use?" in your head, it is a waste of your brainpower. For one thing, catastrophizing (there's no way it's gonna happen for me) and overgeneralizing (nobody is selling anything) are usually inaccurate. Don't predict failure. Try first, complain later—if you have to, because even if by some miracle you make it in spite of your inner critic, your success won't be in congruence with your self-image, and it's possible you might sabotage your success later on.

A friend of mine told me about one of his college buddies ("Jim") who just couldn't make a go of it in the art world despite IMMENSE talent. So I called him up to find out why he was struggling and to see if there was anything I could do to help. Our conversation started something like this (I am changing his name—the last thing he needs is to read this and sink further into the depths of despair): "I saw several of your paintings, you are amazing, man" is how I began. "Oh, those poopy pieces. I did those years ago, before I really knew what I was doing" was his reply. I tried again: "So what are you working on now?" Answer: "I don't know, I can't sell shit. I'm just screwing around with different things. None of it is that good." All-righty, then. A little negative, aren't we? It's bad enough that others are so negative (and sometimes downright cruel). Janis Joplin was voted Ugliest *Man* on Campus by her University of (Austin) Texas classmates. Don't compound it by being negative yourself.

Self-image determines what a person can and can't do. The common thread among the creative people I know who have "made it" is a kind of optimism, a belief that things are going to work out. Rather than worry that they won't, they focus their mental energies on making it happen and are genuinely surprised if things don't. And even then they will say, "But I learned from the setback and now I am stronger/better/smarter. Next time I won't fail." They believe that they can do anything they set their creative minds to. I watch them as adversity makes them try just a little bit harder the next time. In many instances these are not the most talented people, just the most motivated. It is this motivation that others feed off of. People want to be around this kind of positive energy. Like bugs to a light, they attract people and the help they need. These promotable people are confident, and confidence sells!

☆————————

SELF-TEST
Which of the following traits would best describe you?
Competitive, confident, creative, determined, enthusiastic, energized, fun, optimistic, relentless, outgoing, upbeat, unsinkable. (You should be able to circle at least two. The more the better.)
————————————————————

☆————————

THE REAL PAUL BUNYAN
A short, skinny fellow walks into a lumber camp looking for a job. To impress the skeptical foreman, he chops down a towering tree in under a minute. "Where did you learn to do that?" the foreman asks. "In the Sahara Forest," replies the skinny man. "You mean the Sahara Desert," says the foreman. The little man looks him in the eye and says, "Sure, *now* it's a desert." That's self-assuredness! It is a dog-eat-dog world out there. Competition is fierce. What you need to survive is confidence combined with creativity and a competitive fire that refuses to go out.
————————————————————

Stinkin' Thinkin'
"Refuse to sit still for negative thinking."

—SARK

Why are we afraid to pick up the phone and ask for an interview, booking, or to make a sale? The fear that we will fail. We can't let our negative thoughts take control of our physical actions (or lack of actions). It will hold us back—and we can't afford to sit back and wait for things to happen. As a self-promoter, we must speak out and reach out for opportunities. Even if you don't fear failure, you may suffer from limiting (low) expectations. There are so many talented people who have had some success but hit a wall. No matter how hard they try they can't seem to get unstuck. If they keep spinning their wheels they could end up being like many major league baseball players who have a lot of potential but never seem to put it together to become a superstar. (It's not that they lack the physical skills to stand out, it's in their head.) I have seen where a baseball player, for some reason or another, can do extremely well in the minors but can't make it in the majors. They don't see themselves as major league material, and thus they aren't. They are comfortable where they are (in the minors) because there is less pressure, less risk (and far fewer rewards). But their beliefs become reality. Sometimes when it comes to promotion, the creative person will drop the ball at the last minute. So they stay where they are—comfortable, but not nearly as successful as they could be.

The other reason for stinkin' thinkin' is just the opposite—unrealistic expectations. I will read about all these monster advances that authors are getting and think, What's wrong with me? I must be a failure if I don't get that kind of "jack." It's hard to watch others around you succeed. You want what they have and you want it now. (You start to form some really evil thoughts about what you would like to do to the people who are the focus of your envy.) You have to remember that you are competing with yourself. Believe that your time will come. (At least that's what keeps me from doing physical harm to other authors with the big advances.) It also should fill you with hope that hey, if that numbskull can do it, so can I. Learn from them. Ask for their help. (I also take a small bit of comfort from the fact that I don't have to deal with all the pressure they are feeling.) And don't worry, there is plenty to go around. Think abundance, not scarcity. We have to stop feeling sorry for ourselves and start feeling sorry for anyone who stands in our way, because we are going to make it! Besides, like the bumper sticker says, "You shouldn't compare yourself to others—they are more screwed up than you think."

Artist Susan Davis was asked to work for free for six weeks to produce six versions of a presidential holiday card, and all six were rejected without even a comment from the White House. "I'm nobody, but people shouldn't treat anyone like this," says the artist. If you really want to promote yourself and your art, it shouldn't matter what others say or do to you. Confidence comes from within—but then, so does a lack of it. It is the lack of confidence that holds us back. We don't feel we're smart enough, talented enough, savvy enough. It's hard enough to stay confident and upbeat with a regular life, but the creative person is bombarded with assaults on our esteem. Criticism is a part of the art world that will be here forever. Rejection letters, failed auditions, brush-offs from gallery owners, unhappy and demanding clients, slow sales (even though it's your best work), poor reviews—I could go on, but I won't. That's the reality. But let's not dwell on it, because if you do, you'll lose all hope and never try to promote yourself again.

You would think that once you have achieved a certain degree of success the insecurity would pass. For example, if you don't *feel* like a success, it won't matter much what others (fans and friends) say. It won't sink in. Many of us who have been the beneficiaries of rave reviews will still focus on the *one* less-than-stellar review. Why is that? Because we think we can learn something from this disturbed person's point of view? Not likely. We haven't let success go to our head (which we should), and we feel undeserving of positive praise and seek out negative reviews to validate our negative inner feelings. Maybe I am getting a little too Freudian here, but doesn't this ring true with you, too?

I grew up with a family full of negative thinkers, just like their relatives before them. It somehow seems that my ancestry was always looking at half-empty glasses. They could snatch defeat from the jaws of victory. Take my mom as a perfect example. She can't fathom success. She would say things to me like, "Don't get your hopes up, you will just end up being disappointed," or "I hear they are hiring at Wal-Mart." On a recent vacation I pointed out to my mom that she expects the worst and that's usually what she gets. Why not expect the best and see what happens? I mean, if you expect the worst and get it, you just got a double whammy. You wasted all that time worrying and are still powerless to do anything about the outcome. Well, she made a negative remark, and my young nephew pointed his little finger at her and said, "Negative." It was a precious moment. Maybe we *will* be able to break the cycle after all.

You Gotta Believe

"All right, brain, I don't like you and you don't like me—so let's just do this and I'll get back to killing you with beer."

—Homer Simpson

You are what you believe you are, and your success in promoting yourself and how far you will go is determined by that belief—positive or negative. If you don't believe that you have a chance at being a guest on a major talk show, for instance, you won't even try to get on it. No try, no chance. Maybe you believe that you aren't able to work with computers. You are missing some *major* marketing opportunities. You might honestly believe that it is impossible to get your book published, what with the current state of the publishing world. That kind of thinking limits your potential. If you believe in yourself, your abilities, your potential, and your place in the publishing world and say "Why not?" rather than "Why me?" you are well on your way to success. Your beliefs are very powerful—good thoughts lead to good things manifesting themselves in your life. When you think about your future, what do you see?

In the writers' group I belong to, there is a writer who is having a hard time getting his next book published. If you talk to him for a while, you begin to realize that he can't conceive of a positive future for himself. His belief, in my opinion, is that he feels he was a one-hit wonder. As more and more time passes, he is losing faith (and becoming more depressed and disgruntled, and repelling the very people who may be able to help him). His mind-set is making it harder for him to move forward. On the other hand, less talented writers in the same situation see and expect positive outcomes. They see possibilities where my writer friend sees only pessimism. His beliefs have him frozen in place with no positive possibilities. If he could focus on the positive, he would have a better chance of selling his second book. I am not saying don't look at the reality of the situation. No doubt it isn't easy to get a book published today, but it *is* possible (maybe even probable).

Keep Your Head on Straight

"I feel my best when I am happy."

—Winona Ryder

When award-winning mystery writer Laura Lippman worked for the *Baltimore Sun,* her editor told her she wasn't a very good writer. So what did she do? She said, "I'll write a book and prove I can do it!" You gotta believe in yourself! This is your life, so if you don't do something about your situation, who will? "If it's to be, it's up to me" really rings true. You need to have the attitude that you will make it, no matter what. It may take longer than you thought it would and be harder than you hoped, but you will persevere. When everything goes to hell, and it sometimes does (through no fault of your own), you can't cry and say, "Why me?" You have to say, "Yes, why me?" and find a way to fix it (or forget about it). Let it be a wake-up call (or a call to action) and rally yourself. It isn't permanent and it almost never is personal. It's just part of the cycle (of ups and downs) that make up this madness we call a creative career. Push yourself harder. Admit you can do better. Then do get better. When people tell you, "No way," find a way. Say: "Whatever happens, I'm going to go down fighting." I say, get pissed, but don't start blaming people. Nobody is out to get you (I don't think), and it's nobody else's fault. When you take responsibility for your career and promoting yourself, you gain the upper hand. You have power. You aren't the victim, you are on your way to being a victor. Focus on what you can control and then go kick some ass!

I have this inner drive that keeps me going. I don't want a regular job and I don't want to be average. So I often stretch beyond what I am capable of and I get swatted away. At least I tried. It is better to risk some rejection by trying than to stay within your current comfort zone.

Maybe you really did screw up. "It" happens. You have to look at the big picture. I'm sure it was just a blip on the radar screen. You have to move on, move ahead. Keep your eyes on the road (and don't look in the rearview mirror for too long) or you may crash. Maybe you need to make some adjustments—that's moving forward. If you curl up in a fetal position and say, "I'm never going to try that again," you're looking back. Put the pedal to the metal and watch that bad experience fade from view. If you do glance back, look for lessons learned (or rewrite the past) so it doesn't stunt your growth or stop your progress. Maybe you need to work on a certain area. Do it. That can be a nice diversion from dwelling on it. Usually things aren't as bad as they seem once you get some distance between you and them. There must have been some silver lining; find it and focus on it. It's okay to fail now and again. That's how you know what WON'T work for you. (The secret is to fail small.) When you have a clear vision of where you're heading, those speed bumps along the way are minor bumps in the road. Focus on what type of projects you want to work on, how much money you'll make, whom you want to work with, what talk shows you'll appear on, the kind of fans you want cheering you on. That should keep you pointed (and moving) in the right direction. So get rid of the ball and chain you're dragging around and pick up the pace. Dare to be bold! You could be a big star, if you let yourself believe it.

MAD ABOUT YOU

What do the following creative people have in common?
Francis Ford Coppola, Drew Barrymore, Linda Hamilton, Patty Duke, Tennessee Williams, William Faulkner, Ernest Hemingway, Virginia Woolf, T. S. Eliot, Walt Whitman, Anne Sexton, Michelangelo, Vincent Van Gogh, Cole Porter, Kurt Cobain, Brian Wilson, Eric Clapton, Sheryl Crow, Axl Rose, Sarah McLachlan, and Sting.
Answer: All have struggled (at one time or another) with depression.

How to Be Positively Positive

"If you hear a voice within you saying 'You are not a painter,'
then by all means paint and that voice will be silenced."
—*Vincent Van Gogh*

When a chronic worrier finally found a way to overcome his problem, his best friend wanted to know how he made this miraculous change. He didn't seem to be concerned about anything anymore. He explained, "I hired a professional worrier for $1,000 a week and I haven't had a care in the world since." His friend exclaimed, "A thousand a week! How are you going to pay him?" The ex-worrier replied, "That's *his* problem." There are so many things that will kill your confidence, and you need confidence to be a successful self-promoter. Every creative person I know has felt at one time or another that they're "not worthy." Does everybody love Ray Romano? It would seem so. His show is certainly a hit. But it isn't enough. He told *Parade* magazine, "I'm never happy. I have to need something. I need to think the worst, not to become complacent. Are they getting tired of me? I need to worry. Other people have call-waiting. I have worry-waiting." We are almost always better than we give ourselves credit for, and we can do more than we think we can. ("You can *do* it. You can do *it*.") Here are some suggestions to keep you motivated and moving forward, despite all the negativity that swirls around you (and in you).

Good thoughts lead to action. Instead of thinking worst-case scenario (you're not going to end up homeless, come on), think about how it will feel if everything goes fine. Statistically, most things work out, so why waste time worrying? Expect the best and you usually get it.

Be small-minded. Wait until you are ready. Small successes can breed confidence and more success. What promotional activity can you do today where you would be assured some success?

Master your domain. Confidence comes from preparation, mastery, and knowledge. Do everything you can to put yourself in a position to succeed by mastering your craft. Practice, study, find out as much as you can about what is expected, talk to people who have already done what you want to do, get the tools you'll need. Knowledge is power but it's not enough to know what to do, act on it. Annette Bening said, "When I was going up for a part and I didn't know how to deal with it, I'd work on it. That's how I deal with my anxiety and fear. I have a lot of both every time I go to work."

Decide to do it. Make a contract with yourself that states what you will do. Then do whatever it takes. Make up your mind that no matter how frustrated, tired, or discouraged you get you won't quit. This sounds so simple, but it separates the serious from the somewhat committed. (Most people are wishy-washy and don't have the stomach or stamina to see things through.) Make a legal-looking contract with yourself and put in it all the things you're going to do, including a deadline, and sign it.

Do what you do best and forget the rest. Build on existing talents and you gain supreme confidence. Doing what you like to do, do well, and are passionate about breeds confidence, and you have a much better chance at success.

Pet projects. Find projects that turn you on.

Focus on the big picture. Keep your mind on the dream and away from the nightmare. Get in touch with the reasons behind why you want what you want. Get excited again. (It lasts longer than motivation.) It is proven that people are happier when they have a dream and are working toward it rather than letting life push them around.

Plan your work and work your plan. Stay the course. Get lost in the work and it will take your mind off your worries. Then celebrate your success. Set up benchmarks with rewards tied into self-promotion goals.

Don't take criticism personally. Step back and look at the situation objectively. Listen to comments for clues on how you can improve, or better yet, review yourself. If you weren't you, what kind of advice would you give, say, to a friend who was in the same situation? Say to yourself, "It's going to be all right, you'll be fine. Hang in there, champ."

Stumbling blocks are really stepping-stones. You will survive. Matt Lauer was unemployed in the early nineties after failing at five shows. To survive he worked as a tree trimmer before landing a job in front of the camera and eventually the coanchor spot on the "Today" show.

Self-esteem retreat. Take a day for recharging your confidence and come back energized. Do something that gets you back in touch with why you do what you do. Spend the day doing things you are good at. Ask friends, family, and fans to reaffirm why you are wonderful. Reread fan letters, look at your awards, review all of your past successes. Make a list of all of your accomplishments. While promoting her highly successful album *Jagged Little Pill,* Alanis Morissette should have been overjoyed, but she was not. She took some time off and traveled, reconnected with old friends, and even competed in triathlons before getting back to making music.

Hear no evil. Get rid of self-limiting excuses. "It's too hard to break in" or "I don't live in a major city," "I don't have the most modern equipment" or "I don't know anyone" or "I don't have a track record," "I'm too old," "I'm too young," "My agent is a drunk," or whatever. Look for solutions (use your creativity to find ways around a system that is stacked against you). All problems can be solved with innovative thinking. List the biggest problems you fear you may face and come up with one possible solution for each.

Action overcomes fear. Do something, anything. Find a first step and take it. As Coach Lou Holtz once told me, we all face fears. It is how you react to them that determines whether you win or lose. His strategy to W-I-N is this: What's Important Now. Clever, no? All you can control is your attitude—you must remain positive. What are you afraid of? Do that thing now. How will I earn a living? Let fear be the motivator. (Burn the bridges and put yourself in a position in which you HAVE to make it.)

Do a brain dump. Get rid of those irrational thoughts. Write your worries down. Get them out of your head and put them on paper. "I'll never make it." That's irrational. (Unless you quit, then it was a self-fulfilling prophecy.) Singer/songwriter Shawn Colvin spent a decade plying her craft in coffeehouses and bars across the country and didn't release her debut album (which went platinum, won a Grammy Award, and got rave reviews) until she was thirty-three years old. It's never too late.

The Kid Rocks. I'm big on belief. The most important lesson you can learn from success is that you can do it. That you deserve it. Bob Ritchie (better known as Kid Rock) is known for his rap-metal fusion music (a blend of Run-DMC and the Marshall Tucker Band). Kid Rock is also known for his healthy dose of self-esteem (read: full of himself). He had been making commercially unsuccessful albums for years before he made it. "I polished my skills to the point where people had to come around."

Naysayers don't know "nada." Don't listen to the naysayers. Everyone said Nintendo of North America president Minoru Arakawa was crazy. He wanted to import a strange Japanese video game featuring 150 tiny collectible monsters. Research showed that American kids hated it and the game was too confusing. Well, Pikachu and the other Pokémon cards, movies, and games have made Nintendo millions.

It's personal. Get your personal life in order. Focus your energy on your art and promotion and not on your shitty codependent relationship. Any distraction is detrimental to both your motivation and your creativity. Work without worry gives you an edge. Get your spouse involved. Make them an ally, not an enemy.

Loooooosers. Hang out with people who push you rather than pull you down. Surround yourself with supportive people. Look at the people you hang out with. Be brutally honest. Ask yourself if they support and encourage you or suck the energy right out of you. When family and friends want to tell you all the reasons why you can't make it, politely tell them to shut up. You *are* going to make it, with or without them. You'd prefer to do it with them, but if they keep raining on your parade, you will have to dump them. Mastermind and brainstorm with others who can help you with leads, barter services, and offer emotional support. Be with people who keep you focused and charged. If you can't find any supportive friends, you can buy them. Hire a personal coach or listen to a motivational speaker on tape in your car.

Share the fame. "We always felt we would tough it out no matter what. In terms of perseverance we're both really driven. Being a team really helped, because when one was down, the other somehow managed to be up." Matt Damon on himself and Ben Affleck.

A&E "Biography." Read success stories. I am always inspired when I find out that the people I admire (and am envious of) have struggled and had to overcome obstacles before making it big. For example, the *Pioneer Press* in St. Paul, Minnesota, refused to pay a young cartoonist ten dollars a week for his cartoon strip called "Peanuts." Charles Schulz wasn't the only one turned down early on.

The *Kansas City Star* refused to hire a young artist named Walt Disney. The *Lexington Herald-Leader* in Kentucky rejected a young cartoonist, Bill Watterson, when he applied for an editorial cartooning job. He went on to create "Calvin & Hobbs."

Spread some cheer. Helping others with their problems makes yours seem silly. "I'm a shameless dispenser of enthusiasm," said conductor Benjamin Zander. Go to a hospital and volunteer to spread cheer. The creators of *Poor* magazine are putting out a glossy magazine with next to no money and with a staff of homeless people. Actually, that's part of the plan, to empower creative people to think for themselves and be creative and then teach the next ones in line. With the help of artists, designers, and technicians, the people at *Poor* magazine are sidestepping the poverty in their own lives.

Simplify. What do I need to do today? When you get upset, your brain secretes chemicals that increase your heart rate, cause depression, and make you angry. You can counteract this with activities that involve repetition that will cause a relaxation response. The bottom line is, you can't create in an agitated state.

Feng shui is okay. Seeing is believing. Make a wall of fame. Put your past successes where you can see them. Put the books you wrote on the wall, awards on your desk, articles framed and hanging where you can see them. Post your client list. Put up your promotional goals. Enlarge and hang up a fan letter. Keep a journal or scrapbook of your success and leave it out where you can easily pick it up and read through it. Enhance the environment where you create and conduct business. Make it a positive place. Put up posters and positive signs. Make a mock-up of what you want. Make a collage of your goals, accomplishments, or the things that bring you joy. Add some art or color. Maybe your screen saver could be a collage of your creations, goals, words of wisdom.

Start the day off on the right foot. Use a coffee mug with an inspiring message or have one made with your art on it. Read something that inspires you. Review your plans or progress. Find something funny. Keep it going, too. Carry your goals, fan letters, plans, accomplishments, and photos in your planner. Make it a habit to start each month with a review of your successes, your goals, and your marketing plan. Define what would make this month a success. Then work on it. Start a file filled with every resource that can help you achieve your goal.

Keep the faith. "Fear can keep us up all night long, but faith makes one fine pillow." Philip Gulley. Sweet dreams!

ACTION ITEM

Write the kind of review you have always wanted. Paste your product at the top of a best-seller list. (I pasted the name of this book at the top of the *New York Times* best-seller list.)

Parting Thought

"I've had a sense of no limits."

—Carly Fiorina

In the movie *Shawshank Redemption,* one of the movie's central characters, Red (played by Morgan Freeman), becomes "institutionalized" after spending most of his adult life in prison. But his best friend and fellow inmate, Andy (played by Tim Robbins), hasn't lost hope. When Red says, "In here, hope is a dangerous thing," Andy replies with, "Hope is the only thing they can't take away." So he decides to "get busy living rather than get busy dying." Andy escapes (in more ways than one) and leads his dream life on a beach in Mexico. Hope is not a dangerous thing. I probably should write that we need to be careful about getting our hopes up too high—but I can't. I honestly believe that *anything* is possible if you want it badly enough, work at it long enough, and believe it is possible. I am attracted to stories (I think by now you have figured out I am a biography junkie) that show creative people making it against all odds. I'll present just a few examples. There are many more where these came from.

Alfred Butts was an unemployed architect during the Depression when he invented the popular board game Scrabble. Danny DeVito is barely five feet tall, walks with a waddle, is bald and a bit pudgy. He's the most unlikely of movie stars, yet he has made it as a star, director, and producer. What are the odds of that? It's a good thing he didn't listen when people said his height would be an impediment in show business. Newport Beach artist Robb Havassy first picked up a paintbrush when he received a beginner's art kit on his twenty-sixth birthday. Four years later his paintings are selling out and he is heading to New York for his gallery debut. Carly Fiorina's mother taught her the power of positive attitude. Working for AT&T, she became the first-ever female director of AT&T spin-off Lucent Technologies. She was then named chief executive of Hewlett-Packard, one of the nation's top computer companies. Her advice is: "Don't think of yourself as a woman in business. I've never thought in terms of 'men do this' and 'women do that.'" When Sue Miller picked up the paper and read a book review of author Robert Coover's first novel, she thought back to when he was a boarder in her parents' basement a few years earlier. "It suddenly occurred to me that publishing a book was not such a remote thing. It was something to which I could actually aspire." Miller worked as a waitress but had also taught high school English and had a master's degree in creative writing. Her first novel, *The Good Mother,* became a best-seller, and her second book, *Inventing the Abbotts,* was made into a movie. Frank McCourt is another high school English teacher who became a best-selling author and a Pulitzer Prize winner for his book *Angela's Ashes.* Camryn Manheim stood on the stage clutching her Emmy for Best Supporting Actress for her work on "The Practice" and exclaimed, "This is for all the fat girls!" For years people told her that she was never going to be able to achieve her dream—that she didn't have what it takes to make it as an actress. She admits, "You never see parts for large, powerful, sexy women. No one ever thinks of someone like me when they're writing a character." So she is developing scripts and buying the rights to books that she wants to star in. Her own book, *Wake Up, I'm Fat,* was wildly successful. Matt Groening, the creator of the Simpsons, admits that his friends could draw better than he. His teachers ripped his cartoons and talent, telling him he was wasting his time. But he continued to doodle, and it paid off. He first achieved fame with his strip "Life in Hell," which appeared in alternative newspapers and now, thanks to "The Simpsons," he presides over a billion-dollar empire. D'oh!

Ask a Pro

Jason Blume
Songwriter (www.jasonblume.com)

Jason, you are one of the rare songwriters to have songs on the Pop, R&B, and Country charts at the same time, and your songs have been included on albums with sales exceeding thirty million copies. You have made it! How did it begin?

I was so poor during my early days in Los Angeles that I actually ate cat food. I lived in one room (with mice and roaches) and shared a bathroom with the junkies and prostitutes who lived down the hall. I worked more horrible temp jobs than I can count. One of the all-time worst had me shredding paper eight hours per day. But one day the temp agency sent me out on a three-day assignment at a management and public relations firm. The walls were lined with gold records, and I could hardly believe I was going to be paid to make those kinds of connections. I stayed more than a year at that job. I learned how to compose press releases, how to find out whom to send them to, how to write effective cover letters, and much more. That education turned out to be more valuable than I could have imagined.

What lessons did you learn along the way?

I learned how easy it is to contact the media, whether it's to list an upcoming event, request a review of my book or CD, or offer an interview. To a large extent, it's a numbers game. If I send a press release to a dozen media contacts, maybe two or three will run an article. I've had the best success rate in my hometown [Philadelphia]. Your endeavors will likely be of added interest to those in your hometown—especially if you're on the road to becoming a local celebrity.

Did you find it beneficial to have started at the bottom?

Another temp assignment landed me at RCA Records, where I eventually became a permanent employee and worked my way into the position of screening artists for the label and reviewing songs for some of the biggest recording artists in the world. As incredible as that job seemed to others, I was frustrated because what I wanted was to be a successful songwriter. The education I received and the contacts I made were priceless. That position opened the doors to many publishers and songwriters I might otherwise not have found access to. It may sound as though finding these temp jobs was amazing luck. But these opportunities didn't happen by pure chance. First of all, I had to put myself in a major music center. These jobs, and the connections they led to, weren't available in my hometown.

How important was self-promotion in your success?

Self-promotion is critical in every area of my career. While my songs are foremost on my mind, my publisher has tens of thousands of other writers' songs in their catalog. This means that if I want my songs to receive the attention I think they deserve, it's my responsibility to make sure that happens. I accomplish this several different ways.

Like having to hustle and do things for yourself?

Exactly. My publisher does a very good job, but rather than rely solely on my publisher to promote my songs, I schedule meetings and cultivate relationships with the individuals who screen songs at the record labels. I also employ an independent song plugger to augment my publisher's efforts. It was actually an independent plugger who secured the John Berry recording of my song "Change My Mind," which became a top ten country single. While it cost me thousands of dollars in fees and bonuses paid to the song plugger who secured that recording, it was just a fraction of what I earned. It's unlikely that I would have ever had the other opportunities that led to a successful career without that first big recording.

How well do you handle rejection?

I think my mode of dealing with rejection and disappointment played a huge role in my eventual success. I was bound and determined to become successful. I knew it was simply a matter of time until my dreams came true. No one could convince me there would be any other outcome. Persistence is crucial. Without it, you may give up before having a chance to develop your skills, contacts, and understanding of the inner workings of the industry you are targeting. It took me more than sixteen years to accomplish what I initially believed would take a year or two.

5

WALK TALL AND CARRY A BIG SHTICK
(Make Yourself More Memorable)

Shtick: A Yiddish term used to describe a performer's attention-stealing action or gimmick.

"Blahs don't have more fun."
—Unknown

What do Erkle, Drew Carey, and Orville Redenbacher all have in common? Besides being kind of nerdy and wearing horn-rimmed glasses, they are all memorable. They came up with a look, a persona, or a "hook" that helped them stand out and contributed to their marketability. It pays to find a way to make yourself memorable. My agent told me just the other day that publishers are looking for "names" and authors (with writing skills, of course) who are are able to market themselves and build a following. Hmm. So as a creative person it makes sense to build yourself into a brand name that stands out from the competition. "If you're not doing something different, why should anyone buy from you? There are many companies in the field. Many are larger with more resources, and you have to compete with them. You have to find a way to stand out and gain your identity," says J. Peterman. (Yes, *that* J. Peterman.) To stand out and make yourself more marketable includes how you look and act, the car you drive, your name, and much more. "In our industry, you can't be normal. You have to be something odd, or they start making things up," says Debbie Reynolds.

Chonda Pierce is having fun with her faith. (I guess you could call her the "Church Lady.") Chonda, a preacher's daughter, is an evangelical comic who frequently uses f-words like "faith" and has been saved 342 times (just in case). Then there is Reverend Lawrie Adam. This guy is no dummy, but he started using one (named Jake) during sermons to save his struggling parish and fill some empty pews. The first time he spoke through his ventriloquist's dummy, he had 'em rolling in the aisles. The congregation has grown and Reverend Adam is a celebrity in Britain. One man also used marketing for greater good when he wrote a religious message in stones on a mountain in Mexico that was visible from many spots in El Paso, Texas, a border city of 700,000 people. Kinda like a preacher is Tony Robbins, who rose to prominence as a motivational speaker best known for teaching people how to walk across hot coals. This led to infomercials and best-selling books. Dennis Rodman (who is nothing like a preacher) may be a freak, but people talk about him, write about him, and the result is a lot of publicity. Controversy can seem like a crazy thing to mire yourself in—yeah, crazy like a fox.

Take artist Karen Walker, for example. When she first showed her disturbing images of plantation scenes that included rape and lynchings, it shocked the art world. It also launched her career. She began showing her art in and around the Atlanta area, but before long she was exposing her startling images to viewers from coast to coast and into the homes of prominent African-American art collectors' homes at anywhere from $30,000 to $80,000 per piece. "Innovators are inevitably controversial," points out actress and director Eve LeGallienne. The kind of marketing I am referring to is for the open-minded, unconventional, and rebellious creative person. Someone with the balls to go for the unorthodox, and possibly unpopular, promotion. This is for the person who is willing and able to use craftiness and creativity rather than spend money on tried and tired forms of self-promotion. The payoff is a promotional bonanza—if you have the guts to go for it. And the best part is that you use your noggin and not your wallet.

When you hand someone your business card or say your company name, do they say "cool" or just smile and nod? You want them to comment on your card. "Hey, cool card," or "Wow, this is different." Funky is good. Decidedly different is even better. We live in a homogenized world. That's why Apple Computer's slogan, "Think different," and their whole approach to computer design and operating systems makes me smile. When I travel the country giving talks, I have a hard time remembering where I am because every town has the same chain restaurants and stores. It's so sad. But the bright side is that if you put a little thought and effort into being a little off center, you can stand out. Las Vegas gets it! It started with the Mirage. It put an end to tacky. Here was a tropical jungle in the middle of the desert complete with tigers, dolphins, and sharks plus an erupting volcano. It was so cool everyone went home and talked about it and told their friends.

To attract attention to yourself and show off your originality, creativity, resourcefulness, and inventiveness, you can get away with being wild, wacky, original, unusual, and crazy. Tom Wolfe took a very unconventional approach to journalism (at the time) by using a stream-of-consciousness style of writing. His goal was to be anything but boring. He also began dressing in outrageously dapper outfits, sporting custom-made, light-colored suits. He was recognizable (and successful) because of his work and his wardrobe. While I was watching the news today they were talking to a traffic cop in New York City who did a little dance as he directed traffic. The story made it on the wire and all the way to the left coast. That's the power of doing something different. People notice. When Mark Dion was commissioned to create a work for an exhibit at the Museum of Contemporary Art (in La Jolla, California), he went to the municipal dump for materials. Why? The recurring theme of his art is nature and our relationship to it. The completed piece, *Landfill,* was very well received and garnered him a lot of positive press.

You can stand out for your creative uniqueness. Before I was a drummer I played bass, and I was intrigued by the signature sounds of each of my favorite four string heroes. Chris Squire (of Yes) had that crisp Rickenbacker sound, Jaco Pastorious had his melodic fretless thing, and Stanley Clarke created slapping and popping sounds on his alembic bass. Each was known for his own unique sound. Joni Mitchell stopped playing in standard tunings to get chords that didn't sound like anything anybody else was playing. Andrew Cyrille is a drummer's drummer with an "offbeat" approach. Early in his career he suggested that maybe he would play the ride symbol differently. He was told that if he did, it was unlikely he would work again. Of course he found work, but for the past ten years he has performed solo, expanding the realm of creative sounds you can get from the drums. Being unique is a form of self-promotion.

Robert Stephens combined wacky corporate image and exceptional customer service to make his computer consulting company, Geek Squad, super successful. His consultants (called "special agents") dress like Joe Friday of "Dragnet"—black suits and skinny ties—and drive to appointments in old ice cream trucks and vintage cars that are emblazoned with the company's logo. It's hard to forget a company like this, and the media *love* him. (He signed a book deal with Simon & Schuster, too.) When you have the cojones to become an original, it can pay off, BIG-TIME. When Wet Seal (a clothing store) opened a new store, they held a kiss-a-thon. (Sealed with a kiss—clever, huh?) This attracted the media, a younger audience, and launched the then-unknown retailer. I have also found that when pitching designs, you can use humorous touches in the proposal, rough compositions, and presentation. The uniqueness makes an impression. I usually have to scale it back for the final design, but the goal is to get hired, which requires standing out from the competition.

Stick Your Neck Out

"People get used to a diet of beige, and they can't handle it when something shocking pink comes along."

—Rose McGowan

The goal isn't necessarily to be different for the sake of being different. The goal is to make money, and standing out from the crowd is a good way to do it. How? Push the envelope by doing the unexpected, by being bold, daring, unconventional, controversial, and unique. Fashion designer Helmut Lang burst onto the scene by being a pioneer of mixing matte and shiny materials and fabrics. In fact, his most well-known coup is his rubber dress covered in lace, which made the fashion world stand up and take notice after he released it in a Paris show. The press that this piece generated helped him win several awards and won the highest form of flattery—imitation.

Be a pioneer. Cartoonist R. Crumb, producer Phil Spector, and David Filo of Yahoo were all pioneers in their respected mediums. That also meant they were influential, successful, and people sought them out. Break the rules! Unlearn what you know. Go against what you were taught in school. You'll hear naysayers telling you that it never worked before. That may be, but YOU haven't tried it yet, so let's see. Martin Scorsese said: "Not only have I broken all the rules I learned about—I have broken rules I didn't even know existed." Bravo! In the 1960s, soul singer and songwriter Curtis Mayfield went against the flow by singing about black pride and urban landscapes while his contemporaries stuck to love songs and dance tunes. His vision paved the way for funk and rap artists for decades to come.

Sometimes being clueless can be a benefit. Out of curiosity or ignorance you give it a shot. "Well, I'll be damned, you mean you're not s'pose to do that?" Some people are bogged down by too many rules. That's the reason this book is big on ideas, some of them pretty unorthodox, and very light on the "You must do this or that" stuff, because it's up to you to break new ground by breaking the rules when it comes to self-promotion. You do that by being a pioneer with unconventional thinking. Don't let laziness, lack of time, assumptions, rules, conventional wisdom, or the status quo hold you back from being different and trying something new. Experiment. As Henry James once said, "Chaos often breeds life, when order breeds habit."

I am sure that record executives were worried when Melissa Etheridge announced she was a lesbian in 1992. Melissa Etheridge combined her incredible talent and commitment to a cause, which made her more popular than ever. Don't worry what others will think, or that you may make a mistake or two. You have to get past the "But I'll look foolish" and say, "I know I'll have the last laugh." You can't be innovative without making some mistakes. It's part of the process. Sculptor Livio De Marchi noticed how congested the waterways of Venice were becoming with gondolas, ferries, motorboats, and water taxis and decided to do something different. Since the Grand Canal looked like a traffic jam on a freeway, he decided to travel it on a floating bug—a VW-style vessel he carved out of wood and propelled by a ten-horsepower motor (housed in the trunk like the real thing). His mode of transportation has made him a minor celebrity and brought attention to his art—which sells for upward of $10,000.

During one presentation, a meeting planner suggested we—the staff and I, as the speaker—use a seventies theme (because the company and their thinking was stuck in a time warp). So for the meeting we used seventies music, slides, decorations, and attire. (I looked like a pimp on acid.) During the planning stages of this meeting someone said, "This is stupid. It will never work. They won't get it." Well, it was a HUGE hit. The message got through and everyone had FUN. They still talk about it years later. It's risky to try new and bold ideas, but the reward can be big. One guy I know dressed up like Elvis to make a sale. The buyer was a BIG Elvis fan. So he showed up and sang his pitch to an Elvis song. Speaking of Elvis, his television debut was NOT on the "Ed Sullivan Show," as many believe. On January 28, 1956, Elvis blew people away on Tommy Dorsey's "Stage Show" by being bold. He confidently swaggered onstage, despite his startling appearance (eyeliner, long sideburns, thick black hair in a pompadour). That was nothing compared to what happened next. His shoulders twitched and his pelvis gyrated, prompting critics to say he reminded them of a female stripper. Is this not a good example of being out there, outrageous, and original?

Hookers

"There is always room for uniqueness."

—*Tori Amos*

When you have a unique product or service (or odd title), it is easier to stand out. It makes marketing easier. The book *Everything Men Know About Women* sold over 500,000 copies on the strength of the title alone. How do I know that? The book is blank inside! People will perk up and remember you when you are an original. It pays to be a little outrageous or outside the norm. "Success is the child of audacity," said Benjamin Disraeli. When Ginny Rivenberg, who designs custom window products, attends a networking meeting, she carries her remote-controlled miniblinds to stand out more. Candy Caramelo is big, so big she calls herself the "world's biggest showgirl" and jokes with the audience that she can "eat anything that doesn't eat me first."

To stand out I think you have to look at what you do best (and the benefits of those talents and skills) and then look at what your competitors are doing. Is there something you do that they don't? Is there one thing you can honestly say you do differently or better? One self-published author who was unable to get bookstores to carry his titles decided to do something different. The two things he had going for him that his competitors didn't were time and inventory (nobody carried his book but him). So he started selling his books on a busy street corner. A newspaper reporter passing by thought this would make a great story. He wrote a two-page feature story about the upstart author, which led to bookstores stocking his books and eventually to an agent and book deal with a large publisher.

Develop a signature style. Something that is so YOU that nobody can duplicate it. It's your uniqueness. It could be the combination of colors you use in your paintings. Van Gogh created his own color schemes. Your ability to hit the high notes. A style of writing that stands out. (I hope it doesn't annoy you, but my "style" of writing includes the use of a lot of parentheses. I think of it like an actor talking directly into the camera. It's more intimate between me and you. Now, back to the book.) Pete Townshend developed the windmill arm movement when playing. Eddie Van Halen's solos and technique were state-of-the-art. Dave Davies of the Kinks wanted a fuller, more distorted sound for the song "You Really Got Me," so he slashed the speaker in his amp. Voilà, a unique sound was born. With all the octave-shattering singers around today, it's kinda nice to hear someone like Macy Gray. Everything about this hip-hop/old-school soul singer is unconventional. Her delivery and phrasing make her an anomaly amidst today's female-formula music.

How about developing a trademark look? It can be your hair or no hair (Billy Corgin of Smashing Pumpkins), clothes (both Steve Martin and Tom Wolfe wore signature white suits), hats (singer Lou Bega's Italian Borsalinos or Erykah Badu's head wraps), bow ties (Orville Redenbacher), glasses (Elton John and Drew Carey), jewelry (Mr. T, Liberace), props (Alice Cooper's use of snakes), color (Prince and the color purple), a body part (Kiss bassist Gene Simmons's enormous tongue), facial hair (ZZ Top), makeup (Marilyn Manson), voice (Barry White), or make the most of your, um, breasts (Dolly Parton, all 40-20-36 of her. Yowwwwwzzzzzzzaaahhhh!).

I clearly remember when Jack Palance did a one-handed push-up at the Oscars. It was so, well, him. It made him stand out.

I thought it was interesting that Mel Blanc, the voice of Bugs Bunny and many other characters, has a tombstone that reads, "That's All Folks." A hook could be a unique phrase you use in your marketing. Rachel Ashwell may not have as much money as Martha Stewart, but her success isn't shabby, either. Actually, it is shabby. It's called Shabby Chic, and since 1989 she has built her mini-empire to include three books, home furnishing stores, signature fabrics, and an E!-style network television show. Maybe the hook is that you are a big fish in a small pond. Lance Lyons is a woodcarving whiz who has won awards. (He placed second in the world in fish carving.) He also used his artistry in the field of taxidermy (his father was a master taxidermist) to come in second in the World Taxidermy and Fish Carving Championship. (Who knew there was even such a competition?) His carvings sell for thousands of dollars, and he amazes customers when he re-creates a fish's colors to make it look as alive as the day it was pulled from the water. Not having to compete directly with other artists is a nice niche.

In music, having an "act" can be the thing that makes or breaks you. Screamin' Jay Hawkins was performing when a drunk audience member yelled out, "Scream, Jay, scream." Hawkins decided right then, "If I'm gonna make it in this business I'm gonna be a screamer, and I've been destroying songs ever since." His major hit song was "I Put a Spell On You," and his trademark look included a bone in his nose, a skull on a stick, a zebraskin station wagon followed by a hearse, and opening his shows by climbing out of a coffin (until the Drifters, the act that went on before him, locked him inside as a joke). Alice Cooper, in real life the nicest guy you could ever meet and a family man, blackened his eyes and wore a tattered dress on stage and swung around a dead rubber chicken. Jerry Lee Lewis was famous for his over-the-top energy on stage, which included setting his piano on fire. We could write a whole chapter about David Bowie's stage antics.

Some of these "trademark acts" aren't planned. The first time

Chuck Berry was to play in New York City, he wanted to look sharp, so he sent his best suit to the dry cleaners for a rush job. Well, the dry cleaner overcooked the garment and it shrunk—a lot. Berry had to choose between wearing his street clothes or a small suit on stage. He chose the shrunken suit, which was so small he had to hunch over and do a duckwalk on stage to keep the trousers from splitting. This started his signature style of playing in a crouched position and bobbing his head like a chicken.

QUICK QUIZ

Can you name the fitness guru with the perm, tight little shorts, and a tank top? Give up? Richard Simmons. That guy's got a shtick going on.

What's in a Name

"You were born an original. Don't die a copy."

—*John Mason*

One thing has become very clear. If you want to be a successful dotcom, you need a clever name. (That's why squatters are sitting on some of the best domain names and selling them for insane sums.) A good name is gold. There was even a Dallas man who legally changed his name to DotComGuy. More on him later. The same is true for the freelancer or the entertainer or the entrepreneur. There is something to be said for having a powerful and memorable or innovative and fun name. It's a big part of the first impression people have of you and your company. (On the Web it may be the ONLY impression they get.) This is also true for freelancers. You need to think like a business, and that means having a nice name. You want a name that rolls off the tongue, grabs their attention, and is easy to remember. Your name should be an eye-opener and not an eye-roller. It's okay to be a little outrageous. Yes, you want to appear powerful and professional, but *not* boring, puleeze. So don't rush this. It's not easy, but sooooo important. Take the time to do it right, because you will put your name on everything! Robert McMath, who runs the New Product Showcase and Learning Center in Ithaca, New York, believes we can learn a lot from losers. So he has some of the all-time most unsuccessful products ever launched. One of the biggest pitfalls for a product is a poor name. It almost guarantees failure. Brainstorm as many possible names as you can. Narrow it down by writing it out, asking others what they think, and then let it sit for a day or two. Do some research to see if your name is taken. Once you settle on a name, protect it by registering it. Mick Jagger registered his name as a trademark for more than twenty items, including, ha, lip balm. Let's look at what makes for a great name (other than the one you were born with, of course). Ask yourself the following questions regarding a new name for your business, band, project, or piece of art you have created.

Is it easy to spell? (and easy to type?) Do I even need to get into bizarre name changes by an artist who was formerly Prince and is now Prince again? What the hell was that symbol thing all about anyway?

Is it easy to say? In the movie *That Thing You Do,* the band that the movie features was using the name "The Oneders," which was butchered by everyone who said it. When Tom Hanks's character took over managing the band, the first thing he did was change the name to "The Wonderers." Much better. You want a name that rolls off your tongue.

Is it distinctive? You want your customers to say, "Hey, that's a cool name." For an Italian restaurant how about, "Great Impasta"? Or not.

Is it associated with what you do? A pest control company's name is "All Bugged Out." Best if you give at least a hint at what you do.

Does it create a visual picture? If you were in Key West and wanted a nice, quiet dinner for two and you had to choose between Blue Heaven or Sloppy Joe's, which one do you think would get your business?

Is it positive? Gillette didn't call their disposable razors the "Bad News" for good reason. "Good News" is so much more positive. A friend of mine invented a portable hot water shower to use after surfing. He came up with the title "Golden Shower." A few of us had to educate him on the negative meaning of that name.

Does it limit your ability to expand into other areas? Westin Hotels was once called Western International Hotels (an oxymoron if you ask me; you can't be western and international at the same time). AC/DC used its ambiguous name to their favor. Since it is slang for being bisexual, they were hired for gay-themed gigs early in their career. There is a band in San Diego called Dead @ 27, and most of the members are in their mid-twenties. Not good.

Is it powerful? Häagen-Dazs ice cream sounds expensive—and it is. It also sounds imported—it is not. The company was started in

New Jersey by a guy from Brooklyn. The name sounds superior, and so they can charge more.

Is it decidedly different? The band Steely Dan took their name from a William Burroughs book called *Naked Lunch*. Nobody in the band is named Steely or Dan, but Walter Becker and Donald Fagen, the founders, liked the fact that the band's name stood for a steam-powered dildo. I'm not making this up! You also don't want to be confused with the competition. In San Diego we have Mexican restaurants called Roberto's, Royberto's, Alberto's, Umberto's. and about a dozen other 'berto's. So for something different, how about this name for a Mexican restaurant: "Juan in a Million"?

Does it send a message or create a warm fuzzy feeling? For a hair salon "Curl Up and Dye" maybe doesn't give you that warm fuzzy feeling, but it *is* clever.

Does it clearly state your niche? How about this one for Porta-potties: "Johnny on the Spot."

Does it say a little about what you do? "Rhythm and Brews" is a coffeehouse and music venue. How about an exercise and tanning salon in Montana called "Sharon's Shake-N-Bake"?

Make it an A-plus. If you get most of your business from the yellow pages, it may behoove you to start with an A in the name.

The shorter, the better. The most common names of male movie characters are Jack, John, Frank, Harry, and David. Notice how all these names are four and five letters—short. John Anderson, one of the founding members of the band Yes, said, "We wanted a name that was very quick and precise. We wanted a strong conviction in what we were doing. We had to have a strong and straight title for the band." Yes!

Play with words. "Shear Madness" for a hair salon or "Got It Maid" for a maid service or "LeBeastro" for an upscale pet-groomer.

Acronyms can work, as long as they are interesting. (RAD, Robert Alexander Design, or LSD "Lee Silber Design.") The group TLC seems to be doing well. Did you know that if you rearrange the letters of Axl Rose's name it spells oral sex?

Use your name in your business and you can become a celebrity. Every time your business is mentioned, so is your name. The band Crosby, Stills, Nash and Young decided to use their own names so they could continue to build their solo careers. (With a band that breaks up as much as CSN&Y, that was smart thinking.) The problem is, it is difficult to sell a business with a person's name in it. Just ask Wally "Famous" Amos, the cookie king who had to relinquish the rights to his name when he sold his cookie company.

FAST FACT

The most common name for baby boys is Michael, and for baby girls it is Brittany.

You Can Win the Title

"I think the dilemma of being a thirteen-year-old girl is best summed up by a book I've heard about, titled something like I Hate You and I Wish You Would Die, but First Can You Drive Me and Cheryl to the Mall?

—*Tony Kornheiser, author of* Bald As I Wanna Be

The Grateful Dead wanted to call their 1972 live album *Skullfuck*, but Warner Bros. feared no large retail chain would stock the title. So the band relented and the title was changed to *Live Dead*. Come up with a clever title for your product or project and people will want to talk about it. It could be controversial. Metallica changed the title of their first major album from *Metal Up Your Ass* to *Kill 'Em All*. I bet both would get people to take notice. Come up with a cool title for what you do. Gardeners would be better served to say they are plant lovers. A carpenter could use the title "creative woodworking" and ask the question: Got wood?

HOW 'BOUT A NICKNAME?

In addition to gangsters, musicians have used nicknames to make themselves more memorable—Little Richard, Fats Domino, Muddy Waters, Chubby Checker, and The Big Bopper. In 1927, William Basie wanted to make his name known among musicians, so he borrowed a concept from jazzmen like King Oliver and Duke Ellington and coined himself "The Count." He immediately had business cards made with the name Count Basie.

JUST FOR FUN

Many entertainers change their name to make themselves more marketable and memorable. Match the performer's stage name to their real name.

1.	Joan Rivers	a)	Jerome Levitch
2.	Woody Allen	b)	Jerome Silberman
3.	Jerry Lewis	c)	Nathan Birnbaum
4.	Gene Wilder	d)	Judith Tuvid
5.	George Burns	e)	Melvin Kaminsky
6.	Judy Holiday	f)	Eleanora Fagan
7.	Mel Brooks	g)	Betty Jane Perske
8.	Billie Holiday	h)	Leonard Schneider
9.	Lauren Bacall	i)	Joan Molinsky
10.	Lenny Bruce	j)	Stewart Konigsberg

Answers: 1-i, 2-j, 3-a, 4-b, 5-c, 6-d, 7-e, 8-f, 9-g, 10-h

Tag, You're It

"I juxtapose anticipated with anomalous imagery to create visual analogies. Discrepancy and contrast in scale are emphasized as I investigate perception and memory."

—A photographer's artist statement

After reading the above artist's statement, the only thing I could think of saying was, "What the hell are you talking about?" Granted, you want to tell patrons what you stand for and what you are trying to convey with your work, as well as the themes and issues in your art. But there has to be a better way. Here is an example of an artist statement that works well: "My art is dedicated to saving the Florida Everglades." Get to the heart of why you are an artist and convey it quickly to others. What do you want people to understand or feel about your art? All I ever hear from people is how competitive it is today. That's the reason (and the fact that everyone is busy and overloaded with information) you need a statement that makes you stand out and explains what you do in two or three sentences, or thirty seconds or less. An artist statement or tag line helps other people promote and sell you. It helps the media write about you. It leads to self-awareness and helps you talk about what you do, too. When a talk show producer picks up the phone, the first thing she wants to know is: "What do you do and what can you do for me and my listeners/viewers?" That's where a concise statement comes in. It talks about the benefits, characteristics, methods, skills, personality, passions, promises—what you are about. Coming up with a clear, concise (and clever) artist statement or tag line that summarizes what you do gives you a huge advantage over other creative people who don't have one. It quickly states your reason for being in business. It helps others "get it," and it also can help you come up with a clearer understanding of what you offer, and why you do it the way you do, and how you will reach your goal. It focuses your thinking and your promotional efforts. It guides and governs your decisions about how to promote yourself. This short phrase serves as an anchor that helps people remember what you do. Even if they remember your name, that doesn't tell them what you do. A tag line does just that—and more.

The problem is, as creative people we do so many different things. The goal isn't to tell them everything that you do, but rather to tell them what they need to know (and not lose them or waste their time with the trivial stuff). Have you ever asked someone what they do and had to listen to a twenty-minute convoluted explanation that left you more confused than before they began? Nobody has time to hear your whole résumé. What the hell do you do and why the hell should I care? What's your point? Make it clear first and then design around that. Find the right words that best describe what you do. Turn them into a sentence. Use it on all printed material, the Web, and as an oral brochure. Memorize it so that when asked, "Give me one really good reason why I should use you?" you are armed and ready to reply. For instance, on my radio show I am approached by all kinds of people who want to be guests. But the show's title, "Creative Lee Speaking," and tag line, "Helping creative people deal with the business side of creativity," allows me to clearly understand the direction of the show and who should be on it. I also found in the past when people asked, "So, what do you do?" I would reply, "I'm a writer." Then came their next logical question, "Oh, so what do you write about?" And then I would explain about my books. My friends call me "the Rambler" for good reason. I tend to ramble on. I could see their eyes glass over as I explained what my books were about. Then I came up with the line "I write business books for creative people." They now nod (instead of nod off), and I can elaborate if they want. If I am feeling a little feisty or don't want to be categorized and someone asks me what my book is about, I may reply, "It's about fifteen bucks." (Ha ha.) What you need are called sound bites. A fashion designer described his sleekly fitted pantsuits by saying, "They allow a woman to be on the same level as a man in the boardroom, without looking like one. They make a powerful statement, but in a feminine way." Whoa, that's good. What do you offer? What makes you unique or special? What are your strengths? How do you meet the needs of the market? Answer the main question in people's minds, "Why should I do business with you?" and "What is the purpose of your art?" Take the answers to these questions and turn them into a sentence or two that expresses your uniqueness and highlights the single most important thing that you do. You could also say you are a cross between two people or things. Someone described comedian Chris Tucker as a "DNA splice between Jerry Lewis and Little Richard." I heard a Dallas Cowboy cheerleader say, "I'm going to be the female Elvis." Uh-huh. The Pretenders' Chrissie Hynde has been described as "John Wayne crossed with Cleopatra." Obviously it is better to come up with these for yourself. One illustrator, Glen Hilario, describes his unique style of art as "jazz age." You can also come up with a catchphrase that makes you stand out. "Beam me up, Scotty," from Captain Kirk; "Make my day, punk," from Dirty Harry; or "Lucy, I'm home!" from Ricky Ricardo. The U.S. Postal Service has a good one. "Neither snow, nor rain, nor heat, nor gloom of night stays these couriers from swift completion of their appointed rounds."

A simple solution to this dilemma is to find an artist that does what you do and borrow their statement and tweak it until it is your own, or look for an analogy or metaphor that would quickly explain your strength. "We are the Nordstrom of print shops." Syndicated columnist Jane Applegate is known as "the Dear Abby for Small Business." Newsletter guru Elaine Flyod is called "the Martha Stewart of Newsletters." Even strip clubs, er . . . gentlemen's clubs know the value of a position statement. On an HBO special about strippers—I mean dancers—one of the club owners got offended by the characterization of his establishment. He rattled off this statement: "We are an upscale extension of the Las Vegas showgirl experience. We are a gentleman's club and not a bump and grind kind of establishment."

Say It, Don't Spray It

"Join the army, see the world, meet interesting people, and kill them."

—*Anti–Vietnam War slogan*

What we are trying to create is the essence of what you are promoting, and communicating that in a simple, memorable, and positive way. (The shorter it is, the harder it is to write, but an economy of words is key.) Pay attention to tag lines you see every day on ads, billboards, and product boxes. Look for patterns and clues for ideas you can use. Start developing your own statement by asking yourself some questions. Who are you? What business are you in? What do you do? How do you do it? What makes you better or different? What is unique about your background? Whom are you most like? Whom do you serve? What are their needs? Why do people choose you? How do you reach them? What tools do you use? In a perfect world, what would your work look like? Ask others to answer the above questions. Do a brain dump. Make a long list of words (or use mind mapping or index cards) that capture you and what you do or want to do. I like to walk and talk. I took a microrecorder and jogged down the beach rambling on about my books and business. I then went home and transcribed my mumblings until I had a nice list of descriptive words to use for a tag line. List all of your skills and talents and then rank them one to ten by highlighting, circling, or making a new list. For each thing you do, like to do, and do well, ask: What is the benefit? These should include the main benefit for each one. To make sure you make this benefit oriented, ask this question: So what? Play around with the words to describe what makes you special. Be thrifty in your use of words to increase recognition, response, and retention. Is there a metaphor that could help people "get it" by painting a visual picture? For example, "He's a few herbs short of the special recipe" says a lot in a few words. Look through magazines and cut out photos that represent the essence of you or your art or your company (or what you want it to be). Make a collage and look for words that represent what you have created. Try to come up with a new and interesting way to say what you do. Stay away from the clichés like price, service, selection, and replace them with fresh, new words. Otherwise your statement lacks punch. It goes in one ear and out the other. But use familiar words so they can understand more of what you do with less words. Instead of saying, "I'm a writer," I say, "I'm an author," which narrows the focus a lot. Remember, you can always borrow someone else's statement and rework it to be your own. Whom do you want to be most like? Use their success as a model for what you want your work to be like and then write a statement based on what you want to be. Could be "Classical music for real people," for example.

Once you have one, use your tag line on EVERYTHING! Use it as a signature on e-mails, add to it your website, ads, flyers, newsletter, business card, letterhead, and anything else that has your name or logo on it. Don't question, "Just Do It."

Tagged

> *"Wit happens."*
>
> —*Karyn Buxman*

Rodney Dangerfield built a booming career from one line: "I don't get no respect." It's his trademark line. "I don't get no respect. My mother never breast-fed me. She told me she liked me as a friend." "I tell ya, I don't get no respect. My kid goes to a private school. He won't tell me where." Henny Youngman was known as the "King of the One-Liners," and his most famous line was "Take my wife—please!" "I haven't spoken to my wife in three weeks. I didn't want to interrupt her." Jack Eagle is a former big-band trumpet player and Jewish comic. Ironically, he played Brother Dominick in the old Xerox copy commercials. For this reason he calls himself the world's only Jewish monk, or as he likes to say, a "schmonk."

Here are some more examples of tag lines and catchy phrases used by artists and advertisers. See if you can finish them without peeking at the answers.

"Flick my . . ."	(Bic)
"Let Your Fingers . . ."	(Do the Walking)
"The Godfather of . . ."	(Soul, which is James Brown)
"The Queen of . . ."	(Soul, which is Aretha Franklin)
"Snap, Crackle and . . ."	(Pop)
"Melts in Your Mouth, Not . . ."	(In Your Hands)
"Sometimes You Feel Like a Nut . . ."	(Sometimes You Don't)
"Plop, Plop, Fizz, Fizz . . ."	(Oh, What a Relief It Is)
"Good to the Last . . ."	(Drop)
"Reach Out and . . ."	(Touch Someone)

☆
ACTION ITEM

Write a description of what you do in thirty words or less. Now cut that in half to fifteen words or less. Finally, come up with a tag line describing what you do using no more than seven words. Now you have two oral brochures (depending on the time you have to say it) and a tag line. By the way, even if you work for someone else, you should write a tag line for yourself.

Good Gimmicks

> *"A street magician has buried himself in a six-foot by two-foot glass coffin—or, as we refer to it here in Manhattan, a studio apartment."*
>
> —David Letterman

Of course, David Letterman is referring to magician David Blaine, who spent seven days in a coffin buried under six feet of dirt. This prompted Penn and Teller to comment, "Apparently all it takes to be famous is to sit around on your butt all day. Blaine did it for a week. My brother-in-law's been doing it for seven years—he should be huge." Dare to be different. Allow your creativity to guide your promotional efforts. Shatter outdated ideas with breakthrough thinking about self-promotion. The funny thing is, the most innovative promotional stunts happened years ago, before public relations people pulled the plug on some of the more zany ideas. It's partly that public relations people are overworked and overwhelmed so they only have time to do the tried and true. It's also a money thing. Some of the more madcap marketing stunts do cost a few bucks, and if the "suits" don't see how it boosts the bottom line, then it's a no go. What a shame. So it's up to you, the creative person, to find a way to make marketing magic with a fresh and fun approach to promotion. Before you go wild, my only warning would be: Promotion should *always* be professional. Don't do it if it is amateurish or would blemish your good name in some way. One example of a questionable gimmick was a headline on the January cover of *National Lampoon,* which read: "If You Don't Buy This Magazine, We'll Kill This Dog." Be careful, but have fun with it. (And don't threaten to kill anything, please.)

Then and Now, Mild and Wild

> *"Most of us live our lives devoid of cinematic moments."*
>
> —Nora Ephron

Then:

In 1928, Gerber invited artists to submit renderings of happy, healthy babies. The illustration that won was by Dorothy Hope Smith. After the company had their famous "Gerber Baby" in place, they went about promoting. One thing they did was buy a fleet of Austin Mini Cooper cars to promote the food on the East Coast. The horn played "Rock-a-bye Baby" and the Gerber Baby looked out at motorists from the rear windows. Obviously this was the precursor to the "Baby on Board" stickers from a few years ago. The lesson here is that our cars can also be utilized as an advertising "vehicle." Thomas Lipton is probably best known for educating Americans about tea, which he accomplished in part by dropping leaflets from hot air balloons. Lipton also owned a chain of food stores. In 1891, Lipton imported the world's largest cheese and inserted gold coins in the cheese. When the cheese was cut up, the crowd of eager buyers nearly overwhelmed the store. He also had giant sculptures made from sausage and butter. Contests can perk people up. Jim Moran (who recently passed away) was the master of the publicity stunt. To promote products, films, or himself he would come up with classic gimmicks that garnered the attention of the public and the press. For instance, he traveled to Alaska to sell an icebox to an Eskimo at the behest of a refrigerator company. Once, he walked with a live bull through a china shop and had a chimp drive a taxi through the streets of Manhattan to promote a Broadway show. (He was driving from the backseat, but it made *Life* magazine.) Maybe the most outrageous (and successful) promotional stunt was Orson Welles's "War of the Worlds" broadcast. The controversy and publicity led to a movie deal for the movie mogul. Come up with a gimmick to launch your next project. It gets people talking and the press writing about you.

Now:

Before Robert Young became a player in the burgeoning Linux software movement, he published a newsletter. Now his company, Red Hat Inc., is red hot. Young, now a billionaire and a growing threat to Microsoft (he even looks a little like Bill Gates), distinguished himself early by coming up with a trademark look, a red fedora hat. Couldn't you come up with a trademark look or prop? Just when you thought there wasn't anything new under the sun, along come three innovative Seattle women who create made-to-order poems on vintage typewriters as a performance art. It's something old combined with something new. The three poet-performers—a modern dancer/espresso bartender, a new mother, and a grad student—call themselves Typing Explosion Local 898, and stamp their name on every verse they crank out. It all began when a friend asked them to come up with some entertainment for a friend's going-away party. The aspiring poets were then asked to perform at art galleries and coffeehouses. They have developed quite a following—they aren't getting rich (they charge a buck a verse), but they are famous. They made the cover of the Life section of *USA Today*. Look to the past for ideas that will work in the present. When Bill Bradley and Al Gore were both seeking the Democratic presidential nomination in early 2000, there was this guy dressed in a six-foot ear-of-corn costume who hounded or "stalked" Bill Bradley in the Plains states. I never got the guy's real name, he was simply known as Corn Man. Gimmicks are being used all the time and with great success. It seems that brick and mortar stores are fighting back against Internet retailers. And they are fighting with creativity. One of these adventures in shopping can be found at Jordan's Furniture. When you enter, you may see a Louis Armstrong look-alike playing in a room resembling Bourbon Street in the re-created French Quarter of New Orleans. They also pass out fresh-baked cookies to patrons, wash your car windows while you shop, and hand you an umbrella if it's raining. Southwest Airlines was trying to lure interns (and pay them) into a training program. To get the most talented kids to come aboard (without spending a fortune), they tried a novel approach at job fairs. They handed out barf bags and asked, "Sick of your job?" The bottom line is that when done right, gimmicks get people's attention and garner good publicity.

☆ ─────────────

"SLOW" FACT
The record for the longest fart is held by a man from London, England, at an incredible two minutes and forty-two seconds. Now that's an attention-getter.

─────────────────────

Mild

If you're not receiving enough attention, try knocking over some very expensive antique lamps. Or . . .

- One organization sent a reminder to members in an effort to collect photographs for their annual directory. They got a good response. The second reminder brought in all but six photos. Their last effort to collect the photos included an illustration of a gorilla and the note: "If we don't receive your photo by next week we will run your high school yearbook picture." The last six photos all arrived soon after.
- Years ago I put together a booklet called "Cheap Dates" to promote my book and seminar on creative dating. I expanded it to include a booklet called "Coupons For Couples" and T-shirts that said, "I'm a cheap date." I held a contest for cheapest date (a couple went camping in his backyard), most romantic place to make out in San Diego (Mount Soledad), most unusual date (had a picnic in the median of a busy street), and worst first date

(girl accidentally pulled his hairpiece off *and* puked into the dash of his car). The contests were fun and the publicity was fantastic.

- Years ago you were able to win a sailing trip with Jimmy Buffett by donating to his favorite charity.
- A clever company sent crayons and paper and asked respondents to draw their product reviews.
- A woman was getting nowhere trying to get a call-back from a booking agent, so she sent a stuffed puppy and attached a custom collar that read: "I don't mean to hound you, but I would love to work with you." She finally got a call and bookings.
- Letters along with candy seems to work well as a "give me a call" gimmick. Hot Tamales, Good and Plenty, Nerds, Dog Bone (Treat), Testamints, Sweet Tarts, Dots (Dot-com), Lifesavers, Pop Rocks, Red Vine, Goobers, Runts. They could all fit in a clear container and you can make your own label.
- Use money. A penny for your thoughts? Hardly. A dollar bill glued to each letter might do the trick. Better yet, a two-dollar bill.
- Letters glued with a small gimmick are unique. Glue on a ticket to your show, a lottery ticket, a photo. An interior designer includes curtain material glued on.
- An aspiring filmmaker showed his documentary about sharks at night in hotel pools. He invited the media and the public to watch while they floated on inner tubes—with the lights off.
- I made a standee of myself out of foam core that sits on a desk. I think I'll call it . . . Mini-motivator. On it are the words: "You Can Do It! You Can Do IIIIIIttttt!" I give these away for free.
- A landscaper made up his own care and watering signs, and he leaves a free flowering plant on people's doorsteps. It has his name etched in the pot.
- A mountain retreat center included a scented car deodorizer, you know the ones, shaped like a tree. Inside was a brochure with the headline: "Is this the only way you smell the great outdoors?" They were inviting the media to the mountains for a press junket in the hopes they would go back and write nice things—they did!
- A mobile car detailer painted the name of his company on the hood of his van backward so people looking in their rearview mirror could read it.
- You can have custom candles made with your price list embedded in each. I've seen this done. It's pretty cool.

- I'm creating postcards with pictures of creative people and quotes by them in the hope that they'll be put up on the wall in people's offices.
- Jeanine Lobell, the founder of Stila Cosmetics and a makeup artist, includes an inspirational quote from the likes of Emily Dickenson and Amelia Earhart inside each package. (She is also married to Anthony Edwards of "E.R.")
- I got a cool holiday ornament shaped like a company's logo—a shark.
- Send cookies. On the outside of the bag or box it could read, "One tough cookie."
- One consultant did a mailing that said: "Worried all the time about your business's marketing materials? Let me deal with it." He attached worry dolls to the pitch letter. Another one said: "No more headaches," and had a mini–Tylenol packet.
- Write your letter upside down or print the part of your flyer with the special offer or freebie backward so they have to hold it up to a mirror.
- Make custom newspapers with the client's name, photo, and story on the cover. In your letter start with, "This is what I can do for you." This would work well for a publicist.
- Here's a strange one. One author, who had tons of his big book (440 pages), made the extra copies of his books into something he called the "Book Safe" and gave them away as gifts. Then all of a sudden he was getting orders for them and sold out of every last one.
- One clothing company in the lifestyle industry bought a bunch of die-cast metallic VW vans, put a logo sticker on the door of each van, and gave them away as a gimmick.
- Animal themes and gimmicks go good together. Feeling crabby? Let's monkey around. What, are you chicken? No bull. Kiss my bass. I once got a fake fish tank with a message inside.
- How about an empty (and clean) Spam container for an e-mail marketer to enclose their brochure? You could also do Blunder Bread and Bazooka Gum with a Bazooka "Joan" comic for a consulting company.
- A freelance interpreter for the hearing impaired found gold "I Love You" signs in a bargain bin at a swap meet. She bought them all and had them made into jewelry with her name and phone number.
- Stuck up? Make clinging signs that could be attached to a computer with your website.

- A music manager sent potential songwriters sheets of stickers with common song lyrics on them and encouraged the recipient to create a song and send it in. The prize—free management services.
- Create a unique award, "Customer of the Month," and give it to clients. It could be an actual trophy (which is fairly cheap, but lasting), or you could create your own.
- Do your designs need more pop? Give away party poppers with a custom label.
- Create a crossword puzzle that teaches people what you do by completing it.
- Write a free report on the trends in your industry and send it out or post it on the Web.
- Make downloadable free samples.
- How about creating a board game related to what you do?
- Put on your own fashion show with moms and daughters.
- Fill a mesh bag with goodies related to what you do. Maybe beach toys to tie in with your annual summer event.
- Use an empty egg carton and customize it: "Don't put all your eggs in one basket," try our services for a chance. Put a coupon inside.
- Use a mailing tube with a sticker at the top to make your next mailing stand out.
- Create your own welcome wagon basket filled with coupons and samples.
- Create ceramic tiles or cool rocks with interesting info on them and give them away as paperweights.
- I went to waiting rooms of doctors, dentists, and the musicians union and left promo copies of my books along with a stack of postcards and newsletters.
- Post samples of your work on your website.
- Hang flyers or your newsletter over urinals and on stalls.
- An author hid characters in her children's book and offered a prize if readers could find them.
- Take a chance to sing with the band.
- Offer readers a chance to win a free trip to the place where the novel is set.
- Advertise on movie screens.
- Doormats. Customized. "We're one step ahead."
- Feather. "Light as a feather."
- Popcorn to launch website.
- Give away a custom lunch box. "No free lunch."

- Send a barrel of monkeys. "More fun than . . ."
- Mail your offer in a bottle. "Message in a bottle."
- Send a lunch invitation saying, "Let's do lunch together." Include a Twinkie and say, "Just like this Twinkie, this offer never expires."
- Put your business card on a spring in a box.
- Send a G.I. Joe doll. "We'll fight for you."

Wild

"I've never killed a chicken on stage. Well, not purposely, anyway."
—Alice Cooper

No Alice Cooper concert went by without female fans throwing their panties onstage. So Warner Bros. decided to wrap each copy of his 1972 album, *School's Out,* in disposable panties. Unfortunately, they had to stop shipping the panties because, oops, the panties were not up to code (nonflammable). So, at Cooper's concert at the Hollywood Bowl, thousands of panties were dropped on the audience from a crane. Hello, it's raining panties! When good stunts go bad. During every performance the late Keith Moon would destroy his drums. When the Who was invited to appear (and play) on the "Smothers Brothers Show," the producer suggested that Keith detonate his drums using a small packet of explosives. Well, Moon, being the madman that he was, thought it would be fun to increase the charge. He tricked several technicians into giving him additional gunpowder (unbeknownst to each other). Not only did he blow his drum kit completely off the riser, he also burned and deafened guitarist Pete Townshend.

- Pet Rocks were concocted in 1975 by an advertising guy in California named Gary Dahl. What started out as a gimmick became a craze and made the man a millionaire. That's wild!
- Did you know that nearly one million copies of the *Guinness Book of World Records* are sold annually? If you can get in there with some stunt (and not hurt yourself in the process), it could mean some great publicity.
- Attendees showed up for a sales presentation and it was a murder mystery.
- A consultant dressed up like a cop and issued a summons to get a meeting.
- I don't know how many times entrepreneur/adventure-seeker Richard Branson has tried to make it around the world in a balloon, but suffice it to say it's more than a few times, and it's

nearly got him killed. Following in his footsteps is Jeff Taylor, the CEO of Monster.com. He set the world's record for blimp waterskiing. He skied for eleven minutes and forty-three seconds and covered over three miles. The old record holder was . . . Richard Branson.

- One company held a sales presentation at night and made it a pajama party.
- A restaurant charged kids by what they weighed.
- When an ad agency client was in the hospital, instead of flowers or a card they sent Rubio's fish tacos, magazines, aspirin, and old movies.
- A local band gave fake tattoos and glue-on earrings and piercings. Moms didn't dig it, but it was talked about.
- A dog washer parks his logo-ridden van at a place called "Dog Beach" all day.
- With $100 and a little poem he wrote, Marc Gorin won a restaurant. His poem was chosen as the winner by the owners, who wanted to give away the Surfside Café, a successful eatery worth at least $200,000. So they solicited entries at $100 a pop. Mine was "Hey, wow, I love your chow. Can I have the restaurant now?" I guess that's why I didn't win.
- There is a man, formerly known as Mitch Maddox, who has legally changed his name to DotComGuy and has locked himself away in his apartment to see if he can get everything he needs over the Internet for one year. You laugh. We know he can get sex, but can he get medical attention? Or beer, for that matter. Anyway, the stunt has earned him sponsors like Gateway and publicity from *People* magazine and fans (who can watch his every move on the Internet) from as far away as China.

No Money, No Problem
"Outsmart the outspenders."

—Allen Kay

If you don't have big bucks to spend on marketing, you've got to go with what you do have, an unlimited supply of big ideas, creativity, and resourcefulness. You hear the term "guerrilla marketing" used to describe this low-cost, high-hustle kind of marketing, and that's because the analogy works. Since several of my friends are in special forces, I have become somewhat knowledgeable about "hop and pop" strategies. The comparison between military strategy and guerrilla marketing works.

Free

It doesn't cost anything to offer exceptional service, attention to detail, and hustle. Use your creativity to your advantage and save money on marketing. Here are some idea starters. I'm sure you'll think of other clever ideas of your own.

- A consultant or freelancer of almost any kind could answer help-wanted ads to get freelance work. It's cheaper for a corporation to hire an independent contractor than it is to bring in a full-time employee with benefits.
- One designer sends back poorly designed forms along with his brochure and a rough sketch showing how it could be better. With a follow-up call he gets a lot of business this way.
- I've encouraged everyone I know to call bookstores to request copies of my book to build a buzz.
- Autograph everything. It can mean one less book that can be returned.
- Barter and trade for printing, office space—anything you need.
- Tell everyone what you do.
- Keep samples and marketing materials with you at all times. Keep product with you and let people know you have something to sell.
- Offer to inventory or restock shelves as a way of checking to see if your creation has sold.
- Give a free demonstration of what you do, or a sample of your service.
- One designer gives graphic design checkups for past clients.
- Run for city council or even president. Jello Biafra, formerly a singer for the Dead Kennedys, made a bid to be the Green party's presidential nominee. He didn't win, but the debates were televised, and coincidentally he had a brand-new album out. Would you vote for a guy named Jello? His platform included enacting a $100,000 minimum wage and banning SUVs. On his promotional photo he is wearing a T-shirt that reads, "Nobody Knows I'm a Lesbian." Comic Pat Paulsen ran for president so often that people started calling him "Mr. President."
- Call radio talk shows and comment on subjects related to what you do. I mean, if you can't get on as a guest, you can get on as a caller and subtly mention what you do. Listen to popular shows and get involved. I heard on a talk show that actress Molly Shannon covets office supplies and needs to get organ-

ized. I sent her a copy of my book *Time Management for the Creative Person.*

- Stand outside the "Today" show and hold up a sign.
- Get your business listed in the white pages and bump it up to bold type. Cross listings. You can use the yellow pages to build a mailing list. (You'll also need a zip code directory). You can get a free list from the DMV and county clerk.
- Get others to sponsor you. A massage therapist got a company to pay ten dollars per employee for a ten-minute massage.
- Give great service. In 1978 two fresh-out-of-high-school teenagers were doing odd jobs in their neighborhood to make money. They were asked to install an extra hanging rod in a neighbor's closet. The two decided to get creative and build a rack of floor-to-ceiling shelves in the closet as a surprise. When the neighbors got back from vacation they LOVED IT! They wound up doing the whole block's closets and eventually started a business called California Closets, which now has 150 franchises and sales exceeding $100 million.
- Online brochures save you printing costs.
- Let them try it. Fineartlease.com, an Internet upstart, allows people to lease art from anywhere from a few hours to ten years.
- There was this guy sitting with a sign outside a big corporation. I thought the sign would read, "Will Think for Food." Instead it had the address to his website, which delivered food from several restaurants to your office or home.
- When a competing consultant suddenly died of a heart attack, the resourceful (tacky?) guy asked if he could take over the man's phone number and he converted several clients. (The yellow pages had also just come out. Another boon for business.)
- Sell ads in your newsletter to offset printing costs.
- Remember when George Costanza's father invented Festivus Day? Create your own holiday. "Take Your Daughters to Work Day" was created by the Ms. Foundation for Women. Clean Out Your Fridge Day was sponsored by Whirlpool.
- Enclose information about other services you offer when you bill a client. Just don't send it to Andy Rooney. He hates getting junk with his bill. In fact, on "60 Minutes" he commented that he sends junk back when he pays the bill—orange peels, coffee grinds, cigar ashes.
- Get your creation into the hands of influential people. It may be featured in a photo or interview of the celebrity or leader. Presenters at the Oscars all left with baskets full of goodies

like eGo, a portable MP3 player, and Bally Havana loafers, as well as a lifetime AOL VIP membership.

- Have your studio be a part of a tourist tour. Sound silly? A very clever glassblower has his workshop included in the tourist information handed out by hotel concierges.

- Hold an open house. When Simon Finch Rare Books was planning their opening in London's Notting Hill neighborhood, one of the owners invited Hugh Grant to work behind the counter as a clerk for a day (just like he did in the movie called *Notting Hill*). Grant said yes. "I always enjoyed selling things," he said. File that under "You never know unless you ask." Damn, my mother was right.

- Demonstrations in-studio or in-store. At the Gibson Musical Instruments' Guitar Showcase store, you can watch your guitar being built.

- Actors from a rap version of Shakespeare went on subways to sing and pass out flyers to invite people to come to the show.

- Offer your product or service as a raffle prize.

- Donate books to the library. Donate work to a museum (or let them rent it). You may be able to rent art to churches, synagogues, country clubs, businesses, hotels, accountants, dentists, restaurants (commission to the waitress if it sells). Leave sales material behind as well as contact information with the receptionist.

- Don't take no for an answer. Life imitates art. Just like in the movie *Erin Brockovich,* author Clare Boothe Luce (who wrote the play *The Women*) interviewed for a position at *Vogue* but was not hired. She showed up for work anyway and found an empty desk and started working. She convinced people she was an employee, and eventually (and officially) she was one.

- Follow up. So few do it that you can really stand out. One agent asked potential authors to do some research and get back to her. Of the fifty-four whom she asked, only four did it.

- Stay up on the technology and trends in your industry and then offer to keep clients up to speed as you share your knowledge and insights with them. If you can teach them something, they'll treat you well. Have them take you to lunch with the promise that you'll brief them. Put the offer on your website.

- Offer free consulting. Put on a presentation or demonstration. Show them how they can make or save money and you will have won a customer.

- Borrow from the best. "On a rough day you think: 'Everybody is nicking my ideas.' But that's life. The crafty way out of it is to come up with something nobody else has thought of, and seek your identity that way, rather than grumble about what people steal from you. Steal right back!" says guitar hero Jeff Beck.

• A landscaper in Rancho Santa Fe, an upscale community in San Diego where the houses are gated and set back from the street, had a problem. Leaving flyers on the mailboxes wouldn't work because they don't have mailboxes. The post office doesn't allow flyers near the boxes, so he came up with an ingenious idea. He rigged a launcher and weighted the flyer down with a small bag of fertilizer. This way he gives them a little sampler and gets the flyers up near their door. Plus it's fun for him and his workers. (His only worry is that a dog may eat the fertilizer.)

• Wayne's World. Host your own cable access television show or a Web-based radio show.

It's Cheap, But It's Not Free

There are off-season specials for more than travelers. Have you ever considered approaching a gallery during off-season if you can't get in during the peak times? In Palm Springs, which has several successful galleries and a plethora of potential art buyers, one gallery was going to close for the summer (because it's about 155 degrees—in the shade!). An artist came up with a plan that she pitched to the gallery owner. Instead of closing the gallery for the summer, why not let her keep it open with a showing of her work? He agreed, so she worked there five nights a week (after it had "cooled" off and she had got her daily painting in) and sold several expensive pieces to tourists who braved the heat. Since things are so slow during the summer, she also was featured in the news-hungry local paper. The gallery owner got his cut and the artist got her start.

Educate the audience. Jazz-rock fusion is coming back. One record company gave a sampler disc of old classics in this genre with every *Vertu* album—a new release by jazz-rock icons Stanley Clarke and Lenny White. You could also teach a class, hold an open house and show them how you create, educate (or demonstrate to) them about your equipment (and what it means to them), or give away a video or booklet with tips.

Don't be stingy. Richard Evans, author of *The Christmas Box,* gave away thousands of copies of the self-published edition to radio stations at Christmas. His thinking was that the radio stations would talk the book up and the winners would spread word of mouth. He was right. He sold the hardcover rights for $4 million and the book became a best-seller. Supersalesman Joe Girard tosses business cards after every touchdown or home run at ball games. You could create a coupon book for services with other related creative services.

The driving force. Paint your logo on your car and park it where it will be seen. I once saw a picture of David Filo, cofounder of Yahoo, driving around in a Volkswagen Bug painted with the Yahoo logo and address.

Enter contests. Winning one can lead to a movie deal or a grant, and can open doors.

Leftovers. Buy remainder time on radio or TV or remnant space in newspapers.

Timing is everything. When the Super Bowl came to San Diego in 1988, three local artists bought space on city buses for a public-art statement.

Start a festival. In Fallbrook, California, they have an annual avocado festival including the Avocado Olympics, which includes an avocado pit-spitting contest as well as bowling, croquet, and an avocado-on-wheels derby. Then there is the food—best guacamole, salsa, and most creative dish (using the green stuff). Clever.

Final Thought

Dennis Woodruff is possibly Hollywood's most famous unfamous actor. When I came across this story I almost couldn't believe it. Here is a guy who lives in a trailer park in an industrial section of Los Angeles. (At least he has a place to live.) He once was homeless and lived in his car. Now he is a local celebrity posing for pictures with tourists, his cars are in museums and seen in films, he has appeared on TV and film, and there's a documentary being made about him. For years Woodruff has been a tireless self-promoter. He has T-shirts and signs that say, "Dennis Woodruff, Movie Star in Training." His cars are painted (and have giant signs attached to the roof) with his name and phone number as well as the license plate "UNKNWN1" and a bumper sticker saying "Born to Act." He would park outside the studio gates hoping to be discovered. He has put hundreds of flyers about himself on cars that might belong to a VIP. He passes out his head shots with the words "Cast me!" scrawled on them. He hangs out where he is likely to meet Hollywood types, and once struck up a conversation with David Lynch and made a brief appearance in one of his movies. Here is a guy with limited means but unlimited energy, enthu-

WALK TALL AND CARRY A BIG SHTICK

139

siasm, and probably a little eccentricity. But he is going for it! His business card reads: "I Am looking for Work in the Movies. It's Where I Belong." I couldn't agree more!

Ask a Pro

Bart Mendoza
Music writer, producer, musician
mendozab@juno.com

Which musician do you think is the most amazing self-promoter, and how much of a role did it play in his success?

Well, it's not a person—it's the Beatles. And I'm not talking about their sixties heyday, but their late-nineties rebirth—three number-one albums in a year, more than twenty-five years after you broke up, isn't bad. And, with the help of a few trusted aides—most with them since the beginning!—they did it themselves. Although that's the ultimate extreme, self-promotion is the most important thing—really what it's about is seeing things through. It's not just the money, right? We've all seen money thrown at major label releases, or comebacks that actually killed an artist's career. It's not enough to just have a good idea about your career—you've got to see it to the end, without an end in sight—we do this because we love it, right?

In today's music business, what are some of the new means musicians are using to promote themselves?

Well, today, although it really doesn't seem to be adding up to much, the Internet is an obvious thing—it's not the solution, though. I liken it to putting up a flyer—unless someone was going by there anyway, no one is going to see it, and for those that do, you have to change or update the info at least weekly for people to continue to visit. The plus side is that it's much easier to send out a mailing list, though how do you feel about junk mail? Seriously, the best new promotional thing to happen is the networking capability. Those who are making inroads at the moment are making connections, and keeping up on them.

What is the most outrageous, creative, unusual promotional gimmick you can recall a musician (or record label) using to promote a release?

A few years ago I had the great pleasure of spending the day in Balboa Park. As I approached the reflecting pond in front of the Botanical Gardens, I noticed a group of four young men with instruments walking through the crowd playing a song. As they walked the crowd grew larger, and they eventually stopped by the pond and played a quick set of blues before authorities dispersed the rather large throngs. The group continually mentioned that they were promoting their new CD and CD release party—and the response was phenomenal. They mingled, they took their message out of the ordinary, and best of all, they weren't preaching to the converted.

What can musicians with indie labels do to promote themselves on a limited budget?

Network. Meet everybody, expand your horizons. The music of other groups may not always be your cup of tea, but one, you can never have too many friends, and two, you never know where your next drummer is going to come from. Don't send blind promos; they're expensive and the recipient will likely just try to sell it anyway—besides, it will devalue your music locally if a lot of promos end up in the used bins. Make sure if you're going to send something, there's a chance it'll be reviewed. But most of all you have to be willing to put in the legwork, put up the flyers, send out the e-mails, and make the phone calls. I see far too many acts who want to rest on the music alone. Wonderful as it may be, unless it's out there, who will know? And never take it for granted that "a friend" or "the label" will actually do what they said. Occasionally check—politely, of course. It's your career.

6

IMAGE IS EVERYTHING
(You Are the Message)

*"My neighbor was on vacation in Miami and decided to
walk the beach and gather some shells. Mostly he found
.38 Specials and .357 Magnums."*
—Ron Dentinger

The way you run your business is a marketing tool, so be professional in everything you do (including your website, answering machine, attitude, appearance, consistency, charity work, punctuality, punctuation, and how you deal with customers). You are a walking, talking representation of your image, and everything you do reflects that image. Everything you do is an act of marketing. Define that image and obey it. Live it. Make decisions based on it. Package yourself properly to project the image you want to convey. Take a good look at all your points of contact with customers. Do they match the image you want to project? People decide whether they want to work with you based on the image you project—the impression they get. You can mold your image any way you want to. You'll make better marketing decisions by having a long-term, long-range plan and outlook. Don't compromise your artistic, long-range vision for short-range success that may do more harm than good. Knowing the image you want to project and holding true to that is just as important as getting your foot in the door. You can set yourself apart with a professional approach. Make them say "WOW" with your professionalism! (Many artists are flakes, so by being professional you already have an edge.) Being professional means that you do what you say you'll do, when you say you'll do it, and you do it well. Yes, you are an artist, but you are also a creative person in business for yourself.

On August 1, 1981, MTV was launched, and it changed the face of music. Acts like Milli Vanilli could shake and fake their way to a hit. Short-film directors could make or break a musical act. You now had to have "the look" *and* the sound. When you combine good looks with talent you have what is called "marketability." I know, it doesn't seem pure. But what's wrong with using your good looks (and exceptional talent) to show off a little? Diana Krall is a Grammy-nominated, smoky-voiced jazz vocalist who also happens to be beautiful. She is one of the biggest-selling recording artists in jazz, and magazines like *Newsweek* and *Vanity Fair* have taken notice. But in jazz, if you sell more than ten records or play up your looks, you're a sellout. "I'm excited about the music. I play it with integrity, and I don't compromise my vision," Krall says. "But I am also aware of the market and the need to sell records. I'm a girl who likes clothes and likes to look nice. So why shouldn't I have a beautiful cover?" Why not, indeed? In 1996, Katrina Garnett founded Crossworlds Software. What the software did, she felt, was pretty sexy. Others, well, may not have felt the functions of her software were a turn-on. So she hired a famous photographer to shoot the very attractive software mogul in a sexy black dress to use in ads in magazines like *Fortune.* Garnett's nontraditional marketing approach put a face on her company, which was selling an intangible. By putting her face (and body) in the ads, she hoped to attract people who wanted to be associated with someone who is confident, powerful, glamorous, and, as she says, "not a nerd." The ads (and controversy surrounding them) attracted funding from investors and increased sales.

Creating an Image

Soulful singer Barry White calls San Diego home. The last time he performed here we took our boat and watched the show from the bay. It was exactly what you would expect from the voice of love. His stage show was an enormous bedroom suite with black satin and gold trimmings. The band members wore silk pajamas, the dancers were in giant champagne glasses, and the backdrop was shaped like a giant headboard with a crest that read BW. He performed his signature songs (many of them hits and nearly all of them about love) with his trademark basso so profundo. It was just what you'd want from a Barry White concert—romance. Stephen King has built his image as the "King" of gore. Richard Branson, the founder of Virgin Records, is known for taking risks in business and in life. He has attempted to fly around the world in a balloon I don't know how many times. What I'm saying is, you develop a persona and stick with it, and it sticks to you—and that can be a good thing for promotability. How do you want to be known? Take control of that image. Jimmy Buffett is image conscious. He flies around in his own seaplane, surfs, sails, fishes, lives by the beach, travels the world performing in exotic locales, and most of all he's the king of everything hot and tropical. That's his image—laid back. He's not, but that's the image he projects, and it sells records and books. You can create the image you want others to see. This starts with an idea of what you think would appeal to your target market and what you want to project. Look at your website, the signature on your e-mails, your attire, the outgoing message on your voice mail, your agent, your grammar, business cards, head shot, the causes you support, the type of projects you prefer, packages you mail out, your track record, professionalism, persona, portfolio, lifestyle, your color scheme, goals, employees or employer, clients, whom you admire, the car you drive, and so on. Do they convey the image you want? If not, what *is* the image you want to convey?

You Can't Handle the Truth

"Integrity is doing the right thing, even if nobody is watching."
—Jim Stovall

When colleagues describe multiple Oscar-winning actor Tom Hanks, they use adjectives like "decent" and "passionate" and "dedicated." For example, while filming the hit movie *The Green Mile,* Tom Hanks went to put his handprints and footprints into cement at Mann's Chinese Theatre on his lunch break. He came back to the set with cement still on his shoes to read lines (off camera) with one of the young stars. Anyone could have rehearsed with the actor, but Hanks honored his commitment. You can't fake that kind of integrity. To succeed in the long run, you will need more than talent, skill, and ability. You need integrity, honesty, courage, character, empathy, and generosity. You have a code of ethics that says, "I keep the promises I make. I am never late. I always do the right thing." Integrity comes from making tough choices, and making the right choices about how you conduct yourself. Hey, I want to go to the beach *right* now. In fact, three friends have called in the past hour to invite me to go surfing, wakeboarding, and to play tennis—all are very tempting, but this book is (was) due like yesterday. So here I am, the middle of June, sitting in a coffee shop (by the beach) doing what I said I would do, working on my manuscript. That's the image I want to project—hardworking, professional, and dedicated.

All the Right Moves

When you're struggling, it's hard to turn down work. It's tempting to take on jobs that jeopardize your good name. Don't do it. When things are going well you may feel you can do no wrong and may make poor choices about work as well. You get bloated with self-importance and leave a good gig to go solo or reach a little too high too soon. McLean Stevenson played Lieutenant Colonel Henry Blake on the hit show "M*A*S*H" (a great gig), but he left and was never really heard from again. How about David Caruso leaving "NYPD Blue" or Shelley Long leaving "Cheers"? Not great career moves. How do you know what the right thing to do is? Trust your instincts. I had a bad vibe about a client, and I was right—I never got paid and he stole my ideas and used them in a not-so-flattering way. Turn down work with people who are known to be bad (and have proved it in the past) or whom you know nothing about. Turn down work that you aren't suited for. Turn down work with unrealistic deadlines. Turn down work where they could care less about quality and you would be embarrassed to put your name on the work or appalled if anyone found out. If it will take so much time you'll resent them (and maybe lose out on better business). If it goes against your values, just say NO. I heard that Andy Garcia refuses to do nude scenes (much to the chagrin of his female fans).

☆ ————————————————

ACTION ITEM

How do you want others to see you? Which one best describes the image you want to project:

1. Shy, nervous, negative, indecisive, needy, unreliable, boring, self-centered, difficult, fussy, disorganized, untrustworthy.
2. Exciting, clever, charming, amusing, together, well-balanced, well-liked by others, considerate, cheerful, understanding, stylish, interesting, successful, talented, gifted, loyal, reliable, trustworthy, crass, crude, unethical.
3. Write a description of the image you want to project. Ask others to tell you what image you project now.

First and "Lasting" Impressions

"Always give people a friendly greeting; a cold nose in the crotch is very effective."

—All I Needed to Know I Learned from My Dog

Fashionably late. That's an oxymoron, isn't it? Being late is one of THE most disrespectful things you can do. How about when Whitney Houston (who is famous for being tardy or AWOL) arrived two hours late the night she was the featured performer at a White House dinner honoring Nelson Mandela? I mean, if you can't be on time for that!? You have about ten seconds to make a good impression. It can take the rest of your life to undo a bad one. A bad first impression is very hard to shake. You have one shot. Don't miss. Make a strong first and lasting impression. As a time-management expert, I always start (and end) my seminars on time. It's a pet peeve of mine. I also always open with something big like a magic trick, a really good joke, or a powerful story. I realized (by attending other workshops) that a speaker has only a few seconds to connect with an audience. That's why I like to make people laugh or do something entertaining right up front. I can sometimes even hear audience members lean over to the person next to them and say, "This is going to be fun." Yes! People make up their minds whether they will buy from (or into) you in a few seconds. How you look, the gestures you make, what you say, and then the nonverbal messages you send. Knowing that, you can work it to your advantage.

The first thing they notice about you is visual. It's those pesky nonverbal clues you are sending out that can undermine your credibility. Instead, dazzle them. Dress to impress. Do the "do." Make eye contact. Smile. Develop a firm handshake. Don't overdo it with the touching thing. (Remember Francis from the movie *Stripes*? "Anyone touches me . . . I'll kill you.") There are people like that. Carry yourself with confidence. (Get your hands out of your pockets.) It's also better to be upbeat and high energy than a downer and a buzz kill. If your portfolio cover is all ratty and you look like a bag lady or you don't have a business card handy when someone asks for one, you are already off on the wrong foot.

The next signals they're picking up on are the vibrations that come from your lips. Watch what comes out of your mouth. Bad breath. Bad language. (Do something about those Austin Powers teeth.) Make the first few words count. Start with what you can do for them or praise or thanks. Think it through. Come up with an unusual greeting, a signature salutation. Not "Come here often?" as your opening line. Anticipate the "So, what do you do?" and prepare your oral brochure. Stop yapping for a minute and listen. Be a name-caller. Use people's names. Then, to win them over, make a lasting impression with your knowledge. Show them you do your homework. Discuss things they are interested in. Find common ground. Name-drop. "Oh, I was just on that shoot. I was DP on that project. Just worked with him. Looks great. What talent, oy."

Good manners are a must. Actor Stanley Tucci points out the obvious: "Never, and I mean never, use the side of your knife to look and see if you have food wedged in your teeth." A lack of manners stands out. How you handle introductions, farting in the elevator, having your plate piled high and eating like it's happy hour, and never saying thank you all stand out, too. One fledgling writer attended MY book release party and passed out flyers for her book, hit on my editor, and wore this stupid cone-shaped hat. Was that wrong? Let me count the ways. Know what is appropriate etiquette for your industry.

One final thought: Don't go out and try to win people over if you aren't ready. Sometimes you only get one chance. Are you clear about what you do? Can you articulate it concisely? Do you have a body of work and a track record or good references? Are you even ready to sell? Ready to deliver? Ready for feedback (good and otherwise)? Know what price to charge? Have an agreement? Brochure? Prepare, then present.

FAST FACT
The most common cosmetic surgery is (a) breast augmentation, or (b) face-lift, or (c) body reshaping (liposuction and liposculpture)? The answer is . . . (c) body reshaping.

The Image You Project

*"People think you look like the cover of a magazine every day.
But you don't clean the toilet in a red dress that shows your tits."*
—Minnie Driver

1. How do you walk? (Head up or down?)
2. Do you look people in the eye when talking to them, or do you look down or away?
3. Do you dress conservatively or creatively?
4. Is your handshake firm or flimsy?
5. When you sit, do you cross your ankles and slouch or sit up straight?
6. Do you sneak into a room or make a big entrance?
7. Are you considered a good listener? Conversationalist?
8. Do you know how to order and eat without making a mess?
9. Are you punctual?
10. Do you talk like a "Valley Girl" or a professional? (Oh, my gawd.)
11. Do you usually remember and use people's names?

How Others See You

"If women can sleep their way to the top, how come they aren't there yet?"

—Ellen Goodman

There are a few things that you can control regarding your image; most you can't, but that shouldn't stop you from trying. You can't control your physical attributes (at least not without several thousand dollars in plastic surgery) and how people judge you by them. "I have a normal woman's body. I like having a good pair of tits on me and a good ass. If I didn't, I don't think I'd feel attractive," boasts Kate Winslet. Look your best with what you have.

For some people, there's a negative connotation associated with being a creative person. They think: insecure, scatterbrained, flaky, disorganized, unprofessional, neurotic, druggy, selfish, loner, holier than thou, and worse. What are you gonna do? I'll tell you what, prove them wrong! Does your industry have an image problem? Honda had an image problem when they first started selling motorcycles in the United States. People associated motorcycles with a certain type of person—not a pretty picture. To shed the tough guy image, Honda ran ads with very respectable people riding their new bike along with the headline, "You Meet the Nicest People on a Honda." It worked. After the ad ran on television, sales of Honda motorcycles skyrocketed. Culligan water softeners were sold door-to-door. The reputation of door-to-door salesmen was somewhere below that of used-car salesmen. People saw them as untrustworthy. So to overcome the bad rap Culligan wanted to project a more personable and humorous public image. The slogan Culligan came up with in 1959 was "Hey, Culligan man," with that annoying lady's voice. (I thought it should have been "Ohhh, Culligan man," with a sensual voice.) When the salesmen went out after the commercials had run, they opened with "Hi, I'm your Culligan man," and were greeted with a warmer response.

"I'm a trisexual. I'll try anything once," states David Bowie. You obviously can't control what people may think about your particular lifestyle. Coming out of the closet hasn't hurt some artists (Melissa Etheridge, Indigo Girls, K. D. Lang), but others may have wished they kept the doors closed (Ellen DeGeneres, Anne Heche, George Michael). With others it isn't really talked about much (Michael Stipe, David Bowie, Pete Townshend), and to still others it's like duh (Village People, Boy George, Little Richard).

I'm thinking of a musician. Can you guess who it is? Let me give you a few clues. College graduate. Political activist. Active Christian.

Proud father. Pat Boone, you say. Nope. I was thinking of Dave Mustaine, lead singer of Megadeth. Sure, at one time he "smoked, snorted, or shot just about everything." Now he is a model citizen, but the perception is, rock 'n' roller, heavy metal, must be a loser. "People look at me and say, 'Hey, he has long hair, so he must be stupid,'" he says. They would never suspect that he holds a business degree (the band sells millions of records, so it comes in handy) in addition to being a kick-ass guitar player.

On the other hand, you can use perception to your advantage. Play it up. Gene Simmons of Kiss says, "On the road I'm an ambassador of goodwill, here to spread joy to the world." I'm sure Milton Berle and Tom Jones have a reputation as being "stick" men. No need to play that down. Actress Jenna Elfman may be a little bit of a free spirit, but she is not a ditz. "People who are ditzes don't get the job done," says the "Dharma and Greg" star. Her character is a little flaky on the show, but in real life Jenna is just enthusiastic about life.

Cloud 9 Shuttle is winning the shuttle war at the San Diego Airport for a number of reasons, one of which is the professionalism of its operation and operators. Drivers must wear a tie, smile (shower), and keep their radios tuned to soft jazz or classical music. The vans are newer, immaculate, and colorful. This goes against the image of many taxi and shuttle companies. A positive and professional image is good for business.

Decisions, decisions. These are one of the few things you can control (along with your thoughts). Francis Ford Coppola doesn't desire mainstream success. He wants to make good films, and with fifty-four Oscar nominations, he has done just that. By choosing his films based not on box office potential but on personal preference, his credibility quotient is extremely high.

When it comes to politics and religion, don't even go there. Some other areas to avoid include weighty issues. "So, when is the baby due?" Whack. "Oh, you're not pregnant. Geez, I'm so . . ." Whack. Weight is *always* off-limits.

Being too creative with your look can repel people and prospects. Tone it down just a notch. Be a little more conservative (but not Jerry Falwell conservative). Walk into your office or studio as if you're seeing it for the first time. Does your work area convey the "sphere" you were hoping for?

One writer formed his own agency (in name only) and gained more respect in the publishing industry and was able to sell several books and thousands of articles. He also used his brother's New York address to increase his credibility. (He lives in the Midwest.)

Do good work and more good work will come your way. Yes, nobody has appeared in more films in the past few years than Samuel L. Jackson, but William H. Macy is right there as well. He was in *Fargo, Boogie Nights, Magnolia,* and the list goes on and on. He is a consummate pro, constantly in demand, in part because he is highly regarded as a true professional by Hollywood insiders and his fellow actors. Hone your craft to the point of perfection and combine that with a pleasing personality and professional approach and you WILL be in demand.

Let's see, if you marry a second cousin who is only thirteen years old, do you think fans will embrace you? Or worse, you marry your own (adopted) daughter, like Woody Allen did with Soon-Yi Previn. Did that help or hurt his image? At least stay married. Did you know that Zsa Zsa Gabor has been married nine times! Elizabeth Taylor and Mickey Rooney have been married eight times each. Some people choose to do business with you based on factors other than what's in your portfolio. They want to hire people who have character but aren't characters. Actress Jennifer Love Hewitt has that girl-next-door charm and it's no act. Her clean-cut image makes her a favorite among teen audiences, with their moms' endorsement. She takes being a role model seriously, and carefully chooses parts, answers her own fan mail, and does a great deal of charity work. She is devoted to Tuesday's Child, helps children with AIDS. She even contributed a story to the best-selling book *Chicken Soup for the Teenage Soul.* That's nice.

The Company You Keep

"At least they didn't have me involved with one of the Backstreet Boys. Now, that would have been really embarrassing."
—Christina Ricci

Frank Sinatra may have been able to get away with cozying up with known mobsters and become an even bigger celebrity because of it, but the rest of us should be very careful about the company we keep. It's time to lose the losers in our life and be seen with winners, not whiners. Trust your gut. Check out people's track records. (Once a cheater, always a cheater.) Don't be afraid to turn down work that doesn't fit with your morals, standards, or image. It isn't worth the money to associate with people with a bad reputation. It may rub off on you.

I admit that I love Jennifer Lopez and her ass . . . ets. She is multi-talented. Her portrayal as Saleeeeena was so well rounded. Now she is the butt of many jokes because of her past involvement with hip-hop honcho Sean "Puffy" Combs. Just as her album went multiplatinum and her endorsement deal was set (as well as a starring role in a feature film), she was (allegedly) involved in a shooting in Manhattan. Her involvement with "Puffy" could have been a career killer. (I'm sure she'll bounce back, but she needs someone to watch her backside.)

Be careful whom you recommend. Whom you give a blurb to. Whom you share the billing with. Who pays your checks. What you endorse. An artist friend of mine was infamous because he appeared in before and after photos for a hair replacement club. He loved the attention, but because of the ad his "piece" didn't fool anyone. He was a laughingstock. It was not positive promotion. Your reputation is at stake. Do not give away your mailing list to just anyone. This is one of your greatest assets. Guard it very carefully. It takes time to build trust, don't blow it. A powerful agent can be an asset and door opener. A sleazy one and doors start to slam in your face.

A marriage broker offered Morty a beautiful young girl to be his new bride. Morty immediately stated, "I'm a businessman. Before I buy anything, I gotta have a sample. So before I get married, I gotta have a sample also." The broker reluctantly relayed the message to the girl, who replied, "I'm also good at business. A sample I don't give. But I will give him references!" Testimonials give your image an instant boost. They say you're really good, and "don't just take my word for it, I have proof." They vouch for your character and ability and make you seem bigger and better. When you put pictures of yourself with celebrities (or leaders in your field) on your website or your "wall of fame," it is the ultimate gilt by association. Testimonials sell! They carry a lot of clout with customers because they build trust in half the time. Use pictures and quotes from customers in your ads, newsletter, website, video, on the walls of your office. Also, use their real names. It can mean instant trust, and it doesn't have to be the "it" girl or an A-list celebrity. Happy customers will usually do the trick. It means positive word of mouth. Collect as many as you can.

How do you get testimonials? Stay in touch with people so it doesn't seem like you're hitting them up all of a sudden. Ask. That's right. Just ask. People like to see their name in print (or better yet, their photo). Carmella Soprano asked her neighbor for a letter of recommendation to help her daughter Meadow get into Georgetown. When a Soprano asks, people listen. Don't be afraid to ask. What if they decide after thinking about it that they don't like me? Unlikely. You will be surprised. Worst case, you'll get good feedback. Offer people a discount or incentive (contest or drawing) if you can use them in your promotional materials. Do a survey and ask for comments. Ask for specific examples of what you did for them.

Collect and capture all positive press and praise. Save thank-you notes. Don't miss out on an opportunity to get a proof of praise. Keep a camera, tape recorder, and video handy. Do a trade. Endorse their product and they put you in their ad, and vice versa. Don't collect all this positive praise and never use it. Plaster them on everything. Use them. You could even put them on your call waiting. "Push here for testimonials." Make an audiotape of your top testimonials, or even a video. (When my wife was promoted and moved to a bigger store, the employees and managers got together and made her a video loaded with lavish praise.) Print up a booklet of them. Put it on the wall. Get creative when putting it up. Paint on the wall. The goal is to put them out there where people can see. Especially celebrity endorsements. It means instant recognition. Status. Looks great on flyers. Bigger turnouts. More media opportunities. Stands out. Big impact. Whom would your customers respect? Ask for an endorsement. It may not be a mainstream celebrity but someone in your industry that's a big name. (They are easier to reach.) Don't forget that giving a testimonial can be good promotion for you.

How You Look

"I've got taste. It's inbred in me."

—David Hasselhoff

In the movie *Pretty Woman,* Julia Roberts's character goes shopping on Rodeo Drive (with a fistful of cash) for an outfit to wear to dinner with Richard Gere's character. The problem is that the snooty salespeople at the exclusive shops won't give her the time of day (and in fact are downright rude) because she is still dressed like a prostitute. The reality is, people's perception of you IS based on how you look. You can't make them respect you and your funky fashion sense any more than they can change your opinion of their stick-up-their-butt attitude. Since you can't change them or them you, your choices are either to be a bit more flexible and adaptable to what clients and customers expect (and this doesn't have to be a total compromise of your individuality) or fight an uphill battle to gain their respect and business. More and more we have become a visual society. Looking good is a part of marketing. Sorry, some people don't want to hear that. It doesn't mean you have to be handsome or beautiful to make it, but if you are, use it to your advantage. It doesn't mean you have to be fit and fashion forward to make it. "I know I'm this white, lumpy guy that got lucky in the music biz. I'm not hip," says Garth Brooks. (He's sold nearly 100 million records.) But as Thomas Fuller points out, "Good clothes open all doors."

Dress to match your industry. What does your tribe wear? What do the people who sign your paychecks and pay your invoices wear? Find a happy medium between the nose ring and purple hair and looking a bit too conservative and dorky (like Bill Gates, for example). Steve Jobs of Apple Computers is a better example of a well-dressed, stylish guy. Ask yourself, has your look held you back? Could you establish credibility by dressing differently? (That could be long hair, jeans, and a black tee.) As a creative person I find that people expect us to dress differently. (Hallelujah.) They also expect us to be up on trends, know what colors go together, and to show off our creativity in what we wear. Dress to match your personal style. Use your individuality and flair for the unusual. Develop a signature look—funky hat, crazy glasses, or your own signature color.

Always look your best. On planes I am going for comfort. Wouldn't you know I'm seated next to a celebrity, and because I'm dressed like a bum (beach bum), I'm too shy to talk. From that day forward I try to look my best at all times. On another flight the flight attendant was walking down the aisle, eyeing each passenger closely until she got to me. (I was wearing my signature black suit and black mock turtle.) She stops and says, "You were randomly chosen to fly first class." "No way," I said. "Way," she countered. When I was seated in my ultra-comfy first-class seat, she said, "I chose you because you look like you belong in first class." "Thanks, more champagne, please," I said. Just remember, you are always on.

Trisha Yearwood began her career wearing classic country outfits (and belting out straightforward Nashville tunes). Then she adopted a sleeker, more businesslike look and updated her musical style and began to a broaden her fan base. You seem to get more respect and are taken more seriously (treated better) when you dress well. Keep your individuality. *Once Bitten* star Lauren Hutton never fixed her trademark gap between her front teeth, and it didn't discourage fashion magazines from putting her on the cover. Make a statement. When "South Park" creators Trey Parker and Matt Stone arrived at the Oscars dressed like Jennifer Lopez (they were in drag), it made Joan Rivers squirm, but it also got the two a lot of press. (It also meshes with their offbeat sense of humor.)

You Look Mah-vehlous

"I just accept them [her breasts] as a great accessory to every outfit."

—Jennifer Love Hewitt

I admit, everything I know about fashion I learned from my wife. When we first met, she wasn't content to just throw away my lame shoes, no, she had to burn them in the fireplace. (They were THAT bad.) What I do know about fashion is simple. Actually, it's simplicity. Less is more. Restraint. I believe that if the shoe fits (or anything fits right), you wear it. If what you're wearing doesn't fit or flatter, forget about it. Quality over quantity. It's the little things like your belt, shoes, and glasses that can make or break a good outfit. Finally, I believe in black. Designer Christian Dior said (in 1954) that "you can wear black at any time. You can wear it at any age. I could write a book about black." (Somebody did, it's called *Dressed in Black* by Valerie Mendes.) I came across a funny story about the Hollywood people who descend on the Sundance Film Festival in the ski resort town of Park City, Utah, each year. Apparently, their attire is nearly getting them killed. The locals call these "city folk" "PIBs," or people in black. Everything they wear from their head to their toes is black. This has made for several close calls as they cross the street at night. Bottom line: be clean, neat, and alert.

☆————————————

JUST FOR FUN

At the Ritz-Carlton in Boston, kids can take "Social Savvy" classes. These are one-day seminars for ladies and gentlemen ages eight to twelve. Children learn table manners, the art of writing thank-you notes, telephone etiquette, and tips for social conversation. The Ritz should expand this program to include the parents, too!

People Do Judge a Book by Its Cover

"I'm much more than a pair of breasts . . . I represent success, hard work, and fun."

—Pamela Anderson Lee

Many times the way you package something from a proposal to a product can determine its success or failure. If it is attention-grabbing, attractive, and appropriate to the product, it will at least get a second look. This certainly holds true in the book business, where it takes a good cover, a clever or catchy title, and a pleasing page layout to stand out and sell in stores. Publishers tested titles and found that a title change can increase sales by thousands. The book *The Tallow Ball* sold 15,000 copies. When the title was changed to *A French Prostitute's Sacrifice,* sales were 54,700. *The Beverly Hills Diet Book* was once called the *Pineapple Diet Book. The Squash Book* sold less than 2,000 copies, but with a new title, *The Zucchini Cookbook,* it sold 300,000.

Phil Spector couldn't cut the four-minute song "You've Lost That Lovin' Feelin'" down to the standard radio play time of roughly three minutes. (Stations would not have played it at four minutes.) So he simply listed it as 3:05 on the label and it got played. The packaging can position a product or person as either high-end or bargain basement, professional or amateur, creative or generic. If you were a gallery owner who got a massive amount of promotional materials each year, what would work on you? Professional? Polished? Do you think the Pet Rock would have duped so many people in the mid-seventies if it didn't come cleverly packaged with the booklet that parodied dog training, titled, *The Care and Training of Your Pet Rock*? The "Frisbee Player's Handbook" was cut in the shape of a circle and packaged inside a Frisbee. This helped get the book in sporting goods and toy stores. *The Bug Book* comes in a bug-catching bottle. Be creative with how you package and present your ideas. Let your personality show through. One word of caution: appear organized. (Better yet, *be* organized.) When you make a presentation, neatly display your work in a portfolio. When everyone pulls out their planner to pick a date for a follow-up meeting, at least make it look like your scraps of papers and Post-it notes stuffed in between the pages aren't going to spill out all over the floor.

Make everything that you send out match your marketing materials and overall look. Be consistent and clever at the same time. Manischewitz makes matzoh and other kosher foods and has sold it in their orange and forest-green boxes for years. They are a known brand. The company decided to do a makeover of the packaging to try to reach the "goyim," or non-Jews. The look is cleaner but still incorporates much of the old design and colors that people have known for years. Now, if only they could make matzoh taste more interesting.

HOMEWORK

Look at the packaging all around you. Examine how movies, CDs, and clothes are packaged. (Note: CD booklets and covers can be very clever and innovative, but have you ever noticed how poorly the CD case is designed? They are difficult to open—drop it once and the hinges break—and it's nearly impossible to get the booklet back in and under the little plastic hubs.)

LOGO POWER

Get a good logo. (It's a visual representation and expression that describes you and your business, and your uniqueness.) I've heard logos described as your handshake to the world. So make a good first impression with an impressive one. A logo also says a lot about you when you aren't there to say it yourself. Another good reason to get one.

Design 101

> "Computer design is two words, and only one of them is
> important. That word is 'design,' not 'computer.'"
> —Don Sparkman

Design is back! The iMac, the VW Beetle, the Palm Pilot, are all examples of how color and design helped to sell a product and differentiate it in the marketplace. High style isn't highbrow anymore. I noticed this at Target recently. They now stock everything from cool-looking toilet bowl brushes to fabulous frames at "tar-jzay." Computers make it easy for anyone to design, but computers don't design—people do. Design is powerful, and when it is done correctly, it affects your image and your bottom line. In the wrong hands it can do damage. In the right hands a computer is a powerful tool that can make a creative person. When you can design clean, clear, and clever marketing materials for yourself, you will save a bundle and be in complete control of your "look" and your image. Make learning about design part of your ongoing training program.

QUIZ

1. Look at these: websites, press releases, ads, flyers, brochures, reports, package design, photography, illustration, pre-press, résumés, typesetting, PowerPoint presentations.
2. Now look at this: design.
3. Now close your eyes, what do you remember. Exactly. Simplify!!!

Phone Home

"The phone is once again your friend."

—*Pacific Bell ad slogan*

This may be their first impression of you. If it isn't a pleasant and professional one, it can be difficult to undo. Get rid of call waiting. Install a dedicated line for business. Get a rep for returning calls fast. One teenage boy was on an overnight fishing trip with his grandfather. They found a perfect spot under a bridge and secured their boat for the night. The boy promised his girlfriend he would call her every night at ten o'clock sharp. When he tried to use his cell phone to call, it didn't work under the bridge. Since it was a big deal to move the boat, he put the phone in a plastic bag and held it out of the water as he swam away from the bridge. Then, treading water for five minutes, he made his call. We need to have that same kind of dedication when it comes to our clients. As much as we'd like to, we can't just not answer the phone. Sure, e-mail is the best, but it can't replace the interaction and intimacy of an ear-to-ear phone call. How you deal with the phone can be a matter of professional life and death. When Mr. Rizzo got a call from his doctor with the results of his blood test, the doctor said, "I've got bad news and worse news. The bad news is, you've only got twenty-four hours to live." Mr. Rizzo exclaimed, "Oh no, how could it possibly get any worse than that?" to which the doctor replied, "I've been trying to reach you since yesterday."

Answer the phone like a business. (No screaming kids, loud music, eating, or belching.) Be professional but remain personable. Have a signature salutation when you answer the phone. Your voice mail/answering machine is a marketing tool. Treat it as such. (Upbeat and updated is good.) Promote a new book, class schedule, tip of the week, quiz, passage from a new book, sample of new song. Have a foolproof system to write down messages. Blown-off could mean a blown opportunity. Take notes during a call. Prep for important calls and for their voice mail. Assume you are going to get voice mail every time you make a phone call. Have a brief, clear, and detailed message prepared. Even if someone picks up, your thoughts are organized. Leave your number—twice. Respect people's time. Before you begin to ramble, ask the other person if this is a good time to talk. Return calls quickly. Set a time limit for yourself. It could be that you return all calls within twenty-four hours. Get creative. Pick a phone number that spells something and is thus easy to remember. Give away phone cards with your art on them. Have a dedicated line for business calls and one for Internet access. A busy signal is a bugger.

How You Act

"It's not what I do but how I do it. It's not what I say but how I say it—and how I look when I'm saying it."

—Mae West

Creative people are nonconformists. Sometimes this makes us seem like troublemakers. Weirdos. Unorthodox. No need to throw fuel on that fire. To change our image we need to be professional and easy to work with. (Maybe even *appear* to be somewhat normal.) I'm not saying you have to be a saint. You don't have to be a yes person. "If you obey all the rules you miss all the fun," Katharine Hepburn said. It starts by saying I am a professional artist. This is not a hobby. You must take yourself seriously before others will. I mean, if you can't convince yourself you're a professional, it will be nearly impossible to convince others. You can't show fear or they will eat you alive. (Like sharks, low self-esteem is like blood in the water.) Once you lose the amateur mind-set and act professional at all times, you finally get the respect (and pay) you deserve. Start by making answering machine and business cards reflect that you are serious about this. Set up an office or studio you aren't embarrassed to show others. Get a separate business checking account.

People like to work with a winner. Act like you are a success—even if you have to fake it. Unfortunately, nobody wants to work with a struggling artist. One upstart ad agency (it was a one-woman operation) made it appear like business was booming and created the illusion that they were bigger than they were. The founder was sooooooo close to landing her first big account, but he wanted to meet her staff and see her offices. This was a problem since she still lived at home with her parents and did all of the work herself in a corner of the kitchen. She was desperate, so she agreed to a meeting at lunchtime and "borrowed" her brother's office and filled it with her friends, pretending to be her personnel. She quickly showed the client around while her friends called back and forth within the office so it appeared like the phones were ringing off the hook. She spread out artwork all over the place, and her friends held a mock brainstorming session that the potential client sat in on for a few minutes. She landed the account, and now has a thriving business and her own office. The funny thing was the client later admitted he wasn't fooled but was impressed by her creativity, ingenuity, and bravado.

Look at people who have made it in your field. How do they act, talk, and dress? Emulate them (while keeping your personal identity). Be careful whom you emulate. The diva of divas is Barbra Streisand. She has a reputation for demanding control of all details related to her projects. (Down to details like photo approval.) She also has a reputation for blowing people away with her talent. The singer-actor-director-producer has been called "the greatest talent anywhere" by columnist Liz Smith. Her numerous awards and millions of records sold give her a kind of clout many of us will never come close to. It's good to have chutzpah, but only when you can deliver the goods, too. It's not so much what you know, but how much you act like you know what you're talking about. Being confident, decisive, can sell you more than your actual credentials (or lack of). You must think, act, and treat your creative career as a business. (Whether you work for yourself or some schmuck.) Make people feel like they're dealing with a successful and competent company. Prove it's not a hobby, and not a fly-by-night operation. Make clients lives easier. Be considerate (like with editors and deadlines), deliver projects on time or early (in the right format) and customized with a little something extra.

When Bill Haley ("Rock Around the Clock") was arriving at a train station in London in 1956, he saw thousands of screaming fans and wondered what famous person was on the train. That's so refreshing. This guy didn't look like a star. He had squinty eyes (only one was real), a funky hairdo, and his "rock" band included an accordion player. It is so refreshing to work with creative people who have no ego. "I'm not hip, I'm not produced, I'm not slick, and I don't have a big image thing," says Jewel. Or, "I found my inner bitch and ran with her," says Courtney Love. Being a good guy and easy to work with can mean referrals and repeat business. If an editor likes your writing and a pain-in-the-ass writer's stuff equally, they may just refer more work to you because you are professional, personable, and pleasant. We prefer to do business with people we like. Humble people don't think less of themselves—they just think about themselves less. They are a joy to work with, and people want to work with them again and again.

Breaking up is hard to do. There will come a time when you will have to say no to someone; to fire them, let them go, go your own way. Do it with respect for their feelings. Today's hack could be tomorrow's Taylor Hackford. Let them down easy. "Life's a bitch and then they call you one," said Mary Francis Connelly. As they say, you'll see the same people on the way up as you do on the way down, so be careful how you treat them. Oscar winner Michael Caine appeared in nearly a hundred films and won two Oscars, but he has never lost sight of what it was like to grow up impoverished. "I never forget, not for one second, where I come from, and what it would be like to go back." Someone once said that angels can fly because they take themselves lightly. True.

☆ ────────────────────────────────

QUIZ

Check off personality traits you possess that can make you a success. (Promotable characteristics.) Check those that apply: Attention to Details, Communicative, Creative, Efficient, Exciting, Flexible, Fun, Gregarious, Honest, Loyal, Motivated, Organized, Progressive, Reliable, Resourceful, Sharp, Sincere, Trustworthy, Understanding. _____

How Not to Act

"There is such a thing as too much fun. How many times can you wake up and struggle to remember your name, her name, and where you are?"

—Charlie Sheen

Aerosmith (reportedly) liked to bring a chain saw with them on tour so they could chop up hotel rooms with greater efficiency. Sly Stone was so famous for being a no-show at his concerts that they nicknamed him "the man who wasn't there." The onetime San Francisco disc jockey went on to have a profound impact on the music world. Sly and the Family Stone pumped out hit after hit ("Everyday People," "Family Affair," and "I Want to Take You Higher," to name a few), but being a no-show at concerts (or playing for only a short while) prompted riots, and he blew it. His excuse for missing shows: "Sometimes you don't feel your soul at seven-thirty." On the flip side, Sly's bad behavior led to a big break for another band. In September 1968, Sly failed to show up for a gig at Blaise's in England. The club's manager, Roy Flynn, went to the apartment of the yet-to-be-discovered band Yes and literally dragged them out of bed and begged them to play. Yes put on a brilliant performance and launched their career.

See Dick be an out-of-control, irrational, obnoxious, overbearing bully. Watch Dick not get any referrals, reference letters, or repeat business. Get a reputation as a jerk and it's hard to shake. You'll wonder why you don't get calls for work anymore. Nobody wants to be around or work with or hire unreliable people, no matter how talented. One website designer I know made me look bad when he flaked. I vouched for him and he burned me. He never returns photos (and even lost some). I have to threaten him to get anything done. He will say, "The dingo ate my homework." Whatever. I am sure I am not easy to work with ("Authors are easy to get on with—if you like children," says Michael Joseph) because I am demanding, but only because that's what I expect of and do myself.

One actor's career took a serious turn when news surfaced that he had starred in three gay pornos. The actor lost a part on a WB sitcom and Disney passed on casting him in a role as well. (His racy past didn't fit well with their Mickey Mouse image.) Renowned saxophonist Charles McPherson says: "I think the hardest thing to do is to be a so-called creative person, an artist, and still have normal relationships. It's easier to be either the self-destructive and self-centered personality associated with creative genius, or to give up the creative thing and go work at the post office and be a wonderful father and nice husband. The hardest thing to do is to be right in the middle."

What You Charge
"The content of your character is your choice. Day by day, what you choose, what you think, and what you do is who you become."

—Heraclitus

Pricing says a lot about you. You must know your value and act accordingly. If your fees are too low, they think you stink and look second-rate and wonder if there is something wrong with you or your work. If word gets out that you're cheap, it's hard to raise rates. And if they're too high, they feel they can't afford you (and expect a lot for their money). If I had to pick one, I would err on the high side, since you can always come down or throw in a few extras (if you're feeling a twinge of guilt or "seller's" remorse). One freelance ghostwriter I know raised his rates to an insane amount so he could work less, but he actually has more work than ever. It's all about perception. Hairstylist Sally Hershberger charges over $400 for a haircut—and gets it. (She started the coveted choppy do craze in Hollywood with her signature undone cut made famous by Meg Ryan.) What if she charged Supercut prices? Would she have celebrities like Julia Roberts, Cindy Crawford, and Tom Cruise scrambling for appointments? I think not. When Hillary Clinton was going to be on the cover of *Vogue,* it was Hershberger who got the call. Don't be a starving artist. You deserve to make a profit. Don't forget how long it takes you to create. You deserve to be paid for that time. Know what your hourly rate is. (Factor in all those hidden costs: overhead, materials, postage, marketing expenses, taxes, and commissions.) It is usually better to quote a flat fee for a project or a range (and pad or cushion that estimate to take into account unforeseen costs). Don't forget overhead costs. Don't compete on price. Compete by providing the best quality of work anywhere and going way beyond what they expect with service, so they say WOW! (Most people don't not buy because of price. They'll pay for quality. They buy things that satisfy their needs, solve their problems, get emotionally attached to, or if they recognize the brand.) You don't want to be the bottom of the barrel. The funny thing is, when you raise your prices, sales go up. Be the best and they will pay any price. When pricing, keep in mind that it took you half your friggin' life to develop your talent and technique so that you could do a quality job. So don't just give it away. Let's forget about the cost for a minute. What is the client willing to pay? What would you like to get? Then look at the cost. Quality is remembered long after price has been forgotten. Don't give away the store. Don't let people lowball you. They have money. If not, work out a trade. Retain the rights. Create a lower-cost version, but don't do it if you're going to lose money, even if it's a perfect piece for your portfolio. When people find out you'll work for free or are willing to substantially discount your rates, the word gets around. It tarnishes your image. Be very careful about being seen as a discounter. Be consistent. Hold firm to your price. Keep it simple, have one price you work from. Maybe you charge more for customization and quick turnaround, or if they pay cash or pay the entire amount up front. Oh, and say no to work if you feel they want to make crap and you want to make art. It's not worth the money.

What You Say

"What pisses me off is when I've got seven or eight record company fat pig men sitting telling me what to wear."

—Sinead O'Connor

A teacher was telling his speech class to avoid using slang words and expressions, saying, "I'll grade you down if I hear any 'dudes,' 'babes,' 'cools,' 'likes,' or 'you knows.'" "Bummer," exclaimed one of the students. How well you can articulate your thoughts is a part of promotion. That includes the words you use and how well you can string them together into cohesive thoughts. It's a skill worth developing.

Another aspect of speech that pertains to promotion is what you should NOT say. Think before you freak. Sure, you want to tell people to "go f—k themselves." That only works on "The Sopranos." Say it to yourself, in your head, but never out loud. Let it sit and simmer before you make matters worse and boil over. When you want to lash out you MUST take some time to cool off and think about the repercussions of what you are about to say. What will freaking out at someone really get you? Will that person help you then? Speak nicely about you? We don't want enemies. Many in the creative arts are part of very small, tight-knit communities, and people do talk. Take the feud between Joan Crawford and Bette Davis. Davis said about Crawford, "She slept with every male star at MGM except Lassie." A trait that many right-brained creative people use in creating great work can work against us when it comes to wanting to lash out, and that is our tendency to be emotional and take things personally. We need a little left-brain, rational thought at times like these. If you look at the back of any of my books in this series you will notice something is missing— my photo. I begged my previous editor to please put it on there. (It was to be part of my branding campaign.) When the book first came out, I rushed to the bookstore to get a copy. I turned the book over and no photo. I was pissed. I rushed home and called my editor to vent. He wasn't there. I overreacted and left the most inappropriate message on his machine. He called me a couple of days later to tell me he was out of town to be with his father and mother, who were both gravely ill and in the hospital. I regret making that call to this day. I have since made a label and stuck it on the receiver of the phone. It says "Patrick," the name of my old editor. Lesson learned.

Don't let your mouth write a check you can't cash, and honesty is the best policy. These are clichés, because like most clichés, they ring true. If you messed up, can't meet a deadline, can't deliver what you said you would, whatever, tell them you can't. Lies about our accomplishments or background are like wishes. We tell them so we can make ourselves into the kind of person we want to be or to get work we want to do. Rick Rockwell left out a few tidbits of information and embellished some others before he married Darva Conger on national television. Not good. Lies take on a life of their own and usually come back to haunt you. Lie about your credentials or inflate your capabilities and get caught, and it's hard to recover from that. The first time I went bungee jumping we did it from a balloon. The operator asked me what my weight was. I lied, a little. He set up the bungees based on the weight I told him. I was supposed to just graze the water. Well, let me tell you, I was completely submerged. That day I learned that lying can get you killed—and maybe I should shed a few pounds. Oh, by the way, don't forget that August 9 is National Admit You're Lying Day.

What You Write

> "Brevity is the soul of lingerie."
>
> —Dorothy Parker

There is a movement afoot for clearer, simpler writing. This plain language movement, which disdains jargon and celebrates short, conversational sentences with active verbs, is being embraced by both government agencies and big business. It began when President Clinton in 1999 instructed federal agencies to rewrite all documents that the public sees. The reality is that people are overwhelmed by the enormous amount of information they see and must decipher, and the speed in which they must do it in. We know that if people can't quickly discern what the hell you're trying to tell them, they trash it. Hint: You're not communicating very well if your letter is sitting at the bottom of someone's trash can. Know your reader. Spell their name correctly. Make sure you get their title right. The shorter the letter, the better. Before you begin, determine what your goal is. Capture their attention and get to the good stuff fast. (The what's-in-it-for-them part.) Make it clear what you want and tell them what to do next. Make it easy to reply. Don't bore them. Use a conversational tone. Inject some personality. Check for spelling (e-mails, too). Watch what you put in writing: Make it easy to read, with large margins and an easy-to-read font.

Thank You's

Mrs. Finkelstein gave her son two beautiful neckties when he left for college. When he returned home for summer vacation, he wore one of the ties to show his appreciation for the gift. Mrs. Finkelstein took one look at her son and asked anxiously, "What's the matter? The other tie you didn't like?" Saying thank you is so simple, so powerful, and so rare that people remember when you do it. It gives you an edge over 90 percent of your competitors. Others want to be recognized for their efforts. It shows you are responsible, responsive, and it bolsters your reputation. It also shows off your good manners and makes people want to work with you again. It's a perfect way to follow up with somone. It's a low-tech, inexpensive way to spread the word about your business. It's actually a top-notch tool to stay connected to clients. Make it a habit to send a thank-you card for every little thing someone does on your behalf. (Make it easy to do by buying cards in bulk, keeping stamps on hand and some cards with you so you can write when you're waiting somewhere with nothing to do.) You want to get them out quickly, but it's never too late to send one. The advanced creative person will very subtly promote themselves by creating their own thank-you cards and showing off their art and their good manners.

How Well You Do Your Work Is Marketing

"Every man's work, whether it be literature or music or pictures or architecture or anything else, is a portrait of himself."
—Samuel Butler

Tiger Woods is the top-rated golfer in the world, and as a result he is also the most marketable. Glen Keane is one of the best lead animators in the business. His work on Disney's *Tarzan* put him in another league and allows him to pick his projects. It's easier to sell yourself when your skills are stunning, where you stand out from the crowd because nobody does it better than you. Nobody works harder, has as much passion for your profession, is as proficient, does it the same way that you do, is as committed to the craft. These are major selling points. Robert DeNiro comes to mind. He is the best actor of the past few decades. He has turned in amazing (and authentic) performances in *Raging Bull, Taxi Driver* ("You talkin' to me?"), *Cape Fear* (my personal favorite, "counselerrr"), and *Goodfellas*. Not content to just show up and read his lines, he does the kind of mental and physical preparation for a film that makes him the best. The same can be said for Meryl Streep. You can't argue with her eleven Oscar nominations (and two wins). Be the best and people will beat a path to your door. Don't think so? Matt Damon gave such a powerful performance in a small supporting role in *Courage Under Fire,* shedding forty pounds to convincingly play a heroin addict, that it caught the attention of Francis Ford Coppola, who offered him the lead role in *The Rainmaker.* Eric Clapton may be a "god," and you can name a Carlos Santana solo in two notes, but to many of the top guitarists in the world today, Alan Holdsworth is the guitar hero's guitar hero. A fearless improviser with a finely honed sense of texture and dynamics, he is a "god." In fact, it was his masterful musicianship that prompted both George Benson and Eddie Van Halen to help him get record deals. It is his virtuosity that makes him marketable.

As Ralph Waldo Emerson said: "If a man can make a better mousetrap than his neighbor, though he builds his house in the woods, the world will make a beaten path to his door." Being the best at something is a powerful form of promotion. It instills in you the confidence you need to go out and sell yourself and your services.

☆ ───────────────
ACTION ITEM: GETTING FROM GOOD TO GREAT
Part One: Make a list of all of your strengths. This is no time to be modest. List all the things you do well and then narrow that list down to your top ten. Then organize your top ten talents into one-to-ten order, with one being the superior skill.

Part Two: Make a list of the ten top talents needed to get ahead in your field. Are any of your skills the most marketable in your chosen profession? Which skills should you work on improving?

Marketing Your Mastery
"Commitment to Excellence"

—*Oakland Raiders motto*

You are only as marketable as your skills. I mean really, what do you have to sell? Your talent and your track record, your potential and your portfolio. The more potential you have (you ace an audition), and the more powerful your portfolio (proving you have done it in the past), the better your chances for promoting yourself. You must constantly stay up-to-date and one step ahead of the competition. An ongoing program of honing and upgrading your skills is good marketing. Your excellence leads to word-of-mouth referrals and more work. (The opposite is true, too, of course. If you blow things off more than you blow people away, it gets around fast.) Sure, there are many people who have zero talent who have made it big, but in the long run it is talent that takes you to the top and allows you to stay there. Hype is fine for a while, but when you can really perform and consistently do good work, people notice and it pays off. If you are really cynical (and aren't all creative people?), you will point out there are MANY talented people who never get their big break. True, it's a combination of having extraordinary talent and finding a way to let the RIGHT people know about it. Here are some thoughts about how to let your talent take you to the top.

- Every job you do is a form of marketing and promotion. It shouldn't matter if you are paid a dollar or thousands of dollars, you always do your best work. Is that true for you?
- Work on your chops. Blues guitarist Charlie Baty practices two hours a day. "I hate it when I hear a musician say that they never practice. You have to have challenges. If not for themselves, they should be doing it for their craft." After a concert, a fan rushed up to famed violinist Fritz Kreisler and said, "I'd give my whole life to play as beautifully as you do." To which Kreisler replied, "I did." Are you still trying to improve your skills?
- Come up with a signature style. Producer Phil Spector was sought out by the Beatles and the Rolling Stones for his unique "Wall of Sound." He had a track record of producing hits like "You've Lost That Lovin' Feeling" and "Be My Baby," and had created a dense, complex, everything-and-the-kitchen-sink kind of sound. He was a master at what he did, and people wanted to work with him. What do you want to be known for?
- Drop the things you can't brag about. Do what you do best and forget about the rest. Cut out the crap and focus on making your strengths stronger. What are your strengths? In baseball, being labeled a utility player is the kiss of death. It's almost impossible to shake. When you master something, you build up a reputation, a following. Become known for doing great work in some area rather than good work in many areas.
- You never know who may be in the audience. As Lillian Gish once said, "It had been drilled into us that when an audience pays to see a performance, it is entitled to the best performance you can give. Nothing in your personal life must interfere, neither fatigue, illness, nor anxiety—not even joy." You should always set out to do the best show you can do.
- The same is true for your work. It's been said that "if a man is called to be a street sweeper, he should sweep streets even as Michelangelo painted, or Beethoven composed, or Shakespeare wrote poetry. He should sweep the streets so well that all the hosts of heaven and earth will pause to say, 'Here lived a great street sweeper who did his job well.'" Do sweat the small stuff. Do everything with excellence. Give your all. Tentative efforts lead to tentative outcomes. Pay

the price to do something extra well. Go the extra mile. Build something that will stand out for its greatness. Draw attention to yourself because of its magnificence.

• Have you noticed how many anecdotes and quotes and facts and figures and ideas are crammed into my books? I could have just as easily written this and other books off the top of my head. But I go the extra miles to make my books the best books EVER written on a subject. I am driven by the desire to be better than the other books. I will outresearch, outwrite, and outpromote anyone. As Debbi Fields (Mrs. Fields Cookies) says, "Good enough never is." Amen.

Ask a Pro
Tom Morey (starwavs@fea.net)
Inventor of the Morey Boogie Board

Having your name on every Boogie Board is pretty smart.
It is axiomatic in advertising to have and develop a STRONG personal image. Buying is very serious stuff. You are putting out hard-earned money and want real value. You also deserve to know WHO is responsible, just in case something goes wrong. You have to be there out front and say, "Yes, I take full responsibility for this thing, that's why my name's on it. I designed it (or approved the design), I specified the materials and handled the engineering. I am fully responsible for every aspect of the quality. Thus I, Henry Ford, Donald Boeing, or whoever, am the one who gets the credit or the blame. This is my reputation on the line."

What has been the most cost-effective method of promoting yourself and your inventions?
The very best form of promotion is to DILIGENTLY, to the best of one's ability, attempt to give the public major improvements at a very reasonable price. Then simply pick up the phone and call your local newspaper, telling them this. They need good news. I believe that STAYING FOCUSED on being of SERVICE to the public, first and foremost, and all the rest falls into place as a result.

Branding
"About two years ago I realized I was no longer a person but a brand."

—Martha Stewart

Tom Peters accurately describes a brand as a "trust mark." (He should know, he is a brand himself.) In a world of infinite choices, it's a sorting device. It's the buzzword for the new millennium. Everyone must become a brand, which means in essence that you have a loyal following who knows you, likes you, and, most of all, trusts you. The concept is definitely hip. People who can create a buzz about themselves and their products and practices will thrive in the future. It's nothing new to creative people who have been doing it for years. (Corporate America is just catching up, as usual.) Jack Daniel had a dashing mustache, planter's hat, silk vest, and broad bow tie, which became his trademark. Coco Chanel once said, "There are a lot of Duchesses, but only one Coco Chanel." Albert Einstien was branded. He was a symbol of genius and the first intellectual superstar. (And that hair.) Juan Valdez was always real tight with his donkey. Sy Sperling became a celebrity when he appeared in his own ads and said, "I'm not just the Hair Club for Men president, I'm also a client." The Rolling Stones had their lips and the Grateful Dead a skull logo. Apple computer is the ultimate example of branding. Mac users are fiercely loyal. (Not those bandwagoners who jumped ship at the first sign of trouble, but the loyal followers who will NEVER switch to a PC.)

It's not just for big-name acts or big business, either. Geofrey Berliner bought and repaired old pens and became known as "the Pen Doctor." He began writing a column for *Pen World* magazine (I know, who new there was a magazine for pen collectors?), became the director of Pen Collectors of America, founded the Pen Museum and a magazine called *Penfinder,* and even has a website about pens (the guy is like one hundred years old) in additon to his shop. Next he will design and market his own line of pens.

Branding yourself creates loyalty. It creates a following of people who appreciate what you do. They know what to expect, and making a decision about what to buy or whom to hire becomes a no-brainer. Growing up, every kid was into Evel Knievel. This guy was a brand master. He was unique. Nobody was as daring (he jumped the Grand Canyon!), distinctive (red, white, and blue color scheme), a master marketer (he was always on the news), and he parlayed it into endorsements (Wheaties) and licensing (I had the doll, the helmet, and a T-shirt). Jay Conrad Levinson branded his books with a series called "Guerrilla Marketing" and then did Guerrilla Marketing Online, for Home-Based Businesses, and so on. You keep buying them because you know they're good. A friend of mine started a company called "Hello," where they welcome new residents to a community, and local merchants provide samples or discount coupons to entice people to come in and hopefully become loyal patrons. Branding creates habits that are hard to break. A local bar puts pictures of patrons on the wall and gives you a mug with your name on it, and the owner (who looks like Hemingway) remembers your name and is always there to greet you. It's also been called positioning. It's about quickly telling others what makes you distinctive, different. It says to people who are inundated with marketing messages why you are great. It's about being recognizable in a crowd. What do you do better than anyone else? What makes you unique? Build your brand off of that. Branding is actually more important than what you sell. Just look at the Connecticut caterer (better known as Martha Stewart) who teaches the masses how to organize weddings, work in the garden, throw parties, decorate, dress—then sells her fans all the gear they need to do so. She does this with a monthly magazine, website, radio and TV segments, and a newspaper column, as well as her own line of merchandise.

When my parents were looking for a financial planner, they chose Bill Holland. Why? Because he's the best? Maybe. But in reality it's because he has his own radio talk show called "Money Talks," and that promotion led to my parents' preference to pick him over a LOT of other people to manage their money. This happens in a lot of fields. In the speaking world, meeting planners prefer known commodities. There is less risk and they are willing to pay more for a sure thing. Become the undisputed leader or authority in your field. Branding is also about your track record, your portfolio, and projects you've worked on. You need something worth bragging about. Can you name one magazine editor? Probably not, but there is one branded editor who has her name above the title. Not many, if any, magazine editors enjoy the unusual high profile of Tina Brown. The name of the magazine is called *Talk*, but many industry insiders simply call it Tina Brown's magazine. She earned that kind of recognition with a solid track record at *Vanity Fair*, the *New Yorker*, and other magazines. She is darn good at what she does and has developed into a brand that supersedes where she works. It is a long-term-relationship kind of marketing instead of hit-and-run. Instead of a series of one-night stands, it's a serious (and mutually beneficial) long-term committed relationship. You know what they like, what turns them on, and how to please them. Click and Clack (the "Tappet Brothers") have a show called "Car Talk" on NPR and a syndicated column. All John Grisham has to do is turn out a novel and it instantly becomes a best-seller. That is brand power, my friend. Read an old, reliable book if you like legal thrillers. Professional wrestlers are masters at branding. Rambo and Rocky are brands, as are James Bond and Austin Powers.

It can take a long time to build up trust equity, so don't ever do anything that creates ill will. AOL almost blew it when they overpromoted their service and frustrated the hell out of people with busy signals due to an overloaded system a few years ago. A wet-suit manufacturer known for making the best surf suits in the business began having their wet suits made in Mexico. The quality was worse than shoddy, it was . . . well, you know. They quickly quit having their suits made south of the border and avoided blowing their brand name. You can also ruin your reputation in an instant with work you do (poor) and people you associate with (unsavory). Be careful.

The perks of branding are a following that will buy whatever you have to offer, which you can parlay into a nice licensing deal (or in my case, a multicontract book deal). Publishers want authors with a following, a built-in audience. David Bowie even had an IPO offering "Bowie Bonds," and Prudential bought the entire $55 million offering. It could mean a lifetime gig like Desmond Llewelyn's role as Q, Her Majesty's gizmo guru, in the James Bond movies, a role he held for thirty-six years. (Funny thing was, he couldn't even program his own VCR.) You and your creations (and your methods) are the product. Shine the spotlight on yourself. Let people know how wonderful you are. Become known as a reliable and recognizable name brand. Be careful how you deal with others. Produce only quality work. Exude professionalism at all times. Have a hook (like the Motley Fools with their fun and playful approach). Branding starts with a look (Gateway's cow print boxes), a logo, a specialty, being damn good at what you do, creative, different, charismatic (Julia Child), focused, passionate (Martin Luther King), image (Michelle Kwan). Get out there and spread the word. Website, interviews, articles, appear in your own ads (Dave Thomas of Wendy's), and put a face on your product and identify yourself (Orville Redenbacher popcorn). Be consistent (script consultant, everything polished and professional) in what you stand for, and find a way to articulate it (write it down) and live it and love it. Who are you? This is a key question. What do you do? What is your top talent? How do you help people? What do you stand for? What is your passion? What do you offer? How are you different? Better? Best? Ask: What is my color/logo/best-known for? Want to be known for? My goal is to . . . ? My motto is . . . ? Memorable? Brand yourself, or someone else will do it for you. What are the three things you want people to think of when they hear your name? (Turn them into a sign or a T-shirt.) Marilyn Monroe, a brand herself, said: "If I'm going to be a symbol of something, I'd rather have it be sex than some other things we've got symbols of." Yes!

Ask a Pro

Sharilyn Miller
Editor of *Somerset Studio* magazine
smiller@stampington.com

How important is image in the success of an artist?

Image is very important in most lines of work, and perhaps even more so in the art professions. While the idea most of us carry around in our heads of "an artist" may be a sloppily dressed, paint-besplattered genius with a faraway look in his eyes, the truth is that if you want to be respected as a professional artist, you must present yourself professionally.

Does this include your attire?

It does include attire. If you freelance and meet clients face-to-face, present yourself well. Remember, clients are investing a lot of money in your work. Dressing well inspires trust; it sends a message that you are capable and successful. It also signals respect for yourself, your work, and your clients. This holds true whether you are a fine artist, commercial artist, or something in between.

Beyond the obvious of a clean, neat, and tasteful look, any other suggestions?

Keep jewelry to a minimum, but this is one area where an artist may express herself. Add a little splash of something creative. For example, you might add a wildly creative brooch on your lapel. Of course, you made it yourself or you know the artist!

Could you consider your portfolio and marketing materials an image accessory?

Yes. Your portfolio and marketing materials should also be "well-dressed." Your portfolio should be neat, clean, and creatively presented. The first sample should be your very best work, something with a "wow" factor to it. By all means, have a business card professionally printed. Do not rely upon your desktop printer for this. Your résumé and cover letter can be printed at home, but use the best possible paper you can afford. Check all your documents for spelling and grammatical errors before sending them out.

It's Not My Way or the Highway

Now, with all the advice given in this chapter (which will work), there will always be the case of the renegade artist who says, "Screw this, I'm going to get tons of tattoos, wear dreadlocks, dress however the hell I want, announce that I'm bisexual, state my political beliefs in a very public way, shun mainstream success (and major record labels), and say, in essence, I'm going to do it my way"—and then make it big. Singer, songwriter, and businesswoman Ani DiFranco is that artist. The folk-rock-punk musician built up a legion of loyal fans by touring college campuses and bars in a hand-painted car and with rainbow hair and now has fans who wait in freezing rain for tickets to her shows. She was determined to make music her way, and with $1,500 in borrowed money she founded Righteous Babe Records, which is now a fully staffed record label. After fifteen albums she has achieved mainstream success without having to conform or compromise her ideals. It can happen.

7

IT TAKES A VILLAGE TO RAISE
A BUSINESS
(It *Is* Who You Know)

"I get by with a little help from my friends."
—The Beatles

Let's assume for a moment that the Mafia is real. Come on, play along with me. Nobody is gonna know. Isn't the mob the perfect example of networking in action? Think about it. If one of the Godfathers calls an "associate" and tells him, "I got a friend of ours coming to see you, give him anything he wants, *capische?*" you know that the "associate" is going to go out of his way to help this person out of respect for the Godfather. It's the same in a lot of the creative arts. I am not saying that the mob runs the arts, but think about it for a minute. In many areas there is a clear power structure and a close-knit clan built around respect. It *is* who you know. You can move up a lot faster if you become a player or you know someone who has some juice.

I'll be completely honest. I have to force myself to get out and network. That will surprise some of the people who know me best, but like a lot of creative people, I am a loner by nature. (Some would say a recluse, but that's harsh, man.) I am my own best friend. But flying solo will get you only so far. You need several co-pilots to help you reach new heights in your career. It's so much harder and takes so much longer if you try to go it alone in creative careers. It's a myth that if you do good work you will be discovered. You need the help of influential people. Certainly I would prefer to hide out and write all day. But so many of the breaks I've had have come from networking that I decided a long time ago to do a little "reach out and touch someone" every day. An hour a day keeps the "real job" away is what I say. The time you invest in networking will pay off tenfold. Force yourself to make the time. At the very least get out and talk to other creative people. They can point you in the right direction or provide leads you never would have known about otherwise. I never pass up a chance to meet people. You never know. It could be life-changing.

Another reason we don't network is we're too busy doing work for existing clients. The only problem with that is, nothing lasts forever. You need to be on the lookout for new business, or all of a sudden you may be facing a drought. In the acknowledgments section of a book I was reading in preparation for writing this book, I came across the perfect example of how networking can lead to success. The book is called *Selling the Invisible* by Harry Beckwith, which became a best-seller thanks to a little help from his friends. The author begins the acknowledgments by talking about the inception (or is that conception?) of his book. A friend had "unwittingly" started the ball rolling by inviting (and then imploring) the author to give a talk to a strategic planning committee he was a part of. It was a smashing success. But it wasn't until he used the back of his speech notes (to save paper) to write a long letter to a friend that the book began to take shape. The friend, who turned the recycled paper over and read the speech, insisted that this should be published. The speech was edited and revised and run in a magazine. A well-known literary agent came across the article and felt it had the makings of a good book. She contacted the author and sold the book to the publisher. See, this is how it works. And it does work like this all the time.

Networking is marketing, although network marketing (or multi-level marketing) is something else entirely. The goal of networking (and marketing) is to form committed, long-term, mutually beneficial relationships (relax, I'm not talking about marriage) with people whom you can help and who can help *you*. It could be as simple as staying in touch or as involved as sending them referrals and going golfing on weekends. Make it a priority at the beginning of each month to connect with people. Look for opportunities to press the flesh. Set a goal of how many people you will meet, new clients you will connect with and win over, old clients you'll contact, and key people to call. Get out and see and be seen. Even if you don't want to meet new people, stay close to people in your orbit. One of my friends made this statement, which I know will sound sexist, but it's true. He said: Girlfriends come and go, but friends are forever. Only he put it this way: "Bro's before ho's." Treat your friends like gold. They are "money." Stay in touch. Be there for them. Remember important dates. Attend their openings, parties, etc. It's called long-term loyalty. Find friends that encourage you, that cause you to stretch what you think you can do— get you out of your comfort zone. Keep in mind, the goal isn't to see how many people you can contact but to connect with key people and develop a relationship that over time will benefit you both. Another consideration is to consolidate all of your efforts on getting to know a few key people in your industry (and the media) who have a large network of their own.

Networking Quiz
Answer honestly.

1. I have a stack of my business cards with me right now. T or F
2. I use a software program to maintain my mailing list. T or F
3. I send handwritten thank-you notes for even the smallest favors. T or F
4. I keep in touch with key people at least once a month. T or F
5. I have attended an industry-related function in the past month. T or F
6. I believe networking is the key to my success. T or F
7. I am not afraid to contact leaders in my field to ask for help. T or F
8. I am known as a good listener. T or F
9. I go out of my way to meet new people. T or F
10. I have and use e-mail to stay connected with people. T or F

(Any less than eight "True" answers and you will learn a lot from this chapter.)

Is Your Net Working?
"You can't help someone get up a hill without getting closer to the top yourself."

—General H. Norman Schwarzkopf

Networking should be one of your highest priorities, because it is one of the most effective and yet inexpensive forms of marketing. Networking is power. Power to pick up the phone and get things done or connect with people who can get it done for you, people who can open doors for you. They are called "Godfather" calls, because one call from the right person and you can get what you need. Most of the success people have achieved in the arts is a result of relationships. For example, a friend of mine who is an editor at a major magazine admits that he has a stable of writers that he likes to work with and always offers them first crack at assignments. He likes using these same free-lance writers because he knows he can count on them, but more important, he likes them. If you aren't one of the "chosen ones" you would think this stinks. But it's reality. People like to work with people who not only consistently do good work, but whom they know and like (and trust.). It's the difference between a cold call and a warm call. Which sounds better? Exactly. With a call on your behalf or just dropping a name, you can go from a nobody to having your calls returned and proposals read. You have a better chance to get in on the cool projects—projects you want to work on. Knowing the right people can lead to work that is fun, fulfilling, and the first step to launching your career. If you can get to one key person and really WOW! them, they'll tell their influential friends. When someone else is singing your praises, it's music to people's ears. The reason is that people prefer to work with those they know and trust and are comfort-able with. They can be your champion. Keyboardist Chick Corea was earning a reputation as more than just a dependable professional, but also a pianist who added something extra to those he was playing with. He played with Stan Getz and Sarah Vaughan (a great gig), but being in a band with Miles Davis was a coveted spot. When Tony Williams, a friend from Boston and a member of Miles Davis's band, recommended Chick to replace to Herbie Hancock, he played with Davis for several years and on four albums. This led to a great deal of exposure and credibility and eventually a very successful solo career.

Make a good impression with people you work with so they will want to work with you again. Andy Garcia had worked as a waiter and on loading docks while attending open auditions. He also did a little stand-up comedy at the Comedy Store in Los Angeles. A casting agent saw him and gave him a role as a gang member on the show "Hill Street Blues." That led to a movie role as a detective in *The Mean Season.* One of the producers, Fred Roos, developed a friend-ship with Garcia—an important connection because Roos was closely aligned with Francis Ford Coppola, who cast Garcia in *The Godfather III.* You can't make it on your own, no matter how talented you are. That's what Marcus Roberts told a young Wynton Marsalis, who says: "One man can only do so much. That's the first thing Marcus Roberts taught me when he came into the band. He said, 'You can't make it out here alone. Period.' And that's the truth."

It *Is* Who You Know

"At that point, my peers were all gay male dancers. I wanted to be accepted. I wanted to be a gay male dancer."
— Carrie Fisher, on being a teenager in Las Vegas

The creative world is people-oriented and built on relationships. It's really a small community. You want to be able to have someone make a call on your behalf. It's done all the time. Look at the speed dial on your phone. Other than pizza delivery and your mom, who is on it? Being an industry insider with good connections means you know what's happening before it happens. You get the inside track on what projects are in the pipeline, and that inside track gives you an edge when you make your pitch to work on the project.

Magician David Blaine can count Robert De Niro and Leonardo DiCaprio as friends, Woody Allen as a fan, and Fiona Apple as a girl-friend (as of this writing). "I want to do for magic what Ali did for boxing," boasts the personable performer. With goals like that, it's good to have influential friends. In the movie *The Secret of My Success,* Michael J. Fox contacts a distant uncle to get a job—albeit in the mailroom. Start with family and friends. This is an easy first step. (You aren't being a bugger.) Just tell them what you're trying to do and ask if they know anyone who might help. If you don't have a list yet, now is the time to start building one. Make a list of *everyone* you know. Use mind-mapping. Break it down by category. Key contacts. Start with family and friends. They want to support you and see you make it (and move out of the house?) and are usually willing to help. It's great when your family is both large and spread out (and not a bunch of losers). You can mobilize them. One author I know has family and friends all over the country setting up book signings and putting her titles face out. They also contact the media in their towns. (Same could be done for a musician, artist, or any other creative person.) She also offers a family discount on her books and sells literally hundreds of copies (family members give them as gifts). My mother-in-law (who, for the record, is great) sells my books to her customers at her salon. At the very least tell everyone what your dream is. Get them to be a part of it. Build the buzz by letting people you know spread the word. If every friend told two friends (who then told two friends), you could really build some momentum.

It's not how many people you know, but knowing the right people, or at least people who know the right people. Get outside of your comfort zone. Reach out and try to meet and befriend people who are major players in your field. You may be surprised by how much you have in common, how easy it is to reach these people, and how willing many "celebrities" are to help up-and-comers. The worst thing that can happen is that they won't return your e-mail or will say they aren't interested. Big deal. I pay attention to people in *People* magazine, and if they mention they struggle with something I can help them with, *bam,* I mail a book and a letter to them or their agent. This has paid off for me. I have been able to develop relationships with celebrities I would never have had a chance to meet otherwise. Offer samples and services to celebrities (and hope they talk you up in interviews and tell their influential friends. It's like free advertising). Quality, not quantity, counts. In addition to the big-name people on your list, don't forget about networking with their assistants and gate-keepers, and other behind-the-scenes people. Also, network with your peers as well.

Cut the fat and focus on key people. Make a list of ten to twenty people whom you trust, respect (hopefully don't compete with), and want to work with. (I have an alternate list, or "waiting list," of key people, too.) Spend the bulk of your time developing a friendship or working relationship with people you like, can learn from, share leads with, and who can open doors for you. Get rid of the deadweight on your list—the backstabbers, time-wasters, flakes, fuckers, fuckups, and buzz killers. Look at your list (or shuffle through your stack of business cards) and create a "Money List" of top players and what they may represent in dollars and sense. (Good for business, psyche, etc.) It's not enough to just have a list. You have to have a system to follow up with people. Lightning strikes twice. Look at past invoices to see who has been an actual paying customer. It also helps to look back and see who has never shown up at anything, bought anything, or done anything positive for you.

Look in acknowledgments of books and CDs, mastheads, articles, directories, and the Internet for new people to connect with. Don't discount people who can't help you now. Everyone is a client, so treat them like one. Look outside your industry for people to connect with. You never know who's in their network. If you aren't meeting anyone new, try traveling in different circles. Look for up-and-comers, and climb to the top together. Refer clients back and forth. Share contacts and leads. Take advantage of underused but talented people.

Look for people like yourself. Here's a strange one. Raleigh Pinskey, the author of *101 Ways to Promote Yourself,* began going to lunch with another Gemini to celebrate their birthdays. Before she knew it, more and more Geminis started joining them (a friend of a friend of a friend) and it took on a life of its own. In addition to being a lot of fun, it was also a great way to get leads and referrals. Develop friendships with key people. Don't just meet people. Go the extra mile and try to make them your friends. When Bruce Willis and Matthew Perry made a movie together, they became fast friends—so much so that Bruce Willis appeared on "Friends" as a favor to Matthew. You can get people who matter to back you, write a blurb, or be on your album.

You don't want to ask, "Why am I always the last to know?" You need inside information, confidential informants, good intel. You want to turn people into double agents. Stay in touch with your spies. Talk to anyone and everyone. Ken Blanchard (*The One Minute Manager*) talks to cabbies, bellmen, secretaries—anyone. He likes to listen. He gets them going about their lives and uses the material in his books. Tell everyone what YOU do (or are trying to do). Pay attention. Read the newspaper and watch the news and then ask yourself: "How does this affect me?" If someone you know has moved to a bigger, better job, congratulate them. If they won an award, do the same. If you like to be the star, network by performing and giving speeches. Put your contact information on everything. Be accessible. Reach out.

You can buy instant friends and acquaintances. Well, not exactly, but you can purchase lists of contacts. Buy them based on people you want to work with. People with money. The better your list, the better the response.

Networking Is a Contact Sport

"When you can't be seen in elevators, you compensate, so I make a lot of noise."

—Linda Obst, the five-foot-tall producer of
Sleepless in Seattle *and* One Fine Day

Debi Coleman, CEO of the Merix Corporation (and once part of the team that developed the first Mac), founded the Silicon Valley Refugee Club, moving to Forest Grove, Oregon. The group meets periodically at Portland restaurants to gab and gossip about the computer industry. Want to go from a nobody to a somebody in a hurry? Meet as many people as possible in as many places as you can. Not just clients, but peers as well. Where do they hang out? What organizations and clubs do they belong to?

A girl in every port. I built my mailing list by going on the road to promote my books and give seminars. There has to be an easier way. There is, and it's called the Internet. Almost everything I did (the hard way) will be (and already is) easier with e-mail, online seminars and discussion groups, virtual trade shows and websites. The goal is to connect and reconnect with people who can help you further your goals. The method may have changed (no more frequent flier miles) but the results can be better (and easier) to obtain.

Stalking your prey the right way. Whom do you want to know? How can you make them an ally? This is going to sound so simple, but the best way is to initiate contact with them. Why not? You probably have something they want. Figure out what that is (maybe it's just to praise them and boost their already inflated ego) and begin by calling or sending an e-mail. Nothing will happen until YOU make it happen. You may have to be persistent (if they take out a restraining order on you, you went too far), but you can get to just about anyone with a little determination and a dial tone.

There is no free lunch. Find out what charities key people volunteer at and do it, too. Don't just join, get involved. Use your talent. (Do a newsletter and offer to interview the person you want to meet.) Doing good is good for you. You will be making a difference and maybe meet a few like-minded people who can become valuable contacts.

Earn while you learn. One way to build your Rolodex is to take a day job that will put you in position to meet many of the people you will want to do business with later. This could be in the form of an internship, part-time work, apprenticeship, or as a volunteer. You'll be able to interact (and hopefully impress) people who would be otherwise inaccessible. Mark Rappaport tells other inventors, "Don't quit your day job." He worked at Mattel and Parker Bros., where he proved he could develop a $100 million product. Two of the many inventions he can take credit for are the Nerf bow and arrow and a whistling football. He also credits his contacts in the toy business who helped him when he went out on his own. He now pedals his latest invention, a bike/scooter called the California Chariot. "It's 99 percent relationships and one percent product."

Invite people to see you perform and play. Convert them to fans.

Gather around. Organize panel discussions and invite people you would like to get to know better. Organize a brown bag lunch group that gets together; roundtables, mastermind, and brainstorming groups.

Joined at the hip. When I was in art school the dean was the president of the Ad Club. I was a cocky son of a gun and I wanted to meet and maybe even befriend him. It worked out just as I had planned. I became closer to the dean and other advertising people at the Ad Club. There were other perks, too. I heard some powerful presenters, ate at some awesome restaurants, and even made a few friends. You can buy mailing lists from associations and clubs you belong to. Trade leads. Get gossip. Find out inside information. Be in the directory. Listen to speakers and learn. Find a mentor. It gives you credibility. Increase visibility by being a speaker, giving a demonstration, or writing for the newsletter.

End run. Invite the assistant of a key player you want to meet to lunch.

Party crasher. Most newspapers have a calendar-of-events section where you can find out about meetings, book signings, open-mike nights, gallery openings, seminars, charity functions, and other gatherings that could be a place to meet and mingle with VIPs. Also read your trade magazine and association newsletters for industry-specific events.

Funny seeing you here. Bumping into important people outside of traditional networking circles is less stress. Find out where they hang out (and where their kids hang out) and "accidentally" bump into them there.

Just for fun. I heard about "leisure networking," where you arrange golf games, getaways, and gigs for people you want to get to know better. Or just call to invite people to do something fun. I like to take people on my boat for the day. I have also arranged Key West trips, retreats, dive trips, beach cleanups, bike tours, hiking trips, booze cruises, basketball and baseball games, parties, and a few things I could get in trouble for but that were definitely bonding experiences.

Party on, Wayne. When Cameron Diaz was a junior in high school, she attended a Hollywood party where she received a number of business cards from people who told her she could be a model. One of the cards looked legit (it had an actual address on it!), so she followed up and met with an agent, along with her parents, and a week later was signed to a contract with the Elite modeling agency. Do you like to party? Well, alllllllllright. Make it work for you. A lot of the best networking takes place at parties.

Let's get physical. My strategy is to hold big parties so that everyone is in one place at one time. That way I can press the flesh all at once. We also always do networking games, too. (It sounds silly, but it's fun.) At one such party I had everyone write three things about themselves on their name tags and make one of them NOT true. One guy, whom I've known for years, wrote: (1) I'm a pilot, (2) I'm wearing a wig, and (3) I'm gay. I knew for a fact that he was a pilot, but I was afraid to guess which of the other two things were NOT true. (It was number two.) Needless to say, my party was a "coming out" party for him.

Support system. Betty Jurus is well-known in the San Diego writing community as a writer and someone who supports other writers. In 1983 she founded The Writers' Haven, a bookstore and more. It was a place where a writer could buy a book, sell their books, have their books published, put on a workshop, or find solitude in one of the quiet rooms in the back. It should have been called Writer's Heaven and not Haven, if you ask me. One day Gene Wentz walked into the store. The Navy SEAL was looking for a collaborator to help him write about his experiences in Vietnam. Betty, who had a fascination with the SEALs, teamed up with him to write *Men in Green Faces*. Her efforts to help others ended up helping her the most. (Sadly, the store closed a few years ago, but her book is still in print.)

Toasters. Toastmasters and other support groups offer a chance for personal growth, and you can "grow your business" by attending. (For a while AA was the hot networking place in Hollywood. Even people without a drinking problem were attending.)

☆ ————————————————
ORGANIZED OBSESSIONS
Whom do you associate with? Here are a few offbeat associations you may want to team up or network with at their meetings. Or not. Adult Video Association, American Council of Spotted Asses (donkey and burro owners), Beaver Defenders, Beer Drinkers of America, Hug Club, Loners of America (must be some fun meetings, eh?), and the National FRUMPS of America.

Plan and Win/Win
> *"Win-win is a belief in the Third Alternative. It's not your or my way—it's a better way."*
>
> —Steven Covey

When Doug Fieger was a seventeen-year-old high-schooler in Detroit, he wrote a letter to record producer Jimmy Miller ("Gimme Some Lovin' ") and asked him to sign his band, The Sky. Miller didn't sign the band but did look Fieger up when he came to town. Miller asked Fieger to show him around Detroit and take him to Motown Studios. After playing tour guide, Fieger took the producer to his basement, where he and his bandmate played several songs. He got a record deal and moved to Los Angeles, where he founded The Knack and hit it big with the song "My Sharona." You need a plan of attack. Start by clearly defining what your needs are. What do you want help with? How can you best articulate that to others?

Do research into who can help you. Make a list (or mind map) of people you want to meet. Look at the list and ask yourself, "What do I have to offer them? How can I be of service to them?" Not only people who are already successful, but also talented people you can help make successful. Play a game similar to "Six Degrees of Kevin Bacon" and think of who you know who know these people. Then use your creativity to think of backdoor ways to get to these people. How many people (that can help build your business and advance your career) will you contact each day? No matter what, you must contact them. When you go to an event, set a goal of how many new people you will meet. Make it a game. I will attend one industry-related event per month, make five calls to contacts every day, and send out six newsletters this year. Write it in your calendar. You need to treat it seriously, like a creative project. Set specific goals. Do you want to expand your business? Improve your image? Meet influential people? Get paid more? Increase your visibility? Have more respect and power? More work? Get better work? It's also a mind-set. You are always on the lookout and prepared for networking opportunities. A savvy networker always carries business cards. A super duper networker also has brochures, a mini-portfolio, and samples of his work. You don't just call when you need something. You look for ways to help others first, and then when you need help you can call in a favor. You find out how key people prefer to be contacted and communicated with. It shows you care and respect their time. You keep detailed information about your "key" people. These are vital stats like on a baseball card. Hometown, birthday, college, accomplishments, hobbies, spouse and kids' names, and what they may need. When you are invited to their parties, kid's graduation, openings, weddings—you are there.

Get the Ball Rolling: Conversation Starters

"Half the world is composed of people who have something to say and can't, and the other half who have nothing to say but keep on saying it."

—Robert Frost

Remember on the "Peanuts" television specials when the teacher was talking to the class and all you would hear was wha, wha, wha, wha and so on? That's how most people listen until you say something like "nipple" or "penis," then they perk up. How do you break them out of their trance without dropping an "f-bomb"? Be bold and break through the clutter with something clever or outrageous. One artist takes her little dog everywhere. This is quite the conversation starter except for with people who have asthma. You could also come up with your own custom name tag that you bring with you to meetings. Or take the name tag you are given and jazz it up. Make it interactive. Draw a picture of what you do and ask others to try and guess what it is. Write your name in tiny letters but what you DO in larger letters. When someone asks Jeff Smith, a motivational speaker, he'll open up his wallet to grab a business card and all of a sudden it's on fire. (It's a fairly simple magic trick and it gets people talking and asking him for a card. His cards all have burned edges—by design.) Be ready for the inevitable "So, what do you do?" People don't want a long-winded and detailed description. Have a funny one-liner like "I founded LSD . . . Lee Silber Designs, yuk yuk yuk." An electrician had one: "I remove people's shorts." A cleaning service also had one: "I like it when people talk dirty to me." A handyman's was: "I can do anything your husband can do, but I'll do it now." More? A travel agent uses: "People see me for a good time (pause for effect)—I'm a travel agent." I have used "I give people the gift of time" and "I put people in their right mind, and I help others get in touch with their creative side." You could also throw them a curve and talk about your hobbies, pointing out, "I am more than my job." Or maybe you could tell them what you would *like* to be doing.

Keep the Ball Rolling: Avoiding Dead Air

"Talk low, talk slow, and don't say too much."

—John Wayne

Jay Trachman in the book *One to One* shared this story about his networking skills. One night while driving home from a party his wife asked him, "Honey, has anyone ever told you how handsome, sexy, and irresistible to women you are?" "No, not lately," he replied. To which his wife said, "Then what gave you that idea at the party tonight?" Niiiiiice. While some people are flirtatious, others are wallflowers. In a goal-setting group I started with Liz Livingston, we had a lot of very outgoing people, and I think it freaked out some of the shy members. To offset this Liz tried to pair off the shy people with each other as goal partners. Liz also asked them to help out and work on projects like our annual awards show or beach party. That way they could work with other members and get to know them in a nonthreatening way, since the focus isn't on networking but on the project itself. Some of these "shy" members are still friends years later. This is a skill you need to develop. Try role-playing with another creative person.

Another Quiz? Yes!
Check off the following traits that describe you.
—You understand that not everyone will be a good fit with you—
    it's not personal.
—You will work the room rather than sit with friends for
    an entire meeting.
—You are upbeat, supportive, and rarely bad-mouth anyone.
—You stay up on current events in your field and other areas, too.
—You are a good listener and encourage others to talk
    about themselves.
—You are genuinely interested in other people.
—You are good at finding common ground with others.
—You like to look for things you can compliment others on.
—You make other people feel important.
—You avoid arguments whenever possible and instead look
    for common ground.
—You are sympathetic with other people's ideas and desires.

To be a good networker, having at least half of these traits will prove helpful.

BREAK THE ICE

To stand out and break the ice at meetings, one of the best approaches I have seen was by a very creative (and thoughtful) person who brought bundles of flowers and handed them out as he worked the room and introduced himself. Another clever approach was a photographer who brought a Polaroid camera with her to meetings and offered to take people's pictures and hand it to them on the spot. It was a great way to get a conversation going. (She put a sticker with her company name on the back.)

Networking Never Ends

"Unbearable solitude—I cannot believe it or resign myself to it."
—Albert Camus

In Norfolk, England, police sent Christmas cards to ex-cons essentially warning them that Santa may not be watching during this festive period, but the local cops are. The exact wording was: "Wishing you a Merry Christmas and a Happy New Year. Norwich Police will be actively targeting known burglars and car thieves this Christmas—but we are thinking of you throughout the year." The card went on to offer a reward if you "ratted" on a fellow con and called Crimestoppers. This is a great example of good networking skills. Stay in touch with your key people (hopefully they aren't ex-cons) and offer a reward for referrals.

The goal is to build your Rolodex. To turn perfect strangers into partners. To stay connected to key people because out of sight is out of mind. (How many leads or gigs did you miss out on by being incommunicado?)

Make a Top Ten list. Jason McCabe Calacanis is the founder of two magazines that cover the Internet industry: *Silicon Alley Reporter* in New York, and *Digital Coast Reporter* in L.A. In 1997 he came up with the idea to have a kind of "Hot 100" listing of Silicon Alley top Internet companies. Being on this list is a big deal. He also holds conferences and dinner parties that bring together key people in the cyberbusiness community. His mini–media empire has made him an insider's insider. He knows all the players and in many cases has introduced them to each other. It would be easy to do the same thing (on a smaller scale) with your own newsletter, conference, hot list, or dinner parties.

You want a piece of me? Find soft-sell ways to stay in people's faces. Here is a good example. One creative person loves to read those boring business books (if you are even thinking that this is one of them, shame on you), so she takes notes and does a summary (called "What I Learned") and does a review for the people in her network on audiocassette. Not only do people appreciate it, they are encouraging her to write her own book! She now has an agent (based on a recommendation from someone who gets the tapes). She also posts her reviews on her websites and in her newsletter. You could do this for restaurants, CDs, products, or services. Have follow-up materials that are *not* sales pitches.

Be an instigator. Hold an event, throw a party, start a club, organize a roundtable. At events, make networking part of the fun. Be the one who gets things going, keeps it moving, makes it memorable. When you are on the road, make the effort to look people up and invite them out. There is nothing like a personal connection.

Don't call us, we'll call you. Nuh-uh, I will call YOU. Don't wait for them to call you. So few follow up that it actually makes you look impressive. One in a million. Write notes on the back of their card. Do it as soon as you get home. E-mail is the fastest way, but a call or a package the next day is good. Drop it off. Whoa! Keep track of correspondence and follow-ups. Call at off hours or at their home to avoid the gatekeeper. Get organized, or else it is difficult to follow up. (There is a person who can't recall if she mailed me something, so she keeps sending me the same stuff, and it isn't even what I asked for. Aarrrggghhh. I'm thinking FLAKE, not the impression she wanted to make, I am guessing.) Follow up and do what you say you will do. Keep all your supplies on hand. Don't procrastinate your networking responsibilities.

Look for ways to make it memorable. When I found out that a local celebrity was also an avid water-skier (a barefoot skier, no less), I suggested that instead of meeting for lunch in a restaurant (boring), we meet in the morning (when the water is most calm) for skiing, and then have breakfast. Now we have a bond that can't be broken.

Don't ever sell out the people in your network. Guard your mailing list (and reputation) with your life.

Carry your marketing materials with you at all times. Be ready when a networking opportunity presents itself. I made a container with marketing materials and samples that I keep in the trunk of my car.

Look for ways to connect with your A-team. Send articles you think would interest them. Give them referrals (that will get their attention). Remember their birthday or anniversary. Follow-up and staying connected are key. Don't be out of touch too long.

411. You can get people to come to you by being a clearinghouse of information. When someone needs something, they know you're the person who can help. You can do this with your website. You could sponsor a bulletin board where others can post problems and leads and ask for assistance. By providing links to others or an opportunity for people to connect to others, it doesn't really help you. Try to help them out yourself, instead. When they have to call or e-mail you, you can weed out the things you want to do—or pass it on to someone else in your network.

Group therapy. You can't join every networking group (nor should you), so offer to be a speaker at these groups. Not only is it good publicity, but by being a speaker you are elevated to celebrity status in their eyes. You can meet more people by giving one talk than by being a member for months.

Fun to be around. On the set of the film *Virgin Suicides,* young actress Kirsten Dunst turned her trailer into a retreat for the other actresses. She made a collage on the wall of everyone's photos (cast and crew), and instead of hiding out in her trailer, it was a place for everyone to meet, eat, play, paint, and gab.

☆ ————————————————

ACTION ITEM

Of course, you want to try to build up your mailing list. It's even more important to stay in touch with the people you already have as contacts. Make it a weekly thing and make it easy to do. Carry supplies with you, have them accessible. The easier it is to do, the more likely you will do it. Send one note a day. (Send a Blue Mountain card every time you check your e-mail.) Double the number of thank-you notes you are sending now. (Even if they didn't hire you, send one anyway.) Get in the habit of sending personal notes and cards (birthday, sympathy, congratulations, anniversary of time you have been together doing business). Of course, send your newsletter on a regular basis as a way of staying in touch. Finally, I send postcards from the road as a way of staying connected.

How to Be a Mensch

"Diplomacy is to do and say the nastiest thing in the nicest way."
—Isaac Goldberg

What is a mensch? An upright, trustworthy person, worthy of respect. They put people first and go out of their way to help others without even being asked. Here are the five traits that make for a mensch (or menschette).

1. Thoughtful. While I was working on this book, and pulling my hair out, my good friend (and a menschette) Harriet Schechter (also an author) sent me an uplifting article pointing out that many famous authors are late turning in their manuscripts. Boy, that made me feel good. In terms of marketing, all Harriet has to do is ask and I will help her sell, promote, or review her books. Networking, the mensch way, isn't about trying to see how much you can get from the other person. Instead, it's about wanting to help others. Ask not what a contact can do for you, but ask what can you do for your contact. For me, it's not an act. I genuinely want to help other people.

2. Respectful. The mensch treats everyone with respect. At Qualcomm, when the stock went up and split four times, it made many of the people who worked for the wireless company what we call "Quillionares," or put another way, RICH! So, you never know, the janitor at Qualcomm could be a patron of the arts, so treat everyone like gold. Respectful also means that you return calls promptly, follow through when you make a commitment, and you would never do anything to make you look bad. You can refer business to them and know they would never let you down. Be respectful of other's opinions. They try to never piss people off and will go out of their way to patch things up. They are also respectful of the up-and-comers and take the time to help them because, as Cyril Connolly said, "Always be nice to those younger than you because they are the ones who will be writing about you."

3. Loyal. It's been said that friendship is when people know all about you but like you anyway. Martin Scorsese has known Robert De Niro since the two were teenagers. Their collaboration has been beneficial for both the actor and the director. Together they have made *Mean Streets, Taxi Driver, Raging Bull, Goodfellas,* and *New York, New York.* See what I mean? When I first started doing my radio show, I had no trouble choosing guests. I looked at my list of supporters and started there. It was my chance to pay back the people who had supported me. It was a no-brainer.

4. Appreciative. Many performers fail to thank those who have helped them get where they are. One person who always gives her producers public credit is Madonna. It's partly because of self-confidence, and because it makes other collaborators more likely to want to work with her. As a practicing mensch, I am always appalled at those who are the anti-mensch. There is one person in particular who pops into my mind. Bitch. I have helped her get a book published, lined up an ongoing series of talks for her with a seminar company, sent her several consulting clients, had her on my radio show, and mentioned her book in one of my previous books. Has she ever said thanks for all the promotion I have provided her? Noooooooooo. When I finally called her on her behavior and said, "Hey, this is a two-way street, lady," she said, and I quote, "I can't help you, I've got to think of myself first." Well then, screw you! I may be a mensch, but I'm not a schmuck!

5. Generous. A mensch would much rather give than take. They keep a plus balance in their "favor given/received account" with each person and never make a withdrawal on a negative balance (without doing something for them first). They offer advice and help when asked. They will pass on a lead or referral without hesitation. They want to help. Actress Marlee Matlin, who is hearing impaired, sent a note to Aaron Sorkin praising him for a deaf storyline on "Sports Night," a show he created. He wrote her back thanking her and to let her know he was creating a part for her on his other hit TV series, "West Wing." (She has a recurring role as Joey Lucas, a congressional campaign manager.)

Beyond the Basic Business Card

"I may never get an Oscar, but at least I'll have a game."
—Kevin Bacon on the game "Six Degrees of Kevin Bacon"

A business card must be functional (clear about what you do and stand for), but that doesn't mean we can't have a little fun with it. The business card is the most basic and effective networking tool. You almost must have one. It's the minimum piece of equipment for any networker. It's a cheap form of advertising, but that doesn't mean you should skimp here. (No, and I repeat, no preformatted paper should be used for a business card. You deserve better!) This is your chance to make a good first impression. Don't blow it by handing them a boring or flimsy business card. When you hand someone your card you want them to say, "That is soooooo cool." You want a combination of cool-ness, credibility, and contact information. Blow them away with your creativity and bowl them over with your professionalism. (Those two seem diametrically opposed, but they aren't.) It can be clever and rele-vant and stay in keeping with your image. Make your card a work of art. It's a chance to show off your sense of style, taste, creativity, and innovative thinking. Be bold. Be better than the rest.

"Okay, okay, I get it," you may be saying, "but I don't have time." The biggest creativity killer is a lack of time. True, this is *not* something you do in a hurry. Look at books on award-winning designs, go through the stack of cards in your desk drawer for ideas, and then break the mold. The elements you have to work with include size, folds, font, color, art, paper, text, and graphics. Let's explore some ideas in these areas.

Brochure cards. Combine a business card and a brochure. Maybe you make your card into a mini-brochure with several panels. It's better than a regular card and more portable than a big brochure. Chuck Green (who is featured at the end of this chapter) has an outstanding mini, multipage brochure that fits in a wallet.

Hey, I'm royalty. Change your title to something clever like "Grand Poobah" or "Chief Trouble Maker" or "Big Cheese."

Nice backside. Consultant Mary Lea Balsley's business card has a photo and four panels where the recipient can write in, "What I said I would do" and "What you said you would do." Other ideas include putting samples of your art on one side and contact information on the other, a calendar, tour dates, recipes, software shortcuts, related websites or samples of websites you designed, toll-free numbers, coupon, your rates, list of your services, testimonials, list of past clients, or a mini-notepad (so you can write a personal message to them). One artist includes directions to his (hard to find) studio on the back. A comedienne could put her best one-liners on the back or a website where you can see more of her work. The back could include a place to write in an appointment. Include a quiz or interesting tidbits on the back. An author put in a bar code for his book to make it easier to order and check stock on the title as well as the sales history.

It's like a little ad. A business card can be an announcement for a new book— your cover on the front and a summary or table of contents or order information on the back, including the pub date and price.

Rolodex card. Make your business card a Rolodex card as well.

Tell a friend. Cards in three parts with the first and last parts being real cards and the middle one spelling out how to get a $100 gift certificate for referrals.

What are Cub Scouts in the rain? In tents. Your business card could be a freestanding "tent" that people could keep handy. (It folds over and stands on its own.) Especially if you have useful information on the back. A professional editing service might put what all those silly-looking editor symbols mean. I'd keep that where I could see it.

A cut above. Die-cut your letterhead so your card slips right in. Or make your business card a flap on your letterhead. If you use legal-size paper (on card stock), your business cards could be at the bottom of the larger paper (perforated) and could be torn off.

That's odd. Odd materials like transfer paper (clear) or plastic (waterproof) or thin wood (carpenter) stand out. At the least, do not use preperforated paper you run through your ink-jet (if you can help it). It's cheap and it says cheap. If you make it an odd shape or size they have to say, "Hmm, where should I put this?"

Make it stick around. A business card could also be a sticker, magnet, or even window-clinging material (like what the oil-change places use on your windshield). I even saw one with a neon Band-Aid stuck on it. Add a sticker for color and pizzazz. Use a dash of colored ink or paint or even a crayon.

Double duty. If the size of a CD cover or postcard is okay for a card, it can do double duty.

Take one. You can turn cards into a pad (or stack) with a header card that encourages people to take one.

Yummy. How about edible cards made out of chocolate? I used to have one, but I ate it.

Get creative. Odd shapes like a camera or coaster, shaped like a bass amp or an ice cream Popsicle (complete with stick). One card was die-cut (I hope) with a bite taken out of it (for a caterer). Another had the top cut to look like a brown paper bag for company that makes sandwiches for convenience stores. An engineering company's card said "We rule!" and had a ruler on it. A gym had a place on their cards to write in your starting weight and measurements and your ideal weight. (Weigh cool?) Maybe you could make your business card look like a baseball card. A psychologist's card included a stress test. I got one that was a bag of beach sand with a card inside from a travel agent. Put paw prints from your dog. Blow up your card on a copier and use the back as notepaper. Include a mini-article on the back with a link to your website for the rest. Make it look like a parking violation and put them on windshields. Have them printed reversed so you have to hold the back of the card up to a mirror (promised special message). You can now have cards made that play music when opened. For you, the creative thinker, the sky's the limit.

Mentors: Your Mr. Miyagi

"I read biographies of the greats, and they were so messed up that I thought I'd better myself up. But I couldn't, I'm too small."
—*Winona Ryder*

It's good to have friends in high and low places. Van Halen built a solid following in the Los Angeles club circuit, but it wasn't until Gene Simmons of Kiss brought the band to the attention of Warner Bros. that they were signed to a record deal in 1978. It happens all the time in the music business. Creative people can't (and shouldn't) try to go it alone. If you want to cut the amount of time it takes to make it, then get a mentor. They can give you direction, steer you in that direction, and keep you on track and from crashing as you go down the road that they have already driven.

My mentors have been so helpful that I often wonder where I would be without them. One call from my mentor and I'm having lunch with a book industry legend. That kind of says it all. I never knew what doors to open and how to open them when I got there. My mentors escorted me to the correct door, opened it, and then pushed me through. Ride on the coattails of someone who has already made it. A good example is the teaming up of Grammy winners Carlos Santana and Rob Thomas of Matchbox 20. The only question I have is, who was riding whose coattails to success? Madonna has her own label (Maverick Records), and she signed Alanis Morissette. Jimmy Buffett signed some of his band members to record deals with his record label, Margaritaville Records. Shawn Colvin recorded her record in the home studio of Joni Mitchell for professional production.

R-E-S-P-E-C-T. When record producer Jerry Wexler first heard a recording by a thirteen-year-old gospel singer, he knew she had that otherworldly quality that makes some singers stars. Wexler signed Aretha Franklin in 1966 and went on to help her turn that talent into a string of hits.

Step one is to admit that you aren't that smart and that you need help. Everyone can teach you, but it is best to try to get advice from those who have been there and done that. Trey Parker got his big break when he sent Steven Spielberg a "South Park" video Christmas card. Or as Allman Brothers Band member Dickey Betts says, "I'm a dumb-ass guitar player, you know? But I was smart enough to listen to people with ideas."

Step two is to ask for help. Tell them about your project and let them offer to help. If they don't, ask. When Steve Jobs was starting Apple computers, he called Bill Hewlett (Hewlett-Packard) to ask for advice. The two became fast friends. Reportedly, you can now call Steve Jobs and ask for advice. I have got to try that sometime.

Step three is to make them proud by doing what they tell you. Help them help you. Make them look good. Charlie Kaufman's screenplay for *Being John Malkovich* caught the attention of R.E.M.'s Michael Stipe and he coproduced the film. Trisha Yearwood was singing backup and performing solo in a local club when her mentor and friend Garth Brooks introduced her to his producer, who then took her to producer Garth Fundis, who helped her create a slick demo tape. She sang backup on a Garth Brooks album and performed live at a "label showcase," where she caught the attention of Tony Brown, who signed her to MCA Nashville. She was then the opening act for the rising star Garth Brooks, which exposed her to a ton of new fans. To further help out, Garth contributed two tracks to the Yearwood release, helping to boost sales to over two million copies.

Steps four and five. Thank your mentors, often and profusely. The band Luscious Jackson's first show was opening for their mentors the Beastie Boys. They were the first band signed to the Beastie's label, Grand Royal. After the band's success they offered props to the Beastie Boys for helping them get on their feet. Now they are off and running on their own. Other bands are now emulating *them*. Dennis Miller has had a hand in getting so many fellow comics on "Saturday Night Live," he should get some kind of commission. It was Miller who saw Adam Sandler's stand-up act and recommended to Lorne Michaels that Sandler would be a good fit on the show. The rest is history.

If you feel that you don't need no stinkin' mentor's help, okay amigo. But at least study the masters (it's the next best thing to studying *with* the masters). Success leaves clues. Read biographies, put together a time line or flow chart, ask yourself, "What would they do if they were in my shoes?" Gavin Rossdale of the band Bush was having trouble deciding which songs to include on their soon-to-be-released album. He recalled what Mick Fleetwood told him about the same situation Fleetwood Mac had faced with the *Rumours* record. So he followed the advice of Mick Fleetwood and took the same approach. You don't have to actually ask for help, just put it out there. Tell everyone what you want to do.

Get different mentors for different areas you need help with. Specialists. It is also good to have someone older, younger, and the same age as you. It is so great to be able to name-drop. Oh yeah, so-and-so is my mentor. It impresses people and gives you instant credibility. Jazz vocalist Diana Krall added two jazz legends to her band, which caught the attention of the mainstream press (*Newsweek* and *Vanity Fair*) and led to some positive press. It felt so good to have evened the S.C.O.R.E. (Service Corp. of Retired Executives) by having my own "retired executive" just a phone call away. Joseph Oppenheimer, my

S.C.O.R.E. counselor, has given me so much free advice about how to promote myself (before he retired he managed a magazine, and now produces a television show) that it's like having a high-powered consultant on retainer, without having to spend a dime. I highly recommend you look into getting a counselor assigned to you.

Form a board of advisors, mastermind group, or brainstorming club, people who will tell you what you need to hear, not what you want to hear. This is easier than it sounds. You could also form a panel of imaginary mentors. I have Einstein on my imaginary board of directors (strangely, they are all dead), and I can almost hear him saying to me, "Ya, vee should try a little harder, no? See, it is all relative." Put up their picture on your wall along with their philosophies and quotes or mottoes. Actress Lisa Nicole Carson (Carla Reese on "ER" and Renee Radick on "Ally McBeal") could not afford acting classes when she was growing up, so she studied the films and careers of actors she respected. She learned that some of her idols began by attending open casting calls and started in summer stock shows and off-Broadway plays. That's how she got her start as well, eventually landing a guest role on "Law & Order."

Model your career after a role model. Read about them. Research them. Call them. Do what they do and you may just get the same results. Ask yourself whom they associate with. Who is their agent? What was their path and what specific steps did they take to promote themselves? Then reverse-engineer their success. "In a movie, I'd love to have Barbra Streisand play me for my story. Barbra Streisand and I have so much in common. We're Jewish, from Brooklyn, and we both have the same big noses. Barbra Steisand did great as a man in *Yentl*. Cross-dressing is such a rage with the Academy Awards, maybe Barbra would win an Oscar," said Barry Manilow.

You could be a mentor. When you help others succeed they are now in your debt. Like a consultant, no charge. Give seminars, offer to help with their website, do in-house training, sell advice in booklets, books, tapes. Get known in your industry as both helpful and knowledgeable.

Try to land work with people you admire and aspire to be like. Tom Cruise selects his projects (and his directors) with an eye toward self-improvement (and potential commercial success and artistic achievement). Over the years, Cruise has been tutored by some of the best directors, including Martin Scorsese, Barry Levinson, Stanley Kubrick, and Oliver Stone. This has helped him to hone his craft. Paul Thomas Anderson, who directed Cruise in *Magnolia,* said the actor was very inquisitive and curious about all aspects of the shoot, trying to soak up as much information as he could. As a junior in high school, actor Kevin Spacey saw a Katharine Hepburn play. After the performance he waited outside the theater with a bouquet of roses. When she came out a side door, Spacey presented her with the flowers, and she sat on the bumper of her car talking to him for ten minutes about acting. Years later the Oscar winners met again while both were working in Canada and spent Thanksgiving together, where she again gave him advice.

Mentors push you. In high school, Jay Leno was a class clown (no surprise there). One teacher didn't seem to mind, however. The two became close during detention (which Jay was always in and Mr. Walsh was usually supervising). One day the teacher asked (without a hint of sarcasm), "Have you ever thought about going into show business?" The idea had never occurred to Leno. He didn't know anybody in show business. But that teacher's words ignited something in the young comic. A similar situation occurred for acclaimed writer and poet Alice Walker. After going through some difficult times, Walker churned out a stream of poetry and submitted the works to a teacher, the famed poet Muriel Rukeyser. The teacher forwarded them to her agent, which led to the eventual publication of the poems under the title *Once*. Author Alice McDermott's first three books were up for some of literature's top awards, including the Pulitzer Prize. In 1998 her fourth novel won the National Book Award for fiction, stealing it away from Tom Wolfe's *A Man in Full*. McDermott's success is even more amazing considering she had to be prodded by insightful mentors from the very start and almost walked away from writing at one point. Her first mentor encouraged her to take up writing as a living. Her family was less than enthusiastic. They encouraged her to go to secretarial school instead, thinking she could get into publishing and maybe end up as an editor, and if she really wanted to write she could write at night. She actually did work for a short while as a clerk-typist for a vanity publisher before enrolling at the University of New Hampshire, where she enrolled in a writing program. Again, she joined up with a mentor who pushed the reluctant writer (McDermott was unsure of her talent) to submit her work for publication. After several rejections from magazines (McDermott was thrilled to get a letter back from an actual editor at a real magazine), her first piece was published in *Ms.*, and then her stories began appearing in *Redbook, Mademoiselle,* and *Seventeen.* Her mentor then contacted a literary agent on her behalf, who agreed to represent her and subsequently sold all of her books to date. If it wasn't for the encouragement from her mentors, McDermott may never have realized her full potential.

Getting a mentor to help with marketing is nothing new. Elvis Presley had two mentors who helped shape his career: first, Sun Records owner-producer Sam Phillips, and then manager Colonel Tom Parker. Both of these astute individuals recognized the amazing potential of the young singer. Today there is the pop-making machine in Orlando that has turned out some of the biggest boy bands as well as shepherding the career of female teen superstar Christina Aguilera.

Ask a Pro

Chuck Green
Graphic artist/author
www.ideabook.com

What is your advice for aspiring designers?

Numero uno is this: Find talented, experienced people to work with early on. Don't accept a good-paying job where you are the top person. You will profit much more by finding someone in your field who is a real, recognized expert and learning what you can from them. If you are serious about your career, go right to the top. Who do you think is the best designer in the world? The best copywriter? What are the top ten advertising agencies? Go to them and ask for a job—no kidding. Work cheap while you can afford to and take advantage of real-world, on-the-job learning. It's the fast track to knowledge.

As a mentor to aspiring graphic artists, what advice do you give?

If your presentation skills are weak, you must improve them. Not should—must. Today, as you are reading these pages, there are hundreds, perhaps thousands, of truly brilliant ideas being generated in the minds of timid people. They will never see the light of day because the artists are unable to sell them— they are too nervous, too intimidated, or simply lack the skills to communicate their ideas with clarity and enthusiasm. If you fear talking to a group or just have trouble organizing your thoughts—make learning these skills one of your top priorities.

Did you have a mentor when you got your start?

Mr. Kryston, my high school English teacher, got me in touch with a friend of his in Baltimore, Maryland—a guy named Dill Cole. Dill was a designer for the Eucalyptus Tree Studio—to a kid in the sixties, this was the pinnacle of cool. He took a few minutes out of what must have been a very busy schedule to send a young designer a few notes of encouragement—nothing more, nothing less. Yet that encouragement directed my life.

It makes you wonder why we don't all become mentors.

And how little it would take, too. Imagine the positive effect we could have if we just spent thirty minutes more a week encouraging others. No matter who you are, someone is looking to you for direction. Be sure to keep your antenna up for those important moments. Send a note, make a call, help someone get started or redirected.

You seem like someone who walks the talk, too. Have you ever faced a time where you had to put your own advice to the test?

Yes. I got fired from my last job. My family and I had moved into a big mortgage and I was faced with starting over. I was afraid that I was going to lose the house and all that I had worked for. My instinctive reaction was to solve my most immediate hurt—to find something, anything to pay the bills. And then it dawned on me—I had turned my creative dreams into a pursuit of money. I determined then and there that if I was going to start over again, I was going to focus on what I loved doing. If it worked, I'd end up in the catbird seat. If it failed, I'd be no worse off than I was that day.

And?

It worked. Add Chuck Green to the list of people who have said focus on what you love and the money will follow. When you are in tune with what you love, you can't help but grow, be enthusiastic, and get better at what you do. Even if you don't end up making a fortune, you will never regret living an inspired dream.

8

RAVING FANS
(Making the Most of Word-of-Mouth Marketing)

"When writers refer to themselves as 'we' and to the reader as 'you,' it's two against one."
—Judith Rascoe

I hate to admit it, but for the most part self-promotion is a popularity contest, and a strong following proves that you are marketable. In many cases, having a large fan base can be a deal maker (and if you don't have one, a deal breaker). Everyone knows that dedicated and motivated fans will do most of the marketing for you. When people share your vision, and you have won them over, they want to get involved and share you and your work with others. It's a beautiful thing. Hell, if they really like you they'll not only tell their friends about you, they'll even drag them down to see you or purchase your stuff and maybe even buy a bunch to give as gifts over the holidays. (In other words, they'll force you down others' throats.) Most people are too busy and overwhelmed these days and use recommendations from friends and family to simplify the decision-making process about things, like where to go and what to buy. It's a filtering system. If someone tells them, "This is a fantastic book, you should read it," they listen. That's why the more people you have out there spreading the word, the better.

If you can create some sense of organization, you can mobilize your fans into action. With the help of the Internet, a few followers can alert their friends and other fans about upcoming projects, generate publicity, and pass on information about where you'll be appearing and any new projects you are working on. In addition to spreading the word, loyal fans may also donate their time, expertise, and maybe even money if they believe in what you're doing. It is such a powerful thing. (Just look at religion as an example if you have any doubts.) That's why you want to create customers for life. Start small (or local) and build your fan base one person at a time. If you find one person who is a believer, it's equivalent to one hundred who are only mildly interested. These people will be with you for the long haul, the ups and downs. They are the ones who will put up flyers, make calls on your behalf, vouch for you, and pitch in when you need a hand.

If I had a dime for every time someone said, "Why do you go to that much trouble to win people over?" I could retire. I have expended a great deal of energy and have given away a ton of stuff, all in an effort to build a following for my books and talks. On paper it doesn't seem to make financial sense, but the reality is that it has paid off, big-time! I learned this lesson a long time ago. In the early stages of my career I would always help anyone who asked. If someone called and needed advice, information, or encouragement, I was there. Go out of your way to win people over. Maybe you're saying to yourself, "Hell yes, I want people to worship me and love what I do." Good, that's a start. It means you are developing the mind-set that every person you come in contact with can be converted from a casual observer into a raving fan. Guy Kawasaki calls this "evangelizing" people. In theory it should be as simple as doing an amazing job and then waiting for a following to develop. To a degree that *is* how it happens. But I have found that you have to go the extra mile to really win people over. That means you take the time to meet and greet your audience and person- ally answer your e-mails as well as setting an exceptional example with your actions and your art. It also means finding ways to make a difference in people's lives. Whoa, that sounds like a lot of work. I know, but in the long run you will be rewarded for your efforts a hun- dred times over. I promise.

So why wouldn't every creative person start building a fan base? For one, we don't want to be pests, so we let relationships that could have bloomed into something special wither and die. It's also a lot of work and takes discipline and organization skills that, frankly, many creative people haven't developed. You have to build and update a mailing list, return calls and e-mails, when all you really want to do is be left alone. For some it is hard to accept help. When a potential fan reaches out and offers to help, we push them away. The reasons for this may be a fear that we are now obligated to them in some way. It may be a sense that we don't feel as though we deserve their assis- tance. Finally, it is a fear of having to interact with people. Some of these excuses sound silly, but they are real. It can be extremely uncomfortable for some to have others heaping praise upon them, even though that's what they have always wanted—acceptance. It's still a strange feeling. Regardless of the various reasons for not having built a fan base in the past, the time to start is right now. This chapter will show you how to develop fans in a traditional sense (readers, listeners, customers, clients, patrons, and so forth) as well as support people (publishers, publicists, bosses, editors, buyers, distributors, and so on). For example, is there a person between you and a client you'd love to have? Try turning that "middleman" into a fan and they will do most of the marketing for you.

JUST FOR FUN

What do Steven Spielberg, Robin Williams, and Wynton Marsalis have in common? They all collect Roderick Smith's and Linda Miller's remarkable lifelike soft sculptures. I know this because it was on a printed card hanging from each sculpture. I was impressed by the caliber of this sculptor's fans. It's a ringing endorsement. Look at your list of fans. Are there any celebrities, powerful people, or industry leaders that you could get an endorsement from?

Got Fans?

"I was the toast of two continents—Greenland and Australia."
—Dorothy Parker

When I find something or someone I like, I tend to get all geeked up and become a vocal and loyal supporter. (Don't get me started about my Mac, Miata, or mom-and-pop stores.) There are a lot of people like me. We want to be made to feel like part of an exclusive club, to be insiders, to be treated as special. We want to believe in something. Hallelujah, I've seen the light. Maybe you aren't world famous, but a strong following can mean long-term and lasting success. The hip-hop duo Gang Starr would always go "Ghetto Gold" (selling a lot of CDs on their home turf), and earned the respect of hip-hop's hard-core fans. That sustained them before they earned mainstream success for their jazz-influenced music. Gene Simmons of Kiss knows what it takes to win over fans. "It's our job at the end of the night to make sure you walk out of there saying: 'Wow! That's the greatest show I ever saw.' That's the job. And you have to do it as much in Paducah as you do in New York City." To generate a following you have to do it the old-fashioned way, you have to earrrrrrrrn it. It begins by getting their attention. Find ways you can do something worthwhile for them. Establish trust. Keep in contact. Give special offers just for them. Make it personal. Most of all, be interested in and interact with as many fans as possible. In this chapter we will discuss how to recruit, retain, and make it easier for others to rave about you.

Recruiting a Following

What can you do for others that would inspire them and convert them from casual observers into raving fans? Give this question some serious thought. While you are pondering the problem, try these ideas on for size.

It starts with you. Lead by example. Be the real deal. Do what you say you're gonna do when you say you're gonna do it. How many times have you admired someone from afar only to finally meet them and realize they aren't what you thought? Well, I know a photographer who practices what he preaches. Marty Mann was my teacher in design school. (He gave me a C, but I'm over it.) Not only are his photos works of art, but he is a masterpiece himself. Everything about him says professional (and personable). When I was hired by a magazine to interview and profile a local newscaster, of course I chose Marty to handle the photography. The following story is the perfect example of how he wins fans. When we got to the interviewee's house, I did the interview while Marty watched and entertained the newscaster's young daughter. Then Marty took the pictures like a pro. After we were done, Marty said, "Hey, while I'm here and all my gear is set up, how about I take some pictures of you and your daughter." The next thing you know, he was shooting photos of the whole family. This gesture led to a contract doing head shots for all the newscasters at the station and a new niche for him.

Let them take a test drive. That's why listening booths in stores and offering free downloadable music files, sample chapters, and low-resolution samples on the Internet make sense. When I founded several support groups (for goal setters), I always allowed people to attend two meetings to see if it met their needs. Being there and experiencing the power of goal-setting and meeting other members almost always did the trick and I had a new member and a fan.

Make it easy for them to join the club. It starts when you can add their name to your mailing list. Make it easy for them to sign up. Hold a contest or giveaway to start building your mailing list. For example, one established author holds an annual contest for the best short story of the year. He gets a lot of entries and inquiries. He then posts the stories to his website and lets readers vote for their favorite. He also enlists literary agents as judges to choose the five finalists and the winner. Then he pays for the printing of a self-published collection of the final five stories and provides free copies to the winners. If that weren't enough, he then goes out and promotes the book in the media. Wow. The good thing is anyone can participate. He has built a very nice database of readers from entries and voters. (Never, ever do anything illegal, immoral, or irritating with the information they provide you. Trust is a must.)

Start off on the right foot. Win them over right away. If you somehow screw up the first time they work with you, it isn't likely they will give you another shot—unless you go out of your way to correct the problem, and then some. That's the only remedy for being remiss.

Solve their problems. If you can help them in some small way or be there for them in their time of need, they will become a devotee. When one struggling author came to me at wit's end because she could not get her books in stores, I helped her get a distributor, added them to my catalog, and placed them in several stores. Problem solved and a fan for life.

Make them feel special. If you can make your connection more personal, it has a greater impact. This could be a handwritten note with an order, or a card on their birthday or the anniversary of the first time you did business together. Being an author, you would think that a signed book wouldn't mean much to me. Wrong. I get excited when an author takes the time to personalize a book to me. It's a small thing to them, but a big thing to the recipient. It makes them feel special. Maybe you could feature fans on your website, include them in the book you are writing (guess who does that?) or hold a contest or exhibition of some kind and feature as many people as possible. One dry cleaner has their best customers' pictures printed on the paper that covers the hanger. A Florida artist announces an award for art patron of the month and gets the winner's picture in the paper.

Teach them something they didn't know. Who doesn't remember a favorite teacher who turned you on to something new or taught you how to do something special? You know more than you think you know. Everyone has something they can teach others. Find a way to share your knowledge with others. Maybe you could post useful information on your website. Provide links to vital information they may need access to. When people contacted me about self-publishing (which can be overwhelming your first try), I put together a list of important phone numbers and addresses for everything from obtaining a copyright to where to find copies of important forms, and included a checklist of when to do what in the publishing process. Did I charge for this information? No way. It was a way to help others, and by teaching a fellow creative person how to publish, I know that someday soon they will need to know about self-promotion, too. Hey, I heard about this great book. . . .

Touch them deeply. If you can enrich their lives or make a connection with them beyond what is expected or required, it will make for a lasting relationship and create a loyal fan. When a friend of mine wrote to the manager of a star (with ties to San Diego) to ask if she would make an appearance at a function for people with dyslexia (something the star also suffered), he got a form letter back saying the star was too busy, blah blah blah. He wasn't surprised. But when the star showed up unannounced at the banquet, he was *blown away.* Now I have to go see all of her horrible movies because he is a *huge* fan.

Find common ground. Is there a cause that you and the people you want as fans share? Something you are both emotionally and passionately dedicated to? If there is, get involved in some way. Do you share a common enemy with your fans? Do battle together. Do you share the same faith, principles, dreams? Let them know. Whether you share similar views or rally around a common cause, these are the kinds of people who make loyal and supportive fans. They are dedicated, vocal, and action-oriented. Don't believe me? I have two words for you: Melissa Etheridge.

Do more than they expect. When I sent a client to a colleague, I did it because I knew they needed each other. It was a perfect match. When I opened the thank-you card from the colleague, a crisp, new hundred-dollar bill fell out. That wasn't necessary, but it made me take note (and look for other possible leads to pass on to her).

Retaining Your Following

First of all, you want passionate people. Important people. Action-oriented and vocal people. Hell, you just need people, period. No matter whom you're trying to convert, it starts with a mind-blowing experience and exceptional service. Going the extra mile and a half. Bruce Springsteen probably gives the longest and most inspired concert of any performer. Throughout the years, through the good times and the bad, his fans have remained loyal and come to his shows. Other artists, and we won't name names, seem to be just going through the motions on stage. What can you do to show your fans you care about them and are passionate about what you do?

Stay connected. It also means coming up with a way to communicate with your fans on a regular basis and making it possible for them to converse and contact one another. In addition, come up with clever ways to keep them motivated and committed to your common cause—you. It doesn't have to be a big deal. Give them a good reason to visit your website for current, relevant, and useful information. Maybe you could post a work in progress. Have a section for them to post comments and reviews. Answer frequently asked questions. Interview others who may be interesting to your fans. Create a newsletter and post it on your site or e-mail it to them. (1-800-FLOWERS reminds customers of upcoming dates they *don't* want to forget.) Make a postcard with your tour schedule and mail it to them. I am a big Michael Franks fan and I missed the mention of his San Diego concert date. Fortunately, his postcard gave me a heads-up and I got tickets. Get out more and do some "chat and chews" (meet for a meal) or put on an event. Every time author Anne Rice comes to town it is an event (and it's like Halloween all over again). Her fans dress up like characters from her books and hundreds come to her signings like that. It's amazing.

How can others share in your dream? Ask and you shall receive. I wanted to find a way to get readers of my previous books to tell a few friends. So I packaged a newsletter and a letter along with postcards (that had the book cover and order information on them) and prestamped them and asked them to send them to friends. I sent these out, and the results were amazing. With the Internet, this kind of word-of-mouth promotion is even easier, and cheaper. Another way to mobilize supporters (in addition to asking for help and making it easy to do so) is to offer an incentive like a discount if they buy more. (Encourage them to give something you do away as a gift.) Give them the tools so these "enablers" can get the word out. Give them a poster to put up as a subtle way of getting people to inquire about your art. Make sure they are stocked with extra business cards, brochures, newsletters, flyers, posters, mini-brochures, bookmarks, samples, and anything else they may need to spread the word.

Reward them for their loyalty. Offer a reward for any referrals. I did this in the form of a Nordstrom or Borders gift certificate for $100 for leads on speaking engagements. Feature some of your biggest fans on your website or in your newsletter. Hold a banquet and create an award for the most involved and active supporters. Offer free tickets to your shows and encourage them to bring a friend. Above all, thank them (profusely) for any efforts they make on your behalf.

Keep them coming back for more. Marilyn Sherman, an author and speaker, passes out the poem she always closes her talk with and a fax-back form that encourages attendees to share their success stories, which she uses in future talks and books. She also isn't shy about asking for leads and offers discounts on her books and tapes if they are bought in bulk.

Make them feel welcome, special, part of something big. People want to be part of a group that shares a common goal and interest. Arrange for them to chat (online) and maybe meet (club meetings or outings). Maybe even make them a part of the creative process. Ask them what they think. Listen to their needs.

Connect on a personal level. Singer/songwriter Jimmy Buffett commented in an online interview that many of the people who come to see him year in and year out have become friends. One of the top touring acts each summer, Buffett has sold-out shows of 10,000-plus people, so obviously not *everyone* is a close friend. How can you develop deeper relationships with your fans? Let your guard down a little and let them get to know you on a personal level. (That's right, it starts with you.) Send thank-you notes, include a (brief) handwritten note with an order, or throw a customer appreciation party.

Make it fun to do business with you. An enjoyable experience is better than a boring one. Do people say "Ho-hum" when they are done doing business with you, or do they say "Wow!" You want more people who aren't just pleased, but pleasured. (I know what you're thinking. Don't go there.) How can you make it more fun to do business with you?

Learn from multilevel marketing. Use MLM techniques to build a following. Create something so good and that connects so deeply that customers not only want one for themselves, they have to buy one for their friends and family, too. Melissa Bank's debut book *The Girls' Guide to Hunting and Fishing,* seven short stories about a romantically challenged single white female, was that kind of book and ended up on the *New York Times* best-seller list in part from word of mouth from women who gave the books as gifts to their girlfriends and recommended the book to anyone and everyone.

Insider information. When you keep releasing new and neat stuff, customers will call their friends to ask them, "Did you hear about . . . ?" It's the same with a new movie or restaurant. It's human nature to want to be the first to experience it and then tell your friends about it. (For some reason, my mother-in-law likes to tell you the endings to the movies, too. Very annoying.) Hold something back to launch later. Keep putting out new work and let your core fans know about it first and let them spread the word.

Less is more. Focus on your most motivated people and you will be able to better serve them and offer that much-needed one-on-one connection. Maybe you can give out your special "hotline" toll-free number or your private e-mail address that you check regularly so you can respond to their requests for help faster. Help them to help you. It's not necessarily how many people you have as fans, but the quality of them.

Give to get. All take and no give makes for short-term relationships. From time to time give away an idea, referral, help, advice to someone in need. I consider this a sample of what it's like to be a part of my inner circle. If you came to me and said, "How do I get started in public speaking?" I would offer to connect you with some of the meeting planners for groups in your area that use speakers (these meeting planners *need* speakers, so they are grateful for the lead and I have an easy-to-access database).

In with the old. All this talk about converting people is overlooking the obvious. What about the people you already have a relationship with? How can you get them more involved in what you do? Ask them. Ask for their help and support. Tell them what you need. Stay in touch with them. I connected with some old friends, and besides being cool people, they helped me with some material for my last book, the title for an upcoming book, and even set up a signing for me at a local bookstore.

The Magic of Mailing Lists

"If you enjoyed the show tonight, please sign my mailing list at the back of the room. If you hated the show, you should also sign up. This way you'll know where I'm playing next, and you can avoid me with amazing accuracy."

—Don White

To build a fan base you *must* build a mailing list. I believe your promotional ability is determined by the quantity and quality of your mailing list. If you designed the most awesome brochure but sent it to the wrong people (people who could care less about what you do), it would fail. A good in-house mailing list that you compiled yourself of raving fans puts you in the driver's seat and sets you up for long-term success. You can hope they will go to your website to stay connected, but then it's up to them. But when you're able to send announcements, updates, feedback, invites, and more, you control the relationship. Do it cheaply using e-mail. The best way to market a product or service is to have your own list. People you know and who know YOU. Author John Gray has amassed a mailing list of 600,000 followers. He plans to expand his Web offerings to include everything the "Man from Mars" might need (flowers, candles, *lingerie*). Amazon.com is a perfect example of a company compiling (the world's largest) mailing list and database. They may not be making money now, but they are setting themselves up for big things in the future. They have a large list of people and they know what they want, what they need—people who trust them and whom they can reach (via e-mail) at almost no cost. Now they can buy (or create) products based on what the people on their mailing list want and need. Pretty savvy, eh? We can, to a lesser degree, do the same thing, too. Remember, your mailing list is part of your inventory, it's your "goodwill" and has real value, so treat it as you would money.

Granted, as a creative person, maintaining a mailing list is NOT a creative endeavor. It is tedious and boring. But the results make it worthwhile. You can be creative about how you compile your list. One guy snags names and e-mail addresses off incoming e-mails. He looks at who else the e-mails were forwarded to and sees if he can recognize a name in his industry. Or go through your industry trade directory, the yellow pages, back issues of magazines, the Internet, and look for people who may make a good client or contact. (The library is a good place to start.) I once went through one of those awards books for best designs, and among those whose promotional materials won awards (best business card, for example) was the contact information for people who actually appear in stories and interviews in *this* book. Don't ignore those who come to you, either. These are "hot" prospects. If you hate making cold calls, then treat these warm leads with the utmost respect. Guard your list with your life. Sort it so it's manageable. Keep it current. Use some system (on the computer or otherwise) to manage it. A mailing list is the main tool you will use for promoting yourself, so make the time to build and maintain it.

When someone hands you a business card, what do you do with it? Discover it a week later in your pocket after you washed your jeans, or do you enter it into your database? When you are lucky enough to appear on a talk show, do you announce to listeners that you will send them your newsletter if they will write, call, or e-mail you and give you their address? Do you hold contests and drawings to fill your mailing list with new names? When you perform or speak or teach, do you encourage the audience to sign up at the back of the room so you can keep them posted on any new information or trends or notify them about upcoming classes and shows? Do you give out an evaluation form? I find that the feedback is very valuable, but I also need to know if there is anything else they want. For instance, I will ask, "Would you like Lee to speak to your company?" or "Would you be interested in an advanced class on this subject?" and "Would you like to be added to my mailing list?" More times than not, those boxes are checked. At the back of the room you will probably be trying to sell products, but those who don't buy now could still be valuable to you. Do you encourage passersby to drop a business card for a drawing or sign up for your mailing list to receive your free newsletter? Our band started doing just that for song requests when we play. The catch to have us play your favorite song is that you must have your name and address on the request. The people at Palm Pilot headquarters (Palm Pilot users are a good example of a growing cult, er . . . group of loyal followers) build their mailing list of converts by offering free add-ons and software in exchange for your e-mail address. It's a fair trade and likely the start of an ongoing relationship. So, are you doing all you can to build and maintain your mailing list? What are you going to do today to improve in this area? What could you send to your current list (this week) to keep them updated on your activities?

If you are too busy or lazy to build your own mailing list, you can rent one. I am sure you could easily find one specific to your target from a list broker. Maybe you can contact a club, publication, or retailer and ask if you could rent their "house" list. No matter where you beg, borrow, or steal your list from, promise me you will test it out before doing a massive mailing. Send a few (hundred) and see what happens.

☆ ────────────────

ACTION ITEM

List five key people you would really like to add to your mailing list. How can you reach them? Do you already have their address and phone number somewhere? If not, where could you get it? Whom do you know who knows them? Are these "middlemen" on your mailing list? Organize and update your existing list. Plan your next mailing.

Your Fan Club

"Tenk you veddy much."

—Andy Kaufman

Thank people! For me, it's not hard to do. I truly appreciate anyone who takes the time to write, call, or e-mail me. That's why I bend over (backward) for anyone who needs something (advice, encouragement, or information). Then keep on thanking them. You may have to tweak your thinking somewhat. If you believe that once the check clears you're done, you are so wrong. You have just begun. (I will even write a thank-you note in the memo section on the check!) You want to look for additional products and services they may want and need. Martha Stewart is the master at this. She looks for, or creates, additional products and services her audience wants and needs. It's the same audience, but she is able to sell them different stuff. You can do the same thing. One way is the sell-up. (I am usually able to presell my book to meeting planners so that every attendee gets one. I sell myself *and* my books.) Then there is the add-on. ("How about a nice set of custom chairs to go with that table I just made for you?") There is the "Oh, by the way, I have something new I think you'll like." (The sculpture you sold them now has a companion piece that would just look perfect side by side with what they already bought.) Finally, there's the "Let's stay in touch." (This could be in the form of updates about the item they already bought and how to care for it.) The focus is to keep customers longer and sell them more stuff. Amazon does this so well. They know what you like and suggest other things of interest. This is done with updates, discounts, and thank-you notes. For some reason, it doesn't feel contrived or intrusive if it is done right. You actually welcome the contact from them, and their suggestions can be really helpful. In many ways it's like we've gone back in time to more one-on-one marketing with a personalized approach. (It's just that now we use technology to do it.) Some of the tools used today to build a loyal fan base have stayed the same, and some have become better and easier to use. Here are some examples:

Newsletters. The band Phish knows a little something about building and maintaining a following. Their newsletter, "Doniac Schvice," is *anticipated* by their fans. They also have an official website, a telephone hotline for updates, and fan clubs throughout the country. A newsletter is the most essential tool for remaining connected, because when done right, the newsletter is filled with information the fans want. They look forward to receiving it. It's a soft sell.

Surveys. Know your audience. Keep giving them what they want—and things they didn't even know they wanted, but do. Ask them for their preferences. Find out their favorites. What do they like best about what you do? What is their favorite website? Song? Who else are they listening to? What else are they reading? What is their major concern? Biggest challenge? Knowledge is power.

Tours. Go out of your way to meet people. Make *personal* contact. When our band plays, I make it my mission to meet as many people as possible between breaks. I have seen many bands where the moment the set is over they disappear. (I don't think I want to know where they went or what they were up to.) I mean, how hard is it to sit and have a beer with a few fans? I recently saw a documentary about Metallica and was blown away by how they take the time to sign before and after shows. (Sometimes outside in the freezing cold.) That's the attitude! Raquel Welch learned this lesson one day while working with a legend. "Early in my career I thought I could avoid having to sign autographs. But one day Jimmy Stewart took me aside and said, 'N-N-Now, Raquel, ju-ju-just a minute here. They got some folks here wanting to see ya. They're the people who buy the tickets. The least you can do is go over there, smile, and say hello.'" The same thing holds true at book signings. I will stay until the last person has run out of steam telling me their life story. I actually don't mind listening to a reader ramble on. I have always felt that my role is to serve.

Frequency. Frequency equals familiarity, which eventually equals loyal fans. Don't stop staying in touch. Showing them that you care. Reminding them that you rock. Letting them know this is a long-term and mutually beneficial relationship. Win them over with persistence.

Memberships. A small and loyal group of fans is better than a big and fickle group. Come up with some sort of membership club to make the more loyal followers feel like, well, part of the club. I am not suggesting a secret handshake, but how about special T-shirts, a special code to get to a special section of your website, or newsletters, discounts, meetings of members, and more.

Sub-clubs. In the appendix of Julia Cameron and Mark Bryan's awesome book *The Artist's Way,* the authors encourage readers to start an artists' circle to connect with other creative people. This means that readers (fans) are mobilized to get others to join these groups and work through (and buy) the book.

A living trust. Never break their trust! They now call it permission marketing. A lot of it is just marketing mumbo jumbo. What I learned from the latest books on this subject is this: Don't do anything that would diminish their trust in you. Before Nordstrom opened a store in Scottsdale, Arizona, many "zonies" would come to San Diego during the summer to avoid the heat and to shop. Many of these customers had personal shoppers who, during the winter months, would send new stuff to customers in the desert (in the sizes and tastes the customer had specified during earlier shopping sprees). The customers kept what they liked and sent back the rest. That's trust!

Get out there. It seems that bands come and go so fast these days. The ones that seem to have staying power are the ones that put on a great show and tour often. The Dave Mathews band is a perfect example. They continue to win new fans with their amazing live shows.

Action. Mobilize your fans through the power of suggestion. One author asks fans to write reviews online, tell their local librarian about her books, take flyers to their local bookseller, and recommend the author to an organization that may need a speaker. What good is a fan club if all they do is tell you how great you are? Actually, that is pretty cool in and of itself. But if you can also get them to take action on your behalf, wow!

Word of Mouth: From a Whisper to a Scream

"When the product is right, you don't have to be a great marketer."

—Lee Iacocca

Referrals are the fastest and easiest way to build your business and advance your career. Word of mouth is the most important marketing mechanism. (Think of how many jobs or apartments you found this way.) Why? For one thing, almost all of your work comes from people you know or who know you. It's been said that nearly 90 percent of new business comes from word of mouth or referrals. It also happens to be the cheapest form of promotion there is. (How cool is that?) So if you don't have much money for marketing, this is for you! In fact, many freelancers survive (and thrive) on word of mouth alone. Get people excited about what you do and they will want to tell others so they can experience you, too.

Remember the "good old boy" network? It's still alive and well. People don't call it that now because it's not politically correct. Everyone has their network of people they prefer to do business with, and because you have a history and they want to work with you, they will tell their "cronies" about you and what you do. We now call it "relationship selling" or "network marketing." What-evurrrr. If you build a relationship with key people in your field or community and just blow their minds by doing great work and giving good service, they will hire you again and again and also market you to their network of friends. Is this awesome, or what?

This is also called creating a buzz. Getting people to start talking about you (in a positive way) and what you do. Make it your mission to create magic moments for your current clients (blow their friggin' minds!!!) so they can't help but tell others about the amazing things you did for them. You really can't sit back and wait for word of mouth. You have to be proactive (almost audacious) and make it a part of your marketing plan. Martha Stewart said it best: "Don't be embarrassed by your achievements. Being an overachiever is nothing despicable. It is admirable. Never lower your standards." Word of mouth doesn't just happen by itself. You can't just wait around for it to happen, you make it happen. For example, Meg Campbell was going through a difficult time in her life (divorce) and decided to do something about it—no, she didn't do anything violent, she wrote a book of poems called *Solo Crossing* that dealt with divorce. Campbell was then featured on a New York–based website called PoetryCentral.com, and the resulting word of mouth moved copies of the book (on Amazon.com) and led to e-mails from enthusiastic readers and offers to speak all over the country.

Word of mouth can spread like a virus. If the right people are infected, they will pass it on until it becomes so contagious that it is an epidemic (and I mean that in the best possible way). Dava Sobel's book about an eighteenth-century English clock maker became a best-seller based on positive reviews and word of mouth. *Longitude*'s initial print run was less than 8,000 copies (not much) but went on to sell over one million copies worldwide. Word of mouth works! The best example is, of course, *The Blair Witch Project.* The buzz that was generated before the film even hit theaters was supernatural. With no real marketing budget, the creators literally scared up word of mouth about this little independent film. It all began a full year before the film was released, when the creators e-mailed a few friends, who in turn turned on thousands who really believed that these kids were missing. (Later, college campuses were plastered with "Missing Persons" posters that furthered the myth that the characters were in real danger.) The creative marketing team behind this tiny film (which went on to make millions) had everyone talking (and clicking).

How to Get People to Pump You Up

"Success is what sells."

—*Andy Warhol*

Create work that just blows people away and watch what happens. (Hint: great things.) Get so good that others will want to come and check you out (and bring all their friends to see you do what you do). There is a defensive end on the Tennessee Titans whom they call "the Freak" because he is so fast for a big guy. You want to be "the Freak" at what you do, too. That's the best way to build word of mouth.

Exceptional customer service also spreads like wildfire. (Warning! So does bad service.) A landscaper in my area gives clients a dinner for two after he completes a job as a way of saying he's sorry for the mess he created while doing the work. (He doesn't even have to pay for the voucher. He does the restaurants' landscaping for free.) The Border Café shines your shoes while you wait and the valet vacuums your car while you eat. My local editor on previous books made it a habit of giving me more than I expected in the way of service. She made a cheat sheet so I could decipher her scribbles. Since a lot of good stuff had to be cut, she would save it and organize it for future reference and find ways to plug it back in. She'd take care of a lot of the detail stuff so I could focus on writing. She'd call New York and find out what format they needed for the book. She made copies and mailed off my manuscript to the publisher for me and presented me with beautifully bound galleys of my own. The list goes on. In addition to paying her for a great job, I'd also talk her up and give her good referrals. One day when I was in her office, I noticed that of the dozens of books she had worked on which were displayed on a shelf, almost every one of the authors/clients had been referred to her by me. When you are the recipient of super service, you want to tell others. You can't help but tell others. When someone dazzles you with their talent or does the unexpected and pays attention to your needs, you want others to experience this level of service, too.

Customer service and being of service to someone are one and the same. If you are willing to teach what you know through lectures, workshops, in-store demonstrations, adult learning classes, and online, you will find, in my experience anyway, that your students make great fans. Artist and publisher Sharilyn Miller agrees. "Teaching provides the artist the opportunity to give generously, and trust me, students will give back. They will spread the word about your incredible classes, and they will buy your artwork or put you in touch with wealthy friends who will buy your artwork, or direct you to friends who own galleries or publish magazines who may be interested in your work. The bottom line is, disguise self-promotion in acts of generosity. Give as much as you can, and your artistic career will advance in ways you never could have dreamed." She goes on to say that teaching is about building a mutually beneficial relationship (and sometimes friendships), and that by giving of your time and expertise, you will benefit in ways you can't even imagine. I concur. Here are some more thoughts on the subject.

• Make sure that every time they turn around they see your name (in the paper, in their mailbox, on the Internet, in a trade magazine, in person—everywhere). The more people who can experience what you do, the more chances you have for positive word of mouth. Do what you can to get a sample in their hands, have them come see you perform, or look at your portfolio. One speaker rented a ballroom and invited meeting planners (as well as friends and family) to come hear her give a sample presentation. They came for the free food but stayed because she gave a moving and compelling talk. This led to some immediate bookings.

• Everyone is a potential client or knows someone else who is. Tell everyone what you do! People are almost always at least a little intrigued when you tell them that you are a creative person. Use their interest to open a door and start discussing what you do. It could be a family member or a friend of a friend or a complete stranger. Who knows, that person you are seated next to on a plane (usually the BSG or "big sweaty guy") may know someone who needs what you have to offer. It has happened to me—a lot.

• Make sure the people you expect to give good word of mouth know how to do it right. Ask some of your key people if they know what you do. If they aren't clear or up-to-date (and whose fault is that?), you must educate them. Then make it your mission to stay in their face, er . . . stay connected.

• Make your marketing materials available (or easy to obtain). Have others pass out your business card, brochure, newsletter, samples, pamphlets, flyers, postcards, and whatever else you can convince them to use to pimp for you. It makes their word-of-mouth marketing even more impressive. Empower people by giving them the tools (coupons, gift certificates, free samples) they can give to others. One resourceful jewelry designer gave my wife several bracelets she created. My wife wore them to work. The buyer asked, "That bracelet is amazing, where did you get it?" and my wife gave the buyer the designer's brochure, price list, and some samples. Badda bing, a new line of jewelry is now sold at Nordstrom.

• Find an enabler. You don't know anyone you would consider influential? Find someone who does and win them over. This is your champion. It could be someone who gets 15 percent of everything you do (agent) or a geeked-up fan or a celebrity. Entrepreneur Julie Sautter gave a set of curves (lifelike, silicone breast enhancers worn *over* the breasts) to costume designers and televisions stars (including two on "Baywatch"), and it gave the bouncy, lifelike product a big "boost" (sorry) and led to an appearance on "Oprah." The rest is history. Spend time building relationships with the most successful and influential people in your field. It is usually the top 19.5 percent of the people on your mailing list that bring in the 80.5 percent of your word-of-mouth business. (As for the odd percentages, I am sick of the 80/20 rule, so I tweaked it.) Don't know how to meet and mingle with the leaders in your field? Look at your mailing list and see who on it knows who you want to meet.

• Make the most of every opportunity, no matter how small, to win people over. The best salespeople are happy customers. Go out of your way to make sure that everyone you deal with is pleased and will give you positive reviews. Do "exit polls" to find out why they bought from you or why they *didn't*. Present clients are your best source for repeat business, referrals, and raving reviews. They already know you, but do they know all that you can do? Even if they don't need these additional services, it's possible they know someone else who might. Keep them abreast of work you are doing (show off), any new equipment you may have acquired, and let them know when you are available. Remind them when it is time to work on their annual project (that you contribute to) and offer some new ideas.

• What would do it for you if you were them? Put yourself in their shoes. What would it take to get you to give a referral? Think about that last question with the perspective of an outsider looking in and answer it from your customer's perspective. I asked myself that question recently and the answer was: I would give more word of mouth if Lee featured me in his newsletter or on his website or mentioned me in his book. I would want to share that with all my friends. So right away I made a section in my newsletter and a part of my website to post reader comments, stories, examples, samples, and most of all, to publicly thank people for their efforts.

• I am not a big fan of multilevel marketing, but there is a lot to be said for having a motivated sales force out there pitching your products. I'm sure that someone you know has been to a Tupperware party (or if you are a sick puppy like me, a lingerie party) and found that it was a good way to spread the word and sell some product. What if someone you know invited all their friends over for a party (my imagination is on overdrive here) and talked you up and then sold your creations (usually for a commission)? The idea could then possibly spread to several cities.

• If you asked twenty friends to mail or call one person to invite them to your opening, you should have a good turnout. Include a coupon and suggest that they give it as a gift to a friend. I sometimes will ask, "Do you know anyone who might need a band for a birthday party, wedding, corporate party?" All of a sudden a little cartoon lightbulb goes on above their head. "Oh, yeah, my brother-in-law's sister's nephew is looking for a band." Or a more subtle approach is to note on your invoice that such and such makes a great gift, or encourage them to tell a friend (while your phenomenal work is still fresh in their mind). You could also offer a frequent buyer discount. Start a membership club and give points for repeat business (which could be traded in for free products or services). Try the "buy-one-get-one-free approach" in the hopes that they will invite a friend or buy one as a gift for a friend. Give them a VIP card they can give to others. This allows them to avoid lines at a show, get a free drink, get backstage, get a free newsletter, discounts on products, access to special pages on your website, and so forth. Maybe you can make a gift certificate they can buy and give away to a friend or a customer as a birthday present. I know this is going to sound harsh, but my last book on career management was purchased by friends and relatives as a gift for that "creative" person in their family who just couldn't seem to get it together. So I played up the angle that it makes a great gift for your grandson (who can't or won't get a real job), and it worked.

• Ask the people who supply you to refer you. The more work you do, the more supplies and services you will need to buy from them.

• If someone says they are not interested, instead of just saying, "Uh, okay then," just ask them simply if they might know of someone who could benefit from what you have to offer. It lets them off the hook and gives you the bait to try to land another fish. Offer to personally send any information to these people so you are assured the right people get the right stuff. Of course, you name-drop right away.

• Pay for performance. Reward them for their referrals with cash, gift certificates, free product, a commission, credit toward future work, a discount off their invoice. Code coupons, flyers, and any free tickets to see who did what. At the very least, thank them (it reminds them how great you are).

• Get their testimonials and use them on your website, newsletter, ad, press kit, blurb on a book, in a brochure, catalog—everywhere. To a certain extent this is word of mouth.

• Ask for credit on all work you do. That way, when the client shows off their fancy new thing you created for them, it is noted that YOU were the one who made it (and them) look good.

• Give overflow business away (or business that is not up your alley) in exchange for referrals from *them*. Cross-promote with non-competitors (photographer/wedding coordinator/DJ/makeup artist).

• Be a know-it-all. I call my librarian all the time. At her fingertips and off the top of her head is everything I need to know. What if you were like that? When someone needs something you could be "Jeeves." They remember you helped them in a time of need, and you farm out the work you can't do (for a referral fee). Be an industry insider and problem solver.

• Simplify. Have a clear and concise way of saying what you do. Make sure people know you are looking for work. Ask them to spread the word and offer an incentive for doing so. Ask if you can use *their* mailing list.

• Stay connected to past clients through calls, e-mail, mailings. If someone new takes over a client's job, call to congratulate. Call the person who left to wish them well.

To Serve and Protect

"As I get older, I've learned to listen to people rather than accuse them of things."

—Po Bronson

Businesses can nearly double their profits by retaining just 5 percent more of their customers. It's much cheaper to keep customers than to try to get new ones. We all know this, but do we really practice the principle? The definition of marketing is anything you can do to get and *keep* a client. Good customer service is marketing, and all that means is finding ways to make people happy. And a happy customer is the best salesperson you can have. So the goal, then, is to turn a one-time buyer into a repeat customer and eventually into a long-term client and friend. (I know, some people are too weird to be friends, but they make great customers.) To make a customer happy, you put their needs first. Look at things from their perspective. To do that your mind-set has to be that you want the best for them. You have to actually care about and wish them well.

Another factor is being labeled easy to work with. (Not all of us can pull this off, but . . .) If they ask you to do a rewrite, you should say, "Okay, no problem." (You are thinking @#$%!) When they ask for some last-minute changes to a project, grin and say, "Sure, be glad to." (Again, you are thinking $#@#!) Part of being more marketable is a reputation for meeting the needs of clients (and your editor, producer, director, boss are all clients). Nobody said giving good customer service was easy, did they? Making someone say "Wow!" takes extra effort. Maybe you complete a project and turn it in ahead of schedule or you do something better than before. Essentially it is about exceeding their expectations. What this does is get people talking about you and how impressed they were by your exceptional service. So you have to force yourself to go the extra mile, whatever that may be, so they trust you and want to work with you again. You don't have to like it, you just have to do it. When you have a client list that reads like a Who's Who in your industry and you have served them well, you can name-drop. "Oh, yeah, I did the design for so-and-so." The other person is thinking, "Jeez, this person must be amazing." That's the payoff for all the ass-kissing and bending over backward to make clients happy. It's worth it, too.

Besides, with the current state of customer service, just doing a good job, on time, and not ripping them off, impresses people. I don't know about you, but I am sick of walking around a big discount store looking for signs of life. There is nobody there to answer questions or help you in any way. (When you do finally find someone to ask for a little help, they make it seem like some big imposition.) Same thing when ordering on the Web. What if I have questions, how easy (or hard) is it to talk to someone? And when I say "talk" I mean talk—like in the old days, on the phone, live, personal, instead of being sent to a list of frequently asked questions. People want to talk to you. They want competitive prices *and* personalized service. Give it to them. Customer service means making sure clients are happy. Don't assume they are. Ask them for feedback. If you can take the focus off yourself and your problems (and your competition) and just concentrate on what you can do to make your customers happy, exceeding their expectations, you will be fine. Remember, pleasing the customer (first-time or long-term or even one-time) *is* self-promotion.

☆ ——————————————
QUICK QUIZ
What kind of customer service do you expect? Would your own customer service rise to the level of mind-blowing? List ten things that make for excellent customer service. Do you know what your customers want and expect? Where have you gotten exceptional service? What made it so great? What can *you* do better? Pick something you will implement right away.

How to "Do It"
"A customer's not a customer until he's a repeat customer."
—Sam Walton

There are so many similarities between good customer service and relationships that I thought it would be fun to explore them here. On the first date you are working it. You hold the door open for them, pay the bill, make your date feel special. (I know this never should stop, but it does.) You try to discover their likes and dislikes. On the second date you are still on your best behavior. You show up on time, hang on their every word, laugh at their jokes, and try to win over their friends. If all goes well, at the end of the date maybe you end up making out on the doorstep. On the third date you still listen to them, say please, and you are genuinely enthralled by them. Things are going great, which will lead to a relationship where you share your needs, communicate your feelings, talk about the future. You are becoming friends and, hopefully, lovers. You are getting to the point where you know each other, like each other, and *trust* each other. You are affectionate (let them know you *really* like them), considerate (call if you are going to be late), and you do everything you can to please them (if you know what I mean). Then you are a couple. As a couple, the old rules apply, plus you must remember key dates (birthdays and anniversaries) and continue to remind them how much you care. Now reread this and plug in the word "customer" instead of "date." I realize that the goal is different (romance versus building a business), but I believe the analogy holds up.

QUICK QUIZ

Unscramble INTESL. What does it say?

(Listen or Silent) Listen to customers. Ask them and listen to them. Some are cantankerous and crackpots. Others give insight. Either way, unless you shut up and listen, you ain't learnin' nothin'.

Super Service

> "The key to understanding is listening with the eyes and the heart."
>
> —Steven Covey

Super service is an attitude. You would think that Nordstrom, the poster child for exceptional customer service, must have an amazing training program. Well, if you thought that, you were wrong. They simply hire the right people and ask them to use good judgment. I still believe it can be taught and that it's never too early to teach (or too late to learn) good customer service. Here's a good example. One boy had been mowing nearly all the lawns in his neighborhood for the past few years. He took his summer job seriously. Once a week he would get on the phone and call his neighbors, trying to sell them his mowing service at a reduced rate. He took pride in the fact that they always turned him down. See, he was calling his own customers and pretending to be a competitor to see if they were satisfied with his service, and this is a child! (When this kid has his IPO, I'm buying stock.) Competition can be a good thing. If, in the back of your mind, you know there is someone lurking in the shadows, ready and waiting to pounce as soon as you screw up or let your guard down, it can keep you on your toes. You get very protective. Well, I've got some bad news for you about your competition, they're heeerrrreeeeee. Pay attention to your customers. Are they happy? Are you doing all you can do? Listen to them. Really listen to what they want. Ask for performance reviews and improve. The sale is just the beginning. Most people take the money and run (then have to look for new clients). The goal is to have a long list of people who will do business with you again and tell their friends.

A Customer Service Checkup

See how many of these suggestions you are currently using.

— *I am focused on my customers' needs.* It's not about what you want. What do they expect? What are you doing for them now? Is there a gap? Frequently ask: "How can I serve you better?" Promptly add services they request.

— *I underpromise and overdeliver.* Don't make promises you can't keep. "You want this back by next week, no problem." Of course, there is no way in hell you can pull it off. Instead, ask for more time, and if at all possible, turn it in early and underbudget. (I don't need to mention that you also did a bang-up job on it, right?)

— *I am very easily accessible.* Your perspective: There is nothing worse than distractions when you're trying to create. Their perspective: There is nothing worse than not being able to get hold of someone and then not getting a quick reply when leaving a message or sending an e-mail. There is a happy medium. Work on your art early or late and do the drudgery stuff during normal business hours. When you take a break, check messages and reply promptly. Have an assistant handle your calls and answer e-mail. Set a goal that you will respond to requests within twenty-four hours. You get the picture. They want to talk to you, or at least a live, knowledgeable, helpful person.

— *I am friendly and personable.* It costs you nothing to be friendly. When a waitress gives less than her best in the way of service, but does it in a friendly, personable way, it doesn't seem to bother me as much. I like going to this little video store where they know my name. They even call to say, "Hey, that video you were asking about is in." They will give you honest appraisals of videos. They offer off-the-wall and hard-to-get stuff and provide a newsletter with reviews about the latest releases. They let customers review films and talk to the clerk (who is a very vocal film critic), they pop fresh popcorn (for free), and if you're a little late, no big deal. They are convenient, their hours are good, and they have a drive-through window (it used to be a bank) to return rentals.

— *I respond to requests for information as quickly as possible.* I know, I don't dig it, either. Creatives like to be left alone. We're busy. It can be a real drag to have to put a proposal or press kit together. Force yourself. If you wait four or five days to respond, you may lose them (potential clients) to someone else who did reply. The call you don't bother to return and the package you never sent may have been the great opportunity you were waiting for. Sometimes a freelancer will be hired because they were the first to send their portfolio. Have all your materials assembled and ready to go. Make it as pain-free as possible by being prepared. (Use your downtime to do it. It's a fact that tedious and repetitious work actually triggers ideas and creativity.)

— *I look for little things I can do to make life easier for my customers.* Little things do go a long way. Maybe you fix something for free or add in a little something extra. (A service bureau down the road scans things in a couple of different resolutions, just in case you may need a low-resolution version as well as the high-resolution version.) Thoughtful: eToys handwrites its gift cards and attaches them to the packages when they're shipped. Nice touch: When I go to my dentist he always provides a CD player (and even brings in CDs from his home that he knows I enjoy), and he makes it as pain-free as possible. (He gives me the gas for everything. Wahoooooooooo!) A former football player, "Rock" invites me to games, and when I bumped into him at a restaurant, he sent over a round of beers for me and my buddies. What a guy.

— *I always do more than they expect.* When one frantic mother came in with her son, the dry cleaner asked what was wrong. The single mother admitted she didn't know how to knot a tie. The dry cleaner offered to knot the tie for the kid, who was on his way to graduation, and he also found an unclaimed sport coat that fit and gave it to him. One company, Taco Clip Art, can create specialized illustrations in under ninety minutes. This continues to impress clients. Do you do any kind of customer appreciation parties? Do you have an award or section of your newsletter to reward loyal clients?

— *I am good at staying in touch with customers.* Look for ways to stay in touch. Maybe you hold something back and send it a few days later with a note, "Thought you would appreciate this." By all means say "Thank you" even if you didn't get the gig. It's a classy move and it will blow them away. Send a birthday card. One cookbook author who specializes in recipes that go over well with diabetics (she's a diabetic herself) sends updates on the disease and recipe cards (with order information on the back) containing ways to make her regular recipes work for people with diabetes.

— *I am easy to do business with.* Do you offer several payment options? I decided a long time ago that I would offer to bill people rather than make them pay up front. You would think I'd be burned by bad-credit-risk customers. Not once. You can also make life easier by offering free shipping or deliverey. A toll-free number. Free parking. Guarantee all of your work, no questions asked. How else could you make life easier for customers? Take a look at your forms. Try to fill one out yourself. Are they as easy as you thought? Read your ordering instructions. Are they so simple a child could understand them? Can you simplify your pricing?

— *I believe the customer is always right.* The customer *isn't* always right, but so what? If you argue and win, you still lose. Dealing with difficult clients is, well, difficult. What helps is the knowledge that you can't change their behavior. So you have to decide if you want to deal with them or not. What would it take to please these perplexing people, and is it worth it—to you? Some have tried to change the bad behavior of difficult clients by setting up boundaries of what they'll tolerate, with moderate success. I have found that no matter how hard you try to please them, they just don't get it. They don't think they are difficult and then promptly tell you to stop sniveling. So . . . when they really piss you off it is easy to just lash out and tell them to go to hell, but the hangover from that kind of behavior can be a doozy. In my experience, freaking out and telling people to buzz off has never produced a positive result.

— *I always correct my mistakes and go out of my way to make things right.* If you messed up, admit it and fix it. Do NOT argue or try to come up with some lame excuse. Ask how you can make it up to them. Do it. Your ability to handle conflicts with customers can actually increase their loyalty to you. Nearly 95 percent of complaining customers will keep doing business with you if they feel you fixed their problem. Start by hearing them out, then offer solutions to their problem, and finally, follow through on what you agree to do. In a way, maybe you should always pretend you screwed up, even if you do good work. That way you are always in damage control mode and going way beyond what you normally would to please people. Just a thought.

— *I always follow up after the sale.* This alone will make you stand out from 99 percent of all of your competition. Most don't do it. Just a FYI, thank-you, confirmation, update, freebie, coupon, letter, questionnaire—anything to keep the momentum going in a good direction. When it comes to thank-you notes, double what you are now doing.

— *I always show how much I appreciate their business.* The least you should do is send a thank-you note. Food (chocolate and pizza) always seems to go over big. I worked with one client coaching their employees on time management and goal setting. The first training session was a success. The next was a disaster. Not because of anything I did, but on the day of the training the client found out they were being sued. I plunged ahead anyway, with little effect. I offered to do the training over, but the owner was actually pleased. Even so, when my last book came out I went over to the client's office and gave every employee a signed copy of the book as a way of saying thanks. Double your thank-you note output this month and see what happens. It is a good idea to keep this thought in mind, because there are a lot of others competing for their business. Part of being the best isn't so much the work you do, but how you do it and how you treat them.

— *I look for ways to make customers feel special.* When I visited Marty, a photographer friend, I noticed a photo of a celebrity on the wall. I commented that I was a fan (she's a fox), and lo and behold a few days later I got a package and inside was a signed photo, framed, no less. Yowza! How can you make a more personal connection with customers? Do sweat the small stuff. When I travel doing seminars, I am always appreciative of (and remember) the hotels that clean the glass of the overhead machine or remember me from last time and have my water with lemon and no ice up on stage. It is the little things that make a big difference.

— *I demand good service from my suppliers.* You can do everything right and still get tripped up by a supplier who back-orders a key component, a printer who lags, or a manager who continually drops the ball. It's up to you to use your leverage to get the same kind of service from support people that you give to your clients. If they screw you once, shame on them. Twice, shame on you. Drop them.

Stories of Super Service

"How can I serve my competition's customer?"

—Guy Kawasaki

Customer service can be summed up in two words: exceed expectations. When one woman went into her local grocery store and wanted to buy an item on the top shelf that she couldn't reach (she is vertically challenged), she asked a tall stock boy for assistance. He replied, "No problem," as he got down on one knee and intertwined his fingers. "Ready for a boost?" Is that exceptional customer service? It's not bad, but not great, either. Let's look at some super service examples.

When Dale Morrison (now CEO of Campbell Soup Company) worked his first job (delivering papers when he was ten), he didn't just throw the papers on people's lawns, he knocked on their door, said hello, asked how they were doing, then handed them their paper. Contact with your customers can make a HUGE difference. You can better serve your customers if you contact them and listen to what they have to say. Pull your head out of the sand, everything is not fine, and find out what's on their mind. (You'll hear all kinds of positive things, too.)

A waitress at my family's favorite restaurant not only remembers your name, but also what you like (my dad likes lemons with his water and my brother wants his dressing on the side). One time, when the restaurant ran out of ice cream, the waitress got in her car and drove half a mile to get the dessert my dad wanted. I am sure you also have stories of super service. I tell everyone when I get great service. I'm sure you do the same. That's why you want to go out of your way to make clients happy.

After a canceled flight, one angry passenger demanded that the gate agent get him on the next flight, and it better be first class. The fact that he cut in line didn't seem to faze him. The gate agent asked him (nicely) to get in line and she would work something out after helping the other passengers ahead of him. Hearing this, he threw a fit and started screaming, loud enough so everyone could hear. "Do you know who I am? Do you have any idea who I am?" The airline employee smiled and grabbed her public address microphone. "May I have your attention, please?" she began, her message being broadcast throughout the terminal. "We have a passenger here at the gate WHO DOES NOT KNOW WHO HE IS. If anyone can help him find his identity, please come to Gate 17." The people in line lost it and started laughing uncontrollably. The man just glared at the agent and then yelled, "F—k you!" Without flinching, she smiled and said, "I'm sorry, but you'll have to stand in line for that, too."

ACTION ITEM
What are your competitors doing? Find out. How can you one-up them?

Service That Sucks

"It takes months to find a customer and seconds to lose one."
—*Unknown*

When I was in New York visiting my agent and editor, I wanted to try real New York–style pizza. So I went into a place that had multiple locations (each one claiming to be the Original Home of New York Style Pizza). I stared at the menu trying to make up my mind about what I would order (and shocked at New York prices). The guy behind the counter scowled at me and said, "Hey, you gonna orda a piece a pie or you gonna stand there like a idiot?" I couldn't believe it. Of all the nerve. Then I realized where I was (in New York City ordering pizza), so I laughed and said, "Just give me anything." So he slapped down a piece of cheese pizza and yells, "Dat'll be two dollaas." I said, "But there's isn't any meat—" I didn't get to finish the sentence. He picked one slice of pepperoni off another piece of pizza and put it on mine and said, "There, now you got some meat, knucklehead." All righty, then. On "Seinfeld" there is a soup kitchen owner they called the "Soup Nazi" who intimidated customers, and if he didn't like you he would scream "No soup for you!" and you were banned from getting his great soup. As harsh as the Soup Nazi was, there is a lesson to learn. Life is too short to deal with difficult customers. If their demands are unreasonable, they don't pay, or they berate and belittle you, I say get rid of them. Some customers aren't worth the trouble.

Here's something you shouldn't say. "That's not my department, you'll need to call so-and-so." The old car salesman's trick, "Let me check with my manager," doesn't fly anymore. If there is a problem, fix it. Don't say "I'll try," just do it. The other is: "That's not our policy." It reminds me of a story where a guy goes into his bank to cash a check and asks to have his parking validated. The teller tells him that cashing a check isn't really a bank transaction. So he asks to speak to the manager, who backs up the teller, saying, "Sorry, that's our policy." The customer asks if he could make one more transaction. He writes a check for $2 million and closes his account. As he is leaving to go to the bank across the street he says, "Is that a banking transaction?" Ha! The bottom line is this: What people want is R-E-S-P-E-C-T.

FREEBIES

In the late nineteenth century, St. Louis brewer Aldolphus Busch came up with some clever giveaways so bar owners would remember his beer. He distributed novelties like corkscrews, matchboxes, and other gifts (all with the Budweiser name on them). Two of the most successful of these freebies were trays and posters with Budweiser girls on them. These "hotties," who were dressed from head to toe (my, how times have changed), became collector's items. To stand out from the scores of other beer salesmen, he devised a unique calling card. When he would call on tavern owners, he'd leave behind a Budweiser pocketknife with a peephole in it. If you peered inside you would see a picture of Aldolphus looking back at you. Anything they'll keep with your name on it is good. Sending a direct-mail piece with a promotional product generates more than double the response rate. The Hard Rock Cafe in Las Vegas puts rock star faces on their poker chips. If a visitor takes a $25 Jimi Hendrix chip as a souvenir, the Hard Rock Cafe makes $24.50! The best premium items tie in with your business and are either useful, practical, needed, valued, inexpensive, lasting, or seen by others. A good example of this is a T-shirt. It hits all of the above criteria.

FAST FACT

Ninety-five million homes have at least one fridge which they open an average of twenty times a day. (That's 7,300 hits a year.) Make yourself more "magnetic" by putting your logo and contact information on a magnet.

Freebies build customer loyalty, which in turn increases sales. Recognize customers at the end of the year and you create goodwill. If it is something they will see all year long, all the better. Here's how to "give good gift."

It's a sign. One clever company gave signs that people could put on their doors that said, "Out to Lunch," "Do Not Disturb, Genius at Work," and "Beware of Occupant," with their logo and phone number or website at the bottom. Another idea is freestanding flyers that have useful information (software shortcuts or timely tips) that people will put *on top of* the pile of papers on their desk.

Let's get drunk and . . . A bar I go to has *the* best mai tais. So

SELF-PROMOTION FOR THE CREATIVE PERSON

many people asked for the recipe that the bar owner and the rum company got together and made coasters with the recipe on one side and the bar and rum company's logo on the other. Great idea.

Teach a man to fish and you have a customer for life. Tip sheets are cheap, useful, and can lead to more business. An educated customer is a better customer, in my opinion. One tip sheet in particular stands out. It was from a marriage counselor. (It wasn't for me, thank you very much.) It listed twenty-four ways to improve your love life (twelve for him, twelve for her). For example (come on, I know you want to know), number six (for her) talks about how to give a good massage. Another (and not related) example of giving to get is a videographer who gives away a booklet on how to direct a home video (which he also sells and teaches a related class on). He was frequently asked to edit home videos and saw some common mistakes. Now his clients see how much he knows and how much of the equipment needed for making a good video they *don't* have. It's led to a lot of work. That's why I think these are better than a brochure, because by telling them what you can do, you show them a little skin. A little like a striptease.

Inch by inch it's a cinch. A gym could give away a tape measure and a workout log (with their name, hours, class schedules) and free passes for friends and a place for before and after pictures, as well as their workout record and fitness goals.

Stick it. Stickers are both cheap and lasting. I have a copier in my office, and whenever it needs to be serviced I call the same company, even though they aren't the cheapest or the best. Why? Laziness, and the fact that there has been a sticker on the copier since I bought it with this repair company's phone number on it. Another nice feature about stickers is that they are easy for "fans" to put up. Many surfwear companies give away stickers, knowing full well that these mini-ads end up on street signs, in bathrooms, and on boards. It's a very cost-effective form of advertising for them. One progressive church passes out a sheet of stickers at the beginning of the year with the information about upcoming bands and events at the church, and they encourage people to put them on their calendars.

Pin-up calendars. Customize a calendar with creative headings, artwork (yours), facts and figures about your business or industry, and, of course, contact information. Sending a customer a calendar is nothing new. My friend Bruce owned a motorcycle repair shop and he always put up a calendar (or two) from his suppliers. These calendars feature tools and tits. That's not a misprint. The target audience is men. So these tool companies feature scantily clad women posing with various tools. Man, that sounds bad, doesn't it? How about a nice thought-a-day desktop calendar instead with motivational messages? That's nice, isn't it? The goal is to get them thinking about you every day of the year. Custom calendars (nice and otherwise) do just that.

Tchotchkes. It seems like every fast-food chain is giving something away with their meals. It's almost like they are saying, "Do you want fries with that toy?" Yet these little gimmicks get people's attention—if they are clever, related to your business or offer, and have your name on them. One man who wrote a book on the best beaches gave away a little beach in a bag with sand from some of the best beaches in the world. How about a key chain with your art on it? One company that does Navy SEAL workout classes gives away dog tags to promote their classes. I have seen clocks with the face changed and replaced with art, or all the numbers in a pile at the bottom with the word "whatever" painted on. (It also had the artist's website address.) To promote *The Desktop Publisher's Idea Book,* Chuck Green gives away a ruler with picas, inches, fraction-to-decimal conversions, design tips, and of course his website address (www.ideabook.com). It's both creative and useful.

Instructions. Care and cleaning instructions with a painting is smart (and offer to hang it as a bonus and give lighting tips). The better your art looks, the better you look. Why do you think Williams & Sonoma puts recipes in their catalogs? If you said, "So I will want to cook more," you are correct. The more you cook, the more you need their products. Pretty smart. Couldn't you teach your clients more about what you do? When they know more, they buy more. Instead of a brochure, put out an instructional/informational booklet or add tips to your catalog.

Wall posters. When one of my friends showed up at our usual Friday happy hour, it occurred to me: Wouldn't it be great if there was a chart for fashion-impaired people? This could be part of a brochure, on the back of a business card or a wall poster that shows what colors go together, as well as fashion faux pas for, say, an image consultant. (My friend "D" insists on wearing this stupid looking hat and hasn't got the memo that the "Miami Vice" look is OUT! He is a giant fashion emergency, so I am going to make him one of these until he gets a clue.) Posters in general are exceptional "keepers." Who hasn't had a poster on their wall during their teen years? (For many of us it was Farrah Fawcett.) A band could create their own poster that features bios of the band, photos, album covers, tour dates, lyrics, and if they were smart, they'd get a cosponsor to pay for part of it (their label, a music store, equipment company, or a rich parent).

Food. One clever promotion was a chocolate cell phone that said "sweet success" on the wrapper. When these promotional prizes were passed out, one woman muttered, "Just what I need, a cellulite phone." Ha ha ha. To include with orders and pass out as prizes, I came up with my own candy bar. I call it the Bravo Bar. (It's actually a Hershey Bar with the label changed.) I have had only positive feedback from the people who received them.

Coffee cups and more. With ink-jet printers, it is possible to use iron-on transfers and stickers to create custom coffee cups (put your art, tips, quotes, services you provide, interesting websites, and your website on them), or T-shirts, or pillowcases, or use your art or logo to customize bags, wrapping paper, book covers, stickers, hats, and even magnetic signs for your car. Speaking of magnets, I got this magnet that has thirty little cartoon faces, each with a different emotion. It also has a frame that says, "Today I feel," and you slide the frame over the face that best represents your mood. George Willbrandt invented the giant, wide-barreled, narrow-bottomed plastic cup known as "the drive-through." First of all, who needs that much liquid, and why the hell do I care who invented the promotional cups? Just like coffee cups, creating a custom water bottle can be a nice freebie for a fan.

File boxes. A cookbook author could create a custom file box (with her logo on it) and send along recipes with each mailing. A landscaper could do the same for the care of different plants. A consultant could send quick tips or software shortcuts on cards.

Binders. Buy the binders that have a clear sleeve on the front and spine and create your own covers. Then three-hole-punch your sales slicks, newsletters, flyers, announcements, price lists, and updates so people have a safe place to put them. (Gets them out of the pile and into the file.)

Datebooks. You can buy Day Timer pocket planners in bulk imprinted with your name on them. A planner, like a calendar, is something they handle every day, which means you are on their mind. Since I don't use a prepackaged planner myself (I invented my own time-management system for right-brainers), I give away a pad with a month's supply of Right-Brain Things-to-Do lists.

Door hangers. Can also be used on cars, flowers, bags, wine bottles, as well as doors.

Post-it notes. Post-it notes make your message stick. Have some made with your name and contact information on them and use them yourself or give them away.

Personalize it. Write a poem, cartoon, song, or short story and leave it behind.

Dumps. Add more P.O.P. (point of purchase) for your products. A "dump" is a display that retailers use to display your creations (hopefully on the counter). This could also include a custom header card, sign, standee, or a stand to hold your support materials.

Screen savers. These are cheap to produce and very cool! You could do a custom mouse pad, but a screen saver of your own creation (if you know how) could be even better.

Gift certificates. Can't come up with anything creative to give? Go with a gift certificate. It's better than sending something inappropriate. One art director received lingerie from a freelance artist and illustrator. The problem? The art director is a man and NOT a cross-dresser. Besides, even if he did like lace, it's still too weird.

Best bumper stickers. "Real women don't have hot flashes, they have power surges." "IRS: We have what it takes to take what you've got." "The more people I meet, the more I like my dog." Create your own.

Free: the Most Powerful Word in the English Language

"If you have money, you are wise and good-looking and can sing well too."

—Jewish Proverb

Garth Brooks went around the Country Radio Seminar promoting his first single, "Much Too Young to Feel This Damn Old," and pinned buttons on everyone he met. This allowed him to meet and talk to the radio promoters. This is how to build a buzz. Advance copies lead to word of mouth, reviews (positive, we can only hope), and advance orders. The only danger is that a freebie is one less of an item they will buy. (I also have to make sure that books don't get returned to stores, so I doctor the bar code.) Family and friends are the worst. They expect something for nothing. I have found that if they pay for it, they appreciate it more. Besides, a guy's gotta make a living, right? If I gave every one of my family and friends a free book, it would be like me handing them fifteen dollars. I only give books away to people who have, or can, help me in some way, with a few exceptions.

On the other hand, if you have overruns or extras of your creations sitting around your studio or garage, use them. Put them to work for you. Send some as samples or gifts to key people. They aren't doing anything but taking up space. Wouldn't it be better to have them in the hands of the people who can help? If you have only one, hang it where people will see it. Give some samples away to record stores to play. Provide books to bookstore managers and clerks and even librarians to read. Get your samples in the hands of people who can help. If you don't have a product, give a sample performance, a free clinic, free consulting, or a free hour of instruction. Offer to appear at their favorite charity at no charge. Do a free makeover like they do at the MAC cosmetic counter. Don't give away the store, but give them a taste of things to come. Once they experience what you do, they'll pay. The best kind of freebie is when a client buys something of yours in bulk and then THEY give them away to their clients. You sell a ton at once and your customer looks like a very generous person. Or stimulate sales by offering a free gift (something that wouldn't otherwise sell) with every purchase. Or how about this: One appliance retailer gives potential customers a free half gallon of ice cream just for coming in. Sound too generous? The reason he does this is so the customer won't comparison-shop the other stores on the street. If they do, the ice cream will melt, so they go home.

☆ ─────────────────────

JUST FOR FUN
The highest-earning deceased person is . . . Elvis, followed by John Lennon, James Dean, Jimi Hendrix, and Albert Einstein.

─────────────────────

Improve Your Long-Term (Promotional) Health
"I see everyone else working, and I'm not doing dick. I'm in total limbo. I'm a man without a country."

—*Sylvester Stallone*

You are only as good as your last gig, film, book, project—and sometimes even that doesn't seem to matter anymore! What am I trying to do, depress you? Not at all. I'm just warning you that you need fans for long-term security. When you have a vision for the future and fans who will support you, you have a better chance of survival in this disposable world. (It's always the latest greatest thing while the old and outdated is pushed aside. By the way, if you are the new thing, ride it for all it's worth.) Build some momentum. Once you do an exceptional job for a client, start thinking of other ideas for that same client. What else can you offer them? Can you do some kind of maintenance on what you did? Is there anything else they may need to go along with what you have already provided? My brother Mark makes a nice living by training and consulting on the installation of one particular type of software. It's a nice add-on sale for the software maker and a perfect niche for my brother.

Think about the future, but act in the present. Ask yourself: How will what I do today affect my long-range marketability? Carrie Fisher said, "Instant gratification takes too long." I understand. Long-term marketing is not as easy as taking out an ad and then waiting for the phone to ring. Long-term marketing (or relationship selling, as it is sometimes called) is both time-consuming and expensive. (Technology can ease the burden, but . . .) Regardless, you need to think about your overall strategy and long-term marketability when making any decision. "What would happen to Mozart were he alive today?" Cynthia Heimel asks. "After composing his first symphony at the age of four, he would be *Time*'s Man of the Year. He and his family would move to Malibu Colony. He'd host 'Saturday Night Live.' He'd sign with Michael Ovitz, who'd package a sitcom for him. It would fail, as all sitcoms do, and little Mozart would go on drinking sprees and end up in rehab. At the age of seven, Mozart would be a regular on 'Hollywood Squares.'"

FAST FACTS
Examples of creating things with a long shelf life.

1. Which of the following is the best-selling record album of all time? (a) *Thriller* by Michael Jackson, (b) *Rumours* by Fleetwood Mac, (c) *The Beatles* by The Beatles, (d) *The Eagles' Greatest Hits 1971–75* by The Eagles. Answer: (d)

How to Stick Around
Record companies are now creating one-hit wonders by creating a buzz before the music goes on sale. Then they keep promoting the act until we can't stand it anymore. Most of today's acts will barely be remembered a few years from now. Fans' attention spans are not what they used to be. Now it's "one and out." The only way to survive any longer is to have long-term fans or reinvent yourself and win new ones every few years. How? Capture their emotions and take the logic out of it. Another sure way to survive is to have great chops. Tina Turner is still "rollin'" at age sixty. What is it that keeps people coming back for more? The hair? The legs? No, it's that she is an exceptional talent (as a vocalist and performer). People pay to see that. It's also about creativity. Be so unique and avant garde that it captures the attention and imagination of your audience. They wonder: What will you do next? Incorporate some fun into what you do. People want to

have fun, and I think that's why Jimmy Buffett and "Margaritaville" keep chugging along—it's the fun factor.

Stay on top of trends and stay current. Go on a continual program of self-improvement. Change with the times. The Beastie Boys had a nice run in the late eighties and early nineties. But the band won't die. In 1998 their album *Hello, Nasty* hit number one. They not only haven't lost their touch, they've gotten better with age. They were setting new standards for creativity in the music world. Reinvent yourself for the times. Paul Simon has been able to stay popular because his music changes with the tastes of the times.

On the other hand, stay consistent and loyal to your core fans. No matter what trends have come and gone, Neil Young remains. His popularity is due in part to the fact that he has never grown complacent. Study the masters, study the latest and greatest. Learn, practice, improve. Be the Yoda of your field. Be real, and give everything you have, like Bruce Springsteen. Don't sell out for a few bucks that could damage your credibility and reputation. John Cusack chooses his roles carefully. They may not be the most commercial, but they were what he wanted to do. His career began in 1983 with *Class* and is still going strong.

Madonna never grows complacent. She morphs about every two years. It's nice to create something so lasting that it keeps going even after the promotion has stopped. The book *Drawing on the Right Side of the Brain* is in most visual artists' libraries. It was published in 1976, but word of mouth keeps it going. "You gotta get this book."

If you can create something that connects with a core group so they not only have to have it themselves, but will also buy a copy for all their friends and family, you've got a good shot at creative immortality.

Ask a Pro

Jana Stanfield
Recording artist/author
www.janastanfield.com

Without a lot of money how would you start a promotional campaign?

I believe in the promotional power of friends, family, and word of mouth. The people who will be most interested in our projects are the people who care about us. They'll also be most likely to tell others about what we're doing, to help you get a buzz going. When you create something, it's like tossing a little pebble in the water. The first ring that flows out of that will be your family and friends. The second ring will be their family and friends. Soon you'll be known by people you've never met. Here's a way to start the process: Use your holiday card list and send out a letter telling everyone you know about your latest creative endeavor. Ask them to tell everyone they know. Tell them what you're trying to achieve and let them know how they can help. If you feel funny about doing something like this, just imagine that you have a favorite niece or nephew who is a creative person. If he or she wrote you telling you how you could help make a big dream come true, wouldn't you be glad to assist? Then, when the kid succeeds, you can feel great about the fact that you helped. If you're doing art or music, a mailing to everyone you know is a good way to get a good crowd to your next show. If you've written a book, encourage everyone on that list to buy holiday presents from you in bulk and give them a volume discount.

So obviously the goal is to build a better mailing list.

Your mailing list is the list of people who believe in what you do. This is very important, because these are the people who will spread the word about you. Everyone on this list is a potential public relations agent. Think of all the times you read a book, bought a CD, or rented a movie because a friend told you it was good. People respect their friends' recommendations. Don't waste time taking cards from strangers who are unlikely to buy your creations or come to your shows. You just want the people who like you or like your work.

Since maintaining a mailing list is such a pain, how do you recommend doing it?

There are two good ways to keep up with names on your mailing list. If you refuse to put it on a computer, make a mailing list sign-up sheet that has name/address squares the exact size of Avery mailing labels. That's a mailing label brand you can buy at any office supply store. Use the sheet of blank mailing labels as a guide when you create the sheet. Once the sheet is filled with names, you can use a copier to copy the entire page of names onto the sheet of labels. All you have to do is peel the labels off and mail them. If you prefer to collect names on gum wrappers, grocery receipts, and scraps of napkins, there are mailing services that will enter those names into a computer. Look under mailing services in the phone book and call around until you find one that will tolerate you. They'll do mailings for you and will keep your entire database on their computer.

What is the biggest mistake creative people make when marketing themselves?

Exuberant preteens look at life the same way I once did. They say things like, "I want to be a famous singer someday," or, "I want to be a model someday." They want to know how to do that. The answer is so simple, and yet I didn't learn this important life principle until I was in my early thirties. Leave off the word "someday" and start today.

So simple, but so profound. Go on.

A model is one who models. A singer is one who sings. An artist is one who creates art, and a writer is one who writes. The only way to become a famous model, singer, artist, or writer is to start by being *un*-famous. There's a myth that people are "discovered" and that the prize is a great career. The truth is that most people who are discovered have been doing what they do for a long time. By practicing our art, we get better and better at it. The work is the prize. If we get famous at it, that's a bonus.

We think, "If I got that book deal (record deal, artist-in-residence grant, movie funding), then the guy down the street would buy what I create." There are two ways to get your art into the home of the guy down the street. You can spend your time and money sending your art on a circuitous route that takes it all the way around the globe before it gets there, or you can go straight from your house. The people who'll be buying your creations are all around you. Don't waste time waiting for the big company that can send your art around the globe. Your audience is right in front of you.

9

SHOW AND SELL
(Selling Without Selling Out)

"Some of the sharpest traders we know are artists, and some of the best salesmen are writers."
—E. B. White

When one salesman's five-minute meeting with the buyer was over and he didn't get the sale, he knew he needed more time. So he found out where the buyer ate breakfast every morning, what he ordered, and where he sat. The rep bought the buyer a bagel, sat in his seat, and waited for him to arrive. The surprised buyer arrived and the two talked over breakfast (not about business) and then parted ways. The sales rep continued this for seven weeks. The two men ended up becoming friends and finally an order was written. This true example highlights several key points to selling, including following up, coming up with a clever approach, and establishing a relationship. This chapter will show you how to sell without selling out.

We all have the ability to sell. Just think back to when you were a kid. You learned how to sell (manipulate) parents, teachers, and other kids to get what you wanted. Whether it was for a new bike, a later curfew, or permission to drive the car on a Saturday night, you learned how to get what you wanted through selling. You didn't call it sales. You called it things like "the guilt trip," the "rant and rave," and the "I'm gonna cry" technique, but you were selling. And probably pretty well. So what happened? To begin with, many creative people prefer to keep to themselves. This is exactly the opposite of the way things are sold these days. It's about whom you know and who knows you. The more people you know, the fewer cold calls you have to make. The fewer cold calls you have to make, the easier it is to sell. (If you ask me, the less cold calling, the better.) What if all you had to do was call up an acquaintance and say, "How are you? Me? Oh, you know, I'm doing my art and loving it. Hey, you can see my latest creations on my website." That's it. It's not sleazy. It's not pushy. It's not ugly. It's about meeting people, forming a relationship, and staying connected. No problem, you can do *that*. Still, for many of us it just doesn't seem natural. "I mean, I went to all this trouble to create the damn thing and now I have to sell it? That's just not right." Right or wrong, it's a fact of life as a creative person. Maybe all you have to do is sell your agent on the idea and let her do the rest. Then there's one less important sales job you have to make, isn't there? Creative people have to sell to survive. Period. End of discussion. Still, it comes as a shock to some people when I tell them they must learn how to sell their creations (as well as ideas and insights). It's not beneath you, it's not as disgusting as it sounds, and if you use your creativity, it can be an art. When it's done well, selling is an art. The alternative to learning how to sell is even more disgusting in my opinion—having no work and being forced into obscurity. Now, *that* is frightening.

I'll agree that selling isn't usually a strong suit for a lot of creative people, but it can be. Note, there are no "born" salesmen. It's a learned skill and a mind-set. I'm not saying it's easy, because it's not. But it's doable. Did I mention the alternative? So are you ready to learn the secrets to selling? Here's one thing that will improve your attitude toward sales (and make you much more proficient). Think of selling as consulting or teaching. Instead of trying to find ways to shove something down someone's throat, think of it as helping people. "How can I help people by solving their problems?" Who can resist someone who wants to help them solve problems? And it doesn't feel like selling anymore. It can be as easy as saying, "Hey, Jim, I do that kind of work. I'd be happy to do it for you." See, it's not pushy. Think of all the things you're doing for them. Are you bringing art into their lives? Helping them save money? Make money? Improving their lives in some small way? Making them look good?

Make sure you're pitching to the right people. When you find the right fit, it means you have found someone who truly needs what you have to offer, appreciates what you do, and gives you the freedom you need to create great art. There are two schools of thought. Pick the easiest people to pursue first, and build confidence and momentum before going after the "big boys." The other approach is to aim high. If with one sales presentation you could hit the mother lode, why not try? If worse comes to worst, you can regroup and go back to the little fish. Another secret to selling is to do something so freaking fantastic and original that they come to you, and all you have to do is decide whether you want to work with them and how much you're going to make them pay. But until that happens, try finding something that you're proud of and passionate about, and selling will become something you can learn to live with (and maybe even love?).

Finally, shut up and listen to your customers, colleagues, agent, reps, retailers, and anyone else who has ideas about what you could do better to sell your stuff. Most creative people love to talk, but we should also learn to listen to feedback from those with another perspective. Take Joy Hakim, a sixty-eight-year-old grandmother and the author of a series of books about American history. She opened her pitch at a trade show for teachers with this question: "How many of your kids stay up late to read their textbooks?" She hears the moans and groans and then hits them with: "They'll stay up to read mine." She knows what buttons to push because she has tested her approach and adjusted it until it worked.

It's a survival thing. Remember, timid salesmen have skinny kids. Don't be afraid, go for it! If you want to be a freelancer, you MUST be able to sell to some extent. At book signings I was a little unsure of how hard to push (and a little shy) when it came time to ask the audience to buy the book. So the first time I did one I just thanked them and waited for the hordes to come and have their books signed. You can guess what happened. (Don't make me say it. All right, nobody bought a book.) Since that time I have never been shy about asking for the sale, without being obnoxious, of course. Shyness is not a good thing when selling. I'd rather err on the side of audacity. My friend Paula, the author of two books and a busy freelance writer, was so impressed with a speaker that she bought his $100 package, which promised to show her how to write a book in two weeks or less. Paula said she had an out-of-body experience. (Her money was "lifted" right from her pocket, so to speak.) The product stank. She is already an accomplished writer, yet she still was persuaded to buy. Wow! Guy Kawasaki, an evangelist for Apple computers, sent his Macintosh "storm troopers" around the country to attack critics of the Mac's operating system. While in airports, he urged his people to try to convince laptop users on the virtues of the Mac. Sometimes you have to step way outside of your comfort zone to sell, but if it keeps you from being a bag lady (or having to ask, "Paper or plastic?"), I think it's worth it to force yourself to stretch.

Sell what you are passionate and enthusiastic about. Look at what you're working on. Is it possible you're having a hard time selling it simply because it's not your best work, or what you really want to be working on?

Who Cares?

"Kodak sells film, but they don't advertise film. They advertise memories."

—Theodore Levitt

Who cares? Ask yourself that the next time you have something to sell. Then consider, why would they care about what you're peddling? I'm finding that articulating the benefits (to them) of what you have to sell *is* the secret to selling. Ask yourself: What do people care about most? Exactly. Themselves. Show them how what you do will benefit them, and you'll be halfway to getting them to own it. Let's talk about benefits (and features) for a minute. A feature is what a product does, and a *benefit* is what it does for YOU. Features excite the research and development people, but the R&Ds are usually not the buyers. Customers get excited about benefits. Let me put it into a context you can relate to right now. This chapter offers a big benefit by teaching you how to easily convert almost anyone into a buyer. See? Benefits or bust, baby.

When my wife and I were in Cozumel, Mexico, we fell prey to a very personable young man. (I think it was my wife who fell, but I went along.) For a free breakfast, all we had to do was listen to a sales pitch about a time-share. After we chowed down (I was gonna get my money's worth), the salesman sat us down and just started hammering away with the features of the resort. He talked about the property, the pools, the price—he never once inquired about what we wanted or needed. What if we didn't swim? So while he rambled on for an hour, I just went into the deep recesses of my mind and hid until he was done. Then I thanked him and went and had *several* beers. Aye caramba. Before you begin pitching, find out what would be the best approach to take by asking a couple of questions about a prospect's dreams, desires, and even their problems. The best benefits are something they want and need. Why would anyone buy from you? (Why wouldn't they go to your competitors?) What's the benefit to buying your stuff? For example, the slogan "Tastes great, less filling" is all about benefits. What they are saying is, you can drink MORE good beer and not get filled up (or develop a beer gut). As the old saying goes, "Customers don't want a quarter-inch drill bit, they want a quarter-inch hole." Sell them by telling them what they want to hear—bennies. This is nothing new, but most of us forget this important point. People couldn't care less about us and our wants and needs. Instead of saying "me, me, me," it should be "we, we, we." (That doesn't sound quite right, does it?) I often say to myself, "It's not about me, stupid, it's about them and their needs." You know what you do, but what can you do for THEM? Put yourself in their shoes and walk around for a while. How does it feel? What would you need to hear (if you were them) that would make you want to buy?

When Joshua Cowen began marketing Lionel Trains (he had already invented the Eveready flashlight, making him a millionaire), his strategy was: toys bring fathers and sons together. His tag line became: "Lionel Trains make a boy feel like a man and a man feel like a boy." This proved to be very effective. It sells using an emotional appeal, which is a benefit. Technology for technology's sake doesn't sell. I know that when I hear about some technological breakthrough, the first few thoughts that go through my mind are: Why does this matter to me? and What will it do—for me? A close friend had a great idea for a dot-com company. Since I offered to design a logo for him, I needed to know what exactly this thing was that he wanted to launch. (All I had to work with were the name and a vague idea of what it was.) He started rambling about the technology, the facts, figures, and features, you know, blah blah blah. So I stopped him and said, "What are the benefits?" He didn't know. Not good. I ended up giving him more than a logo. I gave him a new way of looking at his proposal and pitch. I was falling asleep when he was telling me about his new company, and I'm his friend! Facts are tedious, and so are details, such as what equipment you use, your background, your location. These are interesting (to you, anyway) but don't sell anything. We went through his list of features to find out what the benefit was for each. We put ourselves in a prospective client's shoes to try to figure out what about these facts would help him serve the client better, make him unique, and save him time and money. Basically, give them what they need and solve their problems.

One professor began his class on marketing by making a point about client needs. As an example, he held up the required book for the course and asked, "When you buy this expensive book, what are you looking for?" One student replied, "Good information." Another said, "Clarity." Then there was a long silence and someone yelled out, "Resale value." Ahhh, yes, benefits again. Start selling what you can do for them and not what you've done in the past. What can you do for me now? Eric Stevens, the marketing director for P. T. Barnum's new, more upscale one-ring circus, said: "Past advertising focused on the circus coming to town and here are the new acts. Now we're selling the emotional experience, looking at the smile on your child's face and sharing something special." The bottom line is, you have to answer the question "What's in it for them?" for everything you offer.

Stating things clearly in benefit form (and not a long list of features) gives you a fighting chance to make a sale. Learning how to turn every feature into a benefit is a skill that gives you a GIANT competitive advantage over others who generally speak about the features.

☆ _____

ACTION ITEM

Write a list of features and benefits for yourself. What are your top ten features? Come up with at least one benefit to each.

Successful Selling Skills

"In the modern world of business it's useless to be a creative, original thinker unless you can also sell what you create."
—David Ogilvy

I know a lot of right-brainers would prefer less preamble and more "just tell me what I freakin' need to know." So I'll get right to the point. Here are some suggestions for hand-to-hand combat, better known as personal selling.

Pit bulls. How do you get past the guard dogs or "handlers" that protect the decision makers? Begin by throwing them a bone so they don't bite. Treat them with warmth, kindness, and respect. Start by learning their names. Then find out what the boss is looking for, how to best reach them, and how decisions are made. Then THANK THEM for their help. Make them an ally. Put yourself in their shoes. If someone like you called, what would it take to get you to put the call through? If all else fails, scratch them behind their ears, they love that.

Prospecting. How do you find people and places to sell to? Usually, there is no shortage of possible prospects. It's finding the *right* ones. The ones that need what you've got (and have the ability to pay). When I was a struggling graphic artist, I would look for the absolute worst brochures, ads, and flyers and offer to redesign them. I would make a mock-up and put together a proposal and then pitch the person. Sure, there were a few times where I would hear, "You think my brochure sucks? Well, my daughter did it. Get out!" But for the most part it was an easy sale. (Plus, I could pick and choose what I wanted to work on.) After several of these makeovers, I made up before and after portfolios and I used these as sales tools to get more clients. Finally, I conducted seminars on the subject (Introduction to Graphic Design) and got more work than I could handle. I found that by educating prospects on what good design is, they wanted me to do it for them. (It's not as easy as it looks.) Another prospecting technique is to look for warm leads. When I was hired by the Marriott Corporation to do training, I asked if they needed training for their Courtyard by Marriott division. Voilà, another sale.

Perform. The last time I was in Key West, I went to the Margaritaville Café for a cheeseburger and a beer. I was excited to see they had live music, too. The band was cooking, and I mean that literally. On stage there was a big pot of gumbo. After each song the singer (Bill Wharton, "The Sauce Boss") would add a few ingredients and talk about *his* secret sauce (available for purchase, of course). I had mixed feelings about this approach to selling. (Now I know where the Jimmy Buffett song title "I Will Play for Gumbo" comes from.) Still, selling from the stage can be very profitable for the performance artist. The goal is to make the audience rush to the back of the room to purchase your products without making yourself seem like a huckster. You could make the argument that if you give a good show, you will automatically sell more. I wish it were that easy. Here are some suggestions to make selling from the stage easier (on them and you). If you really don't want to pitch while you perform, another idea is to build your product into the price of the event so they pay up front. Or you can distance yourself from the sales. Let your introducer do it. Have helpers at the back of the room to handle the sales. Also subtle, and far less stressful, is to distance *them* from the sale. Suggest to an audience that what you are selling would make a good gift for a friend, family member, colleague, stranger, alien—plant the seed that what you are selling doesn't have to be for them, unless they want it to be. Try planting subliminal messages in the audience's heads. Before a song, mention that it is on your new CD. Offer to sign copies of your new book. Wear a hat or T-shirt with your product pictured on it. Give product away as a prize and talk it up so the audience (and winner) knows what she is getting and a little about what you do and have to offer. Anything you can do to try to make it seem like you aren't selling puts them at ease. For example, I would pick up my book and read a little from it during a seminar. It was subtle, and it helped sell books. Offer a special price if they buy today, or throw in a freebie. This is usually the clincher, because it creates a sense of urgency and plays off everyone's weakness—greed. "You mean I get the Butt-Buster *and* the Ab-Blaster if I buy today?" It does something to people when you play on their fear that they may not be able to get a better deal ever again. It's like hitting a switch inside the head of a serious shopper's brain. "It's on sale? Really? Cool, I'm there." Find a way to get them to the back of the room to sign up for a drawing, to pick up a freebie, or to ask questions. Or pass out an evaluation form for feedback and to build your mailing list. Also, nobody should leave an event or presentation empty-handed. Handouts for everyone! Finally, there is the school of thought that if you want to sell something you have to *sell* something. If you really believe in what you are promoting, then what's so wrong with doing a professional sales presentation during or after a performance? Nothing.

Partners. You are only one person with a limited amount of time to sell. To maximize your time, get others to do the selling for you. (At least let them set up the sale so you can close it out, or vice versa.) The most obvious partner is an agent or manager. It could even be an attorney. In the film industry, an appointment to pitch a studio executive is usually arranged by an entertainment attorney or an agent. That's the film industry. In the book business, you are more likely to sell a manuscript through an agent than on your own. In other industries you may need a representative to call on buyers. So find out the protocol for pitching and follow it. If you don't have to use a "professional," then there are all kinds of ways to build a sales staff. Make everyone you know a sales rep (pay for performance) by telling friends and family what you do, what you need, and by keeping them up-to-date and armed with the tools to sell (brochures and business cards) and the motivation (money seems to work well). If you can make them partners (literally or figuratively) in your projects and your plans, they have added incentives. (Parents don't seem to need much prompting. Their motivation is keeping you from moving back home.)

Prepare. Prep work does pay off. The more preparation you are able to do before making a sales pitch, the better your chances of not striking out. I know we (creative people) would prefer to wing it, and we'll get to that in a minute. But just for the sake of discussion, pretend you are willing to do a little prep work. Here are some suggestions that could help. Tony Gwynn, one of the best batters in the history of baseball, prepares for each game by reading a scouting report on an opposing pitcher and reviewing video so he knows what to expect. We should do the same thing. Seek out personal information about the person you are pitching to. What has worked on them in the past? What are they looking for? What are their needs? When is the best time to make a presentation? Tony Gwynn also studies video on himself to make sure he is doing all he can as a hitter. So ask yourself: "Why am I qualified for this job or project? Why should they give me the gig? What do I have that they need? How can I best articulate why they need my stuff?" Your answer becomes your ammunition. Prepare yourself for the tough questions. Professionals prepare and want to work at being the best salesperson they can be. That means practicing your pitch. Tony also is big on batting practice before a game. Many times making a sale means knowing all the facts and figures for the anal-retentive types and the technical stuff for the eggheads. A little advance prep saves me from looking like an idiot later. Besides, people are impressed when you show that you took the time to prepare. It increases your credibility. If you don't want to be bothered by preparing and plan to wing it, use your intuitive powers (a strength the creative person possesses). Just read and react to their body language and level of interest.

Problems. As they say in Jamaica, problems are "No problem, mon." They represent opportunities for you. If you can show how what you have to offer can solve their problems, then you should be able to sell them. At the very least it shows that you understand their needs and opens a dialogue. (You may have to help them understand their needs.) So the first step in selling is the same thing a doctor does. Look for the symptoms (ask questions), then diagnose (help them understand their needs), and then prescribe and treat (show them how you can cure their problem). If they don't have much money to spend, find creative ways to make it work. Even if they have a big budget, be aware of the cost to the client, and if you can find ways to save them money, you may have won a customer for life (or at least have your bid accepted). Sometimes money doesn't matter. A limited budget can stretch your imagination to come up with clever and creative solutions—that's a selling point to ponder.

Presents. One smart salesman brings flowers to salon customers he is calling on for the first time. I've used pizza, bagels, and chocolate. (For people on a high-protein diet, just bring cheese.)

Positive. Just a quick note. Don't depress them by dwelling on the negative. Point out their problems but sell the positive aspects of what you do. Sell solutions. Sell hope. Have a happy ending by proposing a solution to those same problems.

Positive expectations. Anything you can do to get your head on straight before making your sales presentation is a plus. Dress to impress, because when you look good, you feel good. Get there early, test your equipment, and be prepared for every contingency. Eliminate any potential distractions. (I onced unplugged a guy's phone when he wasn't looking so he wouldn't be distracted during my presentation.) Picture success. I used to sit in my car before a sales call and visualize walking out with an order. I felt if I could see it, I could do it. I think it made me more confident. Confident, but not arrogant. William

Wrigley Jr. (think gum) said the key to selling was to "always be polite, always be patient, and never argue." When a potential customer told him "No," he would thank the dealer warmly for having at least listened to him. This approach led to a lot of orders. Steve Oedekerk, a screenwriter (and actor and director) who wrote *Ace Ventura: Pet Detective, The Nutty Professor,* and *Patch Adams,* is one of the many who have made it who said that believing in yourself is just as important as talent. His advice on selling was to approach an editor or agent knowing you've got a million-dollar book (or screenplay) and that no matter how great the advance they offer, you are getting screwed, because your book is that good. That kind of attitude, where you believe you deserve to make a sale and that they need and will benefit from buying from you, makes all the difference in the world.

Personality. We buy from people we like. That's a fact. Buyers don't always make logical decisions, they make emotional ones. I know it's not fair. The most qualified person or the best deal should win, but that's usually not the case. A pleasing personality is definitely a plus for pitching. Do your best to try and click with clients. Be both interesting and interested (in them). Find something you have in common. Look around their office. "I see by that deer head on the wall that you like to kill defenseless little animals. Isn't that special?" Try to be relaxed and get them to relax. Being a good conversationalist is a good thing here. Warm up and build trust. Careful, be personable and professional at the same time. I know this guy that, once he relaxes, so do his manners and his mouth. While it's okay to talk about current events, never talk about politics or religion (or weight loss). Be so easy and fun to work with that they look forward to your next call. By the way, being boring is never good when selling something.

Passion. Passion is a plus when you are selling something. Show them how much you care about *them* and your product or service. Be enthusiastic, it's catching. It's also okay to get emotional. If you can get all teary-eyed to make a sale, or get them all teary-eyed, why not do it? Certain speaking colleagues of mine are so slick when they speak, they are devoid of all emotion. I also have been known to be overprepared. On one occasion I forgot the notes to my talk. It was the best talk I ever gave because I spoke from the heart. I let my emotions and enthusiasm surface and show. People came up and commented that I sounded like I really cared—and I always have—and that they connected with me because I was more real. Remember, you aren't selling *something,* you are almost always selling *yourself.* Sometimes it's not what you say, but how you say it. In the 1960s Tom Watson Jr. (CEO of IBM) was a man on a mission. He believed in the computer and the use of transistors in computers. Some executives expressed doubts about the reliablity of transistors. So he gave each executive a transistor radio and told them to call him when it broke. (He didn't get any calls.) Cool.

Perfect pitch. The perfect pitch starts with benefits and ends with a strong close. That much we know. But what about the middle? For one thing, the shorter the better. Cut the fat and sell the sizzle. When you say "I only need a minute of your time," you should have a sixty-second pitch prepared. That doesn't mean you talk faster, either. Clarity is the key to effective communication. The better they understand what you're saying, the more likely you'll make a sale. How do you make sure they clearly understand you? Start by talking in terms they understand. One way to do that is to tell relevant stories. They are more memorable, more persuasive, more credible, more personal, and, by far, more interesting. Use analogies. "It's like a . . ." Show them what you mean (prototypes, props, PowerPoint, pictures), and if possible let them try it out (samples). Put them in the picture. Don't lose sight of the fact that running through their head is "What does this have to do with me?" and "What can you *do* for me?" Address it early and often. Don't assume they know what you or your product do (or can do). Explain how the things you do can help them solve problems.

Pizzazz. There is nothing wrong with adding a little pizzazz to your presentation. Add a little showmanship. Just don't overdo it. Don't spend so much time preparing a PowerPoint presentation that you forget to focus on their needs. One creative person took out a hundred-dollar bill (who carries around that much cash anymore?) and tore it in half, giving the client the half *without* the serial numbers, and said, "If you can find a better value, I'll give you the other half of this bill." When Southwest Airlines wanted to land an exclusive account with Sea World, they painted a plane to look like Shamu. Sweet.

Prototype. Show them how it works and what it will look like. A demonstration can be a deal maker. Dr. William Scholl wanted to become the "foot doctor to the world." He was a man on a mission. He invented an arch support called the Foot-Eazer. To sell it to dealers, he came up with a unique sales approach. When he walked into a store he would pull out a skeleton of a human foot and toss it on the counter in front of a startled store owner. It was an effective attention-getter. He would then use the prop to demonstrate how his product worked. This guy was a master marketer. He became THE man when it came to podiatry care by writing articles, sponsoring walking marathons, and staging contests in search of the "best pair of feet in America."

Puppy dog. The puppy dog approach is when you let someone hold, play with, and ultimately grow attached to what you're selling by allowing them to sample it. Let them hang one of your paintings in their office for a trial period. This could close the sale. Heck, offer to hang it for them! Offer free shipping. Make it easy for them to say yes and harder for them to say no. When I lived in Hawaii, we would offer free scuba lessons in the pool. Once a tourist had the gear on, it was a done deal. I used this same idea to sell Maui Jim sunglasses (expensive) at the Kapalua Bay Hotel. My sales pitch had to be very subtle because of the caliber of the guests and image of the resort. All I had to do was say, "Hey, try these sunglasses for the day." (They could have stolen them, sure, but that never happened. Instead I sold a lot of glasses, some to big-name celebrities.)

Price. Sell the benefits first, then talk about price. If price is an issue for them (it's usually too high, what else is new?), you must educate them that this is the going rate or a good deal. If your price is too low, you run the risk of losing credibility (and losing money!). Rather than lowering your price, try using a premium. This can be an add-on (let me design your landscaping *and* I'll maintain it for a month free of charge) rather than cutting your fees. Knowledge is power. Find out what your competitors are charging and price yourself accordingly.

Premiums. What if a bank bought a bunch of your books and gave them away to customers for free. For a self-published author, this would be amazing. Having your product used for fund-raisers (picture an army of sweet little kids selling your stuff door-to-door and by the boxload to their neighbors). It's about pitching it once and selling a bazillion. That's why it makes sense to try to land distributors. You make one sales call and sell them cases of stuff, and then they deal with selling and shipping it to the individual outlets. Same thing goes for clubs, catalogs, and any other creative outlet you can uncover. I found out that speakers who don't have a book to sell will gladly sell my book at their seminars. I don't have to do a thing (other than collect on past-due invoices). Just remember this saying: "One call does it all." Whom would you call where you could sell the most stuff?

Push. The close. Everybody knows that in baseball you need a solid reliever to close out a game and hold the lead. The same is true in sales. The difference is, YOU are the closer. Closing a sale is not as complicated or contrived as you may have been led to believe. The simple close is to ASK FOR THE SALE. I know it sounds so simple, but I have done seminars where I forgot to ask for the sale, and after I was done talking, everybody left. Other times I just made sure to mention that the books were available and that I would sign them, and there was a feeding frenzy. (If you can call fifty people a frenzy.) Other aspects of closing out a sale are to have confidence in what you're selling and the belief that the other person needs it. Sometimes to close a sale you need to get over that last hurdle. Try to find out what's holding them back. Do they need a sample, a demonstration, more literature, a tour of your studio, to meet the rest of your staff? One fellow rented an office and had his friends pose as his staff so a prospective client could see how big his company was. (He also had them calling each other to make it seem like the phone was ringing off the hook.) Make it as easy as possible to say yes. Have the paperwork drawn up and ready to sign. Remove the risks by offering a guarantee. Do it on spec. Offer a free sample. Many website designers will do a mock-up so people can see how cool it will look. Once they see it, they want it. There are also some less-than-honest approaches (which I will avoid here), but you may have to resort to "Well, if you don't want it, I can take it to . . ." (their competitor), or "We only have a few left, so if you don't buy now," or the "My schedule is filling up, this may be the only time." Make it *impossible* for them to say no. Ask them, "Would you like that in blue or red (or both!)." I said at the beginning that YOU had to be the closer. Well, that isn't entirely true. You can have your agent deal with the details and dicker on price. Maybe you could have your mentor make a Godfather call on your behalf to clinch the deal. You may want to take the entire team that will be working on the project to meet with a prospect (especially if they can answer more technical questions that you can't). Finally, the person you are pitching to may not be in a position to say yes. You need to know that and then find the person who is authorized to buy.

Plan B. What is your comeback to "I'm gonna think about it" or "I don't think we're interested now"? Have a Plan B. Hold something back so that when they're on the fence, you can push them off and they fall right into your arms. This could be throwing something else in. ("Let me tell ya what I'm gonna do for ya, only because I like ya.") Have something ready like a lower-priced alternative (not a lower price). Have another idea ready in case they aren't ready to buy now. I would not be writing this book if I didn't use this approach. My publisher wasn't interested in the book I proposed originally. They didn't think the timing was right. So I said, "How about a book on self-promotion now, and the other book later." Bam! I sold two books. (Not bad, eh?) When someone says no, instead of just sulking away, ask them, "Do you know of anyone else who might need my services or be a better fit?" Surprisingly, this works more times than not.

Prove it. Show them testimonials, a list of happy clients, a proven track record. Put it on consignment, do it on spec. If you can get the backing of your customers, you can use that as collateral to convince others to buy. Show that there is a market willing to buy what you're selling.

Personally. Don't take a rejection personally. It usually isn't that they are rejecting *you,* they're rejecting your idea. (Sometimes it is personal, but you have to put that out of your mind and move on.) Just because they don't like your play doesn't mean you are worthless. Your play may just need some more work. And this is going to be my main point. Find out exactly WHY they didn't buy. Find the reason behind the "No way." That's the only way to overcome the objection and improve. Say something like: "Just so I understand correctly, you aren't interested because . . ." Or ask them point-blank: "What could I have done to make this sale?" Then regroup and try again. (You should also ask after making a sale, "Is there anything I can do to improve?") And if it really isn't going to be a good fit, say "Thanks" and move on. Don't let them jerk you around when a better fit (and sale) may be out there. Give them a deadline to reply. And hey, you will be turned down from time to time, not have your calls returned; it's all a part of the process. Don't let it get you down. Sure, you'll feel inadequate. Reconnect with your passion and purpose and try again. Want to know someone who doesn't take rejection personally when selling? Arthur Fonzarelli, better known as the Fonz. I know he's not real. Come on. But Henry Winkler, who played the Fonz and is now a producer and deal maker in Hollywood, is known to not take no for an answer. He freely admits he can make himself very annoying until he gets what he wants.

Peace of mind. Make them feel good about their purchase. Reaffirm that they made the right choice. Follow up and ask how they're enjoying what you sold them. Find out if there is anything else they need or you can do for them. Assure them you are there for them if they need you. Maybe just call to say hello. If appropriate, go ahead and get personal. "So, how was your trip to Maui? Wasn't Paiea a quaint little town?" Stay in contact without being a burden. A graphic artist follows up with clients and asks if she can use the client's design in her portfolio and brochure. Other savvy salespeople get audio or video testimonials of happy clients. The same graphic artist does semi-annual checkups (free) of past clients' ads, websites, and newsletters, as a way of following up without being an annoyance.

Persistence. Follow up on a lead immediately. Peavy Electronics has support people for their reps at trade shows to make sure the follow-up gets done in a timely fashion. I started keeping a sales diary to take notes on each person I sold or tried to sell to. I started noting what worked in selling to those who bought and what the objections were by those who didn't. I also made notes and included reminders about following up with both groups. Speaking of follow-up, this is THE most important part of selling. Many people quit after one no. If you can get up the courage to try again, you may just close the sale. I have had people say after a presentation on desktop publishing, "I think I'm just going to do it myself." My reply was always: "Okay, call me if you need me. I'll check back in a week to see how it's going." Sure enough, when I checked back they would say, "Ya know what, I don't have the time or know-how to do this, when can you get started?" "Hmm, well now, I'm really busy, so the price just tripled." (Don't I wish.)

Prize. The prize is making the sale. But some of us need more than that to stay motivated. That's why I have incentive-based games I play with myself that push me to pick up the phone one more time or make another presentation when I really feel like just bailing it. I have set a goal of how many calls I will make in a day. (It can be low pressure: "I just have to call x number of prospects to get the prize," like tennis with a friend.) Involving a friend in your goal gets them to motivate you. "Come on, man, make the calls so we can play!" Then I tie in a prize (weekend in Palm Springs or a day off, for example) if I close a deal. It's also helpful to have a sales goal. As a speaker, I want to make x amount per month. So not only do I have to line up seminars, they must equal a certain dollar amount. Jana Stanfield gave me a great idea. I bought a year-in-review wall calendar where I write in the booking and how much I will be paid. Then I subtract that number from my monthly goal. That way I know where I stand and how far I have to go.

Peaceful. When you get in the right state of mind, you realize it's not life or death, and you can relax a little. Whatever happens, you'll be okay. So don't let them see your sweat.

Different Strokes

You can't sell everyone with the same approach. For example, there is a different style that works for a left-brainer, right-brainer, and a no-brainer ("Just sign here, please"). If you're attempting to sell a left-brainer, it helps to remember they are concerned with the bottom line, details, proof, price, logic (think Spock), and want you to cut to the chase (don't waste my time, don't push me, I need to think things through, is their attitude). A right-brainer needs to see it, touch it (prototypes), and feel it (make an emotional appeal). They respond well to metaphors, stories, and analogies. They are big-picture thinkers and don't really care about the details. Speaking of which, they don't deal well with paperwork, so make it EASY to buy. They are impulsive, so you can play on that. They tend to be easily distracted, so you have to keep them focused. They also procrastinate and have a hard time making decisions, so push a little.

CHECKUP

How is your attitude? Is your portfolio up-to-date? Are you doing work that you are proud of? Passionate about? Is there anything you can do to improve your personality? Is your work marketable? Are you pitching the right people? Name five reasons why someone should buy anything from you.

Point of Purchase

> "To sell something, tell a woman it's a bargain—tell a man it's deductible."
>
> —Earl Wilson

Do you remember walking through the mall and having the Pepperidge Farm girl sitting outside offering free samples of cheese and crackers? That's also how Mrs. Fields originally got people to try her cookies. She stood outside her first store and gave out samples. I know, I have done this at my seminars by putting candy (and not that hard, cheap kind either, the good stuff—chocolate) at the back table among my books. No strings attached, take as much as you want (pig), because my goal was reached, I got you to the product table. (Just like Mrs. Fields and the Pepperidge Farm girl got you to try the goods and go inside the store.) There are plenty of other ways to do this, as well as other tips in this section about selling from the back of the room, trade shows, exhibits, and craft fairs.

Location, location, location. That's what they say about retail stores. The same is true when displaying or selling at shows. Find out where people will be sure to find you. Make it so they almost have to bump into you and your sales table. Maybe it's close to the door, coffee, food stand, or the bathrooms (hey, whatever it takes). One speaker sets up her product tables like a gauntlet you have to walk through to get into the ballroom. That's a bit too presumptuous for me, but it works for her. If you set up the room yourself, get the product tables away from the wall so people can walk around your table (360 degrees of viewing is better than 180 degrees).

Tiki beer bongs, talking parrots, and tropical backdrops. Did that subtitle get your attention? Tailgating before a Jimmy Buffett concert has become an exercise in creativity and gluttony. A bunch of us Parrot Heads got together and came up with the ultimate interactive experience. (See subtitle.) There were all kinds of things for people to see at the preconcert party, but we always drew a crowd. At a trade show or a crafts fair people are passing by, but how do you get them to stop so you can talk to them? Picture this: men running along a sidewalk, and as they pass, an attractive woman smiles at them. They will likely look her way and maybe even slow down. If she flashed them her breasts they'd likely trip and fall, or at least stop and go over to her. "How you doin'?" We need something that has that kind of pulling power for our product tables. How? Celebrities work. If you are a celebrity yourself, even better. Put together a charity event or round-table discussion that would interest a celebrity. Give demonstrations or seminars or clinics (demonstrate watercolor techniques, for example). Sign your books or prints. One very creative person had one of those arcade-style games where you use claws to reach and try to pick up a prize. Another used fair-style games to get people to stop by and talk while they tried to get a basketball in a hoop, get the dart in the bull's-eye, or play the water pistol game. I came up with this idea for a small publisher who wanted to attract writers to her booth. I started a story and we allowed passersby to add a sentence or three of their own to keep the story going (as long as they included their name and e-mail address). Before long there was a line of people waiting to add to it or read what was written after their contribution. It was such a hit, the show's director begged us to read the whole thing at the wrap-up party. (We promised to also mention the contributor's name as we read their passage, so they were all there and beaming.) It was hilarious and touching at times. The whole story was added to her website, and I bet you can guess the ending to this story. Hint, it's a happy one.

Make it easy to buy. Once you get them to the table, how do you get them to buy? Let them take your product for a test drive. Do a demonstration, provide CD players and headphones with your music, have laptops set up so they can sample your software, cook up some of the recipes from your cookbook, have a video loop of your product in action. In retail clothing stores you find entire outfits carefully put together on a rack. You can use this same concept and bundle complementary things together (you'll sell more and for more money). Put prices on things (or post a price list) in case you are too busy to get to everyone right away. Or create "hang tags" attached to items with interesting tidbits and tips or answers to frequently asked questions. If they are "just looking," don't let them leave empty-handed. Give away a freebie like a newsletter, or a tip sheet or a sample recipe, postcard, sticker, price list, catalog, business card, or brochure. Show off your creativity. I love coming up with clever displays for my product tables. For a sign that included handy websites, I attached a plastic surfer. Business cards were displayed in the mouth of a shark. I put out a box with a big button that said, "Don't touch this." Of course, everyone has to push it, and a newsletter pops out the top. Good help isn't that hard to find. Have someone helping with the sales to free you up to schmooze and answer questions. If you are performing and you have help or not, get to your product table before your fans mob you. Make sure to have plenty of inventory as well as change, bags, invoices or receipts, pens, a calculator, and anything else you need to make a sale.

Get your stuff off the shelf. Which do you think would be a better place for a book, on the shelf or on a table at the front of the store? Or in the window! Offer to do a window display for your product or provide the retailer with the props. Ever bought Cliffs Notes? (Not gonna admit it, are you?) Ever notice how they are in their own rack? It works! I made up my own "signed by author" stickers and encouraged stores to make a section for signed books. I also discovered that when I did a signing, my books ended up on display in the window or on an end cap. (And they sold!) So I did as many signings as possible and tried to schedule them at the end of the month, so more people would see the sign or notice it in the store's calendar of events, and so the books would be displayed longer. It worked like a charm. Before I arrived at one bookstore (in Kauai, no less) for a signing, I was told they had sold out of my books, all fifty copies, and had ordered forty more. For a mid-list author like myself, that's pretty good.

Phone Sales

"Many are called but few are called back."

—Mary Tricky

If the thought of having to make a cold call makes you feel sick to your stomach, you can at least take comfort in the fact that you are not alone. Calling somebody you don't really know (or just met at a trade show or through networking) and asking them for something would cause anyone to freeze up as they reached for the phone. Who could blame them? Cold calling (or "cool calling") is possibly the worst part of promotion. You risk rejection every time you say "Hello, my name is . . ." Every time someone gives you the cold shoulder, it's as if they took your self-esteem and stomped on it, kicked it, and punched you in the gut. Before you say "I'm not doing it," you must realize that when done right, it can be huge! One of the keys to phone sales is that the best defense is a good offense. A strategy and even a script can calm your nerves and get you past the first twinge of fear. Knowing what you want to say and having it down cold is one solution. So is the confidence that comes from knowing that this person NEEDS what you are offering. There is another way to go. That is to just do it and figure it out as you go. After a few hang-ups, you quickly realize what NOT to say and begin to mold a phone presentation. Start with the least important candidates for the sale. You don't want to blow it with a VIP (very important prospect). Combining a plan with persistence and flexibility is the key, in my opinion, to selling over the phone.

Ask a Pro

Susan Guzzetta
Booking Agent

Selling over the phone isn't for everyone, but you seem to have a special talent for it. What does it take, in your opinion, to do it well?

I think you have to be self-motivated, disciplined, organized, and, of course, have a thick skin. Persistence and follow-up are really important. That doesn't mean you pester them to death, though. I have what I call "the three strikes rule" with people I cold-call. I give them three chances to return my call, and then I might mail them or give them my toll-free number to make it easier for them to call me back. If that doesn't work, I move on. I honestly believe you can't take the rejection personally or feel like a failure. I look at it this way: By taking them off my call list, it frees me up to work on someone else who is more likely to buy.

Could it be that the person you're pursuing doesn't do business over the phone?

Possibly. Once I get through to someone, I try to find what their comfort level is about how, and how often, they like to be contacted. Some people do prefer to do business via the fax or by e-mail.

How do you deal with those people who put you off?

I ask open-ended questions that they can't easily say no to, like "When would be the best time to call back?" or "When is your next commitee meeting when you'll be discussing your speaker needs?" Then I follow up.

A Good Offense (Outgoing Calls)

Time zone. I know this is obvious, but I did it once so I thought I'd pass it on. Check the time zone you are calling.

Repeat their address. Since you hated calling in the first place, imagine having to call back and ask, "Uh, I can't seem to read my handwriting, is that Clamitia Street or Calmia Street?"

Post your mission or goal on the wall. Chart your success or the number of calls you have made. Focus on the goal and not the call. All that crap about life is a journey doesn't hold true when it comes to cold calling. Life is a destination, and making these damn calls is the bumpy road to get there.

Pep talk. Warm up by reviewing your goals and what you'll get by making the call.

Be prepared. Lenny Kravitz hired his drummer, Cindy Blackman, over the phone. He had her audition using a speakerphone. After playing and chatting, she was part of the band.

What do you want? For a moment, forget about benefits and what *they* need. What's in it for YOU!? Now look at what they need. How do these two things coincide?

Don't get caught with your pants down. When they ask, "What is the purpose of this call?" don't ramble. Have something ready. Outline what you want to say. Or better yet, script it and then learn your lines. Have a checklist of things to cover. Anticipate objections and have responses prepared. Many times producers are screening you. They expect sound bites and a well-spoken guest. If you can't do it on the phone, you ain't gonna get on. The more prepared you are, the more confident you become. Imagine that.

Do your homework. Know a little about them and what they do. "You're the gallery by the ocean, right? Had a showing of . . . ?"

Getting past the gatekeeper. Call at off-hours (really early), and regardless, be ready for them. Try to partner with the gatekeeper. It's better to have them as an ally than an enemy. Do a little fact-finding first. Ask the gatekeeper when it's a good time to call. Find out what is the best approach to get a response. See if you can open a dialogue. Be courteous and kind. And learn their names. These are underpaid, over-worked, and underappreciated *people*. (Even if Hallmark did create a holiday for them.) So respect and thank them with small tokens of your appreciation, thank-you notes, kindness, and compliments. One resourceful consultant would send mailings directly to bigwigs' homes to avoid the gatekeeper. I'm not so sure about that. I am sure you don't want to call them on their home phone.

Name-drop. It is who you know, and if they know that person, too, you have a connection.

When leaving a message. Have a message ready to go. It's nice if you have a number that is easy to remember. (Picture them in their car on their cell phone checking messages.) If all they had to remember was "4badass" (422-3277), it would be much more memorable (in more ways than one).

Getting them to call back. "Hey, Matthew, it's Bruce Willis. Call me back or I'll burn your house down" was the message left for Matthew Perry by his costar in *The Whole Nine Yards.* (If it was someone from TLC, I'd be real concerned.) Tell people a little about the reason for your call, but leave them wanting more. Be a tease and intrigue them enough so they're dying to call you back. Assume you'll get voice mail every time you call. Be ready to deliver a brief, clear, and detailed message BEFORE you call. When you leave a message, slooooooowwww dooooooowwwnn. Don't ramble.

If you are a home-based business. Get a separate phone line so your teenager isn't online while you wait for an important call. If a caller gets a busy signal or voice mail when they try to return your call, it may mean the end. If you are out a lot, it pays to have a cell phone or an assistant to answer your calls. (Leave their number on your outgoing message.) They have toll-free numbers for cell phones, too.

Hey, it's me. Send something unusual so that when you call you can say, "I'm the guy that sent the piggy bank (and mini-hammer) with the brochure inside that said, 'Break me to save money on your . . .'" One woman even sent a phone with all the speed dials set to her number.

When you do talk, respect their time. Introduce yourself and ask an open-ended question. Then listen and learn. In the beginning, the less you say, the better. Ask, "How are things going?" and let them tell you all about their problems and listen for something you can help them with.

Take note. Take notes and highlight the things you said you would follow up with. When they say, "Today is my birthday," write it down. Maybe they mention "I prefer to do deals via e-mail." Write it down. Make notes on their hobbies, preferences, and deadlines. If they mention, "We're looking for . . ." Write it down. Next time you call you can say, "You said you were interested in . . . well, I have just what you're looking for."

Set up supplies. Keep a calculator handy. Have all the information you may need at your fingertips. Get your appointment calendar out before you call to figure out what date would be best for a meeting, and then pick a backup date. (Don't ask them when would be a good time. You suggest your dates.)

Create a strong phone presence. Be confident, interested (and interesting), and enthusiastic. They say you should have a mirror in front of you when you talk on the phone so you remember to smile. Pay attention to inflection, pacing, grammar. Build rapport, but don't get too relaxed. All I know is, I don't want to look at myself in the mirror all day. I wasn't going to mention this, but it just happened to me. Stay away from the bathroom when using your cordless or "hands-free" phone. I could hear this guy a little too clearly.

Persist. Setbacks are temporary. It's a numbers game. Don't bang your phone on the desk and scream "Stupid! Stupid! Stupid!" It's really not you, it's them. You can't follow up on every piece when you do a mass mailing, so limit the amount of a mailing or how many people have your portfolio.

Solid Defense: Incoming Calls

You can't hide forever. Gordon Mathews, the inventor of voice mail, acknowledges that it's a mistake to force callers through voice mail hell. Nothing can replace human contact. Because we have voice mail everywhere we go, people expect speedy replies. Stephen Wright had a good line: "I have an answering machine in my car. It says, 'I'm not home now. But leave a message and I'll call when I'm out.'" Tell them when you're coming back or will be available to call them back.

Your answering machine is a marketing tool. One man leaves daily motivational messages, poems, and tips on his outgoing message. People call just to listen. Make yours informational and upbeat. Announce upcoming events or new projects just completed.

Keep your message short and simple. Have an option for them to talk to a real live person. Give them more than one way to contact you, and leave it on your outgoing message.

Return calls fast. This is a sign of your customer service. The same day is excellent service—same hour is extraordinary.

Shake 'em up. Have your own unique salutation. "This is Mr. Big. I make dreams come true. How can I help you?"

FOR FUN

"There's nobody home now to answer the phone, so please leave a message when you hear the tone. But if you're a burglar, we're not gone at all—we're cleaning our shotguns while screening your call."

Ads: Legalized Lying

"Everyone lives by selling something."

—Robert Louis Stevenson

Lillian Vernon was a pregnant housewife who needed money. She used the $2,000 she and her husband received as a wedding present and took out an ad in *Seventeen* magazine for $495 to promote her line consisting of a leather purse and belt. She got $32,000 worth of orders from that ad and built a $240-million-a-year mail order company—launched with one ad. Tom Morey, the inventor of the Boogie Board, took out an ad in *Surfing* magazine and got his first order for the $37 prototype board. The next day he got five orders, and after that it never stopped. His ads were great, too. The headline was "Surf Morey for a Good Feeling." The ads included action photos and testimonials from happy customers who raved about the boards. Many musicians have started a band or landed a gig using classified advertising. Advertising is everywhere. Why? Because it works. You can reach a lot of people in a hurry. Or you can target a smaller group of people who are likely to be interested in what you have to offer. Advertising can raise the public's awareness of who you are and what you do without your having to do it personally. It builds name recognition, image, familiarity, credibility, and, in a sense, it increases your celebrity status. There are a lot of benefits to advertising. It can also prove to retailers that you are supporting your product (and them). It can also be a colossal waste of money if you don't do it right. For every Monster.com that had success as a result of running one ad during a Super Bowl, there are thousands of examples of businesses that have thrown away millions of dollars on advertising. That's why this section is so important. I can save you a lot of time and money (as we learn from past mistakes).

SELF-PROMOTION FOR THE CREATIVE PERSON

Clever Cuts Through Clutter

Get Your Tongue Out of My Mouth, I'm Kissing You Goodbye
—Title of book by Cynthia Heimel

Over 50,000 books a year are published, but with a clever title like *Don't Pee on My Leg and Tell Me It's Raining* by Judge Judy, a good title gets your attention. If you want your ad to stand out from the crowd, the more clever the headline, the better. I saw one for Santa Claus training that said: "Just say ho." Another good one for a computer company read: "Remember back in high school when fast and easy was considered an insult?" The "Got Milk?" campaign was so successful because the message was so simple (and funny). The punch line is short and concise. It is amusing and says something of substance. At one point, a planner at the ad agency was pushing to change the line to "Got Enough Milk?" That idea was quickly squashed. The whole premise was based on "What kind of pain would it cause if you were without milk?" This idea of being unusual is nothing new, but the trend is now wild, wacky, and weird. That's why you see things like gerbils shooting from a cannon (Outpost.com). However, simple and clever never go out of style.

Skimmers

"The Best Headlines Never Fi . . ."

—Bernard Lewis

Nobody reads anymore. Who has the time? How do you read the paper? Admit it, you skim the headlines to see which couple of articles you have time to read. Headlines are THE most important part of any ad or flyer. Younger people, especially, have very short attention spans. What makes for a good headline? Think powerful, clever, engaging, emotional, startling, and attention-grabbing. Ask a question and you engage the reader. State a startling (and relevant) statistic that can get them interested. Use humor. Play with the words. The perfect companion to a headline is a photograph. A picture is worth a thousand words in promotional materials. It still needs a caption. A photo and a caption (along with the headline) are THE most powerful pulling techniques to slow down a busy reader.

FAST FACT
Adweek's top ad campaign over the last twenty years was . . . Absolut vodka.

How to Advertise Like a Pro
"Marketing is too important to be left to the marketing department."

—David Packard

One savvy businesswoman had the local paper run a two-by-three-inch ad that was blank except for the words: "File this card for future reference." Then the whole family, using double-sided tape, pasted her color cards in place by hand across the top. It was so effective she does it every year. Now, that's creative (and it worked). I love it! Here are a few tips so you will have your own advertising success stories.

Failing to plan is planning to fail. Just like all other aspects of promotion, it helps if you have a plan. If you take a haphazard approach, you will not only fail, you'll also waste a lot of money. All your plan needs to have in it is who your target audience is and what would be the best way to reach them. (Request media guides from the publications. They're free. See who their readers are. Are they right for you? Do they reach enough people? How extensive is their circulation?) You also have to decide how much you're willing to spend. Then find the best way to stretch your dollars so you can consistently (it's a fact that frequency is a key) advertise. Where would your prospects go if they needed what you have to offer? This will determine where you should spend your resources.

Cheap tricks. Run a classified ad first to see if the publication pulls people in, and then decide whether to go with a more costly display ad. Call a current advertiser or two to ask if their ads are working. (Or if you notice competitors putting ads in over a long period of time, it's a safe bet that they're probably pulling.) Offer to trade products or services for ad space. If you start your own ad agency, you'll save 15 percent when placing ads. As Fred Allen said: "Advertising agency: 85 percent confusion and 15 percent commission." Keep the commission for yourself. See if there is any co-op money available from a supplier or retailer. Partner up with a complementary advertiser or group and split the cost.

Avoid the masses. Mass media means you pay to reach a lot of people who aren't likely to be interested in your offer. It's better to use a publication that reaches a target audience geared to the type of person more likely to want what you're advertising. When John Chuang founded MacTemps, he took out a $75, quarter-page ad in a regional Mac newsletter with the headline "You Didn't Buy Just Any Computer. Why Hire Just Any Temp to Use It?" The phones started ringing off the hook and never stopped. Another effective way to stand out and reach a targeted group is to advertise in a publication that doesn't usually run ads for your type of product or service. One artist advertises in travel and airline magazines, business publications, *The Robb Report,* and *Architectural Digest.* He is targeting people with the means (money) and the motive (they appreciate art).

Do it often. Think long-term. When my photographer got hurt, I remembered a gal who had been advertising for several years in my regional paper. I called her and she did a nice job on short notice. Consistency may not pay off right away, but it does build your reputation and recognition.

Sex sells. Reef Brazil makes sandals. Big deal, right? They sold 3,000 pairs in 1985 and two million in 2000. Why the big increase? Well, for one thing they make a really good product. The other is their ads (which have little to do with sandals). In any issue of a surfing-related magazine you will find their ads with amazing models wearing the most incredible thong bikinis, right up in the first few pages.

☆————————

CLEVER CLASSIFIED ADS: IF YOU LOVE PIÑA COLADAS . . .

"Available now! One nice guy, twenty-eight. New merchandise, not used! Limited-time offer. Last one in stock. Don't let this offer pass you by. Call before it's too late."

————————

I read somewhere that the way to begin writing a successful personal ad is to ask yourself these three questions: Whom do you want to meet? What makes you unique? What kind of relationship do you want to have? Hmm. If we applied those same questions to promoting ourselves, we would be well on our way to writing a pretty powerful ad. Of course, you can post classified ads for free on the Web in bulletin board systems, newsgroups, and online services. Then there are classified sections in the back of all kinds of publications, from *USA Today* to your industry's trade magazine. The advantages of both are that they're cheap (or free) and require no production skills (or cost). I have had a lot of success in the past promoting through classified ads. What I discovered is that the best classified sections are divided up by category, that it is hard to sell anything over five dollars by mail, and that doing the two-step (click here or call for a free something) works best. You must have a headline that grabs them (or subject line), and since you're using so few words, you must make each one count.

Directories: Let Their Fingers Do the Walking

"I never made Who's Who, but I'm featured in What's That."
—Phyllis Diller

The shelf life of some sourcebooks and directories is longer than that of a Twinkie (a long, long time). I've had calls years later from someone who said they saw my ad in *Radio-TV Interview Report.* This is a sourcebook distributed to the media nationwide. My ad led to appearances on talk shows, speaking engagements, and other opportunities. The best part is, my publisher paid for it. This can be the easiest way to advertise. What are the yellow pages for your industry? Advertise where lazy people let their fingers do the walking whenever they need some kind of service. In addition to the business it may bring in, it also adds to your credibility within your industry.

Take a Flyer

"Unsolicited advice is the junk mail of life."
—Bern Williams

When you design an attention-grabbing flyer and then put it in the proper place, the return on your investment (next to nothing) can be phenomenal. On the flip side, if you do it poorly (weak headline, no focal point, wimpy call to action) it's a waste of a tree. My favorite flyers are those where the designer thinks so far outside the box you want to say "What box?" For example, when a hairstylist (who specializes in cuts for kids) designed a flyer, it was both clever and a keeper. On the flyer were examples of what kind of cut goes with what shape of face. It included the latest trends in haircuts for kids and a blank face where you could draw in what you wanted. (Where she could, the hairstylist left a box of crayons next to the flyer.) Bravo! What makes for a good flyer?

Headlines. Studies show that four out of five readers don't go past the headline. You want a headline that is big and bold. Bold means the font is big and thick and thus easy to read. Bold could also mean it is controversial or catchy. It could state a startling fact, ask a compelling question, or use humor.

Focal point. Instead of a bunch of stuff thrown on the page, pick one image and make it stand out. Clutter is out, clean is in.

Visual. Pictures of people, animals, babies (and kids) are best. Clip art is a good backup to photographs. And in a pinch, a graph or a chart is better than no visual at all.

Hierarchy. Not everything on the flyer can be big and bold. Decide which information is most important and emphasize it.

Skimmable. A good flyer is easy to read at a glance. Information is broken down by bullets, lists, or sections. (Quickly answer the who, what, why, where, when, and so on.)

Action-oriented. A good flyer tells you what to do and how to do it. It also says DO IT NOW, by giving a deadline ("This offer expires next month" or "If you call now, we'll throw in something for free.") Make it easy to order by phone, fax, e-mail, website, or coupon.

Error free. Double-check your spelling, grammar, and contact information. Better yet, let someone else read it, too.

Size matters. Turn the paper sideways (landscape view) or do it on legal paper, bookmark size, squares (four up), half size (two up), or even poster size (tabloid size).

Backside. One wine merchant made one side of the flyer a "GO PADRES" sign that you could wave in the ballpark, and on the other side was an offer for five dollars off a bottle of wine if the Padres lost. What was the connection? The Padres were playing so poorly that, like most wines, they stayed in the cellar. Ouch!

Put 'em where the sun don't shine. Insert flyers with products you send out. I slip a flyer in the back of every book with every order, advertising all of my other titles. If you're posting them on a bulletin board, put the flyers in a large envelope (10 × 13 inches) and paste one to the front with a note ("Free, Take One"). Or take a large sheet of paper and fold the bottom and staple it to create a pocket. Use tear-away tabs at the bottom. You can also make a pad of flyers fairly cheaply, so one can be torn off at a time. If you live in Seattle, put your flyers in a plastic sheet protector so they'll stay dry. Put them where people will see it. If you want their undivided attention, put them above the men's urinal, the backs of the stalls in the women's rest room, or above the coffeemaker. Don't forget the church, coffee shops, colleges, condo bulletin boards, fairs, Laundromats, lobbies, mailboxes, office buildings, rec room, senior centers, tourist centers, and welcome wagon baskets as places to put them. A copy shop owner and a graphic artist got together to make a calendar of events for a small beach community that lists upcoming events, sponsored by and distributed at area shops. Every day a clever printer crosses a bridge, and in addition to paying his toll, pays for the car behind him, too. He gives the tollbooth operator a flyer to give to the lucky motorist. The printer gets a lot of calls thanking him for his generosity, and some lucrative contracts.

☆————————————————

FAST FACTS
According to a USA.com poll, these were the most effective forms of advertising: (1) Direct mail, (2) Internet ad, (3) Signs and banners.

It's a Sign of the Times
"I didn't think it was physically possible, but this both sucks and blows."

—Bart Simpson

Along the North Scranton Expressway in Pennsylvania, the message on the forty-eight-foot sign attached to a billboard was clear: "Bring in this ad and you'll get a free pair of shoes." So three people decided to do just that. They removed the actual sign (thinking it was the coupon) and brought it to Shoestrings (the store) to claim their free shoes. This is a true story. What makes for a good sign? It's easy to read, short, clever, and in a high-traffic zone. Think "Got Milk?" Speaking of "Got Milk?" one dairy farmer (with a farm by the freeway) sold ads mounted on the sides of his cows, for Ben & Jerry's ice cream. Besides the obvious places, put a sign where people are bored (on a bus or bus bench, subway, movie theater screens, inside an elevator) or where there's a high-traffic area. My brother and I sailed a Hobie Cat around the bay one summer for a radio station because their logo was on the sail. They even PAID us to take the thing out on the water. We can learn from NASCAR people—put your logo and website address on hats and T-shirts. One guy had a plane pulling a sign during the Academy Awards to promote his script. You could sponsor a hot air balloon, adopt a highway and have your sign along the freeway, or sponsor a baseball team and have your sign on the fence or have it appear on the scoreboard. Have you ever thought about hiring a skywriter or having a plane pull a banner by the beach? There are magnetic signs for your car, or better yet, paint your car. One van on the freeway said: "The Blind Man Is Driving." I had to see this. When I got alongside the van I noticed it was a company that installed blinds. Very clever. A creative artist painted footprints on the sidewalk to lead patrons to her out-of-the-way gallery. I've seen signs that were made with plants and rocks alongside the road. One business painted his website address on the roof of his building, which happened to be right in the flight path of a busy airport. A plumber put numbers on the side of his truck (number one on the passenger door, number three on the back) to make it appear he had a whole fleet of trucks. (He only had the one.)

JUST FOR FUN

Some fun and funny signs. Outside a Bar: "Guys: No Shirt, No Service. Girls: No Shirt, No Charge." Dry Cleaner: "Drop Your Pants Here and Receive Immediate Attention." Bait Shop: "Reserved Parking for Casting Director."

The Check Is in the Mail: Direct Mail

> *"The best things in life are postage paid, batteries included, guaranteed forever and tax-free."*
>
> —Jacqueline Schiff

According to a Louis Harris poll, 59 percent of U.S. adults say they are fed up with junk mail, yet direct mail as a form of promotion is on the rise. It's pretty wasteful when 98 percent of your target didn't reply, and that's still considered a success. That's why e-mail is changing the way we market. The electronic media and spamming is sooooooo much cheaper that it is very tempting. No matter what the medium, if you send the most amazing offer to the wrong people, it won't work. And with direct mail, the cost for postage can kill you. So before you begin, do your homework. Then create a dynamic design, clever and concise copy, and close with an offer they can't refuse. The advantage of doing direct mail the old way is you can do more with the design. You can send just about anything through the mail. I've seen a mailing by an illustrator that was on a milk carton. ("Have you seen this guy lately?") One graphic artist mailed Cracker Jack boxes with her offer inside. A website designer wanted to emphasize how fast he could get your site up and running, so he sent a plastic slug to illustrate how slow his competitors were. An insurance salesperson sent nothing. That's right, nothing. She sent an empty envelope and then later calls to ask, "What if your paychecks stopped coming due to illness or injury?" Direct mail can be as simple as a letter. Author

Terry McMillan sent letters to nearly every bookstore in the country, and as a result her book became a best-seller. If a plain letter seems boring: A consultant printed his letter upside down to make his point about potential clients needing to turn things around (with his help).

Just the Fax

"You cannot bore someone into buying your product."

—David Ogilvy

While working as soundstage managers for a Burbank studio, Jeff Hamilton and Robert Platts came across a bunch of flat cardboard figures—most from the seventies. Needing money, the two decided it might be worth their while to recycle the idea and make some new ones. They took photos of three men and a woman, and with a loan from one of their girlfriends, they made up a thousand cardboard standees of each. They then faxed ads to every production company in town and got INSTANT orders. Marketing by fax can still work well.

☆ ———————————————————

PICTURE POSTCARDS

Before the Internet, postcards were the most cost-effective (with the emphasis on "effective") way to market yourself by mail. They still work well to stay in touch and sell. To make the most of this medium, it takes a little creativity. Sure you can send out a postcard with a sample of your work or a photo on one side and tour dates, ordering information, announcements, or a special offer on the other. That will work. But to be better than the rest, you could put a news release on a postcard. Make up some with motivational messages and send them on a monthly basis. Create some suspense by doing one a day and make it like a soap opera—leave them hanging with suspense by including only part of the story, a question with the answer to follow, or part of a picture. Include tips (recipes, hair care tips, how to design website ideas) or directions to your website.

Brochures: The Salesperson You Wish You Had

A brochure is a lot like a business card (on steroids), since as a professional you are expected to have one. Even if the person receiving it never reads it, it's still important to have it when asked. It means they want more information about what you do (and can do for them). There are a lot of ways to present this information to them—a brochure does not have to be a three-fold piece of paper. (More on that in a minute.) Along with the credibility factor, it allows you to elaborate on what you do (and can do for them) beyond what a business card can. (A business card brochure would seem like a pretty good idea, and it is.) A bad brochure is worse than no brochure. (Don't skimp and don't rush it.) It is especially touchy if you do some kind of design work. They'll figure if you don't do your own things with class or creativity, how will you do their project?

Begin by borrowing ideas from your competitors' brochures and books on the best brochures. *How* magazine has a Best Brochure award and related book that is outstanding. I've seen brochures with some very clever approaches, including one that was put on pieces to a puzzle and sent in a box. Another was done comic book style. One was a message in a bottle. Another was done like a birth announcement for a new product. I've seen some done like a children's book, on a CD-ROM and on postcards (so they could be mailed a little at a time, with the final mailing a swatch book–style brochure of all the previous mailings). I'm sure you can come up with even more creative ideas. (Try to get away from the typical three-fold brochure.)

Next, for a minute forget about your ego and focus on the benefits to the reader. Put yourself in their shoes. What would impress you? What kind of information would you want to see? How can you make it unique? Focus on the benefits. What they get. What would it take to make them open it? (A cool cover can't hurt.) What could you include that would make them want to keep it? (Make it valuable to the reader somehow.) Maybe it doubles as a catalog or has timely tips and other interesting information. Maybe you could include a CD-ROM with before and after examples, letters of recommendation, clips or samples, a prototype, or your portfolio. Make up a binder with loose-leaf papers and send regular updates so they look at your binder/brochure on a monthly basis. A booklet may be better than a brochure, because it's usually more in-depth, durable, valuable, and easier to use. Break it up by category, use a table of contents, include a place for notes, be more informational, and make it a teaching tool. It will still fit in an envelope, but it's less likely to be thrown out. I saw a booklet by a music teacher that included the ten most used chords for guitar. Maybe you can create a custom brochure or booklet for each client. It's certainly easier now with laser and ink-jet printers. No matter what, make sure to let them know they can see more of your work on your website, or put addresses to sites where your work appears, or offer to send them your brochure in PDF format.

ACTION ITEM

Take an 8½ × 11-inch piece of paper and see how many unusual folds you can come up with for a brochure. How about a paper airplane, or use flaps to look like doors? ("Behind Door Number Three"), the shape of a napkin, a hat, boat, etc.

Newsletters

For years I have used newsletters to stay connected with customers, and after all this time I have discovered that newsletters are a lousy place to sell stuff but an amazing tool to build goodwill and loyal fans. This is just as true for online versions as for paper versions. In fact, both should be in your marketing plans. Everyone is doing one. There is even a newsletter called the "Supermodel News." Send it to everyone from current clients to prospects, family and friends, the media, your agent, editor, publicist, and anyone who would benefit by knowing what you're up to. Natural Ovens prints a one-page newsletter loaded with health tips, recipes, and letters from consumers, and puts it in with each loaf of bread. Pete's Brewing puts a mini-catalog in each six-pack (bookmark size). It doesn't have to be 8½ × 11 or 11 × 17. There are all kinds of alternative sizes and folds. It could even be a booklet, or on a postcard, with teaser articles and information about how to read the rest of the newsletter online. Come up with a clever name. (The shorter, the better, and it doesn't need to say "Newsletter.") This is your chance to show off your expertise. So give them good, useful information in a quick and easy-to-read format. Make it urgent with time-sensitive information (news, gossip, upcoming events, limited-time specials). A strong lead story gets them to open and read it now. People like to learn from newsletters, so don't skimp on information. (It's a soft sell.) Although one ingenious trainer included ideas about how to get an employer to pay for training and workshops, and got a lot of new attendees. Include a calendar of events, quizzes, FAQ, interviews, tour dates, products for sale, letters to the editor, and don't forget to include a way for them to contact you. A bonus benefit about doing a newsletter is that you have an excuse to interview (and network with) some key people in your field. Lastly, like Metamucil, you must be regular with your newsletter. Choose a quarterly format if monthly is too much work.

Powerful Portfolios

You are your portfolio. It is how clients judge you. Showcase your BEST stuff in the most complimentary way. Make it amazing! Don't skimp. Make it portable so you can always carry it with you. I made a smaller version so I could mail it and it would fit in my Miata. I can also leave it out on the product table to show off and solicit new business, or leave it behind if I have to. Instead of schlepping your portfolio around, you can have your work scanned and saved in digital format, and using a portable portfolio called the Wallet, you can show roughly two hundred images on the four-by-six-inch screen. If you do present it in person, it's nice to have a flip style so it can stand up on its own while you're pitching yourself to a prospect. By the way, I started carrying a camera everywhere I go to document those "magic moments" when you would otherwise say, "Damn, if I only had a camera." Document everything and present it in a clean and professional manner. (Keep your originals in a safe, dry place.) Neatness counts.

Keep it current. Custom-tailor it to the client. Look for what's missing, and take on (make up) projects to fill it in. Sometimes you may even go back and redesign something the way YOU wanted it to be before the pencil pushers got their hands on it. I know one guy who designed a killer book cover using red, black, and gold. It fit the image of the book and the author. However, the client didn't like red— period. Not just the red he chose (red rock), but any red. Arrgggghh. So my friend had to use pink. Pink! Needless to say, the portfolio piece is in red. Add captions and the outcomes of projects. So in addition to them saying, "Wow, that's neat," they can also see that it was highly successful, too. Put in your position statement and a list of things you can do. Make it a show-and-TELL portfolio. Include any awards you have won. Include some before and afters or the stages a project went through. Have some fun and show off your creativity. Choose a cool color, an artistic way of displaying your stuff, or even a crazy cover. (One woman had her portfolio cover made out of fake fur. Hmmm.) The advantage of a cool, clever, or colorful case can make it stand out in a stack on someone's desk. Do it differently, use a laptop. Have your work on the Web and you can access it during a demonstration or direct them to it. Put it on a CD-ROM to leave behind. Another tool is the promotional kit. It's like a portfolio except it is usually a two-pocket folder filled with promotional materials. In your promo kit you would include samples of your work, past articles (written about and by you), biographical information, your brochure, a listing of your services, testimonials, client list, potential interview questions, newsletter, a photo or two, and possibly a premium (a keeper like a custom candy bar).

I've Got a Proposal for You

The bummer about putting together a proposal is that it is a pain in the neck and you may not get any good results for your efforts for a long, long time. Because there is no immediate payoff and no guarantees, it's hard to get excited about working on a proposal. I'm not going to lie and say I enjoy doing them, but I believe if you're a professional, you put them together and send them out promptly. The payoff for doing a proposal can be big. Do it, do it right, do it right now.

"Authors do detailed research on their subject matter, but seldom do any at all on which publishing house is appropriate for their work," says Walter Powell. Keep in mind that most people you send a proposal to have NO time and want to be able to quickly decide whether you're the right person for the project. Make it easy for them to see why you would be perfect for the project and hard for them to say no to you. That's why the layout should highlight key selling points (put them in a sidebar, summary, or make the most important stuff bold). A film producer was bragging in an article about how he doesn't read scripts anymore, he scans them. He reads the first and last part of each piece, so lead with your best stuff and have a strong close. Chuck Palahniuk, the author of *Fight Club,* says about proposals: "Write something so amazing, so audacious, that even the very bored people who read slush pile manuscripts all day, every day, will sit up and take notice. These are people who love books, but so much of what they see is boring. They will be pantingly grateful if you make them laugh, scare them, teach them something interesting, so do all of the above. Make it so good they can't reject it for fear that another house will snap it up and make oodles of money."

Design is everything. Make a good first impression with a cool cover. Maybe go with an unusual size or format to stand out. One author made her proposal smaller than the usual size so that when editors started piling standard-size proposals (larger than hers) on top of her smaller proposal, the pile would fall over. Consequently, her proposal was always on the TOP of the pile, and as a result got read. Another way to give a dull proposal life is in the way you bind it. I've seen several creative bindings, including using a twig and twine (landscaper), a pencil fastened with rubber bands (freelance writer), buttons and thread (seamstress), and a piece of metal tubing (sculptor). Content is also critical. Have something concrete (like a prospectus in the financial world) so a sales force can sell it before it's done. Do your homework. Make sure it's marketable. One of the biggest mistakes is to NOT read all of the requirements before beginning. Other ways you can kill your chances (no matter how compelling your content) is to turn in a sloppy, incomplete, or late proposal. Understand the market. Is there an audience for this? Who are they? Will they buy it? Why will they buy it? Any ancillary markets? Why are you qualified? (Try to make it seem like you are not only the best choice but the only choice, by talking up your capabilities and qualifications.) Don't be vague. Include accurate facts and figures. When friends tell me about their ideas, I usually say to them, "This sounds great, but how will it make money?" Show where the money is to be made. What is the problem you are going to solve for the client? Stating the problem and showing how you'll solve it shows that you understand what you're dealing with and that you have a viable solution. A project overview also shows you understand what they want and how you'll do it. Maybe even provide a time line. Talk about the three to five key concerns and the solutions you can provide. Be clear and concise (maybe even precise). You must have a focus. It shows you have a clear understanding of what you want to sell and whom you want to sell it to. Ask yourself: Do they really need or want to know this? Sell them on the benefits (and you) before getting to price. To reassure them, also include references and a client list. Lastly, have a summary that restates the problem, proposes solutions, and lists the benefits to working with you. If your proposal isn't working, ask the client why they didn't buy and make the appropriate changes.

Video Star

The very first music video on MTV was, ironically, "Video Killed the Radio Star" by the Buggles on August 1, 1981. Videos can be a very effective promotional tool for the creative person (and with an iMac, something you can do by yourself for cheap). A promotional video can descibe (and show) what you do. You can show off your work or have others praising your work. You could show footage from a performance, media clips, works in progress. Do it in an interview style. It could be entertaining, like a documentary. A good video can educate an audience and demonstrate what you do unlike any other medium can. So when you send one out make sure it will get people's attention, that their curiosity will get the best of them and they'll watch it (or part of it) and have a hard time parting with it. They rarely get thrown out. You can also use them when working with the media, or play it at a trade show or in a store that carries your creations. A whole book could be written about how to make a promotional video. Here are a few suggestions that can help make yours more polished and professional: Start by asking to see any promotional videos you can get your hands on for ideas (of what works and what doesn't). Consider using stock footage (much of it is in public domain libraries or you can buy it) to give it an expensive look. Front-load the video with your best stuff in the beginning. Grab their attention fast or they'll hit fast forward (or worse, eject). It is best to work with a professional videographer, but you could also take a class and use the house equipment at a cable access station.

Demos

For the aspiring musician, the most important thing you will use to sell yourself and your songs is a demo tape. This shows record executives what you can do. It pays to put in the effort to do it right. You want your best songs and the best possible production. (With advances in digital technology, you can do a demo yourself for a fraction of the cost.) The problem is that nearly everyone with a credit card has the ability to build a home recording studio that rocks. So record executives are getting spoiled by higher-quality recordings. With that said, production really can't save a bad song. Technology is a tool. (The most important things are your vision and voice, the lyrics and melody.) Work on the quality of your songs and then use technology to make them sound even better. Competition is STIFF, and if you can make your demo sound better (your music is superior and special and the production of the songs is strong), you have a chance to break through the clutter because it puts the artist in the best light. You don't need to put everything you have ever written or recorded on your demo. FOCUS. Include your *best* stuff. Go for something that catches their ear and gets their attention. Something that sets you apart. Something that gets them excited and makes them want to work with you. Finally, a well-produced demo can show a record executive that you are organized and focused enough to get it down on tape. It also gives you something to sell at gigs and online.

STOP THE INSANITY

If you don't want to be the next Susan Powter ("Stop the Insanity"), Suzanne Sommers (Thigh Master), or Jay Kordich (Juiceman), you can do it without having to sign up with Gunthy-Ranker or spend a ton of money to produce your own infomercial. Not that there is anything wrong with doing an infomercial (unless it's for the Flowbee, the hair-cutting vacuum). Infomercials made Tony Robbins, Suze Orman, and John Gray huge. Maybe you could do a demonstration on a smaller cable channel like the Food Network or HGTV.

_____

Not-So-Secret Agents

"My agent gets ten percent of everything I get, except my blinding headaches."

—*Fred Allen*

Upon his death, one actor's will had a strange request. His body was to be cremated and 15 percent of his ashes thrown in his agent's face. The moral of this story is that you don't have to like your agent. As long as they produce results, the relationship works. Naturally, there is resentment among many creative people toward their agents because the artist does all the work and the agent gets a rather large cut for sometimes making just a few calls. That's what you pay them for. Not their time, but the results. You do well, they do well. If you really hate to sell and someone will gladly do it for you, what would that be worth to you? They have the contacts, connections, and credentials. They get meetings with people you never will. A good agent gets you (figuratively) in doors that were otherwise closed. When country music star Trisha Yearwood switched her representation to Ken Kragen, who also manages Kenny Rogers and Travis Tritt, it led to a much higher profile in the industry. They are insiders and understand the industry. My literary agent was an editor at four major publishing houses before representing authors, and because of that experience understands (as well as anyone can) the inner workings at publishing houses and how to approach and sell them. Another nice thing about having an agent is that they negotiate on your behalf. You can distance yourself from the dickering involving dollars. They should be able to get you a better deal than you could have gotten if you represented yourself. (Many creative people get just a little emotional in those situations.) They can fight for promotional dollars and deals on your behalf. They will be tough so you don't have to be. One author said about her agent,

"She's a bitch, but she's my bitch." A good agent will spend time (you don't have to) looking for opportunities, keeping a pulse on your industry, and dealing with details (like handling the licensing, marketing, and selling of your art on, say, posters and mugs). They may even create concepts and project ideas for you.

How to work with your agent depends on each individual agent, but here are a few tips to make sure you get all the promotion you can from them. Your agent is not your mother, your shrink, or even your friend. In fact, they are an employee of yours. It's a business relationship. Still, send thank-you's and remember their birthdays. Be a darling client and easy to work with as well as the squeaky wheel. Maybe you have to *ask* (not demand) that the agent include you on their website or in their directory. It's okay to be proactive, it's not okay to be unprofessional. You want your agent to be making money (for you) and have an appreciation for what you do and the artistic integrity I am sure you want to keep intact. In a way, it's up to you to keep them informed and in the loop. Keep them posted about what you're doing (and want to be doing) with regular updates. Keep them motivated. Make sure they have the tools to promote you (proposals, pictures, portfolios, and so on). One mistake a lot of creative people make is that they think the agent will do all the work and that you are their only client. In many cases you still have to do a lot of the legwork, including generating leads and creating impressive work. One example of the value of having a good agent and doing a lot of the work yourself is author Wally Lamb. He spent twenty-five years teaching high school English before becoming a best-selling author. It wasn't until he had one of his short stories published that he attracted the attention of an agent, who then sent it to an editor in New York. She bought the book *She's Come Undone,* and with the help of Oprah's book club it became a best-seller (five years after the novel first hit stores).

If you believe you are the only one who can make it happen, maybe you should be your own agent. Jimmy Buffett decided that he could negotiate his own book deal without the help of a literary agent, thus saving paying the percentage of his advance and a percentage of the royalties after the book took off and became a best-seller. The reason many people act as their own agent is they can't get one. You have to have a pretty impressive track record or immense talent to get a good agent. You are probably thinking: "But that's why I need an agent, so I can build a body of work." In computer geek lingo it's called an infinite loop–type problem. There is a solution. Do whatever it takes to establish a track record (even if it's on a small scale) to prove you are marketable, and that should attract an agent. I have even heard of stories where the artist has a deal and brings in an agent to negotiate it and handle the details. Does it make sense to give all that commission? Usually an agent will get you a better deal, and when you have a deal in hand it's easier to get a good agent. Other (less expensive) ways to get an agent would be from referrals, submissions, and conferences. Some artists buy space in showcase books that go to agents, buyers, and art directors. You can also use a lawyer or an artists' representative instead of an agent. One final note, don't go overboard with agents, advisors, coaches, publicists, managers, gurus, and other helpers. These people can free you up to do art, but you can end up LOSING money if you aren't careful. Do they generate enough income to justify hiring them?

10

FULL COURT PRESS
(Positive Publicity)

"The only thing worse than being talked about is not being talked about."

—Oscar Wilde

Here's something you may not have known. The media needs YOU (and you need the media). At least the media needs interesting, witty, timely, informative, and irresistible stories. You have more leverage than you think. Ever wonder why some creative people are celebrities and others can't get a break? In most cases it's the creative person who is able to play the media game that wins. A mention in the media (conventional and on the Internet) can mean a boost in sales, larger crowds at your shows, and it can increase your marketability. The media can make you (or break you if you screw up). It's been this way for a long time, ever since Ed Sullivan and his "really big *shew*" launched Elvis and the Beatles. It's the same today, except that there are so many more media outlets than ever before. Let's talk about how to turn the media into a promotional tool that works for greater good—our success! For instance, you could use your positive reviews to convince galleries, distributors, editors, agents, sales reps, clubs, and the public to buy (or buy into you). It drives people to the store, and it also pushes your people (reps, distributors, publishers, publicists) to pick it up, and convinces stores to put it on the shelves. After working my tush off writing these books, I wanted to let people know about them. I'm no fool, I know publicity is the best way. So together let's figure out how to make the media work for us.

One myth I want to explode is that publicity is free. I assure you it is not. It costs you postage, patience, and persistence, but it does pay off—big-time! The cost for spreading the word through positive press is a mere pittance compared to what it would take to run ads. Many authors have to augment what the publisher is willing to do for them by hiring a publicist (very expensive) or hiring an assistant to help deal with the details (not cheap, either). It's so important that it's worth the extra expense. Getting good media gives you instant credibility, makes you appear successful to others—even if you're still driving that old car and can barely pay the bills, people see you as successful because you're in the paper, on TV, or on the radio. It's up to you to turn that into something more than a giant ego massage. People will remember stories in the paper longer than they will an ad, and maybe recognize you. Whoopie. You have to take that notoriety and become a known name and increase your value. Use the exposure to sell yourself and your products and services. The funny thing is, media begets more media, so once you start the wheels in motion, you should find it easier and easier to promote yourself.

Author William Doyle spent five years slaving over a book about modern Presidents and their White House tapes, titled *Inside the Oval Office*. He fully embraced the concept of doing media to support the book and helped to push the book into a second printing. One editor at Doubleday heard an interview with him on the radio and remembered his name. She pulled his proposal from her In box and offered him a sizable advance for his next book. Bravo! Start small and start to build some momentum. Remember, all publicity is valuable. You never know who is reading (or watching or listening) to you and where that will lead. Sister Mary Lisette Valenzuela found her TRUE calling after being a disc jockey for a day. The nun and high school teacher was a natural as she introduced songs and yakked it up with listeners on a Top 40 radio station in Burbank, California. She won the chance to spin records by writing an essay for the station's "Corporate Takeover" promotion, which allows listeners to spend time behind the mike. So use your time in the public eye to get the word out and advance your career. When Fred LaBour was a journalism student at the University of Michigan, he wrote a review in the student newspaper of the Beatles album *Abbey Road*. In his review he observed that if you played the album backward, it gave clues proving that Paul McCartney was dead. National papers picked up the story and interviewed LaBour extensively. He went on to become a songwriter in Nashville. When author and businessman Harvey MacKay got an advance of $250,000 for his book *Swim with the Sharks Without Being Eaten Alive,* he gave back $150,000 and insisted it be used to finance a thirty-city book tour. Then he visited book retailers and wholesalers and outlined his publicity plans and promotional tour. He met with the Waldenbooks CEO and promised to mention that the book was available at Waldenbooks in all interviews, and the retailer increased its initial orders from 2,500 copies to over 10,000 copies.

Media Mind-set

"Journalism is the ability to meet the challenge of filling space."
—Rebecca West

Dealing with the media is like a game—with a lot at stake. If you play by the rules, you'll win. It starts with common courtesy and the ability to put yourself in their shoes. It's not what you want, but what would be attractive to them. Think like an editor, producer, or booking agent. (Hint: Pretend you are underpaid and under pressure, overstressed and over it—jaded.) What do they look for? (Need or want?) As the host of a radio talk show called "Creative-Lee Speaking" that helps creative people deal with the business side of art, I am amazed at the things people send me. (By the way, you should address your press releases to the producer and not the host.) Each time I get one of these off-the-wall (and off-the-mark) pitches, I am tempted to write back and explain what's what when it comes to getting on a show—but then I decided to put it in this book (ha ha). So here's how to develop a media mind-set so both of you are on the same page (so to speak).

Treat the media with respect. (You probably guessed I would say that.) Seriously, they are real people. If you can be friendly but not phony, prepared but able to get to the point, and persistent but not a pest, you will likely land some press.

Get to the point—fast. People in the media are almost always short on time. Get to the point. Ask yourself: Why is this worth their time? Get a handle on your central message. Don't overpitch, but you also don't want to undersell yourself. Remember, they need you, too. It's also a good idea to find the "human" element of a story as part of the pitch. Tell them why you are perfect for their show.

Don't be boring! You are not the first person to pitch them; they are pitched to all day. That's where the expression "Been there, done that" originated, I think. Practice your pitch. Find the angle, hook, or newsworthiness, and then present it in a convincing and compelling way. (Hint: The media loves kids, animals, local, controversial, timely, new, unique, sexy, and David-versus-Goliath angles, among other things.)

Not-so-confidential source. You want them to say, "This is exactly what we need right now. It's interesting, timely, and newsworthy from a credible source." How do you do that? Pay attention to what's happening around you. Read the paper, watch the news, and listen to radio talk shows. As they say, "Be dialed in." (This includes staying abreast of what's happening online. Check out www.mediafinder.com.)

User-friendly. Remember when I said the media is VERY busy? If possible, be available when they call back. You may not get a second chance. In a sense, you want to be easy to work with—user-friendly. Write press releases that are so good they are ready to print. Make their lives easier and they'll love you. (Of course, you e-mailed it so they can just paste it in.) Be a resource they can turn to when they need a "source." Provide interviewers with story ideas, sample questions, fast facts—anything that saves them time is good.

Show that you did your homework. You know their readers. Pay attention to what's on or in a publication you're pitching. You don't want to pitch something they just covered that very day. Show you know them (you sent the right stuff to the right person at the right time *and* spelled their name correctly). Maybe even add a personal touch. I noticed that someone I had surfed with had become the editor of a surfing magazine. First I congratulated him on his promotion, then I pitched him (in that order). Find the tie-in, of course. I mean, sending a pet story to the food critic is not going to work.

Perfect pitch. Call and find out HOW they prefer to be pitched. I've heard many people in the media get perturbed if you fax. (Most media people don't mind being sent e-mail but hate being hit with the same release from all angles—fax, e-mail, and mail.)

Switch the pitch to their audience. Say something like, "Your audience will find this fascinating because it is (fill in the blank)." Then blow them away with your idea. Sure, they want new and newsworthy (or even a new angle on an old theme). When my book on time management came out, I pitched *Maxim* magazine on a story about ways that men (it's a men's magazine) can save time. Although they never used some of my more unusual men-only tips (pee in the shower, drink milk out of the carton, don't undo your tie, and listen to sports on a Walkman while you take the kids to the park), I still got mentioned several times in the article.

Confidence sells. Unwavering belief in a project is hard to resist. Act like you have been there, done that before, but that you also want to do it again. If they say they aren't interested at this time, have a backup pitch or rethink the angle and try again later—or come up with something new. Reinvent yourself, especially if they seem bored or uninterested.

Simplify it. Show them what you do and what makes it exciting or different, timely or useful, funny or fun. Include a tip sheet with your press information. They may just use it as is. The same goes for surveys (attach your name to everything you send).

It's a long-term proposition. Don't burn bridges, even if someone in the media has given you the cold shoulder, misspelled your name, or misquoted you. Trust me, you do not want the media as an enemy. ("The pen is mightier . . ." comes to mind.) It isn't an adversarial situation, unless you make it so. It can be frustrating trying to get your name in print, but when they say no to a story idea (or ignore you), it's almost never personal. If you freak out at them, *then* it may turn personal. If you are frustrated by a lack of media, remember it's a numbers game. It takes timing, persistence, and cleverness to get press. But once the media know they can trust you as a guest or source, there is a good chance they will use you again.

Name-drop. If they don't know you from Adam but you're a friend of so-and-so, use that person's name to open the door. If what you do involves a celebrity of some sort, use that angle, too.

Show and tell. The authors of the book *The Worst-Case Scenario Handbook* went on the "Today" show to demonstrate to Matt and Katie how to land a plane in an emergency, break down a locked door, and fight off a shark or an alligator. This is "good TV" because it is visual. Do you have something you could demonstrate? Film your own behind-the-scenes video and take before and after pictures.

Don't ramble. The media want and need sound bites. Think before you speak, and come up with a couple of really good (and short) sound bites as answers to the most obvious questions.

Bosom buddies. You may not become best buddies, but try to befriend the media. An author friend of mine found out that the book section editor loves cats. So when she wrote an article for *Cat Fancy* magazine, she interviewed *him,* and later he reciprocated with a story about her. You don't have to befriend everyone in the media, but target the key people you feel you need to know. It's the quality of your contacts, not the quantity, that counts. Another savvy media author is a resource for the media. She feeds her contact valuable insider information and went from cold calling to a codependent relationship. In your contact software (or on an index card) jot down some notes about certain media people. For instance, I know that Michael Kinsman of the *San Diego Union-Tribune* loves the blues. Treat the press as you do other valuable business contacts. Meet and greet. In some cities you can frequent media hangouts (but don't follow them home).

Pet peeve. I hate it when someone who's trying to be clever includes things like sprinkles with their press releases. You know, like glitter, for example. I want entertaining, enlightening, or educational guests. Guests that make me look good. Sprinkles just aren't going to cut it.

Work with a charity. The media *loves* the charity angle. LOVES!

Play on any local angle. When singer Chris Isaak announced he would be playing in Stockton, California, his hometown, for the first time in twenty years ("They dropped all the charges so it's wonderful to come back," joked the singer), not only did he make the papers, the mayor gave him the key to the city and proclaimed the date Chris Isaak Day.

Match material to the style of a publication. It shows you've read it. You could even provide a ready-to-run article (with your name and contact information at the bottom). Don't overlook your trade industry's publication or an association newsletter.

Controversial. One tattoo artist gave teens fake tattoos to see what their parents thought before he would do the real deal. It made all the local news shows. A while ago there was a flood of stories about online security, so one brazen computer consultant called and bragged to a news producer that he could hack into the station's computer system. He did (and altered the newscaster's photos to prove he was there), and not only did he appear on the news, he became their "computer guy" and is on all the time.

Send your newsletter to media. Send a sample of your product or offer to give them a free trial. One organizer offered to do a free makeover of one producer's desk. It was a hit, and she landed an ongoing gig with the morning news.

Don't get locked in to only one story idea. Come up with a list of several story ideas that you are an expert on.

Find the "hook." One artist did wood sculpture—with a chain saw! A band held the release party for their new CD—in a haunted house!

How to Get It on . . . TV and Radio (and in Print)

"People aren't interested in reading nice things. A bitchy little comment is far more interesting."

—Mira Sorvino

The number-one excuse for not getting enough publicity that I hear from frustrated people is that they don't have the time to pursue it. Set aside time (thirty minutes a day) and set a goal (one promotion a day). Otherwise, it ain't gonna happen. Garnering publicity requires a lot of little mundane things like stuffing, licking, and faxing. Yuck. Have a

FULL COURT PRESS

pizza party and get some of your family and friends to help out. Remember, winners do what losers don't want to do.

Human contact is critical. Invite the media to your events. (Offer free food and you may just get them to show up.) Send cards when they get promoted or win an award for their journalism. Offer them story ideas or inside information. Do lunch. Get in their face. In support of her debut album, singer/songwriter Treana performed live acoustic sets at music industry magazine offices and radio stations and proceeded to blow them away with her passionate music. This led to write-ups and positive reviews.

Ads in media directories do work. Although this can be very expensive (get your publisher or label to pay), this is one of the best ways to reach the media. The other way is to go to the library (or online) and look up the address of every media source you want to reach, and then send them your press release and press kit. Now, those ads in directories don't sound so bad, do they?

Lead times. Getting press is not a last-minute, haphazard kind of thing. You'll need a calendar of events (yours and theirs), and enter key dates (like your events and deadlines) on a wall calendar. You may want to request a media calendar (to find out when the paper will run a special insert, for example). The other way to see what runs when is to look at back issues for what they ran in the past. Then you can start getting ready well in advance. Have your website ready for hits. Get those head shots taken and reproduced. Line up your tour dates. Remember, timing is everything. (You'll want to hit the media when the time is right for you—and them.) Holiday times are a slow news time, for example, so there is a good chance you can get on an otherwise hard-to-book show if you are available, say, Thanksgiving weekend. Tie it in to the holidays in some way, and voilà— publicity.

Find an upbeat or offbeat angle such as new (technique), local (hometown hero), success (award you won, best-seller status), milestone (anniversary), charitable (proceeds go to good cause), timely (news related or trendy), human interest (overcome adversity, heartwarming), or a new twist on an old theme. The reason *The Worst-Case Survival Handbook* has done so well is both the unusual title and the content (advice on how to survive a leap from a motorcycle to a car and forty other life-threatening situations). The authors also have great sound bites, like "This book helps desk jockeys get in touch with their inner MacGyvers," and "It's really the action hero's handbook." It's got a MacGyver kind of angle. How to fend off a shark is interesting and a nice "hook" for the media. (To fend off a shark, just in case you meet one, hit the shark in the eyes or gills, because that is where they are most sensitive. Hmm.)

Prioritize. Choose the best contacts (you are most likely to land some publicity, or they're so big you want to give it your best shot), and hit them hard. Send your releases early and often. Make a list of potential fits and then pick the best to begin with. Where it will have the most impact? Chicago radio host Milt Rosenberg was dubbed the nation's leading author's interviewer by *Talkers* magazine. I think I will send him a press kit. I'm not kidding. It's better when you already know them and they at least know who you are. Try pitching a new angle or idea to an editor who already knows you. Write a personal letter and have it hand delivered. Offer some freebie that they can pass on to their readers or viewers (that will make them look good). Tie in with some upcoming event (timeliness).

Gimmicks can work. If you wrote a chocolate lover's cookbook, by all means send samples. Be generous. When Epson came out with the first dot matrix printer, they sent printers. Simon & Schuster sent freshly baked cupcakes with review copies of the *Magnolia Bakery Cookbook.* For the movie *Road Trip*—which includes a memorable sperm-bank scene—they mailed a rubber glove, K-Y jelly, a specimen cup, and a dirty photo. For the film *Rocky & Bullwinkle,* they sent the media-cute Rocky slippers.

Hobbies are also an angle you can exploit. Novelist Laurence Shames (*Florida Straits*) is also an avid sailor. In *Men's Journal* he was interviewed about how to dock a sailboat without using an engine while sailing solo.

Don't get too big for your britches. When I appeared on a little cable access TV talk show called "Coffee in Del Mar," I did it because my good friend was the host. Ha, this ended up being more than just a favor for a friend. It led to an article in the newspaper, and when the little cable access show was picked up by all the cable stations in San Diego, over 250,000 people potentially could see the interview.

I realize there is a lot to know when it comes to pitching the press, so here's some more stuff to overwhelm you further. Seriously, here are just a few more items to consider. Get good photos and send them. People look at a picture, and if you send a good one of your product or yourself, there is a far better chance they will run it with the story instead of having to send a photographer for a shoot. If you provide some service (an intangible), see if there is anything tangible you can send—a booklet, tip sheet, or newsletter. If you don't feel comfortable with publicity or can't come up with a "hook," consider pitching one of your clients. If they get on a show, they will talk up you and your services. Consider tie-ins like Scuba Diving Week (the author of a book is also a diver), Gay Pride Week (the central character in the play is gay), timely (a book on life after college is newsworthy around graduation and back-to-school time), holidays (a children's book about the Easter Bunny is news in spring), or an anniversary (a play is more timely when it is the fiftieth anniversary of the famous playwright's death).

Publicity and Persistence Go Hand in Hand

"I would like to take this opportunity to tell the press to kiss my skinny white ass."

—Calista Flockhart

The number-one, MOST important aspect of getting your name in print and on the air is FOLLOW UP. Without it a terrible thing happens—nothing. The problem with this is that it's time consuming, bruising to the ego, and requires good organizational skills and record keeping (three things many creative people do not have enough of). The follow-up call is an art. (I'm using the word "art" to get you interested enough to do it.) I know, I know, you are too busy to be bothered. You think *you* are busy. Ha. The media is more overwhelmed than you are. Trust me on that. If you think you can send a bunch of press releases and then sit back and wait for the media to call, don't wait by the phone in anticipation, I'll end the suspense for you: They ain't gonna call. First you blitz the media (or do a little at a time so you can stay on top of it). Then you follow up. This is a tried-and-true pattern that works. To make it easier, use contact software, a follow-up file, or a wall calendar—but do it. If you really hate the idea of doing follow-up calls, get help. Hire an assistant, use a publicist, or use your publisher's publicist to their full capacity.

If you fail on the first try with a media contact, don't get discouraged and don't even think of giving up. Get to know the gatekeepers (assistants) and then charm and disarm them. Show them respect. You can't, and shouldn't, strong-arm them. Act excited about being on "Good Morning, Boise." Show your gratitude if you get invited, because you'll want to be on again. Send (flowers, nice note, free samples) as a token for their help. Find out when the best (and worst) time to call back would be. If they are on the air or on a deadline, that would be bad. When should you follow up? Wait a few days and call. Don't ask, "Did you get my . . . (whatever you sent)"? Be specific. I like to call with additional information. I'll hold something back for the follow-up call. A little piece of information. Outline or script what you want to say. At least practice your pitch. If they say no, try a new angle. Have it ready. Ask for what they're looking for, then try again later. You don't want to burn any bridges. The goal is to be a good source they will want to work with in the future. When you're bumped, go with the flow, don't go off. "It" happens. Dealing with the media is a long-term approach. Author and spiritual guru Deepak Chopra was bumped from the "Today" show while he was in New York promoting one of his books. The bummer part was that he was bumped by Rick Rockwell ("Who Wants to Marry a Millionaire?"). He didn't lose it. Instead he went into deep meditation. He also turned getting bumped into a news story that was carried by several major papers. Make yourself easy to book and work with. Do not be a prima donna. Be a bulldog. Be a gladiator. Don't be a dick.

Press Kits
"Never believe anything until it has been officially denied."
—Claud Cockburn

The press kit is still alive and well in the electronic age. Press kits are fairly cost-effective ways of reaching not only the media, but also to impress anyone you want to do business with (agent, club owner, clients, sponsors, and so on). No matter who you send them to, the main goal is to get them opened. (No kidding, right?) Well, this is no easy task, believe me. It takes a delicate balance between being as complete as possible and not so complete that you bury them in paper and overwhelm them. No matter what, it must not be boring. Interesting, innovative, and inspiring, yes. Boring, no. I have also found that by customizing it, you can gain their attention. (I know of artists who hand-paint the covers, or create covers that are cut into interesting shapes. Let your creativity shine through.) Create a publicity portfolio, and have some on hand and ready to go, but add or subtract inserts as needed. (Tip: Make them as easy to put together as possible so you won't procrastinate about sending them out, because "Timeliness is next to godliness.")

Make a good first impression with the packaging of your press kit. Start with the way you send it. Create a nice-looking label or unusual envelope. Maybe you could send it in a box meant for something different. When they open the package, the first thing they see is the cover. At the very least, spray-mount (or have printed) something colorful, creative, or cool on the cover. If you send things in a binder, choose the binders with a pocket in front to insert a custom cover.

The second thing they see is your cover letter. It's the first thing they *read*. This is your personal greeting. Make a good first impression. Start by getting their name and title right and personalize it. Keep it clear and simple, warm and friendly, and start and end with the benefits to them. Get to the point quick. Why should they put you on their show? How will they (or their audience) benefit by doing a story about you? Help them "get it" about what you do. (A tag line or *short* artist's statement is handy here.) State your accomplishments in a clever and compelling way, or stated another way: What does it mean to them? Be professional and conversational. Confident, not arrogant. Triple-check for typos, and please, no stupid fonts! Cut out all the irrelevant crap and fit it all on one page. Print it on your letterhead. Close with a call to action. Tell them what the next step is and how to take it.

And then there is the press release. This is probably (in the media's eyes, anyway) the most important piece of paper in a press kit. Sadly, I will many times throw away nearly everything a potential guest sends, but save and file the press release for future reference. Because this is such a staple item in a press kit, every single book ever written about self-promotion or publicity includes several pages on what makes a powerful press release. I grappled with how much space to devote to this subject and decided to give you a checklist to use when writing one yourself. Let's start by calling it a "news" release; it sounds more timely and, well, newsy. As with everything else we have discussed relating to the media, do not be boring! (I got one that was from a marriage counselor who was an expert on families being torn apart by divorce, and the press release was torn. Very clever, just not right for my show.) Anything can be made interesting with the right angle. Find the hook, flush it out somehow, and *focus on it*. A press release should:

- Be no more than one or two pages
- Be double-spaced
- Have a grabber of a headline
- Lead with your best stuff, with less important information at the bottom
- Tell the reader who, what, why, where, and how in the first paragraph
- NOT be an infomercial. (Topic is timely, newsworthy, entertaining, or all three)
- Have a photo on the release if there is room
- Include a letterhead, with contact information on every page
- Be written in the third person

- Focus on the human interest angle, tell a story
- Be custom-tailored to the recipient and audience
- Focus on the most interesting and important information
- Have a local angle
- Not tell them *everything* about an event, just the best stuff—timely, relevant, and interesting
- Glamorize your release by name-dropping (a celebrity endorsement?)
- Have quotes by yourself or other experts
- Be interesting, newsworthy, timely, sexy, involve kids or animals
- Be typo-free
- Include some statistics
- Be appropriate for the publication
- Not be too self-serving. It's not an ad or infomercial
- Not be too late for deadline
- Not have stupid, cheesy, amateur, or hard-to-read fonts
- Have a hook that is imaginative or catchy

Other things to include in your press kit are samples of your work (this could be a mini-portfolio, tear sheets, audio, or a diskette). You may also want to include a sheet with frequently asked questions (and the answers), tickets to a show, or a gimmick item of some kind (like Play-Doh, for example). Just a note: Samples can be downloaded off the Net in compressed format, and all you send are instructions on where to find them and maybe a CD-ROM to put them on. (It's a demo on demand.) Put in press clippings to show you're not an amateur, you are worthy. (But too much coverage could make you look overexposed.) Also include works you have written. You'll also want to include a brief bio and/or your résumé in your press kit. This is no time to be humble. That doesn't mean include *everything* you've ever done, just the latest and greatest or most relevant. There is nothing that says it can't be interesting as well as informative (not just names and dates). Make it clever, cool, relevant, current—let your personality come through. A good bio should tell a little about the person behind the accomplishments. I think a little personal stuff goes a long way; things like your hometown or hobbies are a good example. Use interesting categories to break it up. Be specific about things like your background. This could be your training or facts about your success (over one million sold), whom you have worked with (success by association), any organizations you belong to, and charity work you have done. Never lie on these things, and keep proof in case you ever have to back up one of your claims. Look for things in your background that make you unique and interesting. Match your résumé or bio to your media, maybe even customize it. Have several bios/résumés ready to go, each with a different focus. Show off your creativity. (That does not mean you can use creative spelling. Grammar and neatness do count.)

1-2-3-4-5-6-7 and gone. You have about seven seconds. A summary of activities is fine. Don't overdo it. Make it a short summary, something an editor or producer can quickly scan. (Use bullets, do a time line, or make key accomplishments bold.) Organize it for maximum effectiveness. Front-load it. Succinctly sum up your career in a skimmer-friendly way. If you can't seem to cut it down, have someone else edit or write it. Even if you don't use everything you are doing or have done, by all means document what you're working on and save old sketches, mock-ups, prototypes. (No rough drafts of this book will circulate, however.) Then keep it current (best in, worst out). The best way to do that is to keep a journal or a list of your latest and greatest accomplishments. Create a complete bio/résumé, and then you can pull what you need from it, or have a folder to drop things in as they happen.

Include photographs. That doesn't mean you send snapshots from your personal photo album. Don't skimp here! Think professional. Put contact and credit and caption on the back. You will likely need black-and-white photos, and possibly color, too. Usually five-by-seven or eight-by-ten (head shot). Include before and after photos of a work in progress or a behind-the-scenes shot. Come up with a clever caption and include it with the picture. Videos are necessary for many creative people (like actors). They are also good because you can show-and-tell with video. It's easy to send, and everyone has a VCR. Start with a nice quality cover for the tape. Now let's talk about having high-quality stuff inside as well. Put only high-quality work on it. Professional videos can cost from $500 to $50,000 to make. Don't waste money unless you plan for it to be top-quality. To save money in shooting, you can include existing interview clips, a performance, samples of your work, a tour of your studio; make it into a documentary. Tell a good story and come up with a solid theme that doesn't cost any extra. Make it a little Hollywood. Entertain them! Include cool stuff like animation, graphics, music, special effects, and, by all means, get good sound. It's a lot like a film. You script it, storyboard it, scout locations, cast it, direct it, act in it, edit it—which can all be done on your Mac using Final Cut.

Finally, include an interview with yourself that is ready to print. A fact sheet (fast facts for the interviewer or reporter are handy—for them). Mention who your record label is, your management company. Put in tidbits like your genre, instrument, band members' backgrounds, your client list, tour dates/calendar of events, playlist, a quote page (by you or about you), your philosophy, other interviews, reviews and articles, letters of recommendations, awards, and a SASE if they need more info, or instruct them where to find it on the Internet.

FAST FACT
In the United States alone there are 11,937 magazines, 1,537 daily newspapers, 1,520 television stations, and 9,767 commercial radio stations. (The country with the most daily newspapers is India, with 2,300.)

Where to Pitch Story Ideas

"Writers should be read, but neither seen nor heard."
—Daphne du Maurier

Remember, the media need you. They are always looking for good stories. What is a good story? Put yourself in their shoes and then put yourself in their readers'/viewers'/listeners' shoes. What would I want if I were them? Don't forget, it's not enough just to get publicized, you want to land in a place where your potential clients are going to see it. Find out what the right place is for you. Don't waste your time and energy (at first) on something that is such a stretch or a mismatch that it won't do a lot of good. Read, watch, and listen (and check directories) until you find a fit. (Even if you were turned down by one department of a big paper, hit another one. It might just be the fit you need.) Still not sure? Enlist the help of those with whom you are involved. (Not *that* kind of involved.) Maybe the event organizer knows what media to hit (and has local media and contacts). A gallery, bookstore, or trade show coordinator (as well as the publisher or sponsor) can be your best resource and asset when it comes to getting media. For example, most big bookstores have an event coordinator. Get them your promotional materials and let them do the rest. Find someone who is a champion for what you do. For instance, many established jazz musicians like to see young people get into the genre. It's their cause and they want to see you do well. Get your stuff to them and watch them do the rest. Read bios of talk show hosts and columnists to see if they share a passion for what you do.

Do your homework. According to a Gallup poll, 36 percent of U.S. adults have not visited the library in the past year. Check out magazines and media directories in your library (or the bookstore). Many media listings are online, or you can buy a list. Once you take this seriously, you'll want to build your own list, starting with the local media and industry magazines. Where should you try to get exposure for yourself? Here's a partial checklist.

__ Wire services
__ The Internet has a plethora of opportunities, from Web-based magazines to online versions of print magazines
__ Regional publications
__ General-interest magazines
__ Specialty magazines
__ Hobby magazines
__ Trade magazines
__ In-flight magazines
__ Fanzines
__ Retailers. Even stores (like Borders and Costco) have their own magazines
__ There are also magazines read by the media that would generate more publicity if you got into them
__ Commercial radio (talk radio, news shows, morning shows)
__ National Public Radio ("All Things Considered" and "Fresh Air")
__ College radio
__ Local televsion news, morning shows, cable access shows
__ National talk shows

Start small. Try regional publications first and work the local angle. When you get in a local publication, other national publications may take notice and pick up the story. Make your own mark in the media by writing your own column. Send in a few articles (ready to print) and see what they say. Take advantage of calendar listings. (Send a photo with your calendar release for more impact. They may just run it.) It's not a feature story, but it's better than nothing. (A lot easier to get, too.) A lot of things can qualify for a listing in the paper. Try to get on the regional best-seller list (*Chicago Tribune, Detroit Free Press*). Then try to get it in the hands of a syndicated columnist like Larry King, and if he loves it, watch out. Suggest story ideas. Being quoted in an article is better than nada. Maybe you don't get featured, but being cited as an expert is good, too. Many magazines (non-art-related) use art and photos with articles. Look for publications that match your style or genre (nautical, medical, or comical), and pitch them on the idea of using some of your art with an article (or on the cover!). Find a niche and fill it (military, college, hobby, special interest, employee publications, newsletters, tourist guides, alternative lifestyle). All of them need stories. Find off-the-beaten-path publications to pitch. The top three special-interest magazines are *Car & Travel, Prevention,* and *Sports Illustrated.* Pay attention to which writer writes what. (Write to tell them you like their work.) Don't forget freelancers. Stay in touch and tell them what you're up to. Suggest story ideas. Use regional writers who are contributors for national magazines. Write letters to the editor in local, national, or trade publications. Make an odd connection. A heavy-metal band pitched a steel industry trade magazine. It worked, too.

Know what's what and who's who in your industry by reading trade journals. If you are an actor in New York, you will likely read *Backstage,* and if you're in Los Angeles, read *Back Stage West.* Learn who is doing what (and to whom). Then figure out how YOU can get a mention or a feature story in them. Maybe you're able to get your profile or write a column in a technical magazine like *Modern Drummer.* Get to know columnists in your field. Offer to do artwork or write for them. Maybe you could interview another creative person for a story, and later they will do something for you. Being a part of an industry roundtable dicussion at a conference is a good way to get in. Don't overlook catalogs that also have "how-to" articles and tips sections. Try to get listed as a resource in the back of books, newsletters, and magazines.

Chase's Book of Annual Events (I'm positive there is a copy at your local library) allows you to create and list your own holiday or event. For example, Marissa D'Vari, an author and columnist, created the Shameless Promotion Month (September) and included her website and contact with the listing. I created the Respect for Right-Brainers Month (October). The benefit of doing this is that it's free, it gives you a reason to be interviewed on radio and TV, and it gets you listed in this widely distributed directory.

☆ ————————————————

FAST FACTS

The top magazine in circulation in the United States is the *NRTA/AARP Bulletin* (with over 21 million readers), followed by *Modern Maturity, Readers Digest, TV Guide,* and *National Geographic.*

Interview Skills

"Do you want to pet my pussy?" is what Raquel Welch said on a Johnny Carson show about her pet cat (sitting on her lap). Holy schnikeeeezzz. When the Beatles first arrived in America, they spent the first few minutes answering absurd questions from the media. The public was intrigued by how they looked and, I think, shocked by what they said. One New York reporter asked John Lennon, "Was your family in show business?" His reply was, "Well, me dad used to say me mother was a great performer." And so it began. The media are a jaded bunch; you really have to WOW them. Bring your guitar and perform in studio. Read a poem. Do a demonstration or experiment. Arrive in a limo. Do whatever it takes to go from a talking head to an interesting and compelling interview. I love Charlie Rose. In my opinion he is the best interviewer among the late-night talk show hosts. The only problem is, his show really is a "talk" show in every sense of the word. Some may find that format boring. How can you do something different (entertaining and educational) to make producers beg you to be on the show?

In my experience, most interviewers have NOT read my book and they ask irrelevant questions. I know what I want to say, and I will do my best to weave the discussion back to where it should be. I rarely get confrontational interviewers, but I do get indifferent ones. I am not sure which is more maddening. Many people hire a media coach who does mock interviews to get ready for the real show. After some of the guests I have had on my show (smart people who could not, even if their life depended on it, communicate in a talk show format), I can see why. In a word, they choked once the red light went on. I thought about this a lot. What I like in a guest on my show is a person who is prepared and is able to talk extemporaneously about her topic. I am also a fan of the sound bite. It's so awkward to have to interrupt a rambler to get to a news break. Witty with a good sense of humor is always a nice bonus.

Before the Interview

• Be ready when you call a producer. That's how they screen people who may or may not make it as a guest. If you choke during the call, they feel you will certainly choke on-air (somewhere you'll never be if you blow the phone interview).

• Confirm the date and time. Get directions. Do a dry run to the studio (and factor in traffic). Leave early. Bring a blank video- or audiotape. Print out a card with key information for the announcer/host and one for the station's receptionist. Even if you already sent a sample of your product, bring one with you, too. Give samples to the host, producer, and leave some in the break room. You never know if a producer from another show will pick it up and call you to be a guest on their show also.

- Send sample questions in advance.
- Have friends ready to call in with questions you prepared.
- Prepare! Role-play with a friend. If you sound like an idiot, you can do more harm than good.
- Know a little something about the show. Watch or listen to it before you are on.
- Be on time! (Reliable and ready.)
- Bring a sample of your music or outtakes or clips.

During the Interview

- Bring a pad of paper. Write the host's name down. Create a cheat sheet.
- If doing the interview from home, turn off call waiting and please turn down your radio.
- Have fun. Relax. Be dynamic.
- Do not be boring! Entertaining gets you back on; think Robin Williams. How about this, while being interviewed online, a fan asked Minnie Driver, "How do I download the Minnie Driver. Will it work on Windows 95?" Her reply was "That's funny. I don't know how compatible I am with anything." That's good. Someone asked "X-Files" creator Chris Carter if he read what people write about him and the "X-Files" on the Internet. He said, "Yes I do . . . and no, I am not a cross-dresser!"
- Enthusiastic and passionate about your subject is contagious.
- Sound bites. Anecdotes. Good, useful information. It is NOT an infomercial, but a clever interviewee can weave in their product, service, event, charity, cause, or company name. Don't forget to make a pitch at the end.
- When Trent Dilfer was the quarterback of the Tampa Bay Buccaneers, he was known for throwing interceptions at the worst possible times. A great sound bite about him was, "We'd say he was running around like a chicken with his head cut off, but out of curiosity, when I got home last night I cut the head off a chicken, and it still didn't throw the football."

• It goes by so fast, so plan what point you REALLY want to get across.

• If you don't know, don't guess. Laker center Shaquille O'Neal was asked whether he had visited the Parthenon during a visit to Greece. His answer was, "I can't really remember the names of the clubs that we went to."

• If it's TV, bring props.

• Have a ten- to thirty-second commercial ready.

• Offer a freebie.

• Water is always needed to avoid "cotton mouth." Ick.

After the Interview

• Give samples to the crew and talent. Point out other areas where you may make a good guest. Leave a how-to list, a Rolodex card, a card with your contact information and give to the receptionist in case listeners/viewers call the station wanting more information.

• Send a THANK-YOU note!

Damage Control

"I heard that I walked into another actor's trailer and said, 'You wanna f—k a star?' Like I would socialize with another actor."
—Christina Ricci

Spin control is turning a bad situation into positive press, or at the very least, minimizing the impact of negative publicity. There are so many examples of this in politics that I couldn't decide on a relevant story to use until I was on a plane from San Francisco to San Diego. The plane was delayed from taking off due to fog but finally got into the air well after dark. During the delay passengers ate and drank at the airport bar to pass the time. When we hit some pretty terrible turbulence while in flight, the guy across from me threw up into the lap of the woman sleeping next to him. When she woke and found the mess all over her, he said, "Feel better now?" That, my friends, is spin control. The poster child for bad publicity for a long time was Sinead O'Connor. Her antics were so outrageous on "Saturday Night Live" (emphasis on "live"), she offended everyone (she pulled out a picture of the Pope and tore it to shreds). Even Frank Sinatra offered to kick her ass in a letter to a newspaper. Not good. In addition, she refused to sing at the Garden State Arts Center in New Jersey after the National Anthem was played. She did so much damage that her career was essentially ruined. (Radio abandoned her and sales sucked.) Spin control can't fix everything, so act accordingly.

Controversy can be a way to keep your name in print. Rage Against the Machine are outspoken about many issues (some more popular than others), and the media usually makes room for their diatribes about racism, politics, and economic oppression. Sometimes "bad publicity" is good publicity in disguise, depending on how you handle it. When the Kingsmen's version of the song "Louie, Louie" became a big hit, the indecipherable lyrics created a controversy. Parents, the government, and the media declared the slurred lyrics obscene. There was an FCC investigation (your tax dollars at work), and even the FBI tried to figure out what the heck the band was singing about. (All to no avail, I might add.) So the Kingsmen went to Washington, D.C., to tell the government they were crazy and that they were just singing gibberish. All this attention made the song an even bigger hit. Be who you are. Don't create a false persona and compromise your ideals. Making *some* waves with your work isn't all bad. Pulitzer Prize–winning playwright Paula Vogel has delved into some very controversial topics, everything from pedophilia to domestic violence. She is also openly gay. Many feared the publicity from Anne Heche's off-screen life with Ellen DeGeneres would ruin her career. Others thought it was a publicity stunt. Neither of those two opinions was accurate.

Final Thoughts

"Rock journalism is people who can't write interviewing people who can't talk for people who can't read."

—Frank Zappa

Having been a columnist, talk show host, and publisher, I know what it takes to get my attention. So when I am wearing my other hat (as an author trying to publicize my books), I have a good idea what to do to get the media's attention. Does it always work out? Are you kidding me? It's a lot like a baseball player. If you fail seven out of ten times you are still a .300 hitter, which makes you an all-star. And if you can consistently hit for power, too (land big-time press opportunities), you may end up in the Hall of Fame. I'd like to share some of my personal experiences in trying to publicize my previous book and look at what worked and what did not.

Let's start out with the premise that although I have a publicist provided by the publisher, I still do my own publicity (and was able to get another publicist to work on a pay-for-performance basis as well). When you spend eight months writing a book, you want to make sure you do everything you can to support it. The process began with the "author questionnaire," which the publisher requires authors to complete as a way to look for angles to use to publicize your book. I also included a section in the questionnaire of proposed publicity. (It doesn't hurt to ask.) I suggested several fairly wild and expensive ideas. I followed up with a call to my publicist to ask her what she planned to do for the book in the area of publicity. To my surprise, they agreed to a couple of my requests. They agreed to send a couple of hundred extra review copies of my book, which I planned to use to contact the small media the publisher may overlook. They also agreed to have postcards printed with the book's cover on one side and ordering information on the other, and a couple of hundred press releases printed on the publisher's letterhead. I asked for and received labels for college newspapers from the publicity department as well.

I knew that my publisher would send out review copies to all the major magazines, newspapers, and talk shows. I decided to focus on smaller publications targeted directly to creative people. I used the books the publisher sent and the press releases and started my own publicity campaign. I would send out a dozen kits at a time so I could follow up. This led to some great publicity in a wide range of media. I also sent books to publications and talk shows that had been kind to me before, because lightning does strike twice (and sometimes several times).

To build a buzz I needed a big "opening," so I set up a major book release party (at my own expense). In addition to the resulting book sales, I was able to land a lot of media because of the event, and as a bonus bonded with my editor from New York. (There is nothing like having a few beers with your editor and then having him sing with your band. That was huge.) I was also able to do my radio talk show from the event and hyped the book on the show. All in all, a costly but effective way to build momentum for the book. (I felt great, because I chose a small independent bookstore to handle the book sales and we donated a portion of the book sales to an environmental group I admire and support.) I also used the postcards the publisher provided to do a massive mailing to my list of friends, family, colleagues, acquaintances, past seminar attendees, readers of previous books, and so on. I also mailed out my newsletter to a large portion of the mailing list. It's hard to gauge the success of this type of mailing, because recipients were asked to buy the book from their local bookstore.

My website is a key part of my promotional plans. I built into the site a way to link with Amazon.com and other online booksellers so people could buy, review, or read excerpts from the book. This really paid off. I offered to send a free book to anyone who posts a review (positive or otherwise) on an online bookseller's site. I also used the website to post my book tour (self-financed) and seminar schedule. Since the seminar company I worked for had me going all over the country to teach all-day desktop publishing workshops, I was able to set up signings at night. I also made it a point to seek out bookstores when on the road and sign copies of my new book and encourage them to order more. I would also hand out a free copy to the store manager. This helped, because the next time I was in that town I noticed the signed copies were sold and they had increased their inventory level. Some had even moved the books out onto a table near the door. When a bookstore didn't have my book, I alerted my editor, who in turn talked to the reps.

For some reason, the local libraries do not carry my books—I think because they contain quizzes (readers would obviously take the quiz in the book and ruin it for others). But I know that having your book in a library helps rather than hurts sales. So I donated enough books so every library in my hometown would have at least one copy.

One thing I wanted to do (I heard that author Terry McMillan did this) was to contact the publisher's reps to introduce myself and ask them to push my book. My editor discouraged this. So I went after distributors instead. I called, wrote, and provided them with my book tour schedule to try to increase their inventory levels. To my surprise, some didn't even carry the book, so I did everything I could to convince them they needed this book. I had planned on sending letters to every single bookstore manager I could get an address for, but I decided against it. Instead, I came up with a mini-booklet that told the community relations coordinators of bookstores how to set up a reading group or discussion group around my book. I sent out a test run of twenty-five to see how it would work. I got two stores to build a ten-week course around my book. Not bad, but not great, either.

Some of the other things I did for my last book included becoming a columnist for several e-zines in exchange for plugging the book. My publicist-for-hire set up some radio interviews, and my ad in *TV Radio Interview Report* also got me a few interviews. Of course, I built a seminar around my book and was able to sell books at the back of the room at the Learning Annex as well as for corporate clients. I taught an online class. I sent books to the leaders in the area of creativity, and several wrote back, which was nice, but what made it worthwhile was the one who asked if he could sell my book at his seminars. Uh, yeah!

I left a few things out (I feel like, enough about me, what about *you?*), but suffice it to say, all of these efforts pushed the book into its second printing and set the stage for future contact with the same media.

Ask a Pro

Joan Stewart
Media relations consultant
www.publicityhound.com

What are a couple of hidden gems when it comes to seeking publicity?

My most important piece of advice: write "how-to" and advice articles for print and online publications that are read by your target market—the people you want to buy your products and services. These include newspapers, magazines, trade publications, newsletters, e-zines, and online versions of magazines. Don't expect to be paid for these articles. Rather, give them away for free on the condition that the editor prints an identifier paragraph at the end with your name, phone number, and website URL. Sometimes these newsletters and smaller publications are read by reporters at bigger publications. This happens to me occasionally. A reporter at a large newspaper will see an article I wrote in a newsletter that crosses their desk, and they call me for an interview.

What are the biggest mistakes people make in dealing with the media?

They pitch to a publication they have never seen before. Which means they have no idea of the target audience, the names of the reporters and editors, the various features in the publication, or what the editor needs. They do not understand the first rule of dealing with the media: that is, you must be helpful. If you can't give the media what they need, then don't even bother calling them. Giving them what they need sometimes means offering yourself as a source who can provide background information to a reporter on deadline. It means feeding them news tips. It means giving them story ideas and telling them about trends you are seeing in your industry. It means spending the time to establish a relationship with them, then pitching an idea about your business. Whenever a reporter calls you, never hesitate to ask, "What do you need?" Many businesspeople approach publicity from the wrong angle. They ask, "What can the newspaper do for me?" Instead, they should be asking, "What can I do for the newspaper?"

How has the Internet changed the way people should approach publicity?

Many newspapers and magazines have information about their publications at their websites. With so much information about media outlets available on the Internet, there's no excuse for not researching a publication online. Some reporters (not all) prefer pitches by e-mail instead of phone calls. It is more efficient for them and less time-consuming than talking to people on the phone. The popularity and growing number of e-zines and other e-publications means there are many more media outlets available to publicize your products and services. Sometimes reporters who cover a specific industry hang out at discussion boards devoted to that particular industry. These boards are often an excellent way to become known as an expert. But you must be willing to post free, helpful, valuable information.

Where should you begin if you've never tried to get publicity before?

Don't shoot for the front page of the *Wall Street Journal.* Start by trying to get an item published in a small newsletter. Then try for your weekly newspaper. Then your daily. Then a larger trade journal. Working with editors at smaller publications will give you the experience and confidence you need to work with editors at larger publications.

11

SURF THIS!
(Internet Marketing)

"You go to your television to turn your brain off. You go to the computer when you want to turn your brain on."
—*Steve Jobs*

The more things change, the more they stay the same. Yes, the Internet will completely change the way we promote ourselves. As a tool, the Internet is here to stay, and that's a good thing. Sure, it's scary. Anything new is a little unnerving. But if you embrace it and make it part of your promotional plan, you will see results. There has never been a better way to build a buzz about you and your art. It's comforting to know that what hasn't, and won't, change are basic promotion principles. (All the previous chapters in this book still apply when you incorporate Internet marketing.) Grab their attention, stand out, think creatively, talk in terms of benefits (to them), know your audience, find the most creative (and cheap) way to reach your target audience, form a plan of attack, and then take consistent action. Simple. Now just transfer these ideas to the Net. Where do *your* people go on the Internet? Put yourself in their path. Get the word out with online publicity, a website (your online brochure *and then some*), online newsletters and magazines, put together and post your portfolio or résumé, teach or consult (online), use the Web to give great customer service, build a mailing list of e-mail addresses, build a fan base, and stay in constant contact with clients. You do all this using the same methods and message as before, but with a different medium—the Web.

That said, today's self-promoter must be well-versed in the many capabilities the Internet holds. Don't fight it. It is your ticket to stardom (and a very cost-effective avenue to make it happen!). It's ggrrrrreat! Take the two freelance writers who made an eight-minute short (film), which they were able to have aired on a website for industry professionals. This led to studio executives calling them and an eventual deal with Fox. You don't have to wait around for the perfect time to start taking advantage of the new technology. Be proactive and jump in. You don't have to drop everything else you are doing, but when you can easily find an audience through online research, and distribute your creations and marketing materials to a targeted audience (in a personalized way and on a consistent basis) quickly and inexpensively, the Internet becomes a very sexy and seductive mistress. Just keep in mind that even the best online marketing campaign needs to employ basic marketing principles. (If you opened this book and went right to this chapter, I urge you to go back and read the rest of the book first. I'm not saying this because I'm the author and I want you to read the entire book, but because you need to incorporate everything from previous chapters into your online marketing campaign.)

With the help of a San Diego radio station (co-op), a few feature articles in the paper (publicity), and the Internet, singer Emily Carlsrom is going to get a record deal with a major label. Due to the exposure on the radio, Emily caught the attention of a large record label. They still weren't convinced enough about her marketability, however, to sign her to a recording contract. So the station staged a stunt to get one million clicks for Emily on the station's website—they got seventeen million hits in a month. (We still need to develop a following.) Writers who are frustrated by the current publishing system have taken to the Internet to post their work (and sell it for a fee). There are showcases and contests, too. It is becoming an integral part of promotion. If you aren't using this medium, you should be—and not only because it's easier than ever to be a do-it-yourselfer. Hoorah! It eliminates the codependent relationship an artist has with labels, publishers, and big business. When your sales are a little slow and they can cancel your contract, it isn't the end of the world or certain obscurity. The Internet makes for a somewhat level playing field, theoretically, anyway. You now see mom-and-pop businesses right next to big box stores, and in many ways the mom-and-pop has the edge. Doors that were otherwise closed in the old paradigm are now wide open—even if you aren't an Internet expert. (You just need to know someone who is.)

The best example of this is the success of the film *The Blair Witch Project*—a fake documentary about a legendary witch and the three filmmakers who disappear in the woods making a film about it. It is the most profitable movie ever made. What made the movie so successful? A highly clever marketing campaign that blended traditional marketing with the Web (and a great grassroots strategy). In addition to putting together an amazing website, the guerrilla marketing tactics—missing-persons flyers with the actors' faces on them, comic books featuring *Blair Witch* lore, and T-shirts—drove people (the right people) to the site and created incredible word of mouth for the film (and perpetuated myths about the actors). It all began by e-mailing a few dozen friends, who told two friends, and so on. (Many thought the mythology was real and began putting up their own sites.) The buzz before the film ever reached theaters fueled the success of the movie and launched several film careers. Other filmmakers have used the Internet by submitting trailers, short films, and independent feature films to sites that allow for exposure. Sure, there isn't money to be made from this, but it can lead to bigger and better things. It could be a stepping-stone to a job in the entertainment industry. Or, you can sell your product directly to consumers. In many ways it's like going back to a time when you could interact with your customers directly. (Ever notice that the word "customer" includes the word "custom" right in it?) This is another beautiful thing about the Web. You can customize your marketing materials, products, and approach to match the needs and interests of each customer (if you choose).

Streaming media technology that can send real-time audio and video over the Internet to your computer (and portable devices) is the next big thing. It will turn the clunky Web of today into a sleeker, more powerful promotional tool in the future. Again, technology enables the creative person to create. It will become the ultimate vehicle for building a brand, reputation, presence, following, and freelance business. It will be easy to show off your creativity, create and distribute marketing materials, and sell your work. You can start small (it's cheap and easy to have a Web presence) and decide early on to stay small and survive by being a niche player, and take advantage of others with massive websites. Or maybe you will become the next dot-com gazillionaire. Either way, the Web is *one of* the best ways to promote yourself and your business.

☆ ————————————

FAST FACT

According to an AmericanGreetings.com survey, 60 percent of adult Internet users prefer reading e-mail to snail mail.

A Cautionary Tale or Two

"Computers are useless. They can only give you answers."

—Pablo Picasso

Most companies don't have any specific goals or plans or a way to measure the success of their online activities. Just being on the Web does NOT guarantee success. It can be an expensive failure. Money pit. Don't go nuts too soon. Build as you go. Have you noticed how dot-com companies spend millions of dollars advertising offline? Hint: The Web is not the last word on marketing. It boosts credibility and still works. Don't spend all of your time and money developing a website and ignore other marketing efforts and neglect your business.

Myth Versus Reality of the Internet

"It's going to get worse before it gets worse."

—Lily Tomlin

Myth: Building a *good* website is as easy as it looks.
Reality: Are you kidding me? There are glitches galore, it's time-consuming, takes technical knowledge, and if you hire someone else to do it (and maintain it), it can be very expensive. It is also a headache to have someone else updating it for you. When it comes to regularly maintaining your site (I am not saying most website designers are unreliable), they just may be too busy or just flakes—or both. You can take control of your website by doing it yourself, but it can be a big black hole into which all your time goes. If I haven't scared you off yet, good. If you have the time, technical ability, and the patience, by all means do it yourself.

Myth: A ton of traffic to my website is going to make me wealthy.
Reality: Many of the inquiries I get don't really pay anything. Most of the people coming to the site want something for nothing—which is fine. Selling my books and other products directly to consumers just doesn't happen, at least not for me. (They do buy from Amazon.com, thankfully.) Will people download your music? Sure. But will they pay for it? Uh, not in this lifetime. Think free and you'll be fine. Try to make a living from it, and it's not gonna happen—yet. Maybe that's not your goal. Take Software engineer Linus Torvalds, who created Linux, an operating system that most believe is superior to Windows. The goal was not to make money but to simply build a better, more reliable operating system and provide it to programmers and people to use and improve.

SURF THIS!

Myth: Once I get my site up and list it with search engines, I will be busy.

Reality: Build it and there is a one-in-a-zillion chance they will come. There are zillions of sites now, and getting people to find you is hard. It is not easy to improve your search engine listing. I typed in my name the other day and it took me forever to get to anything remotely related to me. Fortunately, the key word for my site (www.creativelee.com) has to do with "right-brainers" rather than "creativity." I pop up almost right away. You still have to promote yourself and your site the old-fashioned way. Look at how many mainstream ads dot-coms run. Building the website is only the beginning.

Myth: The faster the better.

Reality: Speed kills. Since you can post things so quickly and everyone is rushing to do so as fast as they can, there is a greater risk of doing something damaging to your image and/or reputation. It could be sloppy, inaccurate, or just plain bad. With no time to edit or review things, it may not only be poorly produced, but offensive or all wrong for your audience (also a turnoff).

Note: There's one thing I want to add in front of everything I just said; include the words "At the time this was written . . ." Things change so fast!

☆ ————————————
FAST FACTS
Internet firsts: The first online celebrity chat was in 1989, with two thousand people logging on to Prodigy to ask questions of singer Meatloaf. The first online live concert featured the Rolling Stones, in 1994. The first book sold on Amazon.com was *Fluid Concepts and Creative Analogies* by Douglas R. Hofstadter in 1995.

Making the Most of Online Marketing
"If the Internet marketplace were a city, it would look a lot like New York City at rush hour, and everyone would be blindfolded."
—Jay Conrad Levinson

How to use the power of the Web for promotion. Whether your goal is to be the dominant website in your area—the "hot spot" or "one-stop shop" for everything people need—or you just want to take advantage of other people's sites, here's how to make the most of online marketing.

Offer mind-blowing service. How would you like it if you went into a store with a question and had to wait days for someone to answer it? Exactly. People expect a fast reply when they contact you via the Internet. Give it to them—even if they are a problem—especially if they are problems. Lands' End is innovative in this regard. The clothing company offers immediate responses to questions. You don't have to do it immediately (nobody is open 24/7), but the faster the better. Find ways to make your patrons' lives easier. Southwest Airlines makes it very easy to purchase tickets online. (It's very efficient, without all the frills, just like their flights.)

Make it fast and easy for them. Look for ways that you can do things using the Internet that will save you (and them) time and money. For example, without the cost of printing and postage, you can send just about anything—fast. There is no reason to not stay in touch. You can make changes and update your site in a few minutes to include relevant and recent happenings. You can include a form so people can get quick quotes. You can put in a special "sandbox" page where they can enter a password and see their work in progress and comment on it, or approve it. (Hopefully, it's the latter.) It is easier than ever to become a columnist and contribute to a magazine. You can now easily publish your own novel, or record a song or film and distribute it to a worldwide audience. It's also never been easier or cheaper to let others know about it, either. Send an e-mail announcement (free) and include a link to your work (also free). You can put up an online version of your newsletter (fast and free). Put up the answers to frequently asked questions, post reviews, include links so they will do reviews, post works in progress and ask for feedback, let them download stuff (free), put your art up so it's just a click away.

Make it more personal. In many ways the Internet seems more high-tech and less high-touch. It doesn't have to be that way. I love the fact that Amazon.com allows authors to include their personal comments on the page where the book is featured. There are fewer than a thousand Internet-only radio stations (now), but the potential is there for many more in the near future. (With the Internet soon to be in cars, so will these stations.) The cool thing is that all this can be done on a laptop in your bedroom (or in my case, the beach). You can have several attachments for your e-mails ready to go, and attach the one most appropriate for the reply. Fast and easy, but it seems personal.

Reach a targeted audience. Tennis starlet Anna Kournikova is the undisputed queen of the Internet, with dozens of websites devoted to her. This has made her an international superstar (and promotional powerhouse) even though she has never won a tournament. Whether you want to reach a worldwide audience or just a small targeted group and build a loyal following, it can be done easily and cheaply. Phish, Tori Amos, Christian Bale, Ani DiFranco, and even Barney (the purple dino) have developed cultish followings using the power of the Net. You can also test-market and understand the preferences of an audience early, and shape (if you choose) your creation to their vision. It's pretty powerful when you can bring people together, discover their interests and desires, and be able to respond to those demands. It's doable.

More control over your career. You can now look like a big business on a small budget. You can open your own store or start your own online catalog company. (You don't even need stock.) You can have someone like Amazon.com drop-ship for you and pay you a percentage. Or sell your own creations directly online. It's a chance to reach people who will PAY for your creations. When you sell stuff online, you can keep ALL the profits for yourself. Even if you gave away a free song or chapter of your book, they may just buy the whole album or book later. It's probably better to bundle things together—buy one song, get three free. You can even control your image. Singer/songwriter Jewel has a section on her website called "Rumors and Truth" to squash any ugly rumors and get the facts out. Create your own newsgroups and discussion groups. You can sell items that didn't sell in the traditional marketplace (how many people actually saw your work in a gallery, anyway?) and reach many more online.

Lesson from Lee. When I start to say things like "I remember when . . ." and "In the old days . . ." I feel like a geezer. And like a lot of "older" folk, I have gained some wisdom over the years—at least when it comes to the Web. I do remember that when my first Web-based business, The Success Shop, was launched in 1994 it was a big deal. And in the "old days" (the late nineties) my website www.creativelee.com became my laboratory for experimenting on the Internet. This is what I have learned. Because of the low-cost nature of producing and distributing your art via the Internet, you are able to compete with the big boys. Artists can create and sell their art themselves. This allows the creative person to develop their skills as both an artist and a businessperson (and both skills make them more marketable). Even if you don't want to deal with the actual selling of your art (whatever that may be), you can sell it through online retailers with very little effort on your part. The publicity potential is overwhelming. Start taking advantage of opportunities to "get ink" right away. The Web works very well for building a strong following. Make this a priority. Newsletters and mailings have always been cornerstones of a good marketing plan. You can still do both, but for a lot less money on the Web. Basically, the Internet is *the best* tool ever invented (even more so than the printing press) for marketing yourself and your art. Learn everything you can about its possibilities.

Online Marketing Without a Website

"I'm sure the owner of the breasts, which are beautiful and larger than mine, must be really pissed off, because she paid a lot of money for them and they're giving me the credit."

—Selma Hayek, about a website that had nude photos made to look like her

It seems everyone has their own website. (Even pets have websites dedicated to them!) Although I think you will want one eventually, don't do it if you aren't ready. As with any marketing material, a bad website can do more harm than good. Not having your own site does not mean you can't promote yourself online, however. In fact, there may be more promotional opportunities without using your own website than with one.

Your e-mail is like an electronic business card. Add attachments (with samples of your work or links to samples of your work) or a signature (company name, contact information, a clever quote, or your credits) at the bottom. It can also be used like direct mail to send a newsletter, notices of upcoming events, electronic flyers, press releases, mini-brochures, or catalogs, all via e-mail. Whom do you send it to? Well, you can rent lists (spam, yuck) or create your own (this is the way to go). It's like your electronic Rolodex. These are warm leads. One clever promoter noticed some pretty important people who also got a mass mailing and copied down some of these key people's e-mail addresses and began to build his own VIP e-mail list.

Participating in chat rooms and discussion groups is another example of using the Web without a website for self-promotion. You can participate yourself and help others with advice, answer questions, provide valuable information, post tip sheets, or offer leads or referrals to other websites. It should not be blatant marketing, but the result is that you are promoting yourself in a soft-sell way by making a good impression and proving your knowledge and expertise. Maybe you can have happy customers post a recommendation on your behalf in newsgroups, forums, bulletin boards.

Get chummy with others who have websites. Let them do all the work while you reap the benefits. They create, maintain, and market their sites while you hitch yourself to their wagon. Galleries have websites that will post and sell your art. Team up with other artists and create a co-op gallery site. Tie in with online retailers and have them offer your creations for sale. Stephen King created a small e-book called *Riding the Bullet,* which was downloaded by 500,000 fans (who paid up to $2.50) on its first day of release. Take advantage of sites that offer classified ads, or get listed in directories. Teach a class or hold a seminar or participate in a conference or roundtable discussion. Auction your stuff on eBay. Maybe your agent or publisher or label has a website and will feature you. Maybe the venue you are performing at will feature you or help sell tickets. Offer to be a guest consultant for a week on someone's site. Write articles for e-zines. Provide content for other people's sites. Maybe you could tie in with a charity. Are you getting the idea that there are a lot of opportunities even if you don't have your own website? Good.

☆────────────────
FAST FACTS
According to a Louis Harris poll, the three top reasons people surf the Web are: to gather information about products and services, do research, use e-mail.
────────────────

Getting Them to Your Site Is Half the Battle
"Build it and he will come."
—*"The Voice" in* Field of Dreams

If you have ever been in a band, acted in a play, or had a gallery gala or a grand opening for a retail store, then you know it doesn't matter how great you sound, how well you perform, how nice everything looks—if you don't promote the event, nobody shows up (except a few close friends, family members, and people looking for free food). The truth is, building a website guarantees only one thing—you have built a website. Will people come to see it? That depends on how much promotion you do (online or otherwise). So let's look at the ABC's of how to drive people to your website. (Otherwise you went to a lot of trouble for nothing.)

Address. Make your Web address easy to remember.
Banners. Online ads you can create and place for a fee or free.
Brochures. When someone asks, "Can I have a brochure?" you can now hand them one or give them your Web address and send them

there for samples of your products or a list of your services and testimonials from happy customers.

Chat rooms and discussion groups. Be active in your area of expertise. Where does your audience go to chat?

Contests. Freebies work well online. Hold a contest and give away a prize if they click on every page or submit their e-mail address or vote for something.

Conventional methods. Ads, postcard mailings, a printed newsletter, your answering machine message, or hang a sign with your website address mentioned/featured.

Directories. List with the biggest directories (like Yahoo), and be on the lookout for other ways to be listed and linked. Why not, it's free.

E-mail. Add your website to everything you send out electronically.

Endorsements. Get a celebrity or leader in your field to endorse your site.

Links. Trade links with other related or complimentary sites.

Openings. Hold a grand opening for your site.

Marketing materials. Put your website address on everything (invoice, fax forms, business cards, letterhead, and mailing labels).

Publicity. This is a must, both offline and online. Mention in radio interviews (offline) and put a link at the bottom of every article you write (online).

Search engines. Front-load your descriptions and think about the best keywords and key phrases to submit (and do submit).

Signage. Put your Web address on your license plate, hats, stickers, and T-shirts.

Word of mouth. Encourage and empower others to push your site.

Teasers. Send out postcards, e-mail, or conversations to hint at what's on your site. Leave them wanting more so they will check it out.

Zoophyte. I bet you are wondering, what the hell is a zoophyte? In the real world, it's "any plant or animal, such as a sponge, that looks and grows somewhat like a plant." In the virtual world, it is a way to get people to your site. (I am making this up as I go, by the way.) To "grow" your online presence, you could get alternative domain names that open to your site. (There, I now have an *a* and a *z*.)

FAST FACT

San Francisco leads in the United States (which has the most Internet users in the world) with over 72 percent of their residents (over the age of eighteen) having Internet access. Miami is second with 67 percent, and Raleigh-Durham has 65 percent of its residents wired to the Web.

Catch Them in Your Web (Content)

> *"We don't necessarily get all the tech stuff, but the medium has gotten to the point where it's not about the technology, it's about storytelling."*
>
> —Steve Stanford, CEO of Icebox.com

Someone once said that a website with no content is like watching television with only commercials. Commercials are cool for what, a minute? Then you're over them. So what would make people want to watch longer? Killer programming, or in Web terms, cool content. What this is depends on your people. I'll tell you what it isn't, though: It isn't boring. It isn't all about you. There is something there that they need, want, or think is worth their precious time. And when you give them what they want, guess what? They come back. Why? Maybe it's because you are the place they can go to get everything they need, a kind of one-stop shop. You are linked to all their favorites, so they use you as a launching pad to all the things they want to see. You are their portal to the Web's best. You are the final word on what's hot—the authority of your niche. Since things go bad fast on the Internet, you are known for freshness—the newest and coolest. Again, exactly what that is depends on who your audience is, but here are a few compelling reasons people will keep coming back to your website. Stories sell in any medium—thank God! Make it interesting, for cryin' out loud. Robin Williams has his own radio show of comedy and conversation. You can send a Jeff Goldblum greeting card to a friend. There are countless contests to enter your songs, writings, or art. Check how many of these you are using, or decide which ones you will add to your site.

__ Encourage them to bookmark your site
__ Online newsletter or e-zine
__ Interview leaders in your field and post to your site
__ Get them involved somehow
__ Excerpts from articles you wrote

__ Put together reports or how-to pages and post to your site

__ One-of-a-kind information, hard-to-find items (an online catalog)

__ Travel log (where you've been) or tour dates (where you're going)

__ Free advice in the form of tips, answers to frequently asked questions, or online coaching and consulting

__ Contests and games

__ Links to other things they're interested in

__ Bulletin boards

__ Include instruction or follow-up information after the sale (like upgrades)

__ Chat rooms

__ Personal interaction (you answer e-mails personally)

__ Coupons, discounts, free shipping on orders, specials only available from you

__ Samples of your work (in progress or otherwise)

__ Online greeting cards with your art that people can send electronically

__ Samples of your art (like downloadable songs)

__ Free classifieds

__ Your own radio show

__ Let people see a work in progress or let them in on the creative process

__ Put up your press kit for the media. They can download your head shot, get sample questions and answers for an upcoming interview, read your bio, or see a video clip if they need it

__ Get them involved

__ Put some personal information there

__ Keep your site fresh and new

__ Keep them guessing

Design Checklist

"The Web is a powerful tool, so stupid marketers can use it stupidly with poorly targeted direct mail, irrelevant form letters, and simple rudeness."

—Esther Dyson

Good design increases your credibility and people's confidence in you. Much like a store, your website needs an appealing window display (that's your first page). It needs good signage (navigational buttons), and a logical, interesting layout (page design) where it's easy for them to find what they need. It should, of course, be interesting to wander about in and try things out, and when they're ready, easy to order. Like any store, when they need to find someone who can help with questions they may have, there is someone knowledgeable, helpful, and friendly at their service (contact information on every page). Some people are in a hurry, others want to browse (a text-only version for those in a hurry or one with cool graphics for everyone else). The best and newest stuff that keeps 'em coming back is right up front (you should also highlight your best work with special buttons). Stores offer freebies; ditto for online. Don't worry so much about technology. Make it easy to browse and buy, using classic, pleasing designs, and you'll be fine. I mean, do you really think people come to your site for your graphics? Of course not. Don't overdesign your site by making it confusing, impossible to read, or slow. Use graphics sparingly and artistically. (Important information should be displayed as TEXT.)

Good-looking doesn't always mean it's a good site. Too slow and they're gone. Above all, remember people came for the information. Technical know-how does not a designer make. Still, it is better to have a well-designed site than a boring, ugly, or slow one. So take this quiz to see how your site stacks up (designwise).

True or False?

1. The goal for the first page of my website is to be fast, interesting, and within a few seconds tell the viewer what's in it for them. (True: They are thinking to themselves, "What is this?" and "What's in it for me?" Show and tell them right away.)

2. I should try to collect as many banners as possible and post them to my site. (False: You would think that being affiliated with other cool sites would raise your status—not. Why send people elsewhere for one, and two, the banners slow down your site.)

3. I should err on the side of caution and assume viewers have a slow modem, small screen, aren't able to download the latest plug-in, and may view my site without graphics. (True: Depending on the sophistication of your audience, many people will view your site on a laptop with a modem.)

4. I should use as much animation as possible. The more razzle-dazzle the better. (False: Just because you can doesn't mean you should. People are NOT impressed by silly graphics and cumbersome animation.)

5. I should make it as easy as possible to update my site. (True: Just like anything else in life, the easier you make something to do, the more likely you will do it. Create a theme, templates, and pages that are easy to update.)

6. I shouldn't bother including contact information on each page. (False: Of course, you should make it easy to e-mail you on every page. But what if they print the page out? Put your name and logo, address—Internet and physical—as well as phone and fax numbers.)

7. I should create a "style guide" to stay consistent from page to page and use repeating graphics to speed up the site. (True: A well-organized and functional site is no accident. It doesn't have to be a boring, linear look, but it should be somewhat logical—for the left-brainers out there—and consistent.)

8. I don't want to overwhelm them with choices, so I should make my pages as long as possible so viewers can scroll down for more information. (False: You want to break your site into small, manageable sections with department names that are clear and exciting. Have your navigational buttons make sense and keep them within reach at all times. Idiot-proof your site.)

9. A clean, simple, easy-to-read site without busy backgrounds and a million colors is a professional site. (True: Your number-one goal as a designer is to make your text easy to read. Anything that detracts from that goal must go. As far as colors go, pick three—pleasing and Web-friendly—colors.)

10. I shouldn't bother to tell them to bookmark my site, they will do it anyway. (False: I read somewhere that people are ten times more likely to bookmark your site when you tell them to do it.)

11. When working with photographs (which I know I should), my goal is to make them load as fast as possible. (True: Use photographs, especially of people. Don't use giant photographs that take forever to load. Instead lower the resolution or use a thumbnail and link it to a larger version of the picture.)

12. I should reinvent myself on the Web. I need a look that is totally different from my other marketing materials. (False: Branding comes from consistency, and branding yourself is what the Web is all about.)

Your Score. All the odd-numbered questions are true and the even-numbered questions are all false.

Ask a Pro

Ilise Benun
Author and self-promotion specialist
www.artofselfpromotion.com

In a nutshell, what do you do?

I'm on a mission to teach creative, self-employed people how to promote their talents and services painlessly.

Nicely done. Very concise. I understand you wrote a book on self-promotion.

Yes, I am the author of three books about marketing, including *Self-Promotion Online* (from North Light Books).

Why did you choose to focus on the Internet specifically for this book?

I've noticed that many creative people fight technology (don't ask me why), but isn't it almost a necessity these days to embrace it when it comes to self-promotion? The answer is that it is essential for everyone, including creative people, to embrace technology. Everyone must have some kind of Web presence, whether it's your own domain name or your portfolio posted online somewhere else—in order to be taken seriously by a business prospect. There are many websites that offer portfolio space so you can satisfy your prospect's need to see examples of your work immediately.

How can a creative person use the Internet and technology to gain more publicity?

The media people I've spoken to do prefer e-mailed press releases, though they don't mind them faxed, either. What they really hate is when people send it more than one way: via fax, e-mail, *and* snail mail. In terms of directing people to your website as a substitute for a more substantial press kit, I would not assume they'll make the extra effort to go online. I recommend physically giving them as much information as possible—without overwhelming them, of course.

Do we need printed marketing materials anymore?

Websites are the most common way of providing portfolio samples, but I don't think anyone can avoid having printed materials altogether. There are still many people who either aren't online or who prefer to go online only for what is necessary. If prospects can receive printed materials, they often prefer it, because going online to download anything is time-consuming, no matter how fast your connection.

What are some of the common mistakes in making a website?

I see a lot of sites that have type that's too small, dark backgrounds that make the text illegible, hard-to-find contact information, and too much creativity that confuses visitors. Websites are being used by prospects as a preliminary step to making real contact with a creative professional. So they need to see enough examples and get enough information to encourage them to take the next step, which is picking up the phone or sending an e-mail message that says, "Let's talk."

So what makes a great website from a marketing point of view?

A great website is one that makes it really easy to find samples of the work and offers text and information about the challenge presented, the solution proposed, and, most important, the results of the effort. It should also provide information about the people behind the site—who they are, what they have done, whom they have worked with—which makes a site more personal.

What do you think is key to self-promotion for the creative person?

I think the key to self-promotion, whether online or offline, is to remember that it's not about you, the creative person. Get yourself out of the way, stop being an obstacle to your own work. You must put yourself in the shoes of your prospects and clients, imagine what they need, when they need it, where they'll go looking for it, and how they need to be approached. Figure that out and you have your marketing strategy.

CONTACT INFORMATION

You've made it to the back of the book. Congratulations. (I'm hoping you read the book and didn't just skip right to this part.) Usually when you reach the finish line of a book it will read "The End." Not here. I propose we stay in touch. I promise to post new and creative promotional ideas on my website, and (hopefully) you will share your latest promotional successes with me. (Otherwise, I won't have anything to post to my website. See how this works?) Seriously, if I can help you in any way, don't hesitate to contact me. At the very least, let me send you a free newsletter and resources for right-brainers packet.

Free Bonus Booklet

Want more self-promotion for free? Send an SASE and we will send you the twenty-page booklet *You, Inc.: Promoting Your Way to the Top* absolutely free. This booklet features tips and techniques on how to promote yourself at work.

Lee Silber
c/o CreativeLee Speaking™
4136 Mt. Acadia Boulevard
San Diego, CA 92111

leesilber@earthlink.net
www.creativelee.com

For a complete and updated schedule of workshops for the creative person (many offered free in a bookstore near you) bookmark www.creativelee.com, or better yet, invite Lee to speak to your group by calling 858-792-5312.

BIBLIOGRAPHY

I am staring at the mountainous stack of books that I read before writing this one. I only wish that before I maxed out my credit card ordering from Amazon.com someone could have read and reviewed some of these books for me. (I wasted a lot of time reading several boring books that just rehashed the same old same old.) So in addition to listing each title, I will also comment on and point out which were the best books.

Andrusia, David, and Rick Haskins, *Brand Yourself* (New York: Ballantine, 2000).

Applegate, Jane, *201 Great Ideas for Your Small Business* (Princeton, New Jersey: Bloomberg Press, 1998). Jane Applegate is a shining example herself of what is possible with proper promotion. Her book is filled with functional ideas for freelancers.

Bade, Nicholas, *Marketing Without Money* (Chicago: NTC Business Books, 1994).

Beckwith, Harry, *Selling the Invisible* (New York: Warner Books, 1997). Wow! What a great book. I could not put it down. It was relevant, readable, and an invaluable resource for writing this book.

Benum, Ilise, *Self-Promotion Online* (Cincinnati: North Light Books, 2000). This woman is a genius when it comes to self-promotion for artists. I highly recommend her books and booklets. (www.artofselfpromotion.com)

Black, Roger, *Websites That Work* (San Jose: Adobe Press, 1997). There are so many bad websites, when all a designer needed to do was read this book. It is NOT a how-to-write-HTML-type book, but rather a how-to-DESIGN book. Which is far more valuable, in my opinion.

Crandell, Rick, *1001 Ways to Market Your Services* (Chicago: NTC Business Books, 1998).

Editors of Art Calendar, *Getting the Word Out* (Upper Fairmont, Maryland, 1998).

Fein, Art, *The Greatest Rock & Roll Stories* (Los Angeles: General Publishing Group, 1996). It's funny how you find fantastic books. I was in Guitar Center buying new drumsticks when I saw this book on the counter. This was the most enjoyable reading I did in preparation for writing my book. (Not to mention, the author was very creative with his distribution by selling it in music stores.)

Freeman, Joy Lynn, *Express Yourself* (Boulder, Colorado: Soundstar Productions, 1999).

Godin, Seth, *Permission Marketing* (New York: Simon & Schuster, 1999).

Grant, Daniel, *The Business of Being an Artist* (New York: Allworth Press, 1996).

Hadden, Peggy, *The Artist's Guide to New Markets* (New York: Allworth Press, 1998).

Kawasaki, Guy, *How to Drive Your Competition Crazy* (New York: Hyperion, 1995).

Kawasaki, Guy, *Selling the Dream* (New York: HarperCollins, 1991). Guy Kawasaki is so talented as a writer it's almost intimidating. Both of these books are outstanding!

Kennedy, Dan, *No Rules* (New York: Plume, 1997).

Kremer, John, *1001 Ways to Market Your Books* (Fairfield, Iowa: Open Horizons, 1993). Here is idea number 1002: Buy this book, whether you are a writer or not.

Larsen, Michael, *How to Write a Book Proposal* (Cincinnati: Writer's Digest Books, 1985). A classic and a must-have for most writers.

Lathrop, Tim, and Jim Pettigrew, Jr., *This Business of Music Marketing & Promotion* (New York: Billboard Books, 1999). I found the behind-the-scenes perspective of this book fascinating and very cutting edge.

Levinson, Jay Conrad, and Charles Rubin, *Guerrilla Marketing Online Weapons* (New York: Houghton Mifflin, 1996).

Levinson, Jay, and Seth Godin, *The Guerrilla Marketing Handbook* (New York: Houghton Mifflin, 1994). One of the best books (besides mine, of course) on self-promotion.

Lieber, Ron, *Upstart Start-Ups* (New York: Broadway Books, 1998). I believe we learn deeper by reading real-life stories, especially about others in similar situations. That just about sums up this really good book.

Loeb, Paul Rogat, *Soul of a Citizen* (New York: St. Martin's Griffin, 1999).

McMath, Robert, and Thom Forbes, *What Were They Thinking?* (New York: Times Books, 1998).

Michaels, Nancy, and Debbi Karpowicz, *Off-the-Wall Marketing Ideas* (Holbrook, Massachusetts: Adams Media, 1999). Well-researched and very well-written.

Nelson, Bob, *1001 Ways to Take Initiative at Work* (New York: Workman, 1999).

O'Keefe, Steve, *Publicity on the Internet* (New York: John Wiley & Sons, 1997).

Peters, Tom, *Reinventing Work: The Brand You 50* (New York: Knopf, 1999). Tom Peters knows a little something about "branding." This guy IS a brand himself. His books are always fun to read and full of timely, useful, and creative ideas.

Pinskey, Raleigh, *101 Ways to Promote Yourself* (New York: Avon Books, 1997).

Prior, Teri Lammers with Jacqeline Lapidus, editors, *301 Great Ideas for Selling Smarter* (Boston: Inc. Business Resources, 1998).

Rye, David, *1001 Ways to Get Promoted* (Franklin Lakes, New Jersey: Career Press, 2000).

Salmansohn, Karen, *The 30-Day Plan to Whip Your Career Into Submission* (New York: Broadway Books, 1998). Whenever I go into a bookstore to look for my books, they are often shelved right after Karen's books. ("Sa" and "Si" are very close.) Well, I think it's fitting I follow her. I am a HUGE fan of this truly amazing writer's wit and wisdom.

Schechter, Harriet, *Conquering Chaos at Work* (New York: Fireside, 2000).

Sedge, Michael, *Marketing Strategies for Writers* (New York: Allworth Press, 1999).

Silber, Lee, *Time Management for the Creative Person* (New York: Three Rivers Press, 1998).

Silber, Lee, *Career Management for the Creative Person* (New York: Three Rivers Press, 1999). Do you see a pattern developing here? Good, because there is even more to come in this series. Stay tuned.

Smith, Constance, *Art Marketing 101* (Nevada City, California: Art-Network, 1999). This book *is* a work of art. For the fine artist, it is required reading.

Sparkman, Don, *Selling Graphic Design* (New York: Allworth Press, 1999). As a graphic artist myself, I was made aware by this very thorough book just how much I didn't know about the field—but do now.

Stanfield, Jana, *The Musician's Guide to Making & Selling Your Own CDs & Cassettes* (Cincinnati: Writer's Digest Books, 1997). I was so impressed by this book that I read it *twice.* I wanted to read it again slowly to make sure I didn't miss anything.

Sussman, Jeffrey, *Power Promoting* (New York: John Wiley & Sons, 1997).

Julius, Vitali, *The Fine Artist's Guide to Marketing and Self-Promotion* (New York: Allworth Press, 1996). The author did an excellent job of including contact information and resources that would be otherwise hard to find. A fine book.

INDEX

Aaron Brothers, 55
Abercrombie & Fitch, 35
AC/DC, 119
Ackamoor, Idris, 85
Adam, Lawrie, 111–112
Advertising, 260–267
Aerosmith, 59, 160
Affleck, Ben, 105
Agents, 275–277
Alexander, Elzie, 80
Allen, Fred, 275
"All in the Family," 94
Amazon.com, 35, 77, 208–209, 211,
    214, 307
America Online, 38, 171
Amos, Tori, 15, 115, 308
Amos, Wally "Famous," 120
Amsterdam, Max, 1
Anderson, Helen, 68
Anderson, John, 120
Anderson, Mary, 3
Angela's Ashes (McCourt), 108
Apple Computer, 45, 74–75, 112,
    169, 194, 240
Applegate, Jane, 124
Arakawa, Minoru, 105
Artist statements, 122–126
Artist's Way, The (Cameron
    and Bryan), 212
Ashwell, Rachel, 117
Astaire, Fred, 95
Auld, Doug, 63
Awards, 60–62

Bacon, Kevin, 191
Badu, Erykah, 117
Bailey, Philip, 85
Bale, Christian, 308
Banderas, Antonio, 77
Bank, Melissa, 207
Basie, Count, 121
Baty, Charlie, 167
"Baywatch," 93
Beamer, Keola, 19
Beatles, the, 94, 140, 167, 174,
    278, 294
Becker, Walter, 120
Beckwith, Harry, 93, 175
Bega, Lou, 117
Ben-Ari, Miri, 76
Bening, Annette, 103
Benson, George, 20, 166
Bentley, Wes, 52
Benun, Ilise, 316–317
Bercovitz, Arden, 65
Bergman, Roger, 90
Berliner, Geofrey, 169
Bernbach, William, 5
Berners, Tim, 38
Berry, Chuck, 118
Betts, Dickey, 194
Bezos, Jeff, 35
Biafra, Jello, 135
Black consumers, 24
Blaine, David, 127, 178
Blanc, Mel, 117
Blanchard, Ken, 180

Blume, Jason, 108–110
Blythe, Arthur, 65
Boogie Board, 31–32, 168, 260
Bowie, David, 118, 148, 171
Bozzio, Terry, 24
Branding, 169–172
Brand X, 85
Branson, Richard, 133, 134, 143
Brinkman, Jim, 85
Broadcast.com, 38
Brochures, 268–270
Bronson, Po, 219
Brooks, Garth, 153, 195, 232
Brown, Jerry, 41
Brown, Tina, 170
Brownsey, Maureen, 95
Bruce, Isaac, 96
Bryan, Mark, 212
Buckley, Kathy, 50–51
Buffett, Jimmy, 58, 65, 130,
    143–144, 194, 207, 235, 276
Burns, George, 51
Burton, Tim, 82
Business cards, 191–194
Butler, Samuel, 165
Butts, Alfred, 107

Caine, Michael, 160
Calacanis, Jason McCabe, 187
Cameron, Julia, 212
Campbell, Joseph, 89
Campbell, Meg, 214
Camus, Albert, 187
Caramelo, Candy, 116
Carey, Drew, 111, 117
Carlson, Emily, 83–84, 303
Carson, Lisa Nicole, 196
Carter, Betty, 76
Caruso, David, 145
Case, Steve, 38
Charity events, 65–66
Chase, David, 93
Chopra, Deepak, 287
Christmas Box, The (Evans),
    138–139
Church, Charlotte, 6–7

Churchill, Winston, 87
Clapton, Eric, 68, 85, 165
Clark, Dick, 70
Clarke, Stanley, 113
Clinton, Hillary, 162
Clothes, 152–154, 172
Cockburn, Claud, 287
Cold calling, 255–256
Coleman, Devi, 180
Collins, Phil, 58, 71, 85
Colvin, Shawn, 104, 194
Competitions, entering, 60–61
Cooper, Alice, 117, 133
Coover, Robert, 108
Coppola, Francis Ford, 149,
    165, 177
Corea, Chick, 177
Core customer, description of,
    31–33, 43
Corgin, Billy, 116
Cosby, Bill, 18
Covey, Steven, 24, 183, 221
Cowen, Joshua, 242
Crawford, Joan, 163
Crosby, Stills, Nash and Young, 120
Crossworlds Software, 143
Cruise, Tom, 195–196
Crumb, R., 114
Cusack, John, 75, 235
Customer service, 214–215,
    219–232
Cyrille, Andrew, 113

Dahl, Gary, 133
Damon, Matt, 105, 165
Dangerfield, Rodney, 126
Davies, Dave, 116
Davis, Bette, 85, 163
Davis, Francis, 3
Davis, Susan, 99
Deadlines, 40, 45, 48
Dean Miller Hawaiian print bedding,
    19–20
DeGeneres, Ellen, 148, 297
Dell Computer, 55–56
De Marchi, Livio, 115

Demo tapes, 274
DeNiro, Robert, 165, 190
Denny, Jim, 94
Dentinger, Ron, 142
Depression, 102, 106
Design, 156, 272
DeVito, Danny, 107
Diaz, Cameron, 182
DiFranco, Ani, 173, 308
Diller, Phyllis, 264
Dion, Mark, 113
Direct mail, 267–268
Disney, Walt, 106
Disraeli, Benjamin, 116
Distribution, 29
*Divine Secrets of the Ya-Ya
    Sisterhood* (Wells), 15
Dixie Chicks, 79
DotComGuy (Mitch Maddox),
    118, 134
Doyle, William, 279
Dravecky, Dave, 26
Driver, Minnie, 147, 295
Du Maurier, Daphne, 291
Dunst, Kirsten, 189
Dwell, Charles, 37
Dylan, Bob, 39
Dyson, Esther, 313

Eagle, Jack, 126
Easton, Eric, 94
Eastwood, Clint, 92
Edison, Thomas, 18
Elfman, Jenna, 149
Ellerbee, Linda, 27
Emerson, Ralph Waldo, 166
Ephron, Nora, 127
Erkle, 111
Estefan, Emilio, 25
Etheridge, Melissa, 115, 148, 205
Ethnic target markets, 24–25
Evans, Richard, 138–139
Events, 63–66

Fagen, Donald, 120
Failure, fear of, 5, 82, 98

Fans, 53, 200–237
Faulkner, William, 86
Fieger, Doug, 183–184
Field, Debbi, 168, 253
Filo, David, 114, 139
Fiorina, Carly, 107
First impressions, 145–147
Fisher, Carrie, 178, 234
Fitzgerald, F. Scott, 38
Fleetwood, Mick, 195
Flockhart, Calista, 286
Flyod, Elaine, 124
Follow-up, 84, 251, 286–287
Fox, Vivica A., 51–52
Franklin, Aretha, 194
Freebies, 228–233, 311
Freeman, Morgan, 107
Frost, David, 294
Frost, Robert, 185
Fuller, Thomas, 153

Gabriel, Peter, 85
Gandhi, Mahatma, 47
Garcia, Andy, 145, 177
Gardner, Trent, 24
Garnett, Katrina, 143
Gauguin, Paul, 83
Gayheart, Rebecca, 77
Geek Squad, 113
Genesis, 85
Gerber, 127
Gilliam, Terry, 3
Gimmicks, 127–134, 285
Gish, Lillian, 167
Godek, Greg, 58
Goldberg, Isaac, 189
Gooding, Cuba, Jr., 82
Goodman, Ellen, 148
Good Mother, The (Miller), 108
Gorin, Marc, 134
Graham, Martha, 88
Grant, Hugh, 137
Grateful Dead, 121, 169
Gray, John, 24, 208
Gray, Macy, 116
Green, Chuck, 198–199

Grisham, John, 170
Groening, Matt, 108
Guerrilla marketing, 134–140, 304
Gulley, Philip, 106
Gutenberg, Johann, 38
Guy, Buddy, 59
Guzzetta, Susan, 256–257
Gwynn, Tony, 245–246

Häagen-Daz, 119–120
Hahn, Kurt, 85
Hakim, Joy, 240
Haley, Bill, 159
Halpin, Scott, 51
Hamilton, Katie, 60–61
Hamm, Mia, 92
Hampton, Christopher, 95
Hang Ten, 70
Hanks, Tom, 144
Hanson, Mark Victor, 73
Hapa, 19
Hasselhoff, David, 93, 152
Havassy, Robb, 107
Hawkins, Screamin' Jay, 117
Hayek, Selma, 76–77, 309
Heche, Anne, 148, 297
Heinz, Henry "the Pickle King," 69
Heller, Joseph, 50
Hepburn, Katharine, 158, 197
Heraclitus, 161
Hershberger, Sally, 162
Hewitt, Don, 94, 154
Hewitt, Jennifer Love, 150
Hewlett, Bill, 194
Hilario, Glen, 124
Hilfiger, Tommy, 35
Hirschkop, Dave, 59
Holdsworth, Alan, 165–166
Holiday, Billie, 54
Holmes, Oliver Wendell, 45
Holtz, Lou, 104
Honda, 148
Hootie and the Blowfish, 85
Hopper, Dennis, 62
Houston, Whitney, 145–146

Howe, Steve, 24
Hurok, Sol, 60
Hutton, Lauren, 153
Hynde, Chrissie, 124

Iacocca, Lee, 213
Image, 142–173
Indigo Girls, 148
Infomercials, 275
Internet marketing, 11, 302–317
Interviews, 294–296
Inventing the Abbotts (Miller), 108

Jackson, Phil, 47
Jagger, Mick, 94, 119
James, Henry, 115
Jersey, Katherine de, 78
Jewel, 53, 159, 308
Jobs, Steve, 45, 74–75, 153,
    194, 302
Job Smarts for Twentysomethings
    (Richardson), 27
Job Stores, 20
John, Elton, 117
Johnson, Keyshawn, 96
Johnson, Samuel, 36
Johnston, Kristen, 41
Jones, Rhodessa, 85
Jones, Rickie Lee, 51
Joplin, Janis, 97
Journals, 46
Jurus, Betty, 183

Kane, Ray, 19
Kaufman, Andy, 210
Kaufman, Charlie, 194–195
Kawasaki, Guy, 46, 201, 226, 240
Kay, Allen, 134
Keane, Glen, 165
Keb' Mo', 89–90
Kelley, David E., 51
Kid Rock (Bob Ritchie), 105
King, B. B., 59
King, Stephen, 143, 310
Knievel, Evel, 169–170

Kornheiser, Tony, 121
Krall, Diana, 82, 143, 195
Kreisler, Fritz, 167

LaBour, Fred, 279
Lamb, Wally, 276
Landfill (Dion), 113
Lane Bryant, 19
Lang, Helmut, 114
Lang, Jonny, 59
Lang, K. D., 148
Language, 163, 164
Lauer, Matt, 104
Lazarus, Paul, III, 92
Lebowitz, Fran, 91
Lee, Pamela Anderson, 154
Lee, Tommy, 80
LeGallienne, Eva, 112
Leno, Jay, 197
Letterman, David, 127
Levitt, Theodore, 241
Lewis, Bernard, 261
Lewis, Jerry Lee, 117–118
Lewis, Richard, 26
Liberace, 117
Libraries, 36
Lightyear, Buzz, 78
Lin, Maya, 60
Lincoln, Abraham, 94
Lippman, Laura, 101
Lipton, Thomas, 128
Little Altars Everywhere (Wells), 15
Llewelyn, Desmond, 171
Lobell, Jeanine, 131
Location, 75–77, 253–254
Lochtefeld, Tom, 89
Long, Shelley, 145
Lopez, Jennifer, 150–151
Love, Courtney, 159
Luce, Clare Booth, 137
Lyons, Lance, 117

MacKay, Harvey, 53, 279–280
Macy, William H., 150
Madonna, 6, 94, 190, 194, 235

Manheim, Camryn, 108
Mann, Herbie, 4
Mann, Marty, 203
Manson, Marilyn, 117
Marketing
    age and, 25
    artist statements and tag lines,
        122–126
    awards, 60–62
    branding, 169–172
    core customer, description of,
        31–33, 43
    ethnic target markets, 24–25
    events, 63–66
    fans, 53, 200–237
    focus on effort and action, 8–9
    follow-up, 84, 251, 286–287
    gender and, 25
    gimmicks, 127–134, 285
    guerrilla, 134–140, 304
    hometown, 26
    image, 142–173
    Internet, 11, 302–317
    mentors, 14, 34, 193–199
    money for, 10–11
    networking, 174–199
    niche market, 18, 19, 21, 22, 24
    persistence and, 9, 80–93, 105,
        110, 251–252, 286–287
    planning and organizing, 14–15,
        39–49
    publicity, 9–10, 278–301
    public speaking, 5, 71–74, 78
    rejection, 5, 28, 80–82, 88,
        94–95, 99, 110, 251, 256
    religion and, 26–27
    target market, 18–21, 24–26,
        30–35
    trade shows, 66–70
    unconventional markets, 27
    uniqueness in, 111–118
Marsalis, Wynton, 177, 202
Martin, Ricky, 58
Martin, Steve, 116–117
Mason, John, 118

Mathews, Gordon, 259
Matlin, Marlee, 191
Mayall, John, 54
Mayfield, Curtis, 114
McCourt, Frank, 108
McDermott, Alice, 197–198
McEvoy, Trish, 53
McFarlane, Todd, 81
McGowan, Rose, 114
McMath, Robert, 118
McMillan, Terry, 268, 299
McPherson, Charles, 161
Mendoza, Bart, 140–141
Mendoza, Rudolf, 55
Mentors, 14, 34, 193–199
Mentos breath fresheners, 18
Metallica, 4, 81, 121, 212
Michael, George, 148
Michaels, Lorne, 76, 195
Michelangelo, 84
Michener, James, 9
Millay, Edna St. Vincent, 50
Miller, Dennis, 76
Miller, Jimmy, 183–184
Miller, Sharilyn, 172–173, 215
Miller, Sue, 107–108
Mitchell, Joni, 113, 194
Monroe, Marilyn, 171
Monty Python and the Holy Grail,
    80
Moon, Keith, 51, 133
Moran, Jim, 128
Morey, Tom, 31–32, 168–169, 260
Morissette, Alanis, 104, 194
Morrison, Dale, 226
Mötley Crüe, 80
Mr. T, 117
Murphy, Eddie, 92
Mustaine, Dave, 149

Nadya, 77–78
Names, 118–122
Negative thinking, 96–100, 102
Networking, 174–199
Neuharth, Al, 93
Newsletters, 270

Niche market, 18, 19, 21, 22, 24
Nicknames, 121
Nintendo, 105
No Fear, 22
Nova Menco, 52

Obst, Linda, 180
O'Connor, Sinead, 162, 296
O'Donnell, Rosie, 60
Oedekerk, Steve, 247
Ogilvy, David, 243, 268
Online (*see* Internet marketing)
Orman, Suze, 24
Otis, Alisha, 70

Packaging, 154–156
Packard, David, 262
Pahinui, Cyril, 19
Pahinui, James, 19
Palahniuk, Chuck, 272
Palance, Jack, 117
Parker, Dorothy, 164, 202
Parker, Tom, 14, 198
Parker, Trey, 86, 153, 194
Parton, Dolly, 117
Pass, Joe, 68
Passion, 88–90, 247–248
Pastorious, Jaco, 113
Paulsen, Pat, 135
Perry, Matthew, 180, 258
Persistence, 9, 80–93, 105, 110,
    251–252, 286–287
Personal appearances, 56–59
Peterman, J., 111
Peters, Janice, 81
Peters, Tom, 169
Peterson, Edwin, 3
Peterson, Herb, 3
Pet Rock, 133, 155
Phish, 211, 308
Picasso, Pablo, 305
Pierce, Chonda, 111
Pikachu, 105
Pinskey, Raleigh, 179–180
Planning, 14–15, 39–49
Pokémon, 105

Pollock, Jackson, 75
Popcorn, Faith, 38
Portfolios, 271–272
Positioning, 21, 170
Powell, Walter, 272
PowerPoint, 74, 75, 248
Presentations, 74–75, 248
Presley, Elvis, 14, 94, 115,
    198, 278
Press kits, 56, 69, 287–291
Press release, 288–289
Pricing, 161–162
Prince, 117, 119
Proposals, 272–273
Provenzano, Sam, 80
Publicity, 9–10, 278–301
Public speaking, 5, 71–74, 78

Queen, 64
Quigley, Philip J., 36

Rascoe, Judith, 200
Raymond, Usher, 60
Redenbacher, Orville, 111, 117
Rejection, 5, 28, 80–82, 88, 94–95,
    99, 110, 251, 256
Religion, marketing and, 26–27
Renoir, Pierre-Auguste, 90
Reynolds, Debbie, 111
Ricci, Christina, 150, 296
Rice, Anne, 206
Richardson, Bradley, 27
Rivenberg, Ginny, 116
Robbins, Tim, 107
Robbins, Tony, 24, 112
Roberts, Marcus, 177
Rocky movies, 91, 92
Rodman, Dennis, 112
Rodriguez, Robert, 77
Rogers, Will, 36
Rolling Stones, 59, 167, 169
Romano, Ray, 102
Rooney, Andy, 136
Rose, Axl, 120
Rose, Charlie, 294
Rowling, J. K., 53

Rukeyser, Muriel, 197
Ryder, Winona, 100, 193

Salmansohn, Karen, 81, 93
Sanders, Colonel, 94
Sanders, Dion, 95–96
Sandler, Adam, 38, 94, 195
SARK, 16–17, 98
Sauter, Julie, 216
Schiff, Jacqueline, 267
Scholl, William, 248
Schulz, Charles, 92, 105
Schwarzkopf, H. Norman, 176
Scorsese, Martin, 50, 114, 190
Scott, Jeff, 20–21
Scott, Tom, 41
Sebastian, John, 48
Seidel, Martie, 54
Self-esteem, 28, 104, 105
Self-image, positive, 95–97
Selling, 5, 12–13, 238–277
Selling the Invisible (Beckwith),
    93, 175
Shannon, Molly, 135–136
Sharkproof (MacKay), 53
Shawshank Redemption (movie), 107
Sheen, Charlie, 160
Shepard, Vonda, 51
Sherman, Marilyn, 206–207
Silva, Marla, 68
Simjian, Luther, 3
Simmons, Gene, 117, 149, 194, 202
Simmons, Richard, 88, 118
Simo, Brian, 22
Simo, Mark, 22
Simon, Paul, 235
Simpson, Homer, 100
"Simpsons, The," 108
Sly and the Family Stone, 160
Smith, Barbara, 24
Smith, Chad, 56
Smith, Dorothy Hope, 127
Smith, Jeff, 185
Smith, Liz, 63, 159
Snodgrass, Diana, 38
"Sopranos, The," 93

Sorkin, Aaron, 191
Sorvino, Mira, 283
Sosa, Elaine, 81
Sowell, Thomas, 33
Spacey, Kevin, 197
Spade, David, 76
Sparkman, Don, 156
Spears, Britney, 60, 83
Spector, Phil, 114, 155, 167
Spelling, Aaron, 37
Spelling, Tori, 83
Spielberg, Steven, 194, 202
Spin control, 296
Springsteen, Bruce, 54, 205, 235
Squire, Chris, 113
Stallone, Sylvester, 233
Stanfield, Jana, 84, 235–237
Stanford, Steve, 312
Steel, Danielle, 93
Steely Dan, 120
Stefani, Gwen, 90
Stephens, Robert, 113
Stevens, Eric, 242
Stevenson, McLean, 145
Stevenson, Robert Louis, 260
Stewart, Jimmy, 212
Stewart, Joan, 300–301
Stewart, Martha, 41, 117, 168, 170, 211, 214
Sting, 58
Stipe, Michael, 148, 195
Stone, Matt, 86, 153
Stovall, Jim, 144
Streep, Meryl, 165
Streisand, Barbra, 159, 196

Tag lines, 122–126
Target market, 18–21, 24–26, 30–35
Taylor, Jeff, 134
Taylor Guitars, 68
Telephone calls, 157–158, 255–260
Testimonials, 151–152, 218, 250
Test marketing, 35, 49
Thank you's, 164–165, 189, 210–211, 225
Third Wave, The (Toffler), 38

Thornton, Robert, 86
Time Management for the Creative Person (Silber), 10, 136
Toffler, Alvin, 38
Tomlin, Lily, 54, 305
Torvalds, Linus, 305
Townshend, Pete, 116, 133, 148
Trachman, Jay, 185–186
Trade papers, 34, 35
Trade shows, 66–70
Trends, spotting, 36–38
Tricky, Mary, 255
Tucci, Stanley, 146–147
Tucker, Chris, 124
Turner, Tina, 234
Twain, Mark, 47
Twain, Shania, 87

Uniqueness, 111–118

Van Gogh, Vincent, 102, 116
Van Halen, Eddie, 68, 116, 166, 194
Vernon, Lillian, 260
Videos, 273–274, 290
Viders, Sue, 48–49
Vietnam Veterans' Memorial, 60
Vogel, Paula, 297

Walker, Alice, 197
Walker, Karen, 112
Wal-Mart, 32
Walsh, Steve, 24
Walters, Barbara, 94
Walton, Sam, 32, 220
Warhol, Andy, 214
Warren, Diane, 166
Watson, Tom, Jr., 247–248
Watterson, Bill, 106
Wayne, John, 185
Web sites (see Internet marketing)
Welch, Raquel, 212, 294
Welles, Orson, 128
Wells, Rebecca, 15
West, Mae, 158
West, Rebecca, 280
Wetton, John, 24

Wexler, Jerry, 194
White, Barry, 117, 143
White, Don, 208
White, E. B., 238
Who, the, 51, 133
Wilde, Oscar, 278
Willat, Boyd, 61–62
Williams, Bern, 264
Williams, Robin, 94, 202, 295, 312
Willis, Bruce, 180, 258
Wilson, Earl, 253
Winkler, Henry, 251
Winslet, Kate, 148
Wolfe, Tom, 113, 117, 197
Woodruff, Dennis, 139–140
Woods, Tiger, 165

Wright, Stephen, 259
Wrigley, William, Jr., 246–247
Written plan, 39, 41, 45
Wynne, Arthur, 3

Yearwood, Trisha, 58, 76, 153, 195, 275
Yes, 120, 161
Young, Robert, 128
Youngman, Henny, 126
Yu, Jessica, 72

Zander, Benjamin, 106
Zangwill, Israel, 62
Zappa, Frank, 297
Zuckerman, Mortimer, 18
ZZ Top, 117

ABOUT THE AUTHOR

Lee Silber practices what he preaches using low-cost, highly creative techniques to promote his books, businesses, and band. In addition to being the author of eight books, including the popular *Career Management for the Creative Person* and *Time Management for the Creative Person,* Lee is an accomplished graphic artist, drummer, workshop leader, radio talk-show host, and the founder of five companies, including CreativeLee Speaking™. When not out promoting something or other, Lee resides with his wife in San Diego, California.

FOR MORE OF LEE SILBER'S CREATIVE SOLUTIONS FOR CREATIVE PEOPLE, READ:

Time Management for the Creative Person

0-609-80090-6. $14.00
(Canada: $19.50)

Career Management for the Creative Person

0-609-80365-4. $15.00
(Canada: $21.00)

THREE RIVERS PRESS

Available in paperback wherever books are sold.